The American Pageant

Twelfth Edition

Guidebook

A Manual for Students

Mel Piehl

Valparaiso University

Houghton Mifflin Company   Boston   New York

Sponsoring Editor: Colleen Shanley Kyle
Senior Manufacturing Coordinator: Marie Barnes
Senior Marketing Manager: Sandra McGuire
Editorial Associate: Michael Kerns

Printed in the U.S.A.

ISBN-13: 978-0-618-10355-3   ISBN-10: 0-618-10355-4

15 16 17 18 19 20 21 22 23 - MA - 15 14 13 12 11 10 09 08 07

Contents

To the Student

This revised *Guidebook* is intended to assist you in comprehending American history as presented in *The American Pageant*, Twelfth Edition, by David M. Kennedy, Lizabeth Cohen, and Thomas A. Bailey. The *Guidebook* focuses attention on the central themes and major historical developments of each chapter while presenting a variety of exercises and other material designed to reinforce your comprehension of the text. Factual knowledge of history is important, and some of the exercises will help you to review facts and recall their significance. But the *Guidebook* attempts to demonstrate that facts are best learned when they are understood in relation to key historical events and issues.

The forty-two chapters of the *Guidebook* correspond with those of *The American Pageant* and are best used in close association with the text. Each chapter of the *Guidebook* contains the same sequence of material and exercises, except for the Map Discrimination section, which is omitted from some chapters.

The **Checklist of Learning Objectives** in Part I ("Reviewing the Chapter") of each *Guidebook* chapter provides a summary of the essential chapter themes and underscores the major historical developments to be learned. The **Glossary** defines basic social-science terms and shows their usage in the text. Learning this vocabulary will not only reinforce your understanding of *The American Pageant* but also familiarize you with terms often encountered in the study of politics, economics, geography, military science, and law, as well as history.

The various exercises in Part II ("Checking Your Progress") will assist in your careful reading of the text as well as foster your comprehension and spotlight the essential facts and concepts. **True-False**, **Multiple Choice**, and **Identification** exercises stress reading for understanding of important ideas and terms. **Matching People, Places, and Events** checks your knowledge of key historical figures, locations, and events. **Putting Things in Order** (which is specifically tied to the Chronology section at the end of each chapter of *The American Pageant*) and **Matching Cause and Effect** develop two essential principles of historical understanding: chronological sequence, and the causal relation between events. **Developing Historical Skills** is designed to hone your ability to use the diverse techniques employed in the study of history, including the interpretation of charts, maps, and visual evidence. **Map Mastery** includes Map Discrimination—specific questions focused on map reading—and Map Challenge, which asks you to use maps to discuss a historical issue or problem in a brief essay.

Completion of the exercises in Part II should enable you to handle successfully the crucial questions in Part III ("Applying What You Have Learned"). Your instructor may suggest that you use these questions as guides to study and review or may assign them as essay questions to be answered following your reading of the chapter. The last question is an especially challenging one that often draws on earlier chapters of *The American Pageant* and asks you to make historical comparisons, draw conclusions, or consider broad historical issues.

You and your instructor hence may utilize the *Guidebook* in a variety of ways, to suit a variety of needs. It can be used for class preparation and assignments, for guidance in your reading of the text, or for independent review of course contents. The answers to all the exercises may be found by your careful rereading of the pertinent sections of *The American Pageant*. May your exploration of American history be stimulating and enriching.

M. P.

1

New World Beginnings, 33,000 B.C.–A.D. 1769

PART I: Reviewing the Chapter

A. Checklist of Learning Objectives

After mastering this chapter, you should be able to

√1. describe the geological and geographical conditions that set the stage for North American history.

√2. describe the origin and development of the major Indian cultures of the Americas.

√3. explain the developments in Europe and Africa that led up to Columbus's voyage to America.

√4. explain the changes and conflicts that occurred when the diverse worlds of Europe, Africa, and the Americas collided after 1492.

√5. describe the Spanish conquest of Mexico and South America and identify the major features of Spanish colonization and expansion in North America.

B. Glossary

To build your social science vocabulary, familiarize yourself with the following terms.

1. **nation-state** The form of political society that combines centralized government with a high degree of ethnic and cultural unity. ". . . the complex, large-scale, centralized Aztec and Incan nation-states that eventually emerged." (p. 8)

2. **matrilinear** The form of society in which family line, power, and wealth are passed primarily through the female side. ". . . many North American native peoples, including the Iroquois, developed matrilinear cultures. . . ." (p. 8)

3. **confederacy** An alliance or league of nations or peoples looser than a federation. "The Iroquois Confederacy developed the political and organizational skills. . . ." (p. 8)

4. **primeval** Concerning the earliest origin of things. ". . . the whispering, primeval forests. . . ." (p. 10)

5. **saga** A lengthy story or poem recounting the great deeds and adventures of a people and their heroes. ". . . their discovery was forgotten, except in Scandinavian saga and song." (p. 10)

6. **middlemen** In trading systems, those dealers who operate between the original buyers and the retail merchants who sell to consumers. "Muslim middlemen exacted a heavy toll en route." (p. 11)

✳7. **caravel** A small vessel with a high deck and three triangular sails. ". . . they developed the caravel, a ship that could sail more closely into the wind. . . ." (p. 11)

8. **plantation** A large-scale agricultural enterprise growing commercial crops and usually employing coerced or slave labor. "They built up their own systematic traffic in slaves to work the sugar plantations. . . ." (p. 12)

9. **ecosystem** A naturally evolved network of relations among organisms in a stable environment. "Two ecosystems . . . commingled and clashed when Columbus waded ashore." (p. 14)

10. **demographic** Concerning the general characteristics of a given population, including such factors as numbers, age, gender, birth and death rates, and so on. ". . . a demographic catastrophe without parallel in human history." (p. 15)

11. **conquistador** A Spanish conqueror or adventurer in the Americas. "Spanish *conquistadores* (conquerors) fanned out across . . . American continents." (p. 16)

12. **capitalism** An economic system characterized by private property, generally free trade, and open and accessible markets. ". . . the fuel that fed the growth of the economic system known as capitalism." (p. 17)

13. **encomienda** The Spanish labor system in which persons were held to unpaid service under the permanent control of their masters, though not legally owned by them. ". . . the institution known as *encomienda*." (p. 17)

14. **mestizo** A person of mixed Native American and European ancestry. "He intermarried with the surviving Indians, creating a distinctive culture of *mestizos*. . . ." (p. 21)

15. **province** A medium-sized subunit of territory and governmental administration within a larger nation or empire. "They proclaimed the area to be the province of New Mexico. . . ." (p. 22)

PART II: Checking Your Progress

A. True-False

Where the statement is true, mark **T**. Where it is false, mark **F**, and correct it in the space immediately below.

T   1. The geography of the North American continent was fundamentally shaped by the glaciers of the Great Ice Age.

F   2. North America was first settled by people who came by boat across the waters of the Pacific Strait from Japan to Alaska.

F   3. The early Indian civilizations of Mexico and Peru were built on the economic foundations of cattle and wheat growing.

T   4. Most North American Indians lived in small, seminomadic agricultural and hunting communities.

T   5. Many Indian cultures like the Iroquois traced descent through the female line.

F   6. No Europeans had ever set foot on the American continents prior to Columbus's arrival in 1492.

T   7. A primary motive for the European voyages of discovery was the desire to find a less expensive route to Asian goods and markets.

I F 8. The beginnings of African slavery developed in response to the Spanish conquest of the Americas.

F   9. Columbus immediately recognized in 1492 that he had come across new continents previously unknown to Europeans.

T F 10. The greatest effect of the European intrusion on the Indians of the Americas was to increase their population through intermarriage with the whites.

T 11. Spanish gold and silver from the Americas fueled inflation and economic growth in Europe.

F 12. The Spanish *conquistadores* had little to do with the native peoples of Mexico and refused to intermarry with them.

F 13. The province of New Mexico was first settled by French colonizers from the North.

T 14. Spain expanded its empire into Florida and New Mexico partly to block French and English intrusions.

F 15. The Spanish empire in the New World was larger, richer, and longer-lasting than that of the English.

B. Multiple Choice

Select the best answer and write the proper letter in the space provided.

A 1. The geologically oldest mountains in North America are

    a. the Appalachians.
    b. the Rockies.
    c. the Cascades.
    d. the Sierra Nevada.

B 2. The Indian peoples of the New World

    a. developed no advanced forms of civilization.
    b. were divided into many diverse cultures speaking more than two thousand different languages.
    c. were all organized into the two large empires of the Incas and the Aztecs.
    d. relied primarily on nomadic herding of domesticated animals for their sustenance.

C 3. The Iroquois Confederacy remained a strong political and military influence until

    a. the Spanish conquest of the Americas.
    b. the fur trade was wiped out in the early 1700s.
    c. King Philip's War
    d. the American Revolution.

A 4. Among the important forces that first stimulated European interest in trade and discovery was

    a. the Christian crusaders who brought back a taste for the silks and spices of Asia.
    b. the Arab slave traders on the east coast of Africa.
    c. the Scandinavian sailors who had kept up continuous trade contacts with North America.
    d. the division of Spain into small kingdoms competing for wealth and power.

D 5. Among the most important American Indian products to spread to the Old World were

    a. animals such as buffalo and horses.
    b. technologies such as the compass and the wheel.
    c. economic systems such as plantation agriculture and livestock raising.
    d. foodstuffs such as maize, beans, and tomatoes.

C   6. The primary staples of Indian agriculture were

     a. potatoes, beets, and sugar cane.
     b. rice, manioc, and peanuts.
     c. maize, beans, and squash.
     d. wheat, oats, and barley.

D   7. The number of Indians in North America at the time Columbus arrived was approximately

     a. one million.
     b. four million.
     c. twenty million.
     d. two hundred and fifty million.

C   8. Before Columbus arrived, the only Europeans to have temporarily visited North America were

     a. the Greeks.
     b. the Irish.
     c. the Norse.
     d. the Italians.

A   9. The Portuguese were the first to enter the slave trade and establish large-scale plantations using slave labor in

     a. West Africa.
     b. the Atlantic sugar islands.
     c. the West Indies.
     d. Brazil.

C   10. Much of the impetus for Spanish exploration and pursuit of glory in the early 1500s came from Spain's recent

     a. successful wars with England.
     b. national unification and expulsion of the Muslim Moors.
     c. voyages of discovery along the coast of Africa.
     d. conversion to Roman Catholicism.

A   11. A crucial political development that paved the way for the European colonization of America was

     a. the rise of Italian city-states like Venice and Genoa.
     b. the feudal nobles' political domination of the merchant class.
     c. the rise of the centralized national monarchies such as that of Spain.
     d. the political alliance between the Christian papacy and Muslim traders.

B   12. The primary reason for the drastic decline in the Indian population after the encounter with the Europeans was

     a. the rise of intertribal warfare.
     b. the Indians' lack of resistance to European diseases such as smallpox and malaria.
     c. the sharp decline in the Mexican birthrate.
     d. the sudden introduction of the deadly disease syphilis to the New World.

B 13. Cortés and his men were able to conquer the Aztec capital Tenochtitlán partly because

    a. they had larger forces than the Aztecs.

    b. the Aztec ruler Montezuma believed that Cortés was a god whose return had been predicted.

    c. the Aztecs were peace-loving people who did not believe in war or conquest.

    d. the city of Tenochtitlán already had been devastated by a disease epidemic.

A 14. The primary early colonial competitor with Spain in the New World was

    a. Portugal.

    b. Italy.

    c. France.

    d. England.

D 15. The belief that the Spanish only killed, tortured, and stole in the Americas while doing nothing good is called

    a. the *encomienda*.

    b. the mission of civilization.

    c. the Evil Empire.

    d. the Black Legend.

C. Identification

Supply the correct identification for each numbered description.

Ice Age   1. Extended period when glaciers covered most of the North American continent

Maize   2. Staple crop that formed the economic foundation of Indian civilizations

_____ 3. Important Mississippian culture site, near present East St. Louis, Illinois

_____ 4. First European nation to send explorers around the west coast of Africa

_____ 5. Flourishing West African kingdom that had its capital and university at Timbuktu

_____ 6. Mistaken term that European explorers gave to American lands because of the false belief that they were off the coast of Asia

_____ 7. Animal introduced by Europeans that transformed the Indian way of life on the Great Plains

_____ 8. Among the major European diseases that devastated Native American populations after 1492 (name two)

_____ 9. Disease originating in Americas that was transmitted to Europeans after 1492

_____ 10. Treaty that secured Spanish title to lands in Americas by dividing them with Portugal

_____ 11. Wealthy capital of the Aztec empire

_____ 12. Person of mixed European and Indian ancestry

_____ 13. Indian uprising in New Mexico caused by Spanish efforts to suppress Indian religion

_____ 14. Indian people of the Rio Grande Valley who were cruelly oppressed by the Spanish conquerors

_____ 15. Roman Catholic religious order of friars that organized a chain of missions in California

D. Matching People, Places, and Events

Match the person, place, or event in the left column with the proper description in the right column by inserting the correct letter on the blank line.

D 1. Ferdinand and Isabella
J 2. Cortés and Pizarro
L 3. Lake Bonneville
E 4. Días and da Gama
H 5. Columbus
B 6. Malinche ~~A~~
I 7. Montezuma
A 8. Hiawatha ~~B~~
C 9. Tenochtitlán
F 10. St. Augustine
K 11. John Cabot ~~G~~
G 12. Junipero Serra ~~K~~

A. Female Indian slave who served as interpreter for Cortés
B. Legendary founder of the powerful Iroquois Confederacy
C. Wealthy capital of the Aztec empire
D. Financiers and beneficiaries of Columbus's voyages to the New World
E. Portuguese navigators who sailed around the African coast
F. Founded in 1565, the oldest continually inhabited European settlement in United States territory
G. Italian-born navigator sent by English to explore North American coast in 1498
H. Italian-born explorer who thought that he had arrived off the coast of Asia rather than on unknown continents
I. Powerful Aztec monarch who fell to Spanish conquerors
J. Spanish conquerors of great Indian civilizations
K. Franciscan missionary who settled California
L. Inland sea left by melting glaciers whose remnant is the Great Salt Lake

E. Putting Things in Order

Put the following events in correct order by numbering them from 1 to 5.

3 The wealthy Aztec civilization falls to Cortés.

2 Portuguese navigators sail down the west coast of Africa.

1 The first human inhabitants cross into North America from Siberia across a temporary land bridge.

5 The once-strong Iroquois confederacy divides and collapses.

4 Spanish conquerors move into the Rio Grande valley of New Mexico.

F. Matching Cause and Effect

Match the historical cause in the left column with the proper effect in the right column by writing the correct letter on the blank line.

Cause

D 1. The Great Ice Age

G 2. Cultivation of corn (maize)

B 3. New sailing technology and desire for spices

J 4. Portugal's creation of sugar plantations on Atlantic coastal islands

F 5. Columbus's first encounter with the New World

I 6. Native Americans' lack of immunity to smallpox, malaria, and yellow fever

A 7. The Spanish conquest of large quantities of New World gold and silver

H 8. Aztec legends of a returning god, Quetzalcoatl

C 9. The Spanish need to protect Mexico against French and English encroachment

E 10. Franciscan friars' desire to convert Pacific coast Indians to Catholicism

Effect

A. Rapid expansion of global economic commerce and manufacturing

B. European voyages around Africa and across the Atlantic attempting to reach Asia

C. Establishment of Spanish settlements in Florida and New Mexico

D. Exposure of a "land bridge" between Asia and North America

E. Formation of a chain of mission settlements in California

F. A global exchange of animals, plants, and diseases

G. The formation of large, sophisticated civilizations in Mexico and South America

H. Cortés relatively easy conquest of Tenochtitlán

I. A decline of 90 percent in the New World Indian population

J. The rapid expansion of the African slave trade

G. Developing Historical Skills

Connecting History with Geology and Geography

Because human history takes place across the surface of the earth, both the physical science of geology and the social science of geography are important to historians. Answer the following questions about the geological and geographical setting of North American history.

1. What are the two major mountain chains that border the great mid-continental basin drained by the Mississippi River system?

2. What great geological event explains the formation of the Great Lakes, the St. Lawrence River system, the Columbia-Snake River system, and Great Salt Lake?

3. How did this same geological event isolate the human population of the Americas from that of Asia?

4. Given the original geographical origins of the Indian populations, in which direction did their earliest migrations across North America occur: from southeast to north and west, from southwest to north and east, or from northwest to south and east?

H. Map Mastery

Map Discrimination

Using the maps and charts in Chapter 1, answer the following questions.

1. *Chronological Chart*: The American Declaration of Independence occurred exactly 169 years between what other two major events in American history?

2. *The First Discoverers of America*: When the first migrants crossed the Bering Land Bridge from Siberia to North America, approximately how many miles did they have to walk before they were south of the large ice caps to either side of the only open route? a) 200 miles b) 500 miles c) 2000 miles d) 3000 miles

3. North American Indian Peoples at the Time of First Contact with Europeans: List five Indian tribes that lived in each of the following regions of North America: (a) Southwest (b) Great Plains (c) Northeast (d) Southeast.

4. *Trade Routes with the East*: In the early European trading routes with Asia and the East Indies, what one *common* destination could be reached by the Middle Route, the Southern route, and da Gama's ocean route? a) Constantinople b) Persia c) China

5. *Principal Early Spanish Explorations and Conquests*: Of the principal Spanish explorers—Columbus, Balboa, de León, Cortés, Pizarro, de Soto, and Coronado—which four *never* visited the territory or territorial waters of the land that eventually became part of the United States?

6. *Spain's North American Frontier, 1542–1823*: A) What were the two easternmost Spanish settlements on the northern frontier of Spanish Mexico? B) About how many years was Mission San Antonio founded before the first Spanish settlements in California? a) 10 b) 25 c) 50 d) 100

7. *Principal Voyages of Discovery*: A) Who was the first explorer of the Pacific Ocean?
   B) According to the 1494 Treaty of Tordesillas, about how much of North America was allotted to the Portuguese? a) one-half b) one-third c) one-tenth d) none

Map Challenge

Using the text and the map of *North American Indian Peoples at the Time of First Contact with Europeans*, write a brief essay describing the geographical distributions of the more *dense* North American Indian populations at the time of European arrival. Include some discussion of why certain regions were densely populated and others less so.

Part III: Applying What You Have Learned*

1. How did the geographic setting of North America—including its relation to Asia, Europe, and Africa—affect its subsequent history?
2. What were the common characteristics of all Indian cultures in the New World, and what were the important differences among them?
3. What fundamental factors drew the Europeans to the exploration, conquest, and settlement of the New World?
4. What was the impact on the Indians, Europeans, and Africans when each of their previously separate worlds "collided" with one another?
5. In what ways might the European encounter with the Americas be seen as a disaster or tragedy, and in what ways might it be seen as an inevitable development in the history of humanity with long-run positive results.

---

* Space is provided at the end of each chapter for answering the essay questions. Students needing more room should answer on separate sheets of paper.

2

The Planting of English
America, 1500–1733

Part I: Reviewing the Chapter

A. Checklist of Learning Objectives

After mastering this chapter, you should be able to

1. state the factors that led England to begin colonization.
2. describe the development of the Jamestown colony from its disastrous beginnings to its later prosperity.
3. describe the cultural and social changes that Indian communities underwent in response to English colonization.
4. describe changes in the economy and labor system in Virginia and the other southern colonies.
5. indicate the similarities and differences among the southern colonies of Virginia, Maryland, North Carolina, South Carolina, and Georgia.

B. Glossary

To build your social science vocabulary, familiarize yourself with the following terms.

1. **nationalism** Fervent belief and loyalty given to the political unit of the nation-state. "Indeed England now had . . . a vibrant sense of nationalism and national destiny." (p. 27)
2. **primogeniture** The legal principle that the oldest son inherits all family property or land. ". . . laws of primogeniture decreed that only eldest sons were eligible to inherit landed estates." (p. 28)

moe stocks; moe control of company

3. **joint-stock companies** An economic arrangement by which a number of investors pool their capital for investment. "Joint-stock companies provided the financial means." (p. 28)
4. **charter** A legal document granted by a government to some group or agency to implement a stated purpose, and spelling out the attending rights and obligations. ". . . the Virginia Company of London received a charter from King James I of England. . . ." (p. 28)
5. **census** An official count of population, often also including other information about the population. "By 1669 an official census revealed that only about two thousand Indians remained in Virginia. . . ." (p. 31)
6. **feudal** Concerning the decentralized medieval social system of personal obligations between rulers and ruled. "Absentee proprietor Lord Baltimore hoped that . . . Maryland . . . would be the vanguard of a vast new feudal domain." (p. 34)
7. **indentured servant** A poor person obligated to a fixed term of unpaid labor, often in exchange for a benefit such as transportation, protection, or training. "Also like Virginia, it depended for labor in its early years mainly on white indentured servants. . . ." (p. 34)
8. **toleration** Originally, religious freedom granted by an established church to a religious minority. "Maryland's new religious statute guaranteed toleration to all Christians." (p. 34)

9. **squatter** A frontier farmer who illegally occupied land owned by others or not yet officially opened for settlement. "The newcomers, who frequently were 'squatters' without legal right to the soil . . . ." (p. 40)
10. **buffer** In politics, a small territory or state between two larger, antagonistic powers and intended to minimize the possibility of conflict between them. "The English crown intended Georgia to serve chiefly as a buffer." (p. 41)
11. **melting pot** Popular American term for an ethnically diverse population that is presumed to be "melting" toward some eventual commonality. "The hamlet of Savannah, like Charleston, was a melting-pot community." (p. 41)

PART II: Checking Your Progress

A. True-False

Where the statement is true, mark **T**. Where it is false, mark **F**, and correct it in the space immediately below.

T 1. Protestant England's early colonial ambitions were fueled by its religious rivalry with Catholic Spain.

F 2. The earliest English colonization efforts experienced surprising success.

I F 3. The defeat of the Spanish Armada was important to North American colonization because it enabled England to conquer Spain's New World empire.

T 4. Among the English citizens most interested in colonization were unemployed yeomen and the younger sons of the gentry.

F 5. Originally, the primary purpose of the joint-stock Virginia Company was to provide for the well-being of the freeborn English settlers in the colony.

T 6. The defeat of Powhatan's Indian forces in Virginia was achieved partly by Lord De La Warr's use of brutal "Irish tactics."

F 7. The primary factor disrupting Indian cultures in the early years of English settlement was the introduction of Christianity.

F 8. The Maryland colony was founded to establish a religious refuge for persecuted English Quakers.

T 9. From the time of its founding, South Carolina had close economic ties with the British West Indies.

F 10. The principal export crop of the Carolinas in the early 1700s was wheat.

T F 11. South Carolina prospered partly by selling African slaves in the West Indies.

T 12. In their early years, North Carolina and Georgia avoided reliance on slavery.

T 13. Compared with its neighbors Virginia and South Carolina, North Carolina was more democratic and individualistic in social outlook.

F 14. Britain valued the Georgia colony primarily as a rich source of gold and timber.

_T_ 15. All the southern colonies eventually came to rely on staple-crop plantation agriculture for their economic prosperity.

B. Multiple Choice

Select the best answer and write the proper letter in the space provided.

_C_ 1. After decades of religious turmoil, Protestantism finally gained permanent dominance in England after the succession to the throne of

    a. King Edward VI.
    b. Queen Mary I.
    c. Queen Elizabeth I.
    d. King James I.

_D_ 2. Imperial England and English soldiers developed a contemptuous attitude toward "natives" partly through their colonizing experiences in

    a. Canada.
    b. Spain.
    c. India.
    d. Ireland.

_B_ 3. England's victory over the Spanish Armada gave it

    a. control of the Spanish colonies in the New World.
    b. dominance of the Atlantic Ocean and a vibrant sense of nationalism.
    c. a stable social order and economy.
    d. effective control of the African slave trade.

_B_ 4. At the time of the first colonization efforts, England

    a. was struggling under the political domination of Spain.
    b. was enjoying a period of social and economic stability.
    c. was undergoing rapid economic and social transformations.
    d. was undergoing sharp political conflicts between advocates of republicanism and the monarchy of Elizabeth I.

_B_ 5. Many of the early Puritan settlers of America were

    a. displaced sailors from Liverpool and Bath.
    b. merchants and shopkeepers from the Midlands.
    c. urban laborers from Glasgow and Edinburgh.
    d. uprooted sheep farmers from eastern and western England.

_B_ 6. England's first colony at Jamestown

    a. was an immediate economic success.
    b. was saved from failure by John Smith's leadership and by John Rolfe's introduction of tobacco.
    c. enjoyed the strong and continual support of King James I.
    d. depended on the introduction of African slave labor for its survival.

A   7. Representative government was first introduced to America in the colony of

    a. Virginia.
    b. Maryland.
    c. North Carolina.
    d. Georgia.

D   8. One important difference between the founding of the Virginia and Maryland colonies was that

    a. Virginia colonists were willing to come only if they could acquire their own land, while Maryland colonists labored for their landlords.
    b. Virginia depended primarily on its tobacco economy, while Maryland turned to rice cultivation.
    c. Virginia depended on African slave labor, while Maryland relied mainly on white indentured servitude.
    d. Virginia was founded mainly as an economic venture, while Maryland was intended partly to secure religious freedom for persecuted Roman Catholics.

C   9. After the Act of Toleration in 1649, Maryland provided religious freedom for all

    a. Jews.
    b. atheists.
    c. Protestants and Catholics.
    d. those who denied the divinity of Jesus.

B   10. The primary reason that no new colonies were founded between 1634 and 1670 was

    a. the severe economic conditions in Virginia and Maryland.
    b. the civil war in England.
    c. the continuous naval conflicts between Spain and England that disrupted sea-lanes.
    d. the English kings' increasing hostility to colonial ventures.

C   11. The early conflicts between English settlers and the Indians near Jamestown laid the basis for

    a. the intermarriage of white settlers and Indians.
    b. the incorporation of Indians into the "melting-pot" of American culture.
    c. the forced separation of the Indians into the separate territories of the "reservation system."
    d. the use of Indians as a slave-labor force on white plantations.

A   12. In colonial English-Indian relations, the term "middle ground" referred to

    a. The neutral territory between English soldiers and warring Indian tribes.
    b. The area around the Great Lakes that was contested by the English and French forces.
    c. The economic zone where English and Indian traders met to exchange furs for manufactured goods.
    d. The cultural zone where Indians and whites were forced to accommodate one another by shared practices that included intermarriage.

C 13. After the defeat of the coastal Tuscarora and Yamasee Indians by North Carolinians in 1711–1715,

   a. there were almost no Indians left east of the Mississippi River.
   b. the remaining southeastern Indian tribes formed an alliance to wage warfare against the whites.
   c. the powerful Creeks, Cherokees, and Iroquois remained in the Appalachian Mountains as a barrier against white settlement.
   d. the remaining coastal Indians migrated to the West Indies.

C 14. Most of the early white settlers in North Carolina were

   a. religious dissenters and poor whites fleeing aristocratic Virginia.
   b. wealthy planters from the West Indies.
   c. the younger, ambitious sons of English gentry.
   d. ex-convicts and debtors released from English prisons.

C 15. The high-minded philanthropists who founded the Georgia colony were especially interested in the causes of

   a. women's rights and labor reform.
   b. temperance and opposition to war.
   c. prison reform and avoiding slavery.
   d. religious and political freedom.

C. Identification

Supply the correct identification for each numbered description.

Ireland 1. Nation where English Protestant rulers employed brutal tactics against the local Catholic population

Roanoke colony 2. Island colony founded by Sir Walter Raleigh that mysteriously disappeared in the 1580s

Spanish 3. Naval invaders defeated by English "sea dogs" in 1588

Joint-stock 4. Forerunner of the modern corporation that enabled investors to pool financial capital for colonial ventures

Powhatan wars 5. Name of two wars, fought in 1614 and 1644, between the English in Jamestown and the nearby Indian leader

(1661) Barbados Slave code 6. The harsh system of Barbados laws governing African labor officially adopted by South Carolina in 1696

Charter 7. Royal document granting a specified group the right to form a colony and guaranteeing settlers their rights as English citizens

Indentured servent 8. Penniless people obligated to forced labor for a fixed number of years, often in exchange for passage to the New World or other benefits

Iroquois Confederation 9. Powerful Indian confederation of New York and the Great Lakes area comprised of several peoples (not the Algonquins)

Squatters 10. Poor farmers in North Carolina and elsewhere who occupied land and raised crops without gaining legal title to the soil

Royal 11. Term for a colony under direct control of the English crown

Tobacco 12. The primary staple crop of early Virginia, Maryland, and North Carolina

_____ 13. The only southern colony with a slave majority

_____ 14. The primary plantation crop of South Carolina

Savannah 15. A melting-pot town in early colonial Georgia

D. Matching People, Places, and Events

Match the person, place, or event in the left column with the proper description in the right column by inserting the correct letter on the blank line.

B 1. Powhatan	A. Founded as a haven for Roman Catholics
M 2. Raleigh and Gilbert	B. Indian leader who ruled tribes in the James River area of Virginia
I 3. Roanoke	C. Harsh military governor of Virginia who employed "Irish tactics" against the Indians
L 4. Smith and Rolfe	D. British West Indian sugar colonies where large-scale plantations and slavery took root
K 5. Virginia	E. Founded as a refuge for debtors by philanthropists
A 6. Maryland	F. Colony that was called "a vale of humility between two mountains of conceit"
C 7. Lord De La Warr	G. The unmarried ruler who led England to national glory
D 8. Jamaica and Barbados	H. The Catholic aristocrat who sought to build a sanctuary for his fellow believers
H 9. Lord Baltimore	I. The failed "lost colony" founded by Sir Walter Raleigh
O 10. South Carolina	J. Riverbank site where Virginia Company settlers planted the first permanent English colony
F 11. North Carolina	K. Colony that established a House of Burgesses in 1619
E 12. Georgia	L. Leaders who rescued Jamestown colonists from the "starving time"
N 13. James Oglethorpe	M. Elizabethan courtiers who failed in their attempts to found New World colonies
G 14. Elizabeth I	N. Philanthropic soldier-statesman who founded the Georgia colony
J 15. Jamestown	O. Colony that turned to disease-resistant African slaves for labor in its extensive rice plantations

E. Putting Things in Order

Put the following events in correct order by numbering them from 1 to 5.

1 A surprising naval victory by the English inspires a burst of national pride and paves the way for colonization.

3 A Catholic aristocrat founds a colony as a haven for his fellow believers.

4 Settlers from the West Indies found a colony on the North American mainland.

5 An English colony is founded by philanthropists as a haven for imprisoned debtors.

_a_   A company of investors launches a disaster-stricken but permanent English colony along a mosquito-infested river.

F.   Matching Cause and Effect

Match the historical cause in the left column with the proper effect in the right column by writing the correct letter on the blank line.

<table>
<tr><td colspan="2" align="center">Cause</td><td colspan="2" align="center">Effect</td></tr>
<tr>
<td>B</td>
<td>1. The English victory over the Spanish Armada</td>
<td>A.</td>
<td>Led to the two Anglo-Powhatan wars that virtually exterminated Virginia's Indian population</td>
</tr>
<tr>
<td>F</td>
<td>2. The English law of primogeniture</td>
<td>B.</td>
<td>Enabled England to gain control of the North Atlantic sea-lanes</td>
</tr>
<tr>
<td>E   (J)</td>
<td>3. The enclosing of English pastures and cropland</td>
<td>C.</td>
<td>Forced gold-hungry colonists to work and saved them from total starvation.</td>
</tr>
<tr>
<td>A</td>
<td>4. Lord De La Warr's use of brutal "Irish tactics" in Virginia</td>
<td>D.</td>
<td>Led Lord Baltimore to establish the Maryland colony</td>
</tr>
<tr>
<td>D</td>
<td>5. The English government's persecution of Roman Catholics</td>
<td>E.</td>
<td>Led to the founding of the independent-minded North Carolina colony</td>
</tr>
<tr>
<td>I</td>
<td>6. The slave codes of England's Barbados colony</td>
<td>F.</td>
<td>Led many younger sons of the gentry to seek their fortunes in exploration and colonization</td>
</tr>
<tr>
<td>C</td>
<td>7. John Smith's stern leadership in Virginia</td>
<td>G.</td>
<td>Contributed to the formation of powerful Indian coalitions like the Iroquois and the Algonquins</td>
</tr>
<tr>
<td>G</td>
<td>8. The English settlers' near-destruction of small Indian tribes</td>
<td>H.</td>
<td>Kept the buffer colony poor and largely unpopulated for a long time</td>
</tr>
<tr>
<td>J   (E)</td>
<td>9. The flight of poor farmers and religious dissenters from planter-run Virginia</td>
<td>I.</td>
<td>Became the legal basis for slavery in North America</td>
</tr>
<tr>
<td>H</td>
<td>10. Georgia's unhealthy climate, restrictions on slavery, and vulnerability to Spanish attacks</td>
<td>J.</td>
<td>Forced numerous laborers off the land and sent them looking for opportunities elsewhere</td>
</tr>
</table>

G.   Developing Historical Skills

Understanding Historical Comparisons

To understand historical events, historians frequently compare one set of conditions with another so as to illuminate both similarities and differences. In this chapter, there are comparisons of English colonization in North America with (a) England's imperial activity in Ireland (p. 26), (b) Spanish colonization (pp. 26–27), and (c) England's colonies in the West Indies (pp.34–36). Examine these three comparisons, and then answer the following questions.

1. What similarity developed between the English attitude toward the Irish and the English attitude toward Native Americans?

2. What characteristics of England after the victory over the Spanish Armada were similar to Spain's condition one century earlier?

3. How was the sugar economy of the West Indies different from the tobacco economy of the Chesapeake?

H. Map Mastery

Map Discrimination

Using the maps and charts in Chapter 2, answer the following questions.

1. *Sources of the Great Puritan Migration to New England, 1620–1650*: List any five of the English woolen district counties from which the Puritans came.

2. *Early Maryland and Virginia*: The colony of Maryland was centered around what body of water?

3. *Early Carolina and Georgia Settlements*: Which southern colony bordered on foreign, non-English territory?

4. *Early Carolina and Georgia Settlements*: Which southern English colony had the smallest western frontier?

5. *Early Carolina and Georgia Settlements*: In which colony was each of the following cities located: Charleston, Savannah, Newbern, Jamestown?

Map Challenge

1. Besides the James, what shorter river defines the peninsula where Jamestown was located?

2. What river marked the border between the Virginia and Maryland colonies?

Part III: Applying What You Have Learned

1. What were the diverse purposes of England's American colonies and how were those purposes altered in the early years of settlement?
2. What features were common to all of England's southern colonies, and what features were peculiar to each one?
3. How did the interaction and conflict between English settlers and Indians affect both parties, and contribute to developments that neither group sought?
4. How did the search for a viable labor force affect the development of the southern colonies? What was the role of African-American slavery in the early colonial settlements? Why were two southern colonies initially resistant to slavery?
5. Discuss the relations between the English settlers and the Indians of the southern Atlantic coast.
6. Compare and contrast the early colonial empires of Portugal, Spain, and England in terms of motives, economic foundations, and relations with Africans and Indians. (See Chapter 1.) What factors explain the similarities and differences in the two ventures?

3

Settling the Northern Colonies, 1619–1700

PART I: Reviewing the Chapter

A. Checklist of Learning Objectives

After mastering this chapter, you should be able to

1. describe the Puritans and their beliefs and explain why they left England for the New World.
2. explain the basic governmental and religious practices of the Massachusetts Bay Colony.
3. explain how conflict with religious dissenters, among other forces, led to the expansion of New England.
4. describe the changing relations between the English colonists and Indians.
5. explain why New York, Pennsylvania, and the other middle colonies became so ethnically, religiously, and politically diverse.
6. describe the central features of the middle colonies and explain how they differed from New England.

B. Glossary

To build your social science vocabulary, familiarize yourself with the following terms.

1. **predestination** The Calvinist doctrine that God has foreordained some people to be saved and some to be damned. "Good works could not save those whom 'predestination' had marked for the infernal fires." (p. 44)
2. **elect** In Calvinist doctrine, those who have been chosen by God for salvation. "But neither could the elect count on their predetermined salvation. . . ." (p. 44)
3. **conversion** A religious turn to God, thought by Calvinists to involve an intense, identifiable personal experience of grace. "They constantly sought, in themselves and others, signs of 'conversion.' . . ." (p. 44)
4. **visible saints** In Calvinism, those who publicly proclaimed their experience of conversion and were expected to lead godly lives. "The most devout Puritans . . . believed that only 'visible saints' . . . should be admitted to church membership." (p. 44)
5. **calling** In Protestantism, the belief that saved individuals have a religious obligation to engage in worldly work. "Like John Winthrop, [the Puritans] believed in the doctrine of a 'calling' to do God's work on this earth." (p. 47)
6. **heresy** Departure from correct or officially defined belief. ". . . she eventually boasted that she had come by her beliefs through a direct revelation from God. This was even higher heresy." (p. 48)
7. **seditious** Concerning resistance to or rebellion against the government. "[His was] a seditious blow at the Puritan idea of government's very purpose." (p. 48)
8. **commonwealth** An organized civil government or social order united for a shared purpose. "They were allowed, in effect, to become semiautonomous commonwealths." (p . 53)

9. **autocratic** Absolute or dictatorial rule. "An autocratic spirit survived, and the aristocratic element gained strength. . . ." (p. 59)

10. **passive resistance** Nonviolent action or opposition to authority, often in accord with religious or moral beliefs. "As advocates of passive resistance, [the Quakers] would turn the other cheek and rebuild their meetinghouse on the site where their enemies had torn it down." (p. 60)

11. **asylum** A place of refuge and security, especially for the persecuted or unfortunate. "Eager to establish an asylum for his people. . . ." (p. 60)

12. **proprietary** Concerning exclusive legal ownership, as of colonies granted to individuals by the monarch. "Penn's new proprietary regime was unusually liberal. . . ." (p. 61)

13. **naturalization** The granting of citizenship to foreigners or immigrants. "No restrictions were placed on immigration, and naturalization was made easy." (p. 61)

14. **blue laws** Laws designed to restrict personal behavior in accord with a strict code of morality. "Even so, 'blue laws' prohibited 'ungodly revelers,' stage plays, playing cards, dice, games, and excessive hilarity." (p. 61)

15. **ethnic** Concerning diverse peoples or cultures, specifically those of non-Anglo-Saxon background. ". . . Pennsylvania attracted a rich mix of ethnic groups." (p. 61)

Part II: Checking Your Progress

A. True-False

Where the statement is true, mark **T**. Where it is false, mark **F**, and correct it in the space immediately below.

_T_ 1. The most fervent Puritans believed that the Church of England was corrupt because it did not restrict its membership to "visible saints" who had experienced conversion.

_T_ 2. The Puritans all wanted to break away from the Church of England and establish a new "purified" church.

___ 3. The large, separatist Plymouth Colony strongly influenced Puritan Massachusetts Bay.

___ 4. Massachusetts Bay restricted the vote for elections to the General Court to adult male members of the Congregational Church.

___ 5. Roger Williams and Anne Hutchinson were both banished for organizing political rebellions against the Massachusetts Bay authorities.

_T_ 6. Rhode Island was the most religiously and politically tolerant of the New England colonies.

_T_ 7. The Wampanoag people of New England initially befriended the English colonists.

_T_ 8. Edmund Andros's autocratic Dominion of New England was overthrown in connection with the Glorious Revolution in England.

_F_ 9. King Philip's War enabled New England's Indians to recover their numbers and morale.

___ 10. New York became the most democratic and economically equal of the middle colonies.

___ 11. Dutch New Netherland was conquered in 1664 by Sweden.

___ 12. William Penn originally planned his Pennsylvania colony to be exclusively a refuge for his fellow Quakers.

___ 13. William Penn's benevolent Indian policies were supported by non-Quaker immigrants to Pennsylvania.

___ 14. The middle colonies' broad, fertile river valleys enabled them to develop a richer agricultural economy than that of New England.

___ 15. The middle colonies were characterized by tightly knit, ethically homogeneous communities that shared a common sense of religious purpose.

B.   Multiple Choice

Select the best answer and write the proper letter in the space provided.

___ 1. The principal motivation shaping the earliest settlements in New England was

    a.   the desire for political freedom.
    b.   religious commitment and devotion.
    c.   economic opportunity and the chance for a better life.
    d.   a spirit of adventure and interest in exploring the New World.

___ 2. Compared with the Plymouth Colony, the Massachusetts Bay Colony was

    a.   dedicated to complete separation from the Church of England.
    b.   afflicted with corrupt and incompetent leaders.
    c.   more focused on religious rather than political liberty.
    d.   larger and more prosperous economically.

___ 3. One reason that the Massachusetts Bay Colony was not a true democracy is that

    a.   only church members could vote for the governor and the General Court.
    b.   political offices were dominated by the clergy.
    c.   people were not permitted to discuss issues freely in their own towns.
    d.   the governor and his assistants were appointed rather than elected.

___ 4. The most distinctive feature of the Rhode Island Colony was that

    a.   it enjoyed the most complete religious freedom of all the English colonies.
    b.   it secured an official charter from England.
    c.   it contained a high proportion of well-educated and well-off colonists.
    d.   it had a strong common sense of religious purpose.

___ 5. Before the first English settlements in New England, Indians in the region had been devastated by

    a.   constant warfare with the French.
    b.   harsh weather that reduced the corn harvests and caused severe famine.
    c.   disease epidemics caused by contact with English fishermen.
    d.   intertribal conflicts caused by disputes over hunting grounds.

6. The Indian tribe that first encountered the Pilgrim colonists in New England were the

    a. Iroquois.
    b. Wampanoags.
    c. Narragansetts.
    d. Hurons.

7. The Puritan missionary efforts to convert Indians to Christianity were

    a. weak and mostly unsuccessful.
    b. initially successful but undermined by constant warfare.
    c. similar to the evangelistic efforts of the Catholic Spanish and French.
    d. developed only after the Indians were defeated and confined to reservations.

8. King Philip's War represented

    a. the first serious military conflict between New England colonists and the English King.
    b. an example of the disastrous divisions among the Wampanoags, Pequots, and Narragansetts.
    c. the last major Indian effort to halt New Englanders' encroachment on their lands.
    d. a relatively minor conflict in terms of actual fighting and casualties.

9. The primary value of the New England Confederation lay in

    a. restoring harmony between Rhode Island and the other New England colonies.
    b. promoting better relations between New England colonists and their Indian neighbors.
    c. providing the first small step on the road to intercolonial cooperation.
    d. defending colonial rights against increasing pressure from the English monarchy.

10. The event that sparked the collapse of the Dominion of New England was

    a. King Philip's War.
    b. the revocation of the Massachusetts Bay Colony's charter.
    c. Governor Andros's harsh attacks on colonial liberties.
    d. the Glorious Revolution in England.

11. The Dutch Colony of New Netherland

    a. was harshly and undemocratically governed.
    b. contained little ethnic diversity.
    c. was developed as a haven for Dutch Calvinists.
    d. enjoyed prosperity and peace under the policies of the Dutch West India Company.

12. The short-lived colony conquered by Dutch New Netherland in 1655 was

    a. New Jersey.
    b. New France.
    c. New England.
    d. New Sweden.

13. William Penn's colony of Pennsylvania

    a. sought settlers primarily from England and Scotland.
    b. experienced continuing warfare with neighboring Indian tribes.
    c. actively sought settlers from Germany and other non-British countries.
    d. set up the Quaker religion as its tax-supported established church.

___ 14. Besides Pennsylvania, Quakers were also heavily involved in the early settlement of both

    a. New Jersey and New York.
    b. New Jersey and Delaware.
    c. New Netherland and New York.
    d. Maryland and Delaware.

___ 15. The middle colonies of New York, New Jersey, Pennsylvania, and Delaware

    a. depended almost entirely on industry rather than agriculture for their prosperity.
    b. all had powerful established churches that suppressed religious dissenters.
    c. relied heavily on slave labor in agriculture.
    d. had more ethnic diversity than either New England or the southern colonies.

C. Identification

Supply the correct identification for each numbered description.

Lutheranism   1. Sixteenth-century religious reform movement begun by Martin Luther

_____ 2. English Calvinists who sought a thorough cleansing from within the Church of England

_____ 3. Radical Calvinists who considered the Church of England so corrupt that they broke with it and formed their own independent churches

Mayflower Compact   4. The shipboard agreement by the Pilgrim Fathers to establish a body politic and submit to majority rule

_____ 5. Puritans' term for their belief that Massachusetts Bay had a special arrangement with God to become a holy society

_____ 6. Charles I's political action of 1629 that led to persecution of the Puritans and the formation of the Massachusetts Bay Company

_____ 7. The *two* major nonfarming industries of Massachusetts Bay

_____ 8. Anne Hutchinson's heretical belief that the truly saved need not obey human or divine law

Banished   9. Common fate of Roger Williams and Anne Hutchinson after they were convicted of heresy in Massachusetts Bay

_____ 10. Villages where New England Indians who converted to Christianity were gathered

_____ 11. Successful military action by the colonies united in the New England Confederation

_____ 12. English revolt that also led to the overthrow of the Dominion of New England in America

_____ 13. River valley where vast estates created an aristocratic landholding elite in New Netherland and New York

_____ 14. Required, sworn statements of loyalty or religious belief, resisted by Quakers

_____ 15. Common activity in which the colonists engaged to avoid the restrictive, unpopular Navigation Laws

D. Matching People, Places, and Events

Match the person, place or event in the left column with the proper description in the right column by inserting the correct letter on the blank line.

_____ 1. Martin Luther

_____ 2. John Calvin

_____ 3. Massasoit

_____ 4. Plymouth

_____ 5. Massachusetts Bay Colony

_____ 6. John Winthrop

_____ 7. Great Puritan Migration

_____ 8. General Court

_____ 9. Puritans

_____ 10. Quakers

_____ 11. Anne Hutchinson

_____ 12. Roger Williams

M 13. King Philip

_____ 14. Peter Stuyvesant

_____ 15. William Penn

A. Dominant religious group in Massachusetts Bay
B. Founder of the most tolerant and democratic of the middle colonies
C. Mass flight by religious dissidents from the persecutions of Archbishop Laud and Charles I
D. Small colony that eventually merged into Massachusetts Bay
E. Religious dissenter convicted of the heresy of antinomianism
F. Indian leader who waged an unsuccessful war against New England
G. German monk who began Protestant Reformation
H. Religious group persecuted in Massachusetts and New York but not in Pennsylvania
I. Representative assembly of Massachusetts Bay
J. Promoter of Massachusetts Bay as a holy "city upon a hill"
K. Conqueror of New Sweden who later lost New Netherland to the English
L. Reformer whose religious ideas inspired English Puritans, Scotch Presbyterians, French Huguenots, and Dutch Reformed
M. Wampanoag chieftain who befriended English colonists
N. Colony whose government sought to enforce God's law on believers and unbelievers alike
O. Radical founder of the most tolerant New England colony

E. Putting Things in Order

Put the following events in correct order by numbering them from 1 to 10.

_____ New England Confederation achieves a notable military success.

_____ English separatists migrate from Holland to America.

_____ Swedish colony on Delaware River is conquered by Dutch neighbor.

_____ Manhattan Island is acquired by non-English settlers.

_____ Protestant Reformation begins in Europe and England.

_____ Quaker son of an English admiral obtains a royal charter for a colony.

_____ Puritans bring a thousand immigrants and a charter to America.

_____ England conquers a colony on the Hudson River.

_____ Convicted Massachusetts Bay heretic founds a colony as a haven for dissenters.

_____ James II is overthrown in England and Edmund Andros is overthrown in America.

F. Matching Cause and Effect

Match the historical cause in the left column with the proper effect in the right column by writing the correct letter on the blank line.

Cause	Effect

Cause

____ 1. Charles I's persecution of the Puritans

____ 2. Puritans' belief that their government was based on a covenant with God

____ 3. Puritan persecution of religious dissenters like Roger Williams

____ 4. The Glorious Revolution

____ 5. King Philip's War

____ 6. The Dutch West India Company's search for quick profits

____ 7. Dutch and English creation of vast Hudson Valley estates

____ 8. The English government's persecution of Quakers

____ 9. William Penn's liberal religious and immigration policies

____ 10. The middle colonies' cultivation of broad, fertile river valleys

Effect

A. Led to overthrow of Andros's Dominion of New England

B. Encouraged development of Pennsylvania, New York, and New Jersey as rich, grain-growing "bread colonies"

C. Secured political control of New York for a few aristocratic families

D. Spurred formation of the Massachusetts Bay Company and mass migration to New England

E. Encouraged large-scale foreign immigration to Pennsylvania

F. Led to restriction of political participation in colonial Massachusetts to "visible saints"

G. Spurred William Penn's founding of Pennsylvania

H. Meant that New Netherland was run as an authoritarian fur trading venture

I. Ended New England Indians' attempts to halt white expansion

J. Led to the founding of Rhode Island as a haven for unorthodox faiths

G. Developing Historical Skills

Using Quantitative Maps

Some maps, like *The Great English Migration* on p. 46, present quantitative as well as geographical information. By making a few simple calculations, additional information and conclusions can be derived.

Adding the figures on the map indicates that about 68,000 English people came to North America and the West Indies from about 1630–1642

Study the map and answer the following questions:

1. About what percentage of the total English migration went to New England? (Divide the figure for New England by the total number of immigrants.)

2. How many *more* English settlers went to the West Indies than to New England?

H. Map Mastery

Map Discrimination

Using the maps and charts in Chapter 3, answer the following questions.

1. *Seventeenth-Century New England Settlements*: Which New England colony was largely centered on a single river valley?

2. *Seventeenth-Century New England Settlements*: Which New England colony was made part of Massachusetts Bay in 1641 but separated from the Bay Colony in 1679?

3. *Seventeenth-Century New England Settlements*: When Roger Williams fled Massachusetts to found a new colony, in which direction did he go?

4. *The Stuart Dynasty in England*: Which was the only New England colony founded during the Restoration regime of Charles II?

5. *The Stuart Dynasty in England*: Which New England colony was not founded during the reigns of Charles I or Charles II?

6. *Early Settlements in the Middle Colonies, with Founding Dates*: The territory that was once New Sweden became part of which three English colonies?

Map Challenge

Using the maps on p. 49 and p. 55, write a brief essay on the following question: In what ways did the colony of New Netherland have a historical-geographical relation to its neighboring middle colonies similar to the one Massachusetts Bay had to the other New England colonies, and in what ways were the relations different?

Part III: Applying What You Have Learned

1. Compare and contrast the New England and middle colonies in terms of motives for founding, religious and social composition, and political development.

2. How did the Puritans' distinctive religious outlook affect the development of all the New England colonies?

3. "The dissent from Puritanism was as important in the formation of New England as Puritanism itself." How valid is this statement? Defend your answer.

4. Compare the pattern of relations between colonists and Indians in New England and Pennsylvania. Why did attempts at establishing friendly relations fail?

5. What efforts were made to strengthen English control over the colonies in the seventeenth century, and why did they generally fail?

6. Discuss the development of religious and political freedom in Massachusetts, Rhode Island, New York, and Pennsylvania. How did the greater degree of such freedoms enjoyed by Rhode Island and Pennsylvania affect life in those colonies?

7. What economic, social, and ethnic conditions typical of the early southern colonies (Chapter 2) were generally absent in the New England and middle colonies? What characteristics did the middle colonies have that were not generally present in the South?

4

American Life in the Seventeenth Century, 1607–1692

Part I: Reviewing the Chapter

A. Checklist of Learning Objectives

After mastering this chapter, you should be able to

1. describe the basic population structure and social life of the seventeenth-century colonies.
2. compare and contrast the different populations and ways of life of the southern colonies and New England.
3. explain how the problems of indentured servitude led to political trouble and the growth of African slavery.
4. describe the slave trade and the character of early African-American slavery
5. explain how the New England way of life centered on family, town, and church, and describe the changes that affected this way of life.
6. describe the various conditions affecting women and family life in the seventeenth-century colonies.

B. Glossary

To build your social science vocabulary, familiarize yourself with the following terms.

1. **headright** The right to acquire a certain amount of land granted to the person who finances the passage of a laborer. "Masters—not servants themselves—thus reaped the benefits of land-ownership from the headright system." (p. 67)
2. **disfranchise** To take away the right to vote. "The Virginia Assembly in 1670 disfranchised most of the landless knockabouts. . . ." (p. 68)
3. **civil war** Any conflict between the citizens or inhabitants of the same country. "As this civil war in Virginia ground on . . . ." (p. 68)
4. **tidewater** The territory adjoining water affected by tides—that is, near the seacoast or coastal rivers. "Bacon . . . had pitted the hard scrabble backcountry frontiersmen against the haughty gentry of the tidewater plantations." (pp. 68, 70)
5. **middle passage** That portion of a slave ship's journey in which slaves were carried from Africa to the Americas. ". . . the captives were herded aboard sweltering ships for the gruesome 'middle passage.'. . ." (p. 71)
6. **fertility** The ability to mate and produce abundant young. "The captive black population of the Chesapeake area soon began to grow not only through new imports but also through its own fertility. . . ." (p. 72)
7. **menial** Fit for servants; humble or low. "But chiefly they performed the sweaty toil of clearing swamps, grubbing out trees, and other menial tasks." (p. 73)
8. **militia** An armed force of citizens called out only in emergencies. "[They] tried to march to Spanish Florida, only to be stopped by the local militia." (p. 73)

9. **hierarchy** A social group arranged in ranks or classes. "The rough equality . . . was giving way to a hierarchy of wealth and status. . . ." (p. 73)

10. **corporation** A group or institution granted legal rights to carry on certain specified activities. ". . . the Massachusetts Puritans established Harvard College, today the oldest corporation in America. . . ." (p. 79)

11. **jeremiad** A sermon or prophecy recounting wrongdoing, warning of doom, and calling for repentance. "Jeremiads continued to thunder from the pulpits. . . ." (p. 80)

12. **lynching** The illegal execution of an accused person by mob action, without due process of law. "A hysterical 'witch-hunt' ensued, leading to the legal lynching in 1692 of twenty individuals. . . ." (p. 80)

13. **hinterland** An inland region set back from a port, river, or seacoast. ". . . their accusers came largely from subsistence farming families in Salem's hinterland." (p. 80)

14. **social structure** The basic pattern of the distribution of status and wealth in a society. ". . . many settlers . . . tried to re-create on a modified scale the social structure they had known in the Old World." (p. 83)

15. **blue blood** Of noble or upper-class descent. ". . . would-be American blue bloods resented the pretensions of the 'meaner sort.'. . ." (p. 83)

Part II: Checking Your Progress

A. True-False

Where the statement is true, mark **T**. Where it is false, mark **F**, and correct it in the space immediately below.

____ 1. Life expectancy among the seventeenth-century settlers of Maryland and Virginia was about sixty years.

____ 2. Because men greatly outnumbered women in the Chesapeake region, a fierce competition arose among men for scarce females.

____ 3. By the eighteenth century, the Chesapeake population was growing on the basis of natural increase.

____ 4. Chesapeake Bay tobacco planters responded to falling prices by cutting back production.

____ 5. The "headright" system of land grants to those who brought laborers to America primarily benefited wealthy planters rather than the poor indentured servants.

____ 6. Most of the European immigrants who came to Virginia and Maryland in the seventeenth century were indentured servants.

____ 7. Bacon's Rebellion involved an alliance of white indentured servants and Indians who attacked the elite planter class.

____ 8. African slaves began to replace white indentured servants as the primary labor supply in the plantation colonies in the 1680s.

____ 9. Slaves brought to North America developed a culture that mixed African and American elements.

____ 10. Directly beneath the wealthy slaveowning planters in the southern social structure were the white indentured servants.

____ 11. On average, married women in New England bore about ten children, of whom eight typically survived.

____ 12. New England expansion was carried out primarily by independent pioneers and land speculators who bought up large plots and then sold them to individual farmers.

____ 13. New England women enjoyed fewer rights to inherit and own property than women in the South.

____ 14. New England's commercial wealth was based on overseas shipment of the agricultural products of its rich soil.

____ 15. Seventeenth-century American life was generally simple and lacking in displays of wealth or elaborate class distinctions.

B. Multiple Choice

Select the best answer and write the proper letter in the space provided.

____ 1. For most of their early history, the colonies of Maryland and Virginia

    a. provided a healthy environment for child rearing.
    b. contained far more men than women.
    c. had harsh laws punishing premarital sexual relations.
    d. encouraged the formation of stable and long-lasting marriages.

____ 2. The primary beneficiaries of the "headright" system were

    a. landowners who paid the transatlanic passage for indentured servants.
    b. widows who acquired new husbands from England.
    c. indentured servants who were able to acquire their own land.
    d. English ship owners who transported new laborers across the Atlantic.

____ 3. The primary cause of Bacon's Rebellion was

    a. Governor Berkeley's harsh treatment of the Indians.
    b. the refusal of landlords to grant indentured servants their freedom.
    c. the poverty and discontent of many single young men unable to acquire land.
    d. the persecution of the colonists by King Charles II.

____ 4. African slavery became the prevalent form of labor in the 1680s when

    a. planters were no longer able to rely on white indentured servants as a labor force.
    b. the first captives were brought from Africa to the New World.
    c. blacks could be brought to the New World in safer and healthier condition.
    d. the once-clear legal difference between a servant and a slave began to be blurred.

5. The culture that developed among the slaves in the English colonies of North America was

    a. derived primarily from that of the white masters.
    b. based mainly on the traditions of southern Africa.
    c. a combination of several African and American cultures.
    d. originally developed in the West Indies and spread northward.

6. Political and economic power in the southern colonies was dominated by

    a. urban professional classes such as lawyers and bankers.
    b. small landowners.
    c. wealthy planters.
    d. the English royal governors.

7. Because there were few urban centers in the colonial South,

    a. good roads between the isolated plantations were constructed early on.
    b. a professional class of lawyers and financiers was slow to develop.
    c. the rural church became the central focus of southern social and economic life.
    d. there were almost no people of wealth and culture in the region.

8. Puritan lawmakers in New England prevented married women from having property rights because

    a. they believed that property should be held by towns, not private citizens.
    b. they feared that too much property would fall into the control of the numerous widows.
    c. they feared that separate property rights for women would undercut the unity of married couples.
    d. the Bible plainly prohibited women from owning property.

9. In New England, elementary education

    a. was mandatory for any town with more than fifty families.
    b. failed to provide even basic literacy to most citizens.
    c. was less widespread than in the South.
    d. was oriented to preparing students for entering college.

10. The Congregational Church of the Puritans contributed to

    a. the development of basic democracy in the New England town meeting.
    b. the extremely hierarchical character of New England life.
    c. the social harmony and unity displayed throughout the seventeenth century in New England towns.
    d. the growing movement toward women's rights in New England.

11. In contrast to the Chesapeake Bay colonists, those in New England

    a. had fewer women and more men in their population.
    b. had shorter life expectancies.
    c. practiced birth control as a means of preventing overpopulation.
    d. enjoyed longer lives and more stable families.

___ 12. The focus of much of New England's politics, religion, and education was the institution of

    a. the colonial legislature.
    b. the town.
    c. the militia company.
    d. the college.

___ 13. The "Half-Way Covenant" provided

    a. baptism but not "full communion" to people who had not had a conversion experience.
    b. partial participation in politics to people who were not church members.
    c. admission to communion but not to voting membership in the church.
    d. partial participation in church affairs for women.

___ 14. Those people accused of being witches in Salem were generally

    a. from the poorer and more uneducated segments of the town.
    b. notorious for their deviation from the moral norms of the community.
    c. outspoken opponents of the Puritan clergy.
    d. from families associated with Salem's burgeoning market economy.

___ 15. English settlers greatly changed the character of the New England environment by

    a. raising wheat and oats rather than the corn grown by Indians.
    b. their extensive introduction of livestock.
    c. beating trails through the woods as they pursued seasonal hunting and fishing.
    d. building an extensive system of roads and canals.

C. Identification

Supply the correct identification for each numbered description.

_____ 1. Early Maryland and Virginia settlers had difficulty creating them and even more difficulty making them last

_____ 2. Primary cause of death among tobacco-growing settlers

_____ 3. Immigrants who received passage to America in exchange for a fixed term of labor

_____ 4. Maryland and Virginia's system of granting land to anyone who would pay trans-Atlantic passage for laborers

_____ 5. Fate of many of Nathaniel Bacon's followers, though not of Bacon himself

_____ 6. American colony that was home to the Newport slave market and many slave traders

_____ 7. English company that lost its monopoly on the slave trade in 1698

_____ 8. African-American dialect that blended English with Yoruba, Ibo, and Hausa

_____ 9. Uprisings that occurred in New York City in 1712 and in South Carolina in 1739

_____ 10. Wealthy extended clans like the Fitzhughs, Lees, and Washingtons that dominated politics in the most populous colony

_____ 11. Approximate marriage age of most New England women

_____ 12. The basic local political institution of New England, in which all freemen gathered to elect officials and debate local affairs

_____ 13. Formula devised by Puritan ministers in 1662 to offer partial church membership to people who had not experienced conversion

_____ 14. Late seventeenth-century judicial event that inflamed popular feelings, led to the deaths of twenty people, and weakened the Puritan clergy's prestige

_____ 15. Primary occupation of most seventeenth-century Americans

D. Matching People, Places, and Events

Match the person, place, or event in the left column with the proper description in the right column by inserting the correct letter on the blank line.

_____ 1. Chesapeake

_____ 2. Indentured servants

_____ 3. Nathaniel Bacon

_____ 4. Governor Berkeley

_____ 5. Royal African Company

_____ 6. Middle passage

_____ 7. Ringshout

_____ 8. New York City slave revolt of 1712

_____ 9. Lees, Fitzhughs, and Washingtons

_____ 10. "New England conscience"

_____ 11. Harvard

_____ 12. William and Mary

_____ 13. Half-Way Covenant

_____ 14. Salem witch trials

_____ 15. Leisler's Rebellion

A. Major middle-colonies rebellion that caused thirty-three deaths

B. Helped erase the earlier Puritan distinction between the converted "elect" and other members of society

C. Small New York revolt of 1689–1691 that reflected class antagonism between landlords and merchants

D. Primary laborers in early southern colonies until the 1680s

E. Experience for which human beings were branded and chained, and which only 80 percent survived

F. Some of the "FFVs" who controlled the House of Burgesses in colonial Virginia

G. West African religious rite, retained by African-Americans, in which participants responded to the shouts of a preacher

H. Phenomena started by adolescent girls' accusations that ended with the deaths of twenty people

I. Virginia-Maryland bay area, site of the earliest colonial settlements

J. The legacy of Puritan religion that inspired idealism and reform among later generations of Americans

K. Colonial Virginia official who crushed rebels and wreaked cruel revenge

L. The oldest college in the South, founded in 1793

M. Organization whose loss of the slave trade monopoly in 1698 led to free-enterprise expansion of the business

N. Agitator who led poor former indentured servants and frontiersmen on a rampage against Indians and colonial government

O. The oldest college in America, originally based on the Puritan commitment to an educated ministry

E. Putting Things in Order

Put the following events in correct order by numbering them from 1 to 10.

____ "Legal lynching" of twenty accused witches occurs.

____ Royal slave trade monopoly ends.

____ First colonial college is founded.

____ Landless whites in Virginia lose the right to vote.

____ Major rebellion by African-Americans occurs in one of the middle colonies.

____ Southern slaves in revolt try but fail to march to Spanish Florida.

____ Partial church membership is opened to the unconverted.

____ African slaves begin to replace white indentured labor on southern plantations.

____ Poor Virginia whites revolt against governor and rich planters.

____ First Africans arrive in Virginia.

F. Matching Cause and Effect

Match the historical cause in the left column with the proper effect in the right column by writing the correct letter on the blank line.

Cause		Effect
____ 1. The severe shortage of females in southern colonies	A.	Inspired passage of strict "slave codes"
____ 2. Poor white males' anger at their inability to acquire land or start families	B. C.	Sparked Bacon's Rebellion Produced large number of unattached males and weak family structure
____ 3. Planters' fears of indentured servants' rebellion, coupled with rising wages in England	D.	Thwarted success in agriculture but helped create the tough New England character
____ 4. The dramatic increase in colonial slave population after 1680s	E.	Inspired the Half-Way Covenant and jeremiad preaching
____ 5. The growing proportion of female slaves in the Chesapeake region after 1720	F.	Reduced forests and damaged the soil
____ 6. New Englanders' introduction of livestock and intensive agriculture	G.	Produced high birthrates and a very stable family structure
____ 7. The healthier climate and more equal male-female ratio in New England	H.	Fostered stronger slave families and growth of slave population through natural reproduction of children
____ 8. The decline of religious devotion and in number of conversions in New England	I.	Underlay the Salem witchcraft persecutions
____ 9. Unsettled New England social conditions and anxieties about the decline of the Puritan religious heritage	J.	Caused southern planters to switch from indentured-servant labor to African slavery
____ 10. The rocky soil and harsh climate of New England		

G. Developing Historical Skills

Learning from Historical Documents

The illustrations on pp. 69 and 79 reproduce parts of two colonial documents: excerpts from an indentured servant's contract and some pages from children's school materials.. By carefully examining even these small partial documents, you can learn more about early colonial culture and ideas.

Answering the following questions will illustrate the kind of information that historical documents can provide.

1. What are the principal goals that both the master and the indentured servant are seeking in the contract?

2. What potential problems does each side anticipate?

3. What does the reference to the mother's consent suggest about this servant's condition?

4. What do the children's materials tell us about how the Puritans wanted their children to think about the relation between education and moral behavior?

5. Give two examples from these materials of how the Puritans incorporated religious teaching into their children's instruction.

Part III: Applying What You Have Learned

1. How did the factors of population, economics, disease, and climate shape the basic social conditions and ways of life of early Americans in both the South and New England?

2. How did African-Americans develop a culture that combined African and American elements? What were some of the features of that culture?

3. How did the numbers and condition of women affect family life and society in New England, among southern whites, and among African-American slaves? Compare and contrast the typical family conditions and ways of life among various members of these three groups.

4. How did the harsh climate and soil, stern religion, and tightly knit New England town shape the "Yankee character"?

5. Compare the conditions of seventeenth-century social, economic, and religious life in New England and the Chesapeake region.

6. How did the Salem witch episode reflect the tensions and changes in seventeenth-century New England life and thought?

7. In what ways did the English and Africans who came to America in the seventeenth century have to shape their society and way of life to fit the conditions they faced in the New World?

5

Colonial Society on the Eve of Revolution, 1700–1775

PART I: Reviewing the Chapter

A. Checklist of Learning Objectives

After mastering this chapter, you should be able to

1. describe the basic population and social structure of the eighteenth-century colonies and indicate how they had changed since the seventeenth century.
2. explain how the economic development of the colonies altered the patterns of social prestige and wealth.
3. explain the causes and effects of the Great Awakening.
4. describe the origins and development of education, culture, and the learned professions in the colonies.
5. describe the basic features of colonial politics, including the role of various official and informal political institutions.

B. Glossary

To build your social science vocabulary, familiarize yourself with the following terms.

1. **melting pot** The mingling of diverse ethnic groups in America, including the idea that these groups are or should be "melting" into a single culture or people. "Colonial America was a melting pot and had been from the outset." (p. 85)
2. **sect** A small religious group that has broken away from some larger mainstream church, often claiming superior or exclusive possession of religious truth. (A **denomination** is a branch of the church—usually Protestant—but makes no such exclusive claims.) "They belonged to several different Protestant sects. . . ." (p. 85)
3. **agitators** Those who seek to excite or persuade the public on some issue. "Already experienced colonizers and agitators in Ireland, the Scots-Irish proved to be superb frontiersmen. . . ." (p. 86)
4. **stratification** The visible arrangement of society into a hierarchical pattern, with distinct social groups layered one on top of the other. ". . . colonial society . . . was beginning to show signs of stratification. . . ." (p. 87)
5. **mobility** The capacity to pass readily from one social or economic condition to another. ". . . barriers to mobility . . . raised worries about the 'Europeanization' of America." (p. 87)
6. **elite** The smaller group at the top of a society or institution, usually possessing wealth, power, or special privileges. ". . . these elites now feathered their nests more finely." (p. 87)
7. **almshouse** A home for the poor, supported by charity or public funds. "Both Philadelphia and New York built almshouses in the 1730s. . . ." (p. 87)
8. **gentry** Landowners of substantial property, social standing, and leisure, but not titled nobility. "Wealth was concentrated in the hands of the largest slaveowners, widening the gap between the prosperous gentry and the 'poor whites'. . . ." (p. 90)

9. **tenant farmer** One who rents rather than owns land. ". . . the 'poor whites' . . . were increasingly forced to become tenant farmers." (p. 90)

10. **penal code** The body of criminal laws specifying offenses and prescribing punishments. "But many convicts were the unfortunate victims . . . of a viciously unfair English penal code. . . ." (p. 90)

11. **veto** The executive power to prevent acts passed by the legislature from becoming law. "Thomas Jefferson, himself a slaveholder, assailed the British vetoes. . . ." (p. 90)

12. **apprentice** A person who works under a master to acquire instruction in a trade or profession. "Aspiring young doctors served for a while as apprentices to older practitioners. . . ." (p. 90)

13. **speculation** Buying land or anything else in the hope of profiting by an expected rise in price. "Commercial ventures and land speculation . . . were the surest avenues to speedy wealth." (p. 91)

14. **revival** In religion, a movement of renewed enthusiasm and commitment, often accompanied by special meetings or evangelical activity. "The stage was thus set for a rousing religious revival." (p. 96)

15. **secular** Belonging to the worldly sphere rather than to the specifically sacred or churchly. "A more secular approach was evident late in the eighteenth century. . . ." (p. 98)

Part II: Checking Your Progress

A. True-False

Where the statement is true, mark **T**. Where it is false, mark **F**, and correct it in the space immediately below.

_____ 1. Most of the spectacular growth of the colonial population came from immigration rather than natural increase.

_____ 2. The most numerous white ethnic groups in the colonies were the Germans and the Scots-Irish.

_____ 3. Compared with the seventeenth century colonies, the eighteenth-century colonies were becoming more socially equal and democratic.

_____ 4. The lowest class of whites in the colonies consisted of the convicted criminals and prisoners shipped to America by British authorities

_____ 5. Thomas Jefferson's condemnation of British support of the slave trade was removed from the Declaration of Independence by other members of Congress.

_____ 6. The most highly regarded professionals in the colonies were doctors and lawyers.

_____ 7. Besides agriculture, the most important colonial economic activities were fishing, shipping, and ocean-going trade.

_____ 8. Colonial merchants were generally satisfied to trade in protected British markets and accepted imperial restrictions on trade with other countries.

_____ 9. The established Anglican Church was a more powerful force in colonial life than the Congregational Church of New England.

____ 10. The Great Awakening was a revival of fervent religion after a period of religious decline caused by clerical over-intellectualism and lay liberalism in doctrine.

____ 11. Great Awakening revivalists like Jonathan Edwards and George Whitefield tried to replace the older Puritan ideas of conversion and salvation with more rational and less emotional beliefs.

____ 12. The Great Awakening broke down denominational and sectional barriers, creating a greater sense of a common American identity and a united destiny.

____ 13. Most early colonial education, including that at the college level, was closely linked with religion.

____ 14. The greatest colonial cultural achievements came in art and imaginative literature rather than in theology and political theory.

____ 15. The central point of conflict in colonial politics was the relation between the democratically elected lower house of the assembly and the governors appointed by the king or colonial proprietor.

B. Multiple Choice

Select the best answer and write the proper letter in the space provided.

____ 1. The primary reason for the spectacular growth of America's population in the eighteenth century was

    a. the conquering of new territories.
    b. the natural fertility of the population.
    c. the increased importation of white indentured servants and black slaves.
    d. new immigration from Europe.

____ 2. German settlement in the colonies was especially heavy in

    a. Massachusetts.
    b. Maryland.
    c. New York.
    d. Pennsylvania.

____ 3. The Scots-Irish eventually became concentrated especially in

    a. coastal areas of the Middle Colonies and the South.
    b. the New England colonies.
    c. the frontier areas.
    d. the cities.

____ 4. Compared with the seventeenth century, American colonial society in the eighteenth century showed

    a. greater domination by small farmers and artisans.
    b. greater equality of wealth and status.
    c. greater gaps in wealth and status between rich and poor.
    d. greater opportunity for convicts and indentured servants to climb to the top.

5. The most honored professional in colonial America was the

   a. lawyer.
   b. clergyman.
   c. doctor.
   d. journalist.

6. The primary source of livelihood for most colonial Americans was

   a. manufacturing.
   b. agriculture.
   c. lumbering.
   d. commerce and trade.

7. Indians and African-Americans shared in the common American experience of

   a. migrating westward in search of free land.
   b. creating new cultures and societies out of the mingling of diverse ethnic groups.
   c. forming closed, settled communities that resisted outsiders.
   d. clinging to traditional cultural values brought from the Old World.

8. An unfortunate group of involuntary immigrants who ranked even below indentured servants on the American social scale were

   a. the younger sons of English gentry.
   b. French-Canadian fur traders.
   c. convicts and paupers.
   d. single women.

9. The "triangular trade" involved the sale of rum, molasses, and slaves among the ports of

   a. Virginia, Canada, and Britain.
   b. the West Indies, France, and South America.
   c. New England, Britain, and Spain.
   d. New England, Africa, and the West Indies.

10. The passage of British restrictions on trade encouraged colonial merchants to

    a. organize political resistance in the British Parliament.
    b. find ways to smuggle and otherwise evade the law by trading with other countries.
    c. turn to domestic trade within the colonies.
    d. turn from trading to such other enterprises as fishing and manufacturing.

11. Besides offering rest and refreshment, colonial taverns served an important function as centers of

    a. news and political opinion.
    b. trade and business.
    c. medicine and law.
    d. religious revival.

12. The Anglican Church suffered in colonial America because of

    a. its strict doctrines and hierarchical church order.
    b. its poorly qualified clergy and close ties with British authorities.
    c. its inability to adjust to conditions of life in New England.
    d. its reputation for fostering fanatical revivalism.

13. The two denominations that enjoyed the status of "established" churches in various colonies were the
   a. Quakers and Dutch Reformed.
   b. Baptists and Lutherans.
   c. Anglicans and Congregationalists.
   d. Roman Catholics and Presbyterians.

14. Among the many important results of the Great Awakening was that it
   a. broke down sectional boundaries and created a greater sense of common American identity.
   b. contributed to greater religious liberalism and toleration in the churches.
   c. caused a decline in colonial concern for education.
   d. moved Americans closer to a single religious outlook.

15. A primary weapon used by colonial legislatures in their conflicts with royal governors was
   a. extending the franchise to include almost all adult white citizens.
   b. passing laws prohibiting the governors from owning land or industries.
   c. voting them out of office.
   d. using their power of the purse to withhold the governor's salary.

C. Identification

Supply the correct identification for each numbered description.

_____ 1. Corruption of a German word used as a term for German immigrants in Pennsylvania

_____ 2. Ethnic group that had already relocated once before immigrating to America and settling largely on the Western frontier of the middle and southern colonies

_____ 3. Rebellious movement of frontiersmen in the southern colonies that included future President Andrew Jackson

_____ 4. Popular term for convicted criminals dumped on colonies by British authorities

_____ 5. Term for New England settlements where Indians from various tribes were gathered to be Christianized

_____ 6. A once-despised profession that rose in prestige after 1750 because its practitioners defended colonial rights

_____ 7. Small but profitable trade route that linked New England, Africa, and the West Indies

_____ 8. Popular colonial centers of recreation, gossip, and political debate

_____ 9. Term for tax-supported condition of Congregational and Anglican churches, but not of Baptists, Quakers, and Roman Catholics

_____ 10. Spectacular, emotional religious revival of the 1730s and 1740s

_____ 11. Ministers who supported the Great Awakening against the "old light" clergy who rejected it

_____ 12. Institutions that were founded in greater numbers as a result of the Great Awakening, although a few had been founded earlier

_____ 13. The case that established the precedent that true statements about public officials could not be prosecuted as libel

_____ 14. The upper house of a colonial legislature appointed by the crown or the proprietor

_____ 15. Benjamin Franklin's highly popular collection of information, parables, and advice

D. Matching People, Places, and Events

Match the person, place, or event in the left column with the proper description in the right column by inserting the correct letter on the blank line.

____ 1. Philadelphia

____ 2. African-Americans

____ 3. Scots-Irish

____ 4. Paxton Boys and Regulators

____ 5. Patrick Henry

____ 6. Molasses Act

____ 7. Anglican church

____ 8. Jonathan Edwards

____ 9. George Whitefield

____ 10. Phillis Wheatley

____ 11. Benjamin Franklin

____ 12. John Peter Zenger

____ 13. Quakers

____ 14. Baptists

____ 15. John Singleton Copley

A. Itinerant British evangelist who spread the Great Awakening throughout the colonies

B. Colonial printer whose case helped begin freedom of the press

C. Colonial painter who studied and worked in Britain

D. Leading city of the colonies; home of Benjamin Franklin

E. Largest non-English group in the colonies

F. Dominant religious group in colonial Pennsylvania, criticized by others for their attitudes toward Indians

G. Former slave who became a poet at an early age

H. Scots-Irish frontiersmen who protested against colonial elites of Pennsylvania and North Carolina

I. Attempt by British authorities to squelch colonial trade with French West Indies

J. Brilliant New England theologian who instigated the Great Awakening

K. Group that settled the frontier, made whiskey, and hated the British and other governmental authorities

L. Nonestablished religious group that benefited from the Great Awakening

M. Author, scientist, printer; "the first civilized American"

N. Eloquent lawyer-orator who argued in defense of colonial rights

O. Established religion in southern colonies and New York; weakened by lackadaisical clergy and too-close ties with British crown

E. Putting Things in Order

Put the following events in correct order by numbering them 1 to 10.

____ Epochal freedom of the press case is settled.

____ First southern college to train Anglican clergy is founded.

____ Britain vetoes colonial effort to halt slave importation.

____ Scots-Irish protestors stage armed marches.

____ First medical attempts are made to prevent dreaded disease epidemics.

____ Parliament attempts to restrict colonial trade with French West Indies.

____ Princeton College is founded to train "new light" ministers.

____ An eloquent British preacher spreads evangelical religion through the colonies.

____ Benjamin Franklin starts printing his most famous publication.

____ A fiery, intellectual preacher sets off a powerful religious revival in New England.

F. Matching Cause and Effect

Match the historical cause in the left column with the proper effect in the right column by writing the correct letter on the blank line.

Cause	**Effect**
____ 1. The high natural fertility of the colonial population	**A.** Prompted colonial assemblies to withhold royal governors' salaries
	B. Created the conditions for the Great Awakening to erupt in the early eighteenth century
____ 2. The heavy immigration of Germans, Scots-Irish, Africans, and others into the colonies	**C.** Resulted in the development of a colonial "melting pot," only one-half English by 1775
	D. Was met by British attempts to restrict colonial trade, e.g., the Molasses Act
____ 3. The large profits made by merchants as military suppliers for imperial wars	**E.** Increased the wealth of the eighteenth-century colonial elite
____ 4. American merchants' search for non-British markets	**F.** Led to the increase of American population to one-third of England's in 1775
	G. Forced the migration of colonial artists to Britain to study and pursue artistic careers
____ 5. Dry over-intellectualism and and loss of religious commitment	**H.** Marked the beginnings of freedom of printed political expression in the colonies
____ 6. The Great Awakening	**I.** Reinforced colonial property qualifications for voting
____ 7. The Zenger case	**J.** Stimulated a fervent, emotional style of religion, denominational divisions, and a greater sense of inter-colonial American identity.
____ 8. The appointment of unpopular or incompetent royal governors to colonies	
____ 9. Upper-class fear of "democratic excesses" by poor whites	
____ 10. The lack of artistic concerns, cultural tradition, and leisure in the colonies	

G. Developing Historical Skills

Learning from Map Comparison

By comparing two similar maps dealing with the same historical period, you can derive additional information about the relations between the two topics the maps emphasize. The map on p. 85 shows immigrant groups in 1775, and the map on p. 91 shows the colonial economy. By examining both maps, you can learn about the likely economic activities of various immigrant groups.

Answer the following questions.

1. To what extent were Scots-Irish immigrants involved in tobacco cultivation?

2. What agricultural activities were most of the Dutch immigrants involved in?

3. With what part of the agricultural economy were African-American slaves most involved?

4. Which major immigrant group may have had some involvement in the colonial iron industry?

H. Map Mastery

Map Discrimination

Using the maps and charts in Chapter 5, answer the following questions.

1. Which section contained the fewest non-English minorities?

2. The Scots-Irish were concentrated most heavily on the frontiers of which four colonies?

3. In which colony were German and Swiss immigrants most heavily concentrated?

4. Which colony contained the largest concentration of French immigrants?

5. Which *four* colonies had the greatest concentration of tobacco growing?

6. Which was the larger minority in the colonies: all the non-English white ethnic groups together, or the African-Americans?

7. Which *two* social groups stood between the landowning farmers and the slaves in the colonial social pyramid?

8. Which of the following religious groups were most heavily concentrated in the middle colonies: Lutherans, Dutch Reformed, Quakers, Baptists, Roman Catholics?

9. How many years after the Declaration of Independence in 1776 was the last church officially disestablished?

10. How many of the colonial colleges were originally founded by "established" denominations?

Map Challenge

Using the map on p. 85, write a brief essay in which you compare the "ethnic mix" in each of the following colonies: North Carolina, Virginia, Pennsylvania, New York, Massachusetts.

Part III: Applying What You Have Learned

1. What factors contributed to the growing numbers and wealth of the American colonists in the eighteenth century?

2. Describe the structure of colonial society in the eighteenth century. What developments tended to make society less equal and more hierarchical?

3. What were the causes and consequences of the Great Awakening?

4. What features of colonial politics contributed to the development of popular democracy, and what kept political life from being more truly democratic?

5. How did the various churches, established and nonestablished, fundamentally shape eighteenth-century colonial life, including education and politics?

6. What made American society far more equal than Britain's, but seemingly less equal than it had been in the seventeenth century?

6

The Duel for North America, 1608–1763

PART I: Reviewing the Chapter

A. Checklist of Learning Objectives

After mastering this chapter, you should be able to

1. explain why France and Britain engaged in their great contest for North America and why Britain won.
2. explain how the series of wars with France affected Britain's American subjects and helped pave the way for their later rebellion against the mother country.
3. describe France's North American empire and compare it with Britain's colonies.
4. explain how North American political and military events were affected by developments on the larger European stage.

B. Glossary

To build your social science vocabulary, familiarize yourself with the following terms.

1. **domestic** Concerning the internal affairs of a country. "It was convulsed . . . by foreign wars and domestic strife. . . ." (p. 106)
2. **minister** In politics, a person appointed by the head of state to take charge of some department or agency of government. "France blossomed . . . led by a series of brilliant ministers. . . ." (p. 107)
3. **autocratic** Marked by strict authoritarian rule, without consent or participation by the populace. "This royal regime was almost completely autocratic." (p. 107)
4. **peasant** A farmer or agricultural laborer, sometimes legally tied to the land. "Landowning French peasants . . . had little economic motive to move." (pp. 107–108)
5. **coureurs des bois** French-Canadian fur trappers; literally, "runners of the woods." "These colorful coureurs des bois . . . were also runners of risks. . . ." (p. 108)
6. **voyageurs** French-Canadian explorers, adventurers, and traders. "Singing, paddle-swinging French *voyageurs* also recruited Indians. . . ." (p. 108)
7. **flotilla** A fleet of boats, usually smaller vessels. "The Indian fur flotilla . . . numbered four hundred canoes." (p. 108)
8. **ecological** Concerning the relations between the biological organisms and their environment. ". . . they extinguished the beaver population in many areas, inflicting incalculable ecological damage." (p. 109)
9. **mutinous** Concerning revolt by subordinate soldiers or seamen against their commanding officers. "But he failed to find the Mississippi delta, . . . and was murdered by his mutinous men." (p. 109)
10. **strategic** Concerning the placement and planned movement of large-scale military forces so as to gain advantage, usually prior to actual engagement with the enemy. "Commanding

the mouth of the Mississippi River, this strategic semitropical outpost also tapped the fur trade of the huge interior valley." (p. 109)

11. **guerrilla warfare** Unconventional combat waged by small military units using hit-and-run tactics. ". . . so the combatants waged a kind of primitive guerilla warfare." (p. 110)

12. **sallies (sally)** In warfare, very rapid military movements, usually by small units, against an enemy force or position. "For their part the British colonists failed miserably in sallies against Quebec and Montreal. . . ." (p. 110)

13. **siege** A military operation of surrounding and attacking a fortified place, often over a sustained period. "After a ten-hour siege he was forced to surrender. . . ." (p. 113)

14. **regulars** Trained professional soldiers, as distinct from militia or conscripts. ". . . they had fought bravely alongside the crack British regulars. . . ." (p. 116)

15. **commissions** An official certification granting a commanding rank in the armed forces. ". . . the British refused to recognize any American militia commission. . . ." (p. 117)

Part II: Checking Your Progress

A. True-False

Where the statement is true, mark **T**. Where it is false, mark **F**, and correct it in the space immediately below.

T   1. French colonization was late developing because of internal religious and political conflict.

F   2. The French empire in North America rested on an economic foundation of forestry and sugar production.

T   3. Early imperial conflicts in North America often saw the French and their Indian allies engaging in guerrilla warfare against British frontier outposts.

T   4. Colonists in British North America managed to avoid direct involvement in most of Britain's "world wars" until the French and Indian War.

T   5. In the early seventeenth century, both France and England committed large regular forces to what they considered the crucial struggle for control of North America.

F   6. George Washington's battle at Fort Necessity substantially resolved the issue of control of the Ohio Valley.

T   7. The Albany Congress demonstrated a strong desire among some English colonists to overcome their differences and control their own affairs.

T   8. William Pitt's successful strategy in the French and Indian War was to concentrate British forces and try to capture the strongholds of Louisbourg, Quebec, and Montreal.

F   9. British regular troops under General Braddock succeeded in capturing the key French forts in the Ohio Valley.

T   10. The French and Indian War left France with only Louisiana as a remnant of its once-mighty North American empire.

F 11. American soldiers gained new respect for British military men after the British success against the French.

T 12. The American colonists enthusiastically united in patriotic support of the British cause against the French.

T 13. The removal of the French threat made American colonists more secure and therefore less reliant on the mother country for protection.

T 14. A British commander used the harsh tactics of distributing blankets infected with small-pox to suppress Pontiac's Indian uprising.

T 15. The British government's attempt to prohibit colonial expansion across the Appalachian Mountains aroused colonial anger and defiance of the law.

B. Multiple Choice

Select the best answer and write the proper letter in the space provided.

B 1. Compared with the English colonies, New France was

    a. more wealthy and successful.
    b. better able to maintain consistently friendly relations with the Indians.
    c. more heavily populated.
    d. more autocratically governed.

D 2. The expansion of New France occurred especially

    a. in the interior mountain areas.
    b. along the paths of lakes and rivers.
    c. in areas already occupied by English settlers.
    d. to the north of the original St. Lawrence River settlement.

B 3. Colonial Americans were unhappy after the peace treaty following the "War of Jenkins's Ear" because

    a. it failed to settle the issue that had caused the war.
    b. it gave the Louisbourg fortress they had captured back to France.
    c. it created further conflicts with Spain.
    d. it failed to deal with the issue of Indian attacks on the frontier.

C 4. The original cause of the French and Indian War was

    a. conflict in Europe between Britain and France.
    b. British removal of the "Acadian" French settlers from Nova Scotia.
    c. competition between French and English colonists for land in the Ohio River valley.
    d. a French attack on George Washington's Virginia headquarters.

A 5. The French and Indian War eventually became part of the larger world conflict known as

    a. the Seven Years' War.
    b. the War of Jenkins's Ear.
    c. the War of the Austrian Succession.
    d. King George's War.

A   6. Benjamin Franklin's attempt to create intercolonial unity at the Albany Congress resulted in

a. a permanent cooperative organization of the colonies.
b. rejection of the congress's proposal for colonial home rule both by London and by the individual colonies.
c. a sharp increase in Indian attacks on colonial settlements.
d. a growing colonial sympathy with France in the war against Britain.

A   7. The British forces suffered early defeats in the French and Indian War under the overall command of

a. General Braddock.
b. General Washington.
c. General Wolfe.
d. General Montcalm.

C   8. William Pitt's strategy in the assault on New France finally succeeded because

a. he was able to arouse more support for the war effort from the colonists.
b. he gave full support to General Braddock as commander of the British forces.
c. he concentrated British forces on attacking the vital strong points of Quebec and Montreal.
d. he was able to gain the support of the British aristocracy for the war effort.

A   9. The decisive event in the French-British contest for North America was

a. the British capture of Fort Duquesne.
b. the British victory in the Battle of Quebec.
c. the American capture of the Louisbourg fortress.
d. the British attack on the West Indies.

B   10. Among the factors that tended to promote intercolonial unity during the French and Indian War was

a. religious unity.
b. common language and wartime experience.
c. ethnic and social harmony.
d. improved transportation and settlement of boundary disputes.

____   11. The French and Indian War weakened interior Indian peoples like the Iroquois and Creeks by

a. establishing new American settlements on their territory.
b. eliminating their most effective leaders.
c. ending their hopes for diplomatic recognition in Europe.
d. removing their French and Spanish allies from Canada and Florida.

____   12. Pontiac's fierce attack on frontier outposts in 1763 had the effect of

a. ending good American-Indian relations on the frontier.
b. reviving French hopes for a new war.
c. convincing the British to keep troops stationed in the colonies.
d. stopping the flow of westward settlement.

___ 13. The British Proclamation of 1763

    a. was welcomed by most American colonists.
    b. angered colonists who thought that it deprived them of the fruits of victory.
    c. was aimed at further suppressing the French population of Canada.
    d. halted American westward settlement for several years.

___ 14. The French and Indian War created conflict between the British and the American military because

    a. the American soldiers had failed to support the British military effort.
    b. the British regulars had carried the brunt of the fighting.
    c. British officers treated the American colonial militia with contempt.
    d. American soldiers refused to accept orders from British officers.

___ 15. The effect on the colonists of the French removal from North America was

    a. to increase their gratitude to Britain for defending them in the war.
    b. to create new threats to colonial expansion from Spain and the Indians.
    c. to reduce the colonies' reliance on Britain and increase their sense of independence.
    d. to focus colonial energies on trade.

C. Identification

Supply the correct identification for each numbered description.

_____ 1. French Protestants who were granted toleration by the Edict of Nantes in 1598 but not permitted to settle in New France

_____ 2. Absolute French monarch who reigned for seventy-two years.

_____ 3. Animal whose pelt provided great profits for the French empire and enhanced European fashion at enormous ecological cost

_____ 4. French Catholic religious order that explored the North American interior and sought to protect and convert the Indians

_____ 5. Far-running, high-living French fur trappers

_____ 6. Part of a certain British naval officer's anatomy that set off an imperial war with Spain

_____ 7. Strategic French fortress conquered by New England settlers, handed back to the French, and finally conquered again by the British in 1759

_____ 8. Inland river territory, scene of fierce competition between the French and land-speculating English colonists

_____ 9. Bloodiest European theater of the Seven Years' War, where Frederick the Great's troops drained French strength away from North America

_____ 10. Unification effort that Benjamin Franklin nearly led to success by his eloquent leadership and cartoon artistry

_____ 11. Military aide of British General Braddock and defender of the frontier after Braddock's defeat

_____ 12. Fortress boldly assaulted by General Wolfe, spelling doom for New France

_____ 13. The "buckskin" colonial soldiers whose military success did nothing to alter British officers' contempt

_____ 14. Allies of the French against the British, who continued to fight under Pontiac even after the peace settlement in 1763

_____ 15. The larger European struggle of which the French and Indian War was part

D. Matching People, Places, and Events

Match the person, place, or event in the left column with the proper description in the right column by inserting the correct letter on the blank line.

___ 1. Samuel de Champlain

___ 2. Robert de la Salle

___ 3. Treaty of Utrecht

___ 4. War of Austrian Succession

___ 5. Fort Duquesne

___ 6. George Washington

___ 7. Benjamin Franklin

___ 8. General Braddock

___ 9. William Pitt

___ 10. Plains of Abraham

___ 11. Seven Years' War

___ 12. Pontiac

___ 13. Proclamation of 1763

___ 14. New Orleans

___ 15. Acadians (Cajuns)

A. Advocate of colonial unity at the unsuccessful Albany Congress

B. British document that aroused colonial anger but failed to stop frontier expansion

C. French colonists in Nova Scotia brutally uprooted by victorious British and shipped to Louisiana

D. Conflict that started with the War of Jenkins's Ear and ended with the return of Louisbourg to France

E. Strategic French outpost at the mouth of the Mississippi

F. Indian leader whose frontier uprising caused the British to attempt to limit colonial expansion

G. Blundering British officer whose defeat gave the advantage to the French and Indians in the early stages of their war

H. The Father of New France, who established a crucial alliance with the Huron Indians

I. Site of the death of Generals Wolfe and Montcalm, where France's New World empire also perished

J. Strategic French stronghold; later renamed after a great British statesman

K. Militia commander whose frontier skirmish in Pennsylvania touched off a world war

L. Agreement that ended the War of the Spanish Succession (Queen Anne's War) and awarded Acadia to Britain

M. Conflict in Europe that pitted France against Britain's ally Frederick the Great of Prussia

N. French empire builder who explored the Mississippi Basin and named it after his monarch

O. Splendid British orator and organizer of the winning strategy against the French in North America

E. Putting Things in Order

Put the following events in correct order by numbering them from 1 to 10.

____ A Virginia militia commander attempts an unsuccessful invasion of the Ohio Valley.

____ The "Great Commoner" takes command of the British government and its war effort.

____ Toleration of French Huguenots brings religious peace to France.

____ New France is founded, one year after Jamestown.

____ Britain issues a proclamation to prohibit colonial expansion and thereby prevent another Indian war.

____ The second "world war" between France and Britain ends in British victory and the acquisition of Acadia.

____ British victory on the Plains of Abraham seals the fate of New France.

____ Return of Louisbourg fortress at the end of King George's War angers colonial New Englanders.

____ War begins badly from British when Braddock fails to take Fort Duquesne.

____ A great empire builder explores Louisiana and claims it for the French king.

F. Matching Cause and Effect

Match the historical cause in the left column with the proper effect in the right column by writing the correct letter on the blank line.

Cause	Effect
____ 1. The French fur trade	**A.** Resulted in decisive French defeat and British domination of North America
____ 2. The four "world wars" between 1688 and 1763	**B.** Prompted widespread Indian assaults on the weakly defended colonial frontier
____ 3. Competition for land and furs in the Ohio Valley	**C.** Led to Washington's expedition and battle with the French at Fort Necessity
____ 4. The summoning of the Albany Congress by the British	**D.** Heightened colonial anger and encouraged illegal westward expansion
____ 5. William Pitt's assumption of control of British government and strategy	**E.** Increased American military confidence and resentment of British redcoats
____ 6. Wolfe's victory over Montcalm at Quebec	**F.** Decimated beaver populations while spreading the French empire
____ 7. The colonial militia's military success in the French and Indian War	**G.** Were echoed by four small wars between French and British subjects in North America
____ 8. Colonial American smuggling and trading with French enemy	**H.** Represented the first major attempt at intercolonial unity
____ 9. British issuance of the Proclamation of 1763	**I.** Increased British government's disdain for colonial Americans and raised doubts about their loyalty to the empire
____ 10. Braddock's defeat at Fort Duquesne	**J.** Ended a string of defeats and turned the French and Indian War in Britain's favor

G. Developing Historical Skills

Using a Map to Understand the Text

Reading maps frequently aids in understanding a point being made in the text—especially when it involves geography or strategy. On p.115, the text emphasizes that the British did not turn the tide in the French and Indian War until Pitt altered strategy to concentrate on the strategic points of Louisbourg, Montreal, and Quebec. Examining the map on p. 115 helps you to understand why this was so.

Answer the following questions.

1. Why is Quebec more important than, say, Fort Duquesne in relation to the St. Lawrence River and the Atlantic Ocean?

2. Why was it essential to capture Louisbourg before attacking Quebec?

3. What was the strategic situation of remaining French forces in the Great Lakes area once Montreal and Quebec were captured?

H. Map Mastery

Map Discrimination

Using the maps and charts in Chapter 6, answer the following questions.

1. *France's American Empire at the Greatest Extent, 1700*: Around which great river valley was New France first colonized?

2. *France's American Empire at the Greatest Extent, 1700*: Which French colonial settlement on the Great Lakes linked the St. Lawrence and Mississippi river basins?

3. *Fur-Trading Posts*: Along which river, besides the Mississippi, were the greatest number of French fur-trading posts located?

4. *The Nine World Wars*: How many years of peace did Britain and France enjoy between France's loss of Acadia in the War of Spanish Succession and the beginning of the War of Austrian Succession?

5. *Scenes of the French Wars*: The attacks on Schenectady and Deerfield occurred during attacks from which French Canadian city?

6. *The Ohio Country, 1753–1754*: Fort Duquesne was located at the intersection of which two rivers (which unite at that point to form a third river)?

7. *Events of 1755–1760*: Which French Canadian stronghold did not finally fall until a year after Wolfe's defeat of Montcalm on the Plains of Abraham at Quebec?

8. *North America Before 1754/After 1763*: In the peace treaty of 1763, which nation besides Britain acquired North American territory from France?

9. *North American Before 1754/After 1763*: Which North American territory owned by Spain before 1754 was acquired by Britain in the peace of 1763?

Map Challenge

Using the maps in this chapter, write a brief essay explaining why the St. Lawrence River valley was the strategic key to control of the whole center of North America.

Part III: Applying What You Have Learned

1. Why did the British and their American colonial subjects win the contest with the French for control of North America?
2. In what ways were the American colonists involved in the mother country's struggle with France?
3. How did French relations with the Indians compare with those of Britain and Spain?
4. Why did most Indian peoples fight with the French against Britain and its American colonists in the French and Indian War?
5. Explain why Britain's *success* in defeating the French empire laid the foundations for future failures in dealing with its colonial subjects.
6. How did events in France, England, and elsewhere in Europe affect the history of North America in this period?
7. Compare France's colonizing efforts in the New World with Spain's and England's colonies. (See especially Chapters 1 and 2.) What factors explain France's relatively weak impact on the New World compared with that of England's and Spain's?

7

The Road to Revolution, 1763–1775

PART I: Reviewing the Chapter

A. Checklist of Learning Objectives

After mastering this chapter, you should be able to

1. explain the deeply rooted historical factors that moved America toward independence from Britain.
2. describe the theory and practice of mercantilism and explain why Americans resented it.
3. explain why Britain attempted tighter control and taxation of Americans after 1763 and why Americans resisted these efforts.
4. describe the major British efforts to impose taxes and tighten control of the colonies.
5. describe the methods of colonial resistance that forced repeal of all taxes except the tax on tea.
6. explain how sustained agitation and resistance to the tea tax led to the Intolerable Acts and the outbreak of war.
7. assess the balance of forces between the British and the American rebels as the two sides prepared for war.

B. Glossary

To build your social science vocabulary, familiarize yourself with the following terms.

1. **patronage** A system in which benefits, including jobs, money, or protection are granted in exchange for political support. "The Whigs mounted withering attacks on the use of patronage and bribes by the king's ministers. . . ." (p. 123)
2. **mercantilism** The economic theory that all parts of an economy should be coordinated for the good of the whole state; hence, that colonial economics should be subordinated for the benefit of an empire. "The British authorities nevertheless embraced a theory called mercantilism. . . ." (p. 123)
3. **depreciate** To decrease in value, as in the decline of the purchasing power of money. ". . . dire financial need forced many of the colonies to issue paper money, which swiftly depreciated." (p. 124)
4. **veto** The constitutional right of a ruler or executive to block legislation passed by another unit of government. "This royal veto was used rather sparingly. . . ." (p. 124)
5. **monopoly** The complete control of a product or sphere of economic activity by a single producer or business. "Virginia tobacco planters enjoyed a monopoly in the British market. . . ." (p. 125)
6. **admiralty courts** In British law, special administrative courts designed to handle maritime cases without a jury. "Both the Sugar Act and the Stamp Act provided for trying offenders in the hated admiralty courts. . . ." (p. 126)
7. **virtual representation** The political theory that a class of persons is represented in a lawmaking body without direct vote. "Elaborating the theory of 'virtual representation,' Grenville

claimed that every member of Parliament represented all British subjects, even . . . Americans. . . .” (p. 127)

*8. **nonimportation agreement** Pledges to boycott, or decline to purchase, certain goods from abroad. “More effective than the congress was the widespread adoption of nonimportation agreements. . . .” (p. 127)

9. **mulatto** A person of mixed African and European ancestry. “. . . Crispus Attucks [was] described . . . as a powerfully built runaway ‘mulatto.’. . .” (p. 130)

10. **duty (duties)** A customs tax on the export or import of goods. “. . . finally persuaded Parliament to repeal the Townshend revenue duties.” (p. 131)

11. **propaganda (propagandist)** A systematic program or particular materials designed to promote certain ideas; sometimes but not always the term is used negatively, implying the use of manipulative or deceptive means. (A propagandist is one who engages in such practices.) “Resistance was further kindled by a master propagandist and engineer of rebellion, Samuel Adams of Boston. . . .” (p. 131)

12. **boycott** An organized refusal to deal with some person, organization, or product. “The Association called for a *complete* boycott of British goods. . . .” (p. 134)

13. **inflation** An increase in the supply of currency relative to the goods available, leading to a decline in the purchasing power of money. “Inflation of the currency inevitably skyrocketed prices.” (p. 137)

14. **desert** To leave official government or military service without permission. “. . . hundreds of anxious husbands and fathers deserted.” (p. 137)

Part II: Checking Your Progress

A. True-False

Where the statement is true, mark **T**. Where it is false, mark **F**, and correct it in the space immediately below.

T 1. The republican idea of a just society in which selfish interests were subordinated to the common good took deep root in Britain's North American colonies.

T 2. The theory of mercantilism held that colonies existed primarily to provide the mother country with raw materials as well as a market for exports.

T 3. British mercantilism forbade the importation of any non-British goods into the colonies.

T 4. In practice, British mercantilism provided the colonies with substantial economic benefits such as military protection and guaranteed markets for certain goods.

T 5. The fundamental motive behind the steep new taxes in the 1760s was to repay the large debt that Britain had incurred in defending its North American colonies.

F 6. Americans generally accepted the right of Parliament to tax the colonies to provide money for defense but denied its right to legislate about colonial affairs.

T 7. When Americans first cried “no taxation without representation,” what they wanted was to be represented in the British Parliament.

F 8. The colonies finally forced repeal of the Stamp Act by organizing political protests and enforcing nonimportation agreements against British goods.

F   9. Colonial rebellion against the new Townshend Acts was more highly organized and successful than the earlier Stamp Act protests.

F   10. The Boston Massacre led the British government to pursue even harsher enforcement of the Townshend Acts.

T   11. Massachusetts Governor Thomas Hutchinson provoked a crisis in Boston by enforcing the importation of British tea even though he believed that the tea tax was unjust.

T   12. The colonists considered the Quebec Act especially oppressive because they thought it would extend the domain of Roman Catholicism.

F   13. The First Continental Congress proclaimed that the colonies would declare independence from Britain unless their grievances were redressed.

F   14. One fundamental American asset in the impending war with Britain was a small but well-trained professional military force.

T   15. A key British advantage was that they did not have to defeat all the American forces but only fight to a draw in order to crush the Revolution.

B.   Multiple Choice

Select the best answer and write the proper letter in the space provided.

C   1. The British theory of mercantilism, by which the colonies were governed, held that

    a.   the economy should be shaped by market forces, without government interference.
    b.   the colonies should develop by becoming as economically self-sufficient as possible.
    c.   the colonial economy should be carefully controlled to serve the mother country's needs.
    d.   colonists should promote economic growth by free trade with other countries.

D   2. One of the ways in which mercantilism harmed the colonial economy was

    a.   by prohibiting colonial merchants from owning and operating their own ships.
    b.   by inhibiting the development of banking and paper currency in the colonies.
    c.   by forcing the colonists to fall into debt through the purchase of goods on credit.
    d.   by forcing Virginia tobacco planters to sell their product only in Britain.

B   3. The mobilization of "nonimportation" policies against the Stamp Act was politically important because

    a.   it aroused the first French support for the American cause.
    b.   it aroused revolutionary fervor among many ordinary American men and women.
    c.   it reinforced the completely nonviolent character of the anti-British movement.
    d.   it helped stimulate the development of colonial manufacturing.

A   4. The British troops killed in the Boston Massacre had been sent to the city as a result of

    a.   colonial protests against the Stamp Act.
    b.   the illegal activities of the Committees of Correspondence.
    c.   colonial resistance to the Quartering Act of 1767.
    d.   colonial resistance to the Townshend Acts' tax on tea and other products.

B   5. The British reacted to the Boston Tea Party by

    a. shipping the colonial protestors to Britain for trial.
    b. closing the Port of Boston until damages were paid and order restored.
    c. passing the Quebec Act prohibiting trial by jury and permitting the practice of Catholicism.
    d. granting a monopoly on the sale of tea to the British East India Company.

B   6. American colonists especially resented the Townshend Acts because

    a. they strongly disliked the British minister, "Champagne Charley" Townshend, who proposed them.
    b. the revenues from the taxation would go to support British officials and judges in America.
    c. they called for the establishment of the Anglican church throughout the colonies.
    d. the taxes were to be imposed directly by the king without an act of Parliament.

C   7. The passage of the Quebec Act aroused intense American fears because

    a. it put the French language on an equal standing with English throughout the colonies.
    b. it involved stationing British troops throughout the colonies.
    c. it extended Catholic jurisdiction and a non-jury judicial system into the western Ohio country.
    d. it threatened to make Canada the dominant British colony in North America.

A   8. The most important action the Continental Congress took to protest the Intolerable Acts was

    a. forming The Association to impose a complete boycott of all British goods.
    b. organizing a colonial militia to prepare for military resistance.
    c. forming Committees of Correspondence to commnicate among all the colonies and develop political opposition to British rule.
    d. sending petitions to the British Parliament demanding repeal of the laws.

A   9. The event that precipitated the first real shooting between the British and American colonists was

    a. the British attempt to seize Bunker Hill and the Old North Church.
    b. the British attempt to seize colonial supplies and leaders at Lexington and Concord.
    c. the Boston Tea Party.
    d. the Boston Massacre.

D   10. The British parliamentary government at the time of the American Revolution was headed by

    a. William Pitt.
    b. "Champagne Charley" Townshend.
    c. Edmund Burke.
    d. Lord North.

A   11. The American rebellion was especially dangerous to the British because they were also worried about

    a. possible revolts in Ireland and war with France.
    b. labor unrest in British industrial cities.
    c. maintaining sufficient troops in India.
    d. their ability to maintain naval control of the oceans.

_D_ 12. The British political party that was generally more sympathetic to the American cause was

    a. the Tory Party.
    b. the Labor Party.
    c. the Country Party.
    d. the Whig Party.

_B_ 13. One of the advantages the British enjoyed in the impending conflict with the colonies was

    a. a determined and politically effective government.
    b. the ability to enlist foreign soldiers, Loyalists, and Native Americans in their military forces.
    c. a highly motivated and efficiently run military force in America.
    d. the concentration of colonial resistance in a few urban centers.

_A_ 14. One of the advantages the colonists enjoyed in the impending conflict with Britain was

    a. fighting defensively on a large, agriculturally self-sufficient continent.
    b. a well-organized and effective political leadership.
    c. a strong sense of unity among the various colonies.
    d. the fact that nearly all Americans owned their own firearms.

_C_ 15. In the Revolutionary War, African-Americans

    a. unanimously supported the American patriot cause.
    b. were generally neutral between the British and American forces.
    c. fought in both the American patriot and British loyalist military forces.
    d. took the opportunity to stage substantial slave revolts.

C. Identification

Supply the correct identification for each numbered description.

_____ 1. The basic economic and political theory by which seventeenth- and eighteenth-century European powers governed their overseas colonies

_____ 2. The set of Parliamentary laws, first passed in 1650, that restricted colonial trade and directed it to the benefit of Britain

_____ 3. The term for products, such as tobacco, that could be shipped only to England and not to foreign markets

_____ 4. Hated British courts in which juries were not allowed and defendants were assumed guilty until proven innocent

_____ 5. British governmental theory that Parliament spoke for all British subjects, including Americans, even if they did not vote for its members

_____ 6. The effective form of organized colonial resistance against the Stamp Act, which made homespun clothing fashionable

_____ 7. The product taxed under the Townshend Acts that generated the greatest colonial resistance

_____ 8. Underground networks of communication and propaganda, established by Samuel Adams, that sustained colonial resistance

_____ 9. Religion that was granted toleration in the trans-Allegheny West by the Quebec Act, arousing deep colonial hostility

_____ 10. British political party opposed to Lord North's Tories and generally more sympathetic to the colonial cause

_____ 11. German mercenaries hired by George III to fight the American revolutionaries

_____ 12. Paper currency authorized by Congress to finance the Revolution that depreciated to near worthlessness

_____ 13. Effective organization created by the First Continental Congress to provide a total, unified boycott of all British goods

_____ 14. Rapidly mobilized colonial militiamen whose refusal to disperse sparked the first battle of the Revolution

_____ 15. Popular term for British regular troops, scorned as "lobster backs" and "bloody backs" by Bostonians and other colonials

D. Matching People, Places, and Events

Match the person, place, or event in the left column with the proper description in the right column by inserting the correct letter on the blank line.

F 1. John Hancock
A 2. George Grenville
B 3. Stamp Act
M 4. Sons and Daughters of Liberty
G 5. "Champagne Charley" Townshend
K 6. Crispus Attucks
J 7. George III
H 8. Samuel Adams
O 9. Boston Tea Party
I 10. Intolerable Acts
N 11. Thomas Hutchinson
C 12. First Continental Congress
E 13. Marquis de Lafayette
L 14. Baron von Steuben
D 15. Quartering Act

A. British minister who raised a storm of protest by passing the Stamp Act

B. Legislation passed in 1765 but repealed the next year, after colonial resistance made it impossible to enforce

C. Body led by John Adams that issued a Declaration of Rights and organized The Association to boycott all British goods

D. Legislation that required colonists to feed and shelter British troops; disobeyed in New York and elsewhere

E. Nineteen-year-old major general in the Revolutionary army

F. Wealthy president of the Continental Congress and "King of the Smugglers"

G. Minister whose clever attempt to impose import taxes nearly succeeded, but eventually brewed trouble for Britain

H. Zealous defender of the common people's rights and organizer of underground propaganda committees

I. Harsh measures of retaliation for a tea party, including the Boston Port Act closing that city's harbor

J. Stubborn ruler, lustful for power, who promoted harsh ministers like Lord North

K. Alleged leader of radical protesters killed in Boston Massacre

L. Organizational genius who turned raw colonial recruits into tough professional soldiers

M. Male and female organizations that enforced the nonimportation agreements, sometimes by coercive means

N. British governor of Massachusetts whose stubborn policies helped provoke the Boston Tea Party.

O. Event organized by disguised "Indians" to sabotage British support of a British East India Company monopoly

E. Putting Things in Order

Put the following events in correct order by numbering them from 1 to 10.

3 Britain attempts to gain revenue by a tax on papers and documents, creating a colonial uproar.

9 Britain closes the port of Boston and opens the western frontier to Catholicism.

6 Crispus Attucks leads a crowd in an attack on British troops, and eleven people are killed.

10 Colonial Minute Men fire "the shot heard around the world" in the first battle of the Revolution.

5 A British minister cleverly attempts to gain revenue and dampen colonial protest by imposing an import tax only on certain specialized products.

2 A British agency is established with broad but generally ineffective power over colonial commerce.

7 Samuel Adams and others organize revolutionary cells of communication and agitation across the colonies.

4 Parliament repeals a direct tax in response to colonial protest but declares that it has the right to tax colonies.

8 A band of "Indians" dumps the rich cargo of the British East India Company into Boston Harbor, provoking a harsh British response.

1 First acts are passed by Parliament to regulate colonial trade based on mercantilist principles.

F. Matching Cause and Effect

Match the historical cause in the left column with the proper effect in the right column by writing the correct letter on the blank line.

	Cause		Effect
H	1. America's distance from Britain and the growth of colonial self-government	A.	Prompted the summoning of the First Continental Congress
G	2. British mercantilism	B.	Led Grenville to propose the Sugar Act, Quartering Act, and Stamp Act
B	3. The large British debt incurred defending the colonies in the French and Indian War	C.	Precipitated the Battle of Lexington and Concord
J	4. Passage of the Stamp Act	D.	Fired on colonial citizens in the Boston Massacre
D	5. British troops sent to enforce order in Boston	E.	Prompted passage of the Intolerable Acts, including the Boston Port Act
I	6. The British government's attempt to maintain the East India Company's tea monopoly	F.	Resulted in the printing of large amounts of paper currency and skyrocketing inflation
E	7. The Boston Tea Party	G.	Enforced restrictions on colonial manufacturing, trade, and paper currency
A	8. The Intolerable Acts	H.	Led to gradual development of a colonial sense of independence years before the Revolution
		I.	Spurred patriots to stage Boston Tea Party

___C___ 9. A British attempt to seize the colonial militia's gunpowder supplies

___F___ 10. The Continental Congress's reluctance to tax Americans for war

J. Was greeted in the colonies by the nonimportation agreements, the Stamp Act Congress, and the forced resignation of stamp agents

G. Developing Historical Skills

Interpreting Historical Illustrations

Contemporary illustrations of historical events may not only give us information about those events but tell us something about the attitude and intention of those who made the illustrations. The caption to the engraving of the Boston Massacre by Paul Revere (p.130) observes that it is "both art and propaganda." Drawing on the account of the massacre in the text (pp. 129–130) enables you to see the ways in which Revere's engraving combines factual information with a political point of view.

Answer the following questions.

1. What parts of the encounter between the British redcoats and the colonists does the engraving entirely leave out?

2. The text says that the British troops fired "without orders." How does the engraving suggest the opposite?

3. How does Revere's presentation of the colonial victims seem especially designed to inflame the feelings of the viewer?

Part III: Applying What You Have Learned

1. Why did the American colonies move from loyalty to protest to rebellion in the twelve years following the end of the French and Indian War?

2. How and why did the Americans and the British differ in their views of taxation and of the relationship of colonies to the empire?

3. What was the theory and practice of mercantilism? What were its actual effects on the colonies, and why did the colonists resent it so much?

4. What methods did the colonists use in their struggle with British authorities, and how did the British try to counteract them?

5. What advantages and disadvantages did the American rebels and the British each possess as the war began? What did each side do to mobilize its resources most effectively?

6. Given the history of the colonies' founding and British "benign neglect" until the period just before the Revolution, was the American Revolution inevitable? Or could the thirteen colonies have remained peacefully attached to Britain for many years, as Canada did?

8

America Secedes from the Empire, 1775–1783

PART I: Reviewing the Chapter

A. Checklist of Learning Objectives

After mastering this chapter, you should be able to

1. describe how America moved from engaging in military hostilities with Britain even while proclaiming loyalty to declaring its independence.
2. explain the principal ideas of "republicanism" developed by Thomas Paine and other American leaders.
3. explain the specific reasons and general principles used in the Declaration of Independence to justify America's separation.
4. explain why some Americans remained loyal to Britain and what happened to them during and after the Revolution.
5. describe how the British attempt to crush the Revolution quickly was foiled, especially by the Battle of Saratoga.
6. describe the military and political obstacles Washington and his generals had to overcome before the final victory at Yorktown.
7. describe the terms of the Treaty of Paris and explain how America was able to achieve such a stunning diplomatic victory.

B. Glossary

To build your social science vocabulary, familiarize yourself with the following terms.

1. **mercenary** A professional soldier who serves in a foreign army for pay. ". . . the Americans called all the European mercenaries Hessians." (p. 143)
2. **indictment** A formal written accusation charging someone with a crime. "The overdrawn bill of indictment included imposing taxes without consent. . . ." (p. 148)
3. **dictatorship** A form of government characterized by absolute state power and the unlimited authority of the ruler. "The [charges] included . . . establishing a military dictatorship. . . ." (p. 148)
4. **neutral** A nation or person not taking sides in a war. "Many colonists were apathetic or neutral. . . ." (p. 148)
5. **civilian** A citizen not in military service. "The opposing forces contended . . . for the allegiance . . . of the civilian population." (p. 148)
6. **traitor** One who betrays a country by aiding an enemy. ". . . they regarded their opponents, not themselves, as traitors." ((p. 152)
7. **confiscate** To seize private property for public use, often as a penalty. "The estates of many of the fugitives were confiscated. . . ." (p. 152)

8. **envoy** A messenger or agent sent by a government on official business. "Benjamin Franklin, recently sent to Paris as an envoy, truthfully jested that Howe had not captured Philadelphia. . . ." (p. 155)

9. **rabble** A mass of disorderly and crude common people. "This rabble was nevertheless whipped into a professional army. . . ." (p. 155)

10. **arsenal** A place for making or storing weapons and ammunition. "About 90 percent of all the gunpowder . . . came from French arsenals." (p. 155)

11. **isolationist** Concerning the belief that a country should take little or no part in foreign affairs, especially through alliances or wars. "The American people, with ingrained isolationist tendencies, accepted the French entanglement with distaste." (p. 156)

12. **hereditary** Passed down from generation to generation. "They were painfully aware that it bound them to a hereditary foe that was also a Roman Catholic power." (p. 156)

13. **blockade** The isolation of a place by hostile ships or troops. "Now the French had powerful fleets. . . in a position to jeopardize Britain's blockade and lines of supply." (p. 157)

14. **privateer** A private vessel temporarily authorized to capture or plunder enemy ships in wartime. "More numerous and damaging than ships of the regular American navy were swift privateers." (p. 159)

15. **graft** Taking advantage of one's official position to gain money or property by illegal means. "It had the unfortunate effect of . . . involving Americans, including Benedict Arnold, in speculation and graft." (p. 159)

Part II: Checking Your Progress

A. True-False

Where the statement is true, mark **T**. Where it is false, mark **F**, and correct it in the space immediately below.

F   1. George Washington was chosen commander of the American army primarily because of his military abilities and experience.

F   2. Following the Battle of Bunker Hill, King George and the Continental Congress made one last attempt at reconciliation.

T   3. The American army that invaded Canada falsely believed that oppressed French Canadians would join them in revolt and make Canada the fourteenth state.

T   4. Tom Paine's *Common Sense* was most important because it pushed the colonies into violent rebellion against the king as well as against Parliament.

T   5. The Declaration of Independence was especially important because it enabled the Americans to appeal for direct aid from France.

F   6. American militiamen proved politically very effective in pushing their apathetic or neutral fellow citizens into supporting the Patriot cause.

T   7. The Loyalists considered the "Patriots" to be the traitors to their country and themselves to be the true patriots.

T   8. Most Loyalists were executed or driven from the country after the Patriot victory.

F   9. The Loyalists were strongest in New England and Virginia.

T   10. General Burgoyne's defeat at Saratoga in 1777 was critical for the American cause because it led to the alliance with France.

T   11. French entry into the war turned the American Revolutionary War into a world war involving most of the European great powers.

T   12. During much of the Revolutionary War, the British controlled cities like New York, Boston, Philadelphia, and Charleston, while the Americans conducted their campaigns primarily in the countryside.

F   13. At Yorktown, the Americans finally showed that they could win an important battle without French assistance.

F   14. American diplomats were successful in guaranteeing American political independence but failed to gain the territorial concessions they wanted.

T   15. American success in the Revolutionary War and the peace treaty was due in significant measure to political developments in Europe.

B. Multiple Choice

Select the best answer and write the proper letter in the space provided.

B   1. During the period of fighting between April 1775 and July 1776, the colonists claimed that their goal was

    a. the removal of all British troops from America.
    b. to restore their rights within the British Empire.
    c. complete independence from Britain.
    d. to end the power of King George III to rule them.

C   2. George Washington proved to be an especially effective commander of American forces in the Revolution because

    a. he was able to rally previously skeptical New Englanders to the Patriot cause.
    b. of his exceptionally brilliant military mind.
    c. of his integrity, courage, and moral forcefulness.
    d. his humble background inspired the ordinary soldiers in the Revolutionary army.

B   3. The bold American military strategy that narrowly failed in December 1775 involved

    a. a two-pronged attack on British forces in New York.
    b. an invasion of Canada by generals Arnold and Montgomery.
    c. an attack on British forts in the Ohio country.
    d. a naval assault on British warships in Boston harbor.

D   4. Many of the German Hessian soldiers hired by King George III to fight for the British

    a. hated the American revolutionaries and their cause.
    b. helped draw in the Prussian King Frederick II as a British ally.
    c. were ineffective in battle against American militiamen.
    d. had little loyalty to the British cause and ended up deserting.

A   5. Thomas Paine's appeal for a new republican form of government attracted many Americans because

     a. they believed that social class differences promoted by monarchy were wrong.
     (b.) their own experience with local and colonial democratic governance had prepared them for the idea.
     c. they were impressed that Paine was drawing on the best classical ideas from Plato's *Republic*.
     d. they were fearful that wealthy southern planters like Washington wanted to establish nobility in America.

D   6. Paine's *Common Sense* was crucial in convincing many Americans that what they should fight for was

     a. American representation in the British Parliament.
     b. an alliance with the French against Britain.
     c. a federal constitution and bill of rights.
     d. an independent and republican America separate from Britain.

A   7. The Loyalists were particularly strong among

     a. conservative and well-off Americans.
     b. the younger generation.
     c. Presbyterians and Congregationalists.
     d. citizens of New England.

A   8. Besides George Washington, the most militarily effective American officer in the early campaigns of 1776 and 1777 was

     a. General Nathanael Greene.
     b. General von Steuben.
     (c.) General Benedict Arnold.
     d. General William Howe.

B   9. The Battle of Saratoga was a key turning point of the War for Independence because

     a. it prevented the British from keeping control of the key port of New York City.
     b. it brought about crucial French assistance to the Revolutionary cause.
     c. it ended the possibility of a peaceful settlement with Britain.
     d. if effectively destroyed British military power in the middle colonies.

A   10. The primary French motive in aiding the American cause was

     a. to weaken the British Empire.
     b. to promote republican government and the principles of the Declaration of Independence.
     c. to test new forms of military weaponry and tactics.
     d. to gain the economic advantage of trade with the former British colonies.

D   11. The British especially relied on the numerous Loyalists to aid them in fighting the Patriots

     a. in Rhode Island and the rest of New England.
     b. in the western Illinois country.
     c. in the warfare at sea.
     d. in the Carolinas.

B 12. Most of the Six Nations of the Iroquois under Joseph Brant fought against the American revolutionaries because

    a. they disagreed with the principles of the Declaration of Independence.
    b. they believed that a victorious Britain would contain westward American expansion.
    c. they were paid as mercenary soldiers by the British government.
    d. they hoped to drive the American colonists off the North American continent.

A 13. The British defeat at Yorktown was brought about by George Washington's army and

    a. the French navy under Admiral de Grasse.
    b. the American navy under John Paul Jones.
    c. the American militia under George Rogers Clark.
    d. the Armed Neutrality under Catherine the Great.

D 14. In the peace negotiations at Paris, the French wanted the Americans

    a. to stop short of demanding full independence.
    b. to negotiate a separate peace with Britain.
    c. to acquire only the territory east of the Appalachian Mountains.
    d. to help them regain Quebec from the British.

B 15. The British yielded the Americans a generous peace treaty that included the western territories primarily because of

    a. the desire of the weak Whig ministry in London for friendly future relations with the United States.
    b. the threat of further war with France.
    c. the military power of the United States.
    d. the willingness of the Americans to yield on other issues like trade and fishing rights.

C. Identification

Supply the correct identification for each numbered description.

_____ 1. The body that chose George Washington commander of the Continental Army

_____ 2. The British colony that Americans invaded in hopes of adding it to the rebellious thirteen

_____ 3. The inflammatory pamphlet that demanded independence and heaped scorn on "the Royal Brute of Great Britain"

_____ 4. The document that provided a lengthy explanation and justification of Richard Henry Lee's resolution that was passed by Congress on July 2, 1776

_____ 5. The term by which the American Patriots were commonly known, to distinguish them from the American "Tories"

_____ 6. Another name for the American Tories

_____ 7. The church body most closely linked with Tory sentiment, except in Virginia

_____ 8. The river valley that was the focus of Britain's early military strategy and the scene of Burgoyne's surrender at Saratoga in 1777

_____ 9. Term for the alliance of Catherine the Great of Russia and other European powers who did not declare war but assumed a hostile neutrality toward Britain

_____ 10. The region that saw some of the Revolution's most bitter fighting, from 1780 to 1782, between American General Greene and British General Cornwallis

_____ 11. "Legalized pirates," more than a thousand strong, who inflicted heavy damage on British shipping

_____ 12. British political party that replaced Lord North's Tories in 1782 and made a generous treaty with the United States

_____ 13. The western boundary of the United States established in the Treaty of Paris

_____ 14. The irregular American troops who played a crucial role in swaying the neutral civilian population toward the Patriot cause

_____ 15. The other European nation besides France and Spain that supported the American Revolution by declaring war on Britain

D. Matching People, Places, and Events

Match the person, place, or event in the left column with the proper description in the right column by inserting the correct letter on the blank line.

J 1. George Washington

H 2. Bunker Hill

B 3. Benedict Arnold

M 4. Thomas Paine

N 5. Richard Henry Lee

D 6. Thomas Jefferson

I 7. Loyalists

O 8. General Burgoyne

A 9. General Howe

E 10. Benjamin Franklin

L 11. George Rogers Clark

C 12. John Paul Jones

G 13. Saratoga

K 14. Yorktown

F 15. Joseph Brant

A. British general who chose to relax in New York and Philadelphia rather than march up the Hudson to fight

B. Brilliant American general who invaded Canada, foiled Burgoyne's invasion, and in 1780 betrayed his country

C. American naval commander who harassed British shipping

D. Author of an explanatory indictment, signed on July 4, 1776, that accused George III of establishing a military dictatorship

E. Shrewd American diplomat who established the French alliance and worked with Jay and Adams to win a generous peace treaty

F. Mohawk chief who led many Iroquois to fight with Britain against American revolutionaries

G. The decisive early battle of the American Revolution that led to the alliance with France

H. Military engagement that led King George III officially to declare the colonists in revolt

I. Americans who fought for King George and earned the contempt of Patriots

J. A wealthy Virginian of great character and leadership abilities who served his country without pay

K. The British defeat that led to the fall of North's government and the end of the war

L. Leader whose small force conquered key British forts in the West

M. A radical British immigrant who put an end to American toasts to King George

N. Fiery Virginian and author of the official resolution of July 2, 1776, formally authorizing the colonies' independence

O. Blundering British general whose slow progress south from Canada ended in disaster at Saratoga

E. Putting Things in Order

Put the following events in correct order by numbering them from 1 to 6.

5   Lord North's military collapses, and Britain's Whigs take power ready to make peace.

2   Thomas Jefferson writes an eloquent justification of Richard Henry Lee's resolution.

3   Burgoyne and Howe are defeated both by the generalship of Washington and Arnold and by their own blundering.

6   The Treaty of Paris is signed, guaranteeing American independence.

1   The British launch a frontal attack on entrenched American forces near Boston and suffer drastic losses in their "victory."

4   Washington's army and the French navy trap General Cornwallis, spelling the end for the British.

F. Matching Cause and Effect

Match the historical cause in the left column with the proper effect in the right column by writing the correct letter on the blank line.

Cause	Effect
B 1. The Battle of Bunker Hill	A. Led to American acquisition of the West up to the Mississippi River
I 2. Thomas Paine's *Common Sense*	B. Caused King George to proclaim the colonies in revolt and import Hessian troops to crush them
E 3. Jefferson's Declaration of Independence	C. Led to a favorable peace treaty for the United States and the end of French schemes for a smaller, weaker America
J 4. The Patriot militia's political education and recruitment	D. Caused the British to begin peace negotiations in Paris
G 5. The blundering of Burgoyne and Howe and the superb military strategy of Arnold and Washington	E. Inspired universal awareness of the American Revolution as a fight for the belief that "all men are created equal"
H 6. The Battle of Saratoga	F. Caused the British defeat at Yorktown and the collapse of North's Tory government
A 7. Clark's military conquests and Jay's diplomacy	G. Led to the failure of Britain's grand strategy and the crucial American victory at Saratoga
F 8. The trapping of Cornwallis between Washington's army and de Grasse's navy	H. Made France willing to become an ally of the United States
D 9. The collapse of the North ministry and the Whig takeover of the British government	I. Stirred growing colonial support for declaring independence from Britain
C 10. Jay's secret and separate negotiations with Britain	J. Won neutral or apathetic Americans over to the Patriot cause

G. Developing Historical Skills

Distinguishing Historical Fact and Historical Meaning

Some historical events can be understood as simple facts requiring little explanation. But other historical events have meaning only when their significance is analyzed. The text on pp. 142–148 contains examples of both kinds of historical events. Comparing them will help sort out the difference between the two.

Indicate which of these pairs of historical events is (a) a simple factual event requiring little explanation and which is (b) an event whose meaning needs to be interpreted in order to be understood. In each case, list the meaning the text gives to the second kind of event.

1. The British burning of Falmouth (Portland), Maine, and King George's proclamation that the colonies were in rebellion.

2. Tom Paine's *Common Sense* and the death of General Richard Montgomery.

3. Richard Henry Lee's resolution of July 2, 1776, and Thomas Jefferson's Declaration of Independence.

H. Map Mastery

Map Discrimination

Using the maps and charts in Chapter 8, answer the following questions.

1. *Revolution in the North, 1775–1776*: Which two British strong points in Canada did the American generals Arnold and Montgomery attack in 1775?

2. *New York-Pennsylvania Theater, 1777–1778*: When Washington recrossed the Delaware River before the Battle of Trenton on December 26, 1776, which state did he come from, and which state did he go to?

3. *New York-Pennsylvania Theater, 1777–1778*: Which of the three British generals who were supposed to meet near Albany, New York moved in the opposite direction and failed to get to the appointed gathering?

4. *Britain Against the World*: Besides France, which two European nations directly declared war on Britain during the American Revolution?

5. *War in the South, 1780–1781*: Name three cities in the South occupied at one time or another by General Cornwallis.

6. *George Rogers Clark's Campaign, 1778–1779*: Which river did George Rogers Clark move down as he went to conquer western forts from the British?

7. *George Rogers Clark's Campaign, 1778–1779*: Which three British posts did Clark capture?

Map Challenge

Using the maps on p. 144 and p. 154 as a basis, write a brief essay explaining why control of the Hudson River–Lake Champlain Valley was strategically crucial to both the British and the Americans in the Revolutionary War.

PART III: Applying What You Have Learned

1. Why was the Battle of Saratoga such a key to American success in the Revolutionary War?
2. What were the causes and consequences of the American Declaration of Independence in 1776?
3. Describe the different courses of the Revolutionary War in New England, the middle Atlantic states, and the South. What role did the battles in each region play in the eventual American victory?
4. Why did Americans choose not only to break from Britain, but to adopt a republican form of government in 1776? What republican ideas did they share, and what did they disagree about?
5. Who were the Loyalists, what role did they play during the Revolution, and what happened to them afterward?
6. What role did France play in winning America's independence? How does the American Revolution fit into the series of "world wars" described in Chapter 6?

9

The Confederation and the Constitution, 1776–1790

PART I: Reviewing the Chapter

A. Checklist of Learning Objectives

After mastering this chapter, you should be able to

1. explain the political and social movement toward "equality" that flourished after the Revolution, and understand why certain social and racial inequalities remained in place.
√ 2. describe the government of the Articles of Confederation and indicate its achievements and failures.
√ 3. explain the crucial role of Shays's Rebellion in sparking the movement for a new Constitution.
√ 4. describe the basic intentions and ideas of the Founding Fathers, and how they incorporated their fundamental principles into the Constitution.
√ 5. grasp the central concerns that motivated the antifederalists, and indicate their social, economic, and political differences with the federalists.
√ 6. describe the process of ratification of the Constitution, and explain why the federalists won.
√ 7. indicate the ways in which the new Constitutional government was "conservative," yet preserved the central principles of the American Revolution.

B. Glossary

To build your social science vocabulary, familiarize yourself with the following terms.

1. **disestablish** To separate an official state church from its connection with the government. ". . . the Protestant Episcopal church . . . was everywhere disestablished." (p. 167)
2. **emancipation** Setting free from servitude or slavery. "Several northern states . . . provided for the gradual emancipation of blacks." (p. 167)
3. **chattel** An article of personal or movable property; hence a term applied to slaves, since they were considered the personal property of their owners. ". . . a few idealistic masters freed their human chattels." (p. 167)
4. **abolitionist** An advocate of the end of slavery. "In this . . . were to be found the first frail sprouts of the later abolitionist movement." (p. 167)
5. **ratification** The confirmation or validation of an act (such as a constitution) by authoritative approval. "Massachusetts . . . submitted the final draft directly to the people for ratification." (p. 168)
6. **bill of rights** A list of fundamental freedoms assumed to be central to society. "Most of these documents included bills of rights. . . ." (p. 168)
7. **speculators (speculation)** Those who buy property, goods, or financial instruments not primarily for use but in anticipation of profitable resale after a general rise in value. "States seized control of former crown lands . . . although rich speculators had their day." (p. 169)
8. **township** In America, a surveyed territory six miles square; the term also refers to a unit of local government, smaller than a county, that is often based on these survey units. "The six-

teenth section of each township was set aside to be sold for the benefit of the public schools. . . ." (p. 174)

9. **territory** In American government, an organized political entity not yet enjoying the full and equal status of a state. ". . . when a territory could boast sixty thousand inhabitants, it might be admitted by Congress as a state. . . ." (p. 174)

10. **annex** To make a smaller territory or political unit part of a larger one. "They . . . sought to annex that rebellious area to Britain." (p. 175)

11. **requisition** A demand for something issued on the basis of public authority. "The requisition system of raising money was breaking down. . . ." (p. 176)

12. **foreclosure** Depriving someone of the right to redeem mortgaged property because the legal payments on the loan have not been kept up. ". . . Revolutionary war veterans were losing their farms through mortgage foreclosures." (p. 176)

13. **quorum** The minimum number of persons who must be present in a group before it can conduct valid business. "A quorum of the fifty-five emissaries from twelve states finally convened at Philadelphia. . . ." (p. 177)

14. **anarchy** The theory that formal government is unnecessary and wrong in principle; the term is also used generally for lawlessness or antigovernmental disorder. "Delegates were determined to preserve the union [and] forestall anarchy. . . ." (p. 179)

15. **bicameral, unicameral** Referring to a legislative body with two houses (bicameral) or one (unicameral). ". . . representation in both houses of a bicameral Congress should be based on population. . . ." "This provided for equal representation in a unicameral Congress. . . ." (p. 179)

PART II: Checking Your Progress

A. True-False

Where the statement is true, mark **T**. Where it is false, mark **F**, and correct it in the space immediately below.

T   1. The American Revolution created a substantial though not radical push in the direction of social and political equality.

T   2. The movement toward the separation of church and state was greatly accelerated by the disestablishment of the Anglican church in Virginia.

F   3. After the Revolution, slavery was abolished in New York and Pennsylvania, but continued to exist in New England and the South.

T   4. Drawing up a written fundamental law in a special constitutional convention and then submitting the document directly to the people for ratification was an important new idea of the Revolutionary period.

T   *F*   5. The state governments after the Revolution stayed mostly under the tight political control of the eastern seaboard elite.

T   6. The United States experienced hard economic times and some social discontent during the years of the Confederation (1781–1787).

F   7. The greatest failure of the national government under the Articles of Confederation was its inability to deal with the issue of western lands.

T 8. The Articles of Confederation were weak because they contained neither an executive nor power to tax and regulate commerce.

T F 9. The Northwest Ordinance originally attempted to make the western territories permanent colonial possessions of the United States.

T 10. Shays's Rebellion significantly strengthened the movement for a stronger central government by raising the fear of anarchy among conservatives.

F 11. The states sent their delegates to Philadelphia in 1787 for the purpose of writing a new Constitution with a strong central government.

F 12. The delegates to the Constitutional Convention were all extremely wealthy slaveholders.

T 13. The "Great Compromise" between large and small states at the convention resulted in a bicameral legislature with different principles of representation in each.

F 14. The antifederalists opposed the Constitution partly because they thought it gave too much power to the states and not enough to Congress.

T 15. The federalists used tough political maneuvering and the promise of a bill of rights to win a narrow ratification of the Constitution in key states.

B. Multiple Choice

Select the best answer and write the proper letter in the space provided.

C 1. Among the important changes brought about by the American Revolution was

    a. the abolition of slavery everywhere except South Carolina and Georgia.
    b. a strong movement toward equality of property rights.
    c. the increasing separation of church and state.
    d. full equality and voting rights for women.

C 2. A major new political innovation that emerged in the Revolutionary era was

    a. the election of legislative representatives capable of voting on taxation.
    b. the shifting of power from the legislative to the executive branch of government.
    c. the idea of a written constitution drafted by a convention and ratified by direct vote of the people.
    d. the regulation of land sales by the courts.

C 3. Despite the Revolution's emphasis on human rights and equality, the Founding Fathers failed to abolish slavery because

    a. they saw it as necessary to maintain American power.
    b. they feared black rebellion if slavery were removed.
    c. of their fear that a fight over slavery would destroy fragile national unity.
    d. almost none of them believed that slavery was wrong.

B   4. The ideal of "republican motherhood" that emerged from the American Revolution held that

     a. women should be rewarded politically for having helped establish the American republic.
     b. women had a special responsibility to cultivate the "civic virtues" of republicanism in their children.
     c. the government should establish social services to help mothers raise their children.
     d. mothers should be granted full political and economic rights in the American republic.

A   5. In the new state constitutions written after the Revolution, the most powerful branch of government was

     a. the legislative branch.
     b. the executive branch.
     c. the judicial branch.
     d. the military branch.

A   6. One way that American independence actually harmed the nation's economic fortunes was by

     a. ending British trade and investment in America.
     b. abolishing the stable currency system that had existed under the empire.
     c. cutting off American trade with the British empire.
     d. weakening the manufacturing efforts begun under the British.

B   7. Attempts to establish strong governments in post-Revolutionary America were seriously hindered by

     a. the lack of strong leadership available in the new nation.
     b. the revolutionary ideology that preached natural rights and suspicion of all governmental authority.
     c. the hostility of the clergy toward the idea of separation of church and state.
     d. the fear that a strong government would suppress economic development.

B   8. The primary political obstacle to the formation of the first American government under the Articles of Confederation was

     a. disputes among the jealous states over control of western lands.
     b. disagreement over the relative power of Congress and the executive branch.
     c. conflict over the right of Congress to regulate trade and manufacturing.
     d. conflict over slavery between northern and southern states.

B   9. The greatest weakness of the government under the Articles of Confederation was that

     a. it was unable to deal with the issue of western lands.
     b. it had no power to regulate commerce or collect taxes from the sovereign states.
     c. it had no power to establish relations with foreign governments.
     d. there was no judicial branch to balance the legislative and executive branches.

C 10. The Northwest Ordinance of 1787 provided that

     a. the states should retain permanent control of their western lands.
     b. money from the sale of western lands should be used to promote manufacturing.
     c. after sufficient population growth, western territories could be organized and then join the union as states.
     d. the settlers in the northwest could vote on whether or not they should have slavery.

B   11. Shays's Rebellion contributed to the movement for a new constitution by

    a. demonstrating the desire of western farmers for a strong government to assist them.
    b. raising the fear of anarchy and disorder among wealthy conservatives.
    c. raising the prospect of British or French interference in American domestic affairs.
    d. demonstrating that the Northwest Ordinance had failed to resolve western land issues.

D   12. Besides George Washington, among the most influential figures in the Constitutional Convention were

    a. John Jay, Thomas Jefferson, and John Hancock.
    b. Samuel Adams, Patrick Henry, and Thomas Paine.
    c. John Adams, Abigail Adams, and Gouverneur Morris.
    d. Benjamin Franklin, James Madison, and Alexander Hamilton.

D   13. The "Great Compromise" in the Constitutional Convention provided that

    a. the House of Representatives would be elected by the people and the Senate by the state legislatures.
    b. the large states would be taxed on the basis of population and the small states on the basis of territory.
    c. there would be separation of powers between the executive and legislative branches of government.
    d. there would be representation by population in the House of Representatives but equal representation of all states in the Senate.

C   14. Antifederalists generally found their greatest support among

    a. small states like Delaware and New Jersey.
    b. the commercial areas of the eastern seaboard.
    c. the poorer debtors and farmers.
    d. the wealthy and well educated.

B   15. The crucial federalist successes in the fight for ratification occurred in the states of

    a. Georgia, Maryland, and Delaware.
    b. Massachusetts, Virginia, and New York.
    c. Pennsylvania, North Carolina, and Rhode Island.
    d. Connecticut, South Carolina, and New Hampshire.

C. Identification

Supply the correct identification for each numbered description.

_____ 1. New name for the Anglican Church after it was disestablished and de-Anglicized in Virginia and elsewhere

_____ 2. The idea that American women had a special responsibility to cultivate "civic virtue" in their children

_____ 3. A type of special assembly, originally developed in Massachusetts, for drawing up a fundamental law that would be superior to ordinary law

_____ 4. The first constitutional government of the United States

_____ 5. The territory north of the Ohio and east of the Mississippi governed by the acts of 1785 and 1787

_____ 6. In the new territories, six-mile by six-mile square areas consisting of thirty-six sections, one of which was set aside for public schools

_____ 7. The status of a western area under the Northwest Ordinance after it established an organized government but before it became a state

_____ 8. A failed revolt in 1786 by poor debtor farmers that raised fears of "mobocracy"

_____ 9. The plan proposed by Virginia at the Constitutional Convention for a bicameral legislature with representation based on population

_____ 10. The plan proposed by New Jersey for a unicameral legislature with equal representation of states regardless of size and population

_____ 11. The compromise between North and South that resulted in each slave being counted as 60 percent of a free person for purposes of representation

_____ 12. The opponents of the Constitution who argued against creating such a strong central government

_____ 13. A masterly series of pro-Constitution articles printed in New York by Jay, Madison, and Hamilton

_____ 14. The official under the new Constitution who would be commander in chief of the armed forces, appoint judges and other officials, and have the power to veto legislation

_____ 15. A list of guarantees that federalists promised to add to the Constitution in order to win ratification

D. Matching People, Places, and Events

Match the person, place, or event in the left column with the proper description in the right column by inserting the correct letter on the blank line.

C 1. Society of the Cincinnati

E 2. Virginia Statute for Religious Freedom

O 3. Articles of Confederation

J 4. Northwest Ordinance of 1787

G 5. Dey of Algiers

F 6. Daniel Shays

M 7. George Washington

B 8. James Madison

D 9. federalists

A. Group that failed to block the central government they feared but did force the promise of a bill of rights

B. Father of the Constitution and author of *Federalist No. 10*

C. An exclusive order of military officers that aroused strong democratic opposition

D. Wealthy conservatives devoted to republicanism who engineered a nonviolent political transformation

E. Legislation passed by an alliance of Jefferson and the Baptists that disestablished the Anglican church

F. Revolutionary War veteran who led poor farmers in a revolt that failed but had far-reaching consequences

G. North African leader who took advantage of the weakness of the Articles of Confederation to attack American shipping

H. The only state to allow a direct vote on the Constitution

I. Frustrated foreign affairs secretary under the Articles; one of the three authors of *The Federalist*

J. Legislation that provided for the orderly transformation of western territories into states

A 10. antifederalists

L 11. Patrick Henry

N 12. Alexander Hamilton

I 13. John Jay

K 14. Massachusetts

H 15. New York

K. First of key states where federalists won by a narrow margin over the opposition of antifederalist Sam Adams

L. Virginia antifederalist leader who thought the Constitution spelled the end of liberty and equality

M. Unanimously elected chairman of the secret convention of "demi-gods"

N. Young New Yorker who argued eloquently for the Constitution even though he favored an even stronger central government

O. Document of 1781 that was put out of business by the Constitution

E. Putting Things in Order

Put the following events in correct order by numbering them from 1 to 5.

4 Fifty-five "demi-gods" meet secretly in Philadelphia to draft a new charter of government.

2 The first American national government, more a league of states than a real government, goes into effect.

1 At the request of Congress, the states draft new constitutions based on the authority of the people.

5 The Constitution is ratified by the nine states necessary to put it into effect.

3 Debtor farmers fail in a rebellion, setting off conservative fears and demands for a stronger government to control anarchy.

F. Matching Cause and Effect

Match the historical cause in the left column with the proper effect in the right column by writing the correct letter on the blank line.

Cause	Effect
E 1. The American Revolution	**A.** Forced acceptance of the "Three-Fifths Compromise," counting each slave as three-fifths of a person for purposes of representation
J 2. Agreement among states to give up western land claims	**B.** Made the federalists promise to add a bill of rights to the Constitution
C 3. The weakness of the Articles of Confederation	**C.** Nearly bankrupted the national government and invited assaults on American interests by foreign powers
I 4. Shays's Rebellion	**D.** Laid the basis for the Virginia Statute for Religious Freedom and the separation of church and state
H 5. The conflict in the Constitutional Convention between large and small states	**E.** Brought about somewhat greater social and economic equality and the virtual end of slavery in the North
A 6. The North-South conflict in the Constitutional Convention over counting slaves for representation	**F.** Finally brought New York to ratify the Constitution by a narrow margin
G 7. A meeting in Annapolis to discuss revising the Articles of Confederation	**G.** Issued a call to Congress for a special convention to revise the Articles of Confederation
B 8. Antifederalist fears that the Constitution would destroy liberties	**H.** Forced the adoption of the "Great Compromise," which required a bicameral

F . 9. *The Federalist* and fears that New York would be left out of the Union

D 10. The disestablishment of the Anglican Church

I. legislature with two different bases of representation

I. Scared conservatives and made them determined to strengthen the central government against debtors

J. Made possible the approval of the Articles of Confederation and the passage of two important laws governing western lands

G. Developing Historical Skills

Interpreting a Chart

Analyzing a chart in more detail can enhance understanding of the historical information in the text and add further information. The chart on p. 182 provides information on the voting for ratification of the Constitution in the states.

Answer the following questions.

1. Look carefully at the vote in the five most populous states. What conclusions can you draw about the relation between population and support for ratification?

2. Look at the vote in the five least populous states. In what ways would the figures support your conclusion about the relation between population and support for ratification in #1? How would the results in New Hampshire and Rhode Island partially qualify that conclusion?

3. Look at the relation between region and date of ratification. Which region—New England, the middle Atlantic states, or the South—had only *one* state ratify after January of 1788? Which region had only *one* state ratify before April of 1788? In which region was opinion more evenly divided?

4. The text indicates that four states—Pennsylvania, Massachusetts, Virginia, and New York—were the keys to ratification. How many *total* delegates would have had to switch sides in order for all of those states to have opposed ratification? (Remember that each change subtracts from one side and adds to the other.)

H. Map Mastery

Map Discrimination

Using the maps and charts in Chapter 9, answer the following questions.

1. *Western Land Cessions to the United States*: Which two of the thirteen states had the largest western land claims?

2. *Western Land Cessions to the United States*: Which states had claims in the area that became the Old Northwest Territory?

3. *Surveying the Old Northwest*: How many square miles were there in each township established by the Land Ordinance of 1785?

4. *Main Centers of British and Spanish Influence After 1783*: Which nation exercised the greatest foreign influence in the American Southwest from 1783 to 1787?

5. *Strengthening the Central Government*: Of the measures that strengthened the central government under the Constitution as compared with the Articles of Confederation, how many dealt with economic matters?

6. *Ratification of the Constitution*: In which three states was there no opposition to the Constitution?

7. *Ratification of the Constitution*: In which state was there only slender opposition?

8. *Ratification of the Constitution*: In which four states was support for the Constitution strong—by a ratio of two to one or three to one—but not overwhelming?

9. *Ratification of the Constitution*: In which five states was the Constitution ratified by very slender margins?

10. *Ratification of the Constitution*: Of the top five states in population, how many had extremely narrow votes in favor of the Constitution (less than twenty votes difference)?

11. *The Struggle Over Ratification*: The map shows that western frontier residents were generally antifederalist. In which two large states, though, was western opinion divided over, or even inclined to favor, adoption of the Constitution?

Map Challenge

Using the map of *The Struggle over Ratification* on p.183, write a brief essay describing how the factors of (a) nearness to the commercial seacoast and (b) size of state influenced profederalist or antifederalist views. Indicate which states were exceptions to the general pattern.

PART III: Applying What You Have Learned

1. How did the revolutionary American ideas of natural human rights, equality, and freedom from governmental tyranny affect developments in the immediate post-Revolutionary period (1783–1789)?

2. How were women and African-Americans affected by the ideas of the American Revolution? Why was slavery abolished in the North but not in the entire nation?

3. Which problems of the post-Revolutionary period and weaknesses of the Articles of Confederation lead to the adoption of a new Constitution?

4. What were the basic features of the new Constitution, and how did they differ from the government under the Articles of Confederation?

5. Who were the federalists and the antifederalists, what were the issues that divided them, and why did the federalists win?

6. Should the Constitution be seen as a conservative reaction to the Revolution, an enshrinement of revolutionary principles, or both? What was most truly *original* about the Constitution?

7. In Chapters 4 and 5, the basic structure of early American society and economy was described. How was that structure changed by the political developments during the period after the Revolution? How did the Constitution itself reflect issues concerning social structure, economic equality, and the distribution of power?

10

Launching the New Ship
of State, 1789–1800

PART I: Reviewing the Chapter

A. Checklist of Learning Objectives

After mastering this chapter, you should be able to

1. indicate why George Washington was pivotal to inaugurating the new federal government.
2. describe the various means Alexander Hamilton used to put the federal government on a sound financial footing.
3. explain how the conflict over Hamilton's policies led to the emergence of the first political parties.
4. describe the polarizing effects of the French Revolution on American foreign policy and politics from 1790 to 1800.
5. explain why Washington negotiated the conciliatory Jay's Treaty with the British and why it provoked Jeffersonian outrage.
6. describe the causes of the undeclared war with France and explain Adams's decision to move toward peace rather than declare war.
7. describe the poisonous political atmosphere that produced the Alien and Sedition Acts and the Kentucky and Virginia resolutions.
8. describe the contrasting membership and principles of the Hamiltonian Federalists and the Jeffersonian Republicans.

B. Glossary

To build your social science vocabulary, familiarize yourself with the following terms.

1. **census** An official count of population; in the United States, the federal census occurs every ten years. ". . . the first official census of 1790 recorded almost 4 million people." (p. 190)
2. **public debt** The debt of a government or nation to individual creditors, also called the national debt. ". . . the public debt, with interest heavily in arrears, was mountainous." (p. 190)
3. **cabinet** The body of official advisers to the head of a government; in the United States, it consists of the heads of the major executive departments. "The Constitution does not mention a cabinet. . . ." (p. 191)
4. **circuit court** A court that hears cases in several designated locations rather than a single place. "The act organized . . . federal district and circuit courts. . . ." (p. 193)
5. **fiscal** Concerning public finances—expenditures and revenues. "His plan was to shape the fiscal policies of the administration. . . ." (p. 193)
6. **assumption** The appropriation or taking on of obligations not originally one's own. "The secretary made a convincing case for 'assumption.' " (p. 194)
7. **excise** A tax on the manufacture, sale, or consumption of certain products. "Hamilton . . . secured from Congress an excise tax on a few domestic items, notably whiskey." (p. 195)

8. **stock** The shares of capital ownership gained from investing in a corporate enterprise; the term also refers to the certificates representing such shares. "Stock was thrown open to public sale." (p. 196)

9. **medium of exchange** Any item, paper or otherwise, used as money. "They regarded [whiskey] as a . . . medium of exchange." (p. 196)

10. **despotism** Arbitrary or tyrannical rule. "The American people, loving liberty and deploring despotism, cheered." (p. 198)

11. **impress** To force people or property into public service without choice; conscript. "They . . . impressed scores of seamen into service on British vessels. . . ." (p. 200)

12. **assimilation** The merging of diverse cultures or peoples into one. "The drastic new law violated the traditional American policy of open-door hospitality and speedy assimilation." (p. 205)

13. **witch-hunt** An investigation carried on with much publicity, supposedly to uncover dangerous activity but actually intended to weaken the political opposition. "Anti-French hysteria played directly into the hands of witch-hunting conservatives." (p. 206)

14. **compact** An agreement or covenant between states to perform some legal act. "Both Jefferson and Madison stressed the compact theory. . . :" (p. 207)

15. **nullification** In American politics, the assertion that a state may legally invalidate a federal act deemed inconsistent with its rights or sovereignty. "[The] resolutions concluded that . . . 'nullification' was the 'rightful remedy.' " (p. 207)

PART II: Checking Your Progress

A. True-False

Where the statement is true, mark **T**. Where it is false, mark **F**, and correct it in the space immediately below.

____ 1. One immediate concern for the new federal government was the questionable loyalty of people living in the western territories of Kentucky, Tennessee, and Ohio.

____ 2. The passage of the first ten amendments to the Constitution demonstrated the Federalist determination to develop a powerful central government.

____ 3. Hamilton's basic purpose in all his financial measures was to strengthen the federal government by building up a larger national debt.

____ 4. Both "funding at par" of the federal debt and assumption of state debts were designed to give wealthier interests a strong stake in the success of the federal government.

____ 5. Hamilton financed his large national debt by revenues from tariffs and excise taxes on products such as whiskey.

____ 6. In the battle over the Bank of the United States, Jefferson favored a "loose construction" of the Constitution and Hamilton favored a "strict construction."

____ 7. The first American political parties grew mainly out of the debate over Hamilton's fiscal policies and U. S. foreign policy toward Europe.

____ 8. The French Revolution's radical political goals were greeted with great approval by both Jeffersonian Republicans and Federalists.

___ 9. Washington's Neutrality Proclamation was based on his confidence in America's military strength in comparison to potentially hostile powers.

___ 10. The Indians of the Miami Confederacy northwest of the Ohio River were easily defeated by U.S. forces and removed across the Mississippi.

___ 11. Washington supported John Jay's unpopular treaty with Britain because he feared a disastrous war if it were rejected.

___ 12. Adams decided to seek a negotiated peace with France in order to unite his party and enhance his own popularity with the public.

___ 13. The Alien Laws were a conservative Federalist attempt to prevent radical French immigrants and spies from supporting the Jeffersonians and stirring up anti-British sentiment.

___ 14. Jeffersonian Republicans believed that the common people were not to be trusted and had to be led by those who were wealthier and better educated.

___ 15. The Jeffersonian Republicans generally sympathized with Britain in foreign policy, while the Hamiltonian Federalists sympathized with France and the French Revolution.

B. Multiple Choice

Select the best answer and write the proper letter in the space provided.

___ 1. A key addition to the new federal government that had been demanded by many of the ratifying states was

    a. a cabinet to aid the president.
    b. a written bill of rights to guarantee liberty.
    c. a supreme court.
    d. federal assumption of state debts.

___ 2. One immediate innovation not mentioned in the Constitution that was developed by George Washington's administration was

    a. the cabinet.
    b. the military joint chiefs of staff.
    c. the Supreme Court.
    d. the vice presidency.

___ 3. The Bill of Rights is the name given to provisions whose actual form is

    a. an executive proclamation of President George Washington.
    b. Article II, Section 3 of the U.S. Constitution.
    c. a set of rulings issued by the Supreme Court.
    d. the first ten amendments to the federal Constitution.

___ 4. Which of the following sets of rights are *not* included in the Bill of Rights?

    a. freedom of religion, speech, and the press.
    b. rights to freedom of education and freedom of travel.
    c. rights to bear arms and to be tried by a jury.
    d. rights to assemble and petition the government for redress of grievances.

5. The Ninth and Tenth Amendments partly reversed the federalist momentum of the Constitution by declaring that

   a. the federal government had no power to restrict the action of local governments.
   b. the powers of the presidency did not extend to foreign policy.
   c. all rights not mentioned in the federal Constitution were retained by the states or by the people themselves.
   d. the Supreme Court had no power to rule in cases affecting property rights.

6. Hamilton's first financial policies were intended

   a. to finance the new government through the sale of western lands.
   b. to fund the national debt and to have the federal government assume the debts owed by the states.
   c. to repudiate the debts accumulated by the government of the Articles of Confederation.
   d. to create a sound federal currency backed by gold.

7. The essential disagreement between Hamilton and Jefferson over the proposed Bank of the United States was

   a. whether the Constitution granted the federal government the power to establish such a bank.
   b. whether it would be economically wise to create a single national currency.
   c. whether the bank should be under the control of the federal government or the states.
   d. whether such a Bank violated the Bill of Rights.

8. The first American political parties developed primarily out of

   a. the disagreement of Jefferson and his states' rights followers with Hamilton's economic policies.
   b. the belief of the Founding Fathers that organized political opposition was a necessary part of good government.
   c. the continuing hostility of the antifederalists to the legitimacy of the new federal Constitution.
   d. patriotic opposition to foreign intervention in American domestic affairs.

9. The Whiskey Rebellion was most significant because

   a. it showed that American citizens would rise up against unfair taxation.
   b. it showed that the new federal government would use force if necessary to uphold its authority.
   c. it demonstrated the efficiency of the American military.
   d. it showed the strength of continuing antifederalist hostility to the new constitutional government.

10. Regarding the French Revolution, most Jeffersonian Democratic-Republicans believed that

   a. the violence was regrettable but necessary.
   b. the overthrow of the king was necessary, but the Reign of Terror went much too far.
   c. the Revolution should be supported by American military aid.
   d. the Revolution represented a complete distortion of American ideals of liberty.

____ 11. Washington's foreign policy rested on the basic belief that

    a.   there should be an end to European colonialism in the Americas.

    b.   it was in America's interest to stay neutral in all European wars.

    c.   America needed to adhere to its Revolutionary alliance with France.

    d.   America ought to enter the French-British war only if republican ideals were at stake.

____ 12. The United States became involved in undeclared hostilities with France in 1797 because of

    a.   fierce American opposition to the concessions of Jay's Treaty.

    b.   American anger at attempted French bribery in the XYZ Affair.

    c.   French interference with American shipping and freedom of the seas.

    d.   President Adams's sympathy with Britain and hostility to Revolutionary France.

____ 13. The Alien and Sedition Acts were aimed primarily at

    a.   the Jeffersonians and their allegedly pro-French activities and ideas.

    b.   the opponents of President Adams's peace settlement with France.

    c.   Napoleon's French agents who were infiltrating the country.

    d.   the Hamiltonian Federalists and their pro-British activities and ideas.

____ 14. Jefferson's Kentucky resolutions argued that

    a.   the Alien and Sedition Acts were necessary and constitutional.

    b.   states ought to secede from the federal government if their rights were violated.

    c.   the states had the right to nullify unconstitutional federal laws.

    d.   the Supreme Court had the right to declare legislation unconstitutional.

____ 15. The Federalists essentially believed that

    a.   most governmental power should be retained by the states.

    b.   government should provide no special aid to private enterprise.

    c.   the common people could, if educated, participate in government affairs.

    d.   there should be a strong central government controlled by the wealthy and well educated.

C. Identification

Supply the correct identification for each numbered description.

_____ 1. The official body designated to choose the President under the new Constitution, which in 1789 unanimously elected George Washington

_____ 2. The constitutional office into which John Adams was sworn on April 30, 1789

_____ 3. The cabinet office in Washington's administration headed by a brilliant young West Indian immigrant who distrusted the people

_____ 4. Alexander Hamilton's policy of paying off all federal bonds at face value in order to strengthen the national credit

_____ 5. Hamilton's policy of having the federal government pay the financial obligations of the states

_____ 6. The first ten amendments to the Constitution

_____ 7. Political organizations not envisioned in the Constitution and considered dangerous to national unity by most of the Founding Fathers

8. Political and social upheaval supported by most Americans during its moderate beginnings in 1789, but the cause of bitter divisions after it took a radical turn in 1792

9. Agreement signed between two anti-British countries in 1778 that increasingly plagued American foreign policy in the 1790s

10. Alliance of eight Indian nations led by Little Turtle that inflicted major defeats on American forces in the early 1790s.

11. Document signed in 1794 whose terms favoring Britain outraged Jeffersonian Republicans

12. The nation with which the United States fought an undeclared war from 1798 to 1800

13. The political theory on which Jefferson and Madison based their antifederalist resolutions declaring that the thirteen sovereign states had created the Constitution

14. The doctrine, proclaimed in the Virginia and Kentucky resolutions, that a state can block a federal law it considers unconstitutional

15. The nation to which most Hamiltonian Federalists were sentimentally attached and which they favored in foreign policy

D. Matching People, Places, and Events

Match the person, place, or event in the left column with the proper description in the right column by inserting the correct letter on the blank line.

___ 1. Census of 1790

___ 2. Alexander Hamilton

___ 3. Thomas Jefferson

___ 4. James Madison

___ 5. Supreme Court

___ 6. Funding and assumption

___ 7. Bank of the United States

___ 8. Whiskey Rebellion

___ 9. Federalists

___ 10. Republicans

___ 11. XYZ

A. A protest by poor western farmers that was firmly suppressed by Washington and Hamilton's army

B. Body organized by the Judiciary Act of 1789 and first headed by John Jay

C. Brilliant administrator and financial wizard whose career was plagued by doubts about his character and belief in popular government

D. Political party that believed in the common people, no government aid for business, and a pro-French foreign policy

E. Effort that counted 4 million Americans

F. Skillful politician-scholar who drafted the Bill of Rights and moved it through the First Congress

G. Institution established by Hamilton to create a stable currency and bitterly opposed by states' rights advocates

H. Hamilton's aggressive financial policies of paying off all federal bonds and taking on all state debts

I. Harsh and probably unconstitutional laws aimed at radical immigrants and Jeffersonian writers

J. Agreement between the United States and Miami Indians that ceded much of Ohio and Indiana while recognizing a limited sovereignty for the Miamis.

K. Message telling America that it should avoid unnecessary foreign entanglements—a reflection of the foreign policy

    ____ 12. Treaty of Greenville   of its author

                                                L.   Secret code names for three French agents who attempted

    ____ 13. Alien and Sedition   to extract bribes from American diplomats in 1797

               Acts   **M.** Washington's secretary of state and the organizer of a

                                                    political party opposed to Hamilton's policies

    ____ 14. Bill of Rights   **N.** Ten constitutional amendments designed to protect

                                              American liberties

    ____ 15. Farewell Address   **O.** Political party that believed in a strong government run by

                                                the wealthy, government aid to business, and a pro-British

                                                foreign policy

E. Putting Things in Order

Put the following events in correct order by numbering them from 1 to 5.

____ Revolutionary turmoil in France causes the U.S. president to urge Americans to stay out of foreign quarrels.

____ Envoys sent to make peace in France are insulted by bribe demands from three mysterious French agents.

____ First ten amendments to the Constitution are adopted.

____ Western farmers revolt against a Hamiltonian tax and are harshly suppressed.

____ Jefferson organizes a political party in opposition to Hamilton's financial policies.

F. Matching Cause and Effect

Match the historical cause in the left column with the proper effect in the right column by writing the correct letter on the blank line.

Cause		Effect
____ 1. The need to gain support of wealthy groups for the federal government	**A.**	Led to the formation of the first two American political parties
____ 2. Passage of the Bill of Rights	**B.**	Caused the Whiskey Rebellion
	C.	Led Hamilton to promote the fiscal policies of funding and assumption
____ 3. The need for federal revenues to finance Hamilton's ambitious policies	**D.**	Guaranteed basic liberties and indicated some swing away from Federalist centralizing
____ 4. Hamilton's excise tax on western farmers' products	**E.**	Led to imposition of the first tariff in 1789 and the excise tax on whiskey in 1791
____ 5. Clashes between Hamilton and Jefferson over fiscal policy and foreign affairs	**F.**	Aroused Jeffersonian Republican outrage at the Washington administration's pro-British policies
____ 6. The French Revolution	**G.**	Created bitter divisions in America between anti-Revolution Federalists and pro-Revolution Republicans
____ 7. The danger of war with Britain	**H.**	Caused an undeclared war with France
	I.	Led Washington to support Jay's Treaty
____ 8. Jay's Treaty	**J.**	Caused passage of the Alien Acts

___ 9. The XYZ Affair

___ 10. The Federalist fear of radical French
immigrants

G. Developing Historical Skills

Reading for Main Idea and Supporting Details

Any historical generalization must be backed up by supporting details and historical facts. For example, the text states that "the key figure in the new government was smooth-faced Alexander Hamilton. . ." (p. 193). This generalization is then supported by details and facts showing Hamilton's importance, such as his policy of funding and assumption, his customs and excise taxes, and his establishment of the Bank of the United States. (pp. 193–196)

List at least two supporting details or facts that support each of the following general assertions in the text.

1. "President Washington's far-visioned policy of neutrality was sorely tried by the British." (p. 200)

2. "True to Washington's policy of steering clear of war at all costs, [President Adams] tried again to reach an agreement with the French. . . ." (p. 203)

3. "Exulting Federalists had meanwhile capitalized on the anti-French frenzy to drive through Congress in 1798 a sheaf of laws designed to reduce or gag their Jeffersonian foes." (p. 205)

4. "Resentful Jeffersonians naturally refused to take the Alien and Sedition Laws lying down." (p. 207)

5. "As the presidential contest of 1800 approached, the differences between Federalists and Democratic-Republicans were sharply etched." (p. 207) (Indicate two clear differences between the parties.)

PART III: Applying What You Have Learned

1. What were the most important issues facing the new federal government, and how did the Washington administration address them?

2. Explain the purpose and significance of the Bill of Rights. Did these Ten Amendments significantly weaken federal authority, or actually enhance it?

3. What were Hamilton's basic economic and political goals, and how did he attempt to achieve them?

4. What were the philosophical and political disagreements between Hamilton and Jefferson that led to the creation of the first American political parties?

5. What were the basic goals of Washington's and Adams's foreign policies, and how successful were they in achieving them?

6. How did divisions over foreign policy create the poisonous political atmosphere that produced both the Alien and Sedition Acts and the Kentucky and Virginia resolutions?

7. Although Federalists and Republicans engaged in extremely bitter political struggles during this period, they both retained their basic commitment to republican government, and at the end of the decade, the Federalists peacefully handed over power to the Republicans. What characteristics of American politics and society enabled them to keep their conflict within bounds?

11

The Triumphs and Travails of Jeffersonian Democracy, 1800–1812

PART I: Reviewing the Chapter

A. Checklist of Learning Objectives

After mastering this chapter, you should be able to

1. explain how Jefferson's moderation and compromises turned the "Revolution of 1800" into a relatively smooth transition of party control from Federalists to Republicans.
2. describe the conflicts between Federalists and Republicans over the judiciary and the important legal precedents that developed from these conflicts.
3. describe Jefferson's basic foreign-policy goals and how he attempted to achieve them.
4. analyze the causes and effects of the Louisiana Purchase.
5. describe how America became entangled against its will in the turbulent international crisis of the Napoleonic Wars.
6. describe the original intentions and actual results of Jefferson's embargo and explain why it failed.
7. explain the complex causes of the War of 1812.

B. Glossary

To build your social science vocabulary, familiarize yourself with the following terms.

1. **lame duck** A political official during the time he or she remains in office after a defeat or inability to seek another term, and whose power is therefore diminished. "This body was controlled for several more months by the lame-duck Federalists. . . ." (p. 214)
2. **commission** The official legal authorization appointing a person to an office or military position, indicating the nature of the duty, term of office, chain of command, and so on. "When Marbury learned that his commission was being shelved by the new secretary of state, James Madison, he sued for its delivery." (p. 218)
3. **writ** A formal legal document ordering or prohibiting some act. ". . . his Jeffersonian rivals . . . would hardly enforce a writ to deliver the commission. . . ." (p. 218)
4. **impeachment** The charge of a public official with improper conduct in office. "Jefferson urged the impeachment of an arrogant and tart-tongued Supreme Court justice. . . ." (p. 219)
5. **pacifist** Characterized by principled opposition to all war and belief in nonviolent solutions to conflict. "A challenge was thus thrown squarely into the face of Jefferson—the non-interventionist, the pacifist. . . ." (p. 220)
6. **consulate (consul)** A place where a government representatives is stationed in a foreign country, but not the main headquarters of diplomatic representation headed by an ambassador (the embassy). "The pasha of Tripoli . . . informally declared war on the United States by cutting down the flagstaff of the American consulate." (p. 220)
7. **cede** To yield or grant something, often upon request or under pressure. (Anything ceded is a *cession*.) "Napoleon Bonaparte induced the king of Spain to cede to France . . . the immense trans-Mississippi region. . . ." (p. 220)

8. **precedent** In law and government, a decision or action that establishes a sanctioned rule for determining similar cases in the future. ". . . the transfer established a precedent that was to be followed repeatedly. . . ." (p. 222)

9. **secession** The withdrawal, by legal or illegal means, of one portion of a political entity from the government to which it has been bound. "Burr joined with a group of Federalist extremists to plot the secession of New England and New York." (p. 223)

10. **conscription** Compulsory enrollment of men and women into the armed forces. "Impressment . . . was a crude form of conscription. . . ." (p. 226)

11. **broadside** The simultaneous firing of all guns on one side of a ship. "The British warship thereupon fired three devastating broadsides. . . ." (p. 226)

12. **embargo** A government order prohibiting commerce in or out of a port. "The hated embargo was not continued long enough or tightly enough to achieve the desired result. . . ." (p. 227)

PART II: Checking Your Progress

A. True-False

Where the statement is true, mark **T**. Where it is false, mark **F**, and correct it in the space immediately below.

_____ 1. The "Revolution of 1800" involved a radical transfer of power from the Federalist merchant class to farmers and urban artisans and craftsmen.

_____ 2. An unexpected deadlock with Aaron Burr meant that Jefferson had to be elected by the House of Representatives.

_____ 3. Jefferson and his Treasury Secretary, Albert Gallatin, kept in place most of the Federalist financial policies.

_____ 4. The Jeffersonian Republicans showed their hostility to the Federalist Supreme Court by trying to impeach Chief Justice John Marshall.

_____ 5. The case of _Marbury_ v. _Madison_ established the principle that the president could appoint but not remove Supreme Court justices.

_____ 6. Jefferson cut the size of the United States Army to twenty-five hundred men because he believed that a large standing army was a threat to liberty and economy.

_____ 7. Jefferson's envoys to Paris initially intended to buy only New Orleans and the immediate vicinity.

_____ 8. Jefferson's deepest doubt about the Louisiana Purchase was that the price of $15 million was too high.

_____ 9. The Lewis and Clark expedition demonstrated the viability of an overland American route to the Pacific.

_____ 10. Aaron Burr's various conspiracies to break apart the United States demonstrated the fragility of the American government's control of the trans-Appalachian West.

_____ 11. The most explosive issue between Britain and the United States was the British blockade of American shipments to Europe.

____ 12. After the *Chesapeake* affair, Jefferson could easily have declared war on Britain with the enthusiastic support of both Federalists and Republicans.

____ 13. Jefferson's embargo badly hurt southern and western farmers as well as Federalist New England.

____ 14. New Englanders overcame the effects of the embargo by conducting illegal trade with Canada and developing more domestic manufacturing.

____ 15. The War of 1812 was promoted largely by New Englanders angry over British violation of American freedom of the seas.

B. Multiple Choice

Select the best answer and write the proper letter in the space provided.

____ 1. The most "revolutionary" development in the critical election of 1800 was

    a. the nasty campaign smears against Jefferson.
    b. Jefferson's radical proposals for overturning the existing political system.
    c. the peaceful transition of power from one political party to its opponent.
    d. the electoral stalemate between Jefferson and his running mate, Burr.

____ 2. One Federalist policy that Jefferson quickly overturned was

    a. funding and assumption.
    b. the excise tax.
    c. the Bank of the United States.
    d. the protective tariff.

____ 3. The case of *Marbury* v. *Madison* established the principle that

    a. the Supreme Court has the right to determine the constitutionality of legislation.
    b. federal laws take precedence over state legislation.
    c. the president has the right to appoint the federal judiciary.
    d. the Supreme Court is the final court of appeal in the federal judiciary.

____ 4. Jefferson was forced to reverse his strong opposition to substantial military forces because of

    a. growing French intervention in Santo Domingo and Louisiana.
    b. the plunder and blackmailing of American shipping by North African states.
    c. the threat to America posed by the British-French wars.
    d. the political attacks by his Federalist opponents.

____ 5. Jefferson's greatest concern in purchasing Louisiana was

    a. whether it was in America's interest to acquire the territory.
    b. whether the cost was excessive for his small-government philosophy.
    c. whether the purchase was permissible under the Constitution.
    d. how to defend and govern the territory once it was part of the United States.

6. The greatest political beneficiary of the Louisiana Purchase was

    a. Thomas Jefferson.
    b. Aaron Burr.
    c. the Federalist party.
    d. Napoleon.

7. Although greatly weakened after Jefferson's election, the Federalist party's philosophy continued to have great influence through

    a. the propaganda efforts of Federalist agitators.
    b. the Federalist control of the U.S. Senate.
    c. the Federalist judicial rulings of John Marshall.
    d. Federalist sympathies within the U.S. army and navy.

8. The term "midnight judges" refers to

    a. Federalist judges appointed by President John Adams at the last moments of his administration.
    b. federal judges who held late-night court sessions to hear controversial cases.
    c. judges like William Marbury who sued to have their late-night appointment commissions confirmed.
    d. states' rights judges appointed by President Jefferson moments after his inauguration.

9. The Republicans' failure to impeach Supreme Court Justice Samuel Chase established the principle that

    a. the Supreme Court had the power to declare laws unconstitutional.
    b. presidents could appoint but not remove federal justices.
    c. impeachment should be used only for "high crimes and misdemeanors" and not as a political weapon.
    d. the constitutional power of impeachment was in effect impossible to carry out.

10. Jefferson focused his military construction policy primarily on

    a. building large naval frigates like the *Constitution*.
    b. building several hundred small gunboats.
    c. building up coastal forts and defense works.
    d. constructing light and medium artillery capable of use on land or sea.

11. Which of the following was *not* among the consequences of the Louisiana Purchase?

    a. the geographical and scientific discoveries of the Lewis and Clark expedition.
    b. the weakening of the power of the presidency in foreign affairs.
    c. Former Vice President Aaron Burr's attempt to break off the West from the United States.
    d. a strengthening of national unity and the decline of the Federalist party.

12. Jefferson's Embargo Act provided that

    a. America would not trade with Britain until it ended impressment.
    b. American goods could be carried only in American ships.
    c. America would sell no military supplies to either warring nation, Britain or France.
    d. America would prohibit all foreign trade.

___ 13. A crucial foreign policy goal for many "war hawks" in the War of 1812 was

    a. the end of all Spanish colonization in the Americas.
    b. the capture and annexation of Canada.
    c. the conquest and settlement of Texas.
    d. the destruction of the British navy.

___ 14. Besides creating a pan-Indian military alliance against white expansion, Tecumseh and Tenskwatawa (the Prophet) urged American Indians to

    a. resist white ways and revive their traditional culture.
    b. demonstrate their legal ownership of the lands that whites were entering.
    c. adopt the whites' culture and technology as a way of resisting their further expansion.
    d. declare independence and form an alliance with Spain.

___ 15. Most Indian military resistance east of the Mississippi River was effectively crushed in the two battles of

    a. the Thames and Lake Erie.
    b. Fort McHenry and New Orleans.
    c. Tippecanoe and Horseshoe Bend.
    d. Plattsburgh and Bladensburg.

C. Identification

Supply the correct identification for each numbered description.

_____ 1. Hamiltonian economic measure repealed by Jefferson and Gallatin

_____ 2. Action Jefferson took toward Republican "martyrs" convicted under the Federalist Sedition Law

_____ 3. Derogatory Republican term for Federalist judges appointed at the last minute by President Adams

_____ 4. Precedent-setting Supreme Court case in which Marshall declared part of the Judiciary Act of 1789 unconstitutional

_____ 5. The principle, established by Chief Justice Marshall in a famous case, that the Supreme Court can declare laws unconstitutional

_____ 6. Action voted by the House of Representatives against Supreme Court Justice Samuel Chase

_____ 7. Branch of military service that Jefferson considered least threatening to liberty and most necessary to suppressing the Barbary states

_____ 8. Sugar-rich island where Toussaint L'Ouverture's slave rebellion disrupted Napoleon's dreams of a vast New World empire

_____ 9. Territory beyond Louisiana, along the Columbia River, explored by Lewis and Clark

_____ 10. Price paid by the United States for the Louisiana Purchase

_____ 11. American ship fired on by British in 1807, nearly leading to war between the two countries

_____ 12. Jefferson's policy of forbidding the shipment of any goods in or out of the United States

_____ 13. Militantly nationalistic western congressmen eager for hostilities with the Indians, Canadians, and British

_____ 14. Battle in 1811 where General Harrison defeated the Indian forces under Tecumseh and Tenskwatawa (the Prophet)

_____ 15. Derisive Federalist name for the War of 1812 that blamed it on the Republican president

D. Matching People, Places, and Events

Match the person, place, or event in the left column with the proper description in the right column by inserting the correct letter on the blank line.

____ 1. Thomas Jefferson

____ 2. Albert Gallatin

____ 3. John Marshall

____ 4. *Marbury* v. *Madison*

____ 5. Samuel Chase

____ 6. Pasha of Tripoli

____ 7. Napoleon Bonaparte

____ 8. Robert Livingston

____ 9. Toussaint L'Ouverture

____ 10. Lewis and Clark

____ 11. Aaron Burr

____ 12. *Chesapeake* affair

____ 13. Embargo Act of 1807

____ 14. Tecumseh

____ 15. William Henry Harrison

A. Former vice-president, killer of Alexander Hamilton, and plotter of mysterious secessionist schemes

B. Military leader who defeated Tecumseh's brother, "the Prophet," at the Battle of Tippecanoe

C. Swiss-born treasury secretary who disliked national debt but kept most Hamiltonian economic measures in effect

D. American minister to Paris who joined James Monroe in making a magnificent real estate deal

E. Strong believer in strict construction, weak government, and antimilitarism who was forced to modify some of his principles in office

F. Shawnee leader who organized a major Indian confederation against U.S. expansion

G. Federalist Supreme Court justice impeached by the House in 1804 but acquitted by the Senate

H. British attack on American sailors that aroused angry demands for war

I. Explorers who crossed the Louisiana Purchase territory and went on to Oregon and the Pacific coast

J. Restrictive trade policy that hurt Britain but hurt American shippers and farmers even more

K. Ruling based on a "midnight judge" case that established the right of the Supreme Court to declare laws unconstitutional

L. North African leader who fought an undeclared war with the United States from 1801 to 1805

M. Gifted black revolutionary whose successful slave revolution indirectly led to Napoleon's sale of Louisiana

N. French ruler who acquired Louisiana from Spain only to sell it to the United States

O. Federalist Supreme Court justice whose brilliant legal efforts established the principle of judicial review

E. Putting Things in Order

Put the following events in correct order by numbering them from 1 to 5.

____   Rather than declare war after a British attack on an American ship, Jefferson imposes a ban on all American trade.

____   President Adams appoints a host of "midnight judges" just before leaving office, outraging Republicans.

____   The foreign difficulties of a French dictator lead him to offer a fabulous real estate bargain to the United States.

____   After four years of naval war, the Barbary state of Tripoli signs a peace treaty with the United States.

____   A deceitful French dictator and aggressive western Congressmen maneuver a reluctant president into a war with Britain.

F. Matching Cause and Effect

Match the historical cause in the left column with the proper effect in the right column by writing the correct letter on the blank line.

Cause

____   1. Jefferson's moderation and continuation of many Federalist policies

____   2. Adams's appointment of "midnight judges"

____   3. Marshall's ruling in *Marbury* v. *Madison*

____   4. The Barbary pirates' attacks on American shipping

____   5. France's acquisition of Louisiana from Spain

____   6. Napoleon's foreign troubles with Britain and Santo Domingo

____   7. The Louisiana Purchase

____   8. British impressment of American sailors and anger at American harboring of British deserters

____   9. French compliance with Macon's Bill No. 2

____   10. Western war hawks' fervor for acquiring Canada and removing resisting Indians

Effect

A. Provoked Federalists to charge Jefferson with unconstitutional expansionism

B. Aroused Jeffersonian hostility to the Federalist judiciary and led to repeal of the Judiciary Act of 1801

C. Forced Madison to declare a policy of nonimportation that accelerated the drift toward war

D. Led to an aggressive and deadly assault on the American ship *Chesapeake*

E. Created stability and continuity in the transition of power from one party to another

F. Caused Harrison's and Jackson's military ventures and contributed to the declaration of war in 1812

G. Established the principle of "judicial review" of laws by the Supreme Court

H. Made Americans eager to purchase New Orleans in order to protect their Mississippi River shipping

I. Led to a surprise offer to sell Louisiana to the United States for $15 million

J. Forced a reluctant Jefferson to send the U.S. Navy into military action

G. Developing Historical Skills

Reading and Election Map: Reading an election map carefully yields additional information about voting patterns and political alignments. Using the map of the *Presidential Election of 1800* on p. 214, answer the following questions:

1. How many electoral votes did Adams get from the five New England states?

2. Which was the only state north of Virginia that went completely for Jefferson?

3. How many electoral votes were there in the three states that divided between Adams and Jefferson?

4. The text records the final electoral vote as 73 for Jefferson to 65 for Adams, and notes that Jefferson carried New York only by a very slender margin. *If* Adams had carried New York, what would the electoral result have been?

PART III: Applying What You Have Learned

1. What was the significance of the Jeffersonian "Revolution of 1800" in relation to the new republican experiment and the fierce political battles of the 1790s? (See Chapter 10.)

2. How did the conflict between Federalists and Republicans over the judiciary lead to a balance of power among political interests and different branches of government?

3. What were the political and economic consequences of the Louisiana Purchase? What did Aaron Burr's conspiracies reveal about the condition of American power west of the Mississippi River?

4. What was the essential idea behind Jefferson's imposition of the embargo, and why did it finally fail?

5. What were the real causes of the War of 1812? Was the declaration of war a "mistake," or the result of deliberate policies by new American political forces?

6. What were the central principles animating American government in the years 1800–1812? Was the War of 1812 a violation of the principles of the "Revolution of 1800" or its fulfillment?

12

The Second War for Independence and the Upsurge of Nationalism, 1812–1824

PART I: Reviewing the Chapter

A. Checklist of Learning Objectives

After mastering this chapter, you should be able to

1. describe the failed American attempts to conquer Canada and their consequences.
2. describe the crucial military developments of the war and explain why Americans experienced more success on water than on land.
3. describe the major issues and terms of the Treaty of Ghent and explain the long-term results of the War of 1812 for the United States at home and abroad.
4. describe and explain the burst of American nationalism that followed the War of 1812.
5. describe the major economic developments of the period, particularly the tariff, finances, and the panic of 1819.
6. describe the conflict over slavery that arose in 1819 and the terms of the Missouri Compromise that temporarily resolved it.
7. indicate how John Marshall's Supreme Court promoted the spirit of nationalism through its rulings in favor of federal power.
8. describe the Monroe Doctrine and explain its real and symbolic significance for American foreign policy.

B. Glossary

To build your social science vocabulary, familiarize yourself with the following terms.

1. **regiment** A medium-sized military unit, larger than a company or battalion and smaller than a division. "Among the defenders were two Louisiana regiments of free black volunteers. . . ." (p. 236)
2. **mediation** An intervention, usually by consent of the parties, to aid in voluntarily settling differences between groups or nations. (**Arbitration** involves a *mandatory* settlement determined by a third party.) "Tsar Alexander I of Russia . . . proposed mediation between the clashing Anglo-Saxon cousins in 1812." (p. 237)
3. **armistice** A temporary stopping of warfare by mutual agreement, usually in preparation for an actual peace negotiation between the parties. "The Treaty of Ghent, signed on Christmas Eve in 1814, was essentially an armistice." (p. 237)
4. **dynasty** A succession of rulers in the same family line; by extension, any system of predetermined succession in power. "This last clause was aimed at the much-resented 'Virginia Dynasty.' . . ." (p. 239)

5. **reaction (reactionary)** In politics, extreme conservatism, looking to restore the political or social conditions of some earlier time. ". . . the Old World took the rutted road back to conservatism, illiberalism, and reaction." (p. 240)

6. **protection (protective)** In economics, the policy of stimulating or preserving domestic producers by placing barriers against imported goods, often through high tariffs. "The infant industries bawled lustily for protection." (p. 241)

7. **raw materials** Products in their natural, unmanufactured state. "Through these new arteries of transportation would flow foodstuffs and raw materials. . . ." (p. 241)

8. **internal improvements** The basic public works, such as roads and canals, that create the structure for economic development. "Congress voted . . . for internal improvements." (p. 242)

9. **intrastate** Something existing wholly within a state of the United States. (**Interstate** refers to movement between two or more states.) "Jeffersonian Republicans . . . choked on the idea of direct federal support of intrastate internal improvements." (p. 242)

10. **depression** In economics, a severe and very prolonged period of declining economic activity, high unemployment, and low wages and prices. "It brought deflation, depression, [and] bankruptcies. . . ." (p. 243)

11. **boom** In economics, period of sudden, spectacular expansion of business activity or prices. "The western boom was stimulated by additional developments." (p. 244)

12. **wildcat bank** An unregulated, speculative bank that issues notes without sufficient capital to back them. "Finally, the West demanded cheap money, issued by its own 'wildcat' banks. . . ." (p. 244)

13. **peculiar institution** Widely used term for the institution of American black slavery. "If Congress could abolish the 'peculiar institution' in Missouri, might it not attempt to do likewise in the older states of the South?" (p. 245)

14. **demogogic (demagogue)** Concerning a leader who stirs up the common people by appeals to emotion and prejudice, often for selfish or irrational ends. ". . . Marshall's decisions bolstered judicial barriers against democratic or demogogic attacks on property rights." (p. 250)

15. **contract** In law, an agreement in which each of two or more parties binds themselves to perform some act in exchange for what the other party similarly pledges to do. ". . . the legislative grant was a contract . . . and the Constitution forbids state laws 'impairing' contracts." (p. 250)

PART II: Checking Your Progress

A. True-False

Where the statement is true, mark **T**. Where it is false, mark **F**, and correct it in the space immediately below.

_____ 1. President Madison cleverly manipulated Napoleon into repealing his blockade decrees.

_____ 2. The large western delegation in Congress was not concerned about foreign-policy issues such as Canada and maritime rights.

_____ 3. Western hostility to Britain arose partly because the war hawks believed the British were supplying Indians with weapons for war.

_____ 4. New Englanders opposed the War of 1812 because they believed that Canada should be acquired by peaceful negotiation rather than war.

_____ 5. The most effective branch of the American military in the War of 1812 proved to be the U.S. Army.

___ 6. The American strategy for conquering Canada was well conceived but failed because of a lack of equipment and troops.

___ 7. American naval forces under Perry and Macdonough thwarted British-Canadian invasion threats to Detroit and upstate New York.

___ 8. Andrew Jackson's victory at the Battle of New Orleans was crucial to the American military and political gains in the Treaty of Ghent.

___ 9. Clay's and Calhoun's plans for an extensive system of federally funded roads and canals were blocked by the western states' objections to federal involvement in their affairs.

___ 10. The "Era of Good Feelings" under President Monroe was a period of sustained economic prosperity.

___ 11. Because of its wildcat banking practices and land speculation, the West was hit especially hard in the panic of 1819.

___ 12. The Missouri Compromise admitted Missouri to the Union as a free state, in exchange for the admission of Louisiana as a slave state.

___ 13. John Marshall's Supreme Court rulings generally defended the power of the federal government against the power of the states.

___ 14. Secretary of State John Quincy Adams successfully acquired both Oregon and Florida for the United States.

___ 15. The Monroe Doctrine prohibiting European colonialism in the Americas was most enthusiastically welcomed in Latin America.

B. Multiple Choice

Select the best answer and write the proper letter in the space provided.

___ 1. The greatest American military successes of the War of 1812 came

    a. in the land invasions of Canada.
    b. in the campaign fought around Washington and Baltimore.
    c. in the naval battles on the Great Lakes and elsewhere.
    d. in the defense of Fort Michilimackinac.

___ 2. Two prominent American military heroes during the War of 1812 were

    a. Tecumseh and Henry Clay.
    b. Oliver Hazard Perry and Andrew Jackson.
    c. Thomas Macdonough and Francis Scott Key.
    d. Isaac Brock and John Quincy Adams.

3. The American victory in the Battle of New Orleans proved essentially meaningless because

   a. General Jackson was unable to pursue the British any further.
   b. the British continued their attacks on the Mississippi Valley region.
   c. the peace treaty had been signed several weeks before.
   d. the British navy retained control of the shipping lanes around New Orleans.

4. The terms of the Treaty of Ghent ending the War of 1812 provided

   a. that there would be a buffer Indian state between the United States and Canada.
   b. that Britain would stop impressment of American sailors.
   c. that the United States would acquire western Florida in exchange for guaranteeing British control of Canada.
   d. that the two sides would stop fighting and return to the status quo before the war.

5. One significant domestic consequence of the War of 1812 was

   a. a weakening of respect for American naval forces.
   b. an increased threat from Indians in the West.
   c. an increase in domestic manufacturing and economic independence.
   d. a decline of nationalism and a growth of sectionalism.

6. One significant international consequence of the War of 1812 was

   a. a growth of good relations between the United States and Britain.
   b. a growth of Canadian patriotism and nationalism.
   c. the spread of American ideals of liberty to much of western Europe.
   d. increased American attention to the threat of attack from European nations.

7. The Era of Good Feelings was sharply disrupted by

   a. the bitter political battles over the Tariff of 1816.
   b. the rise of international tensions with Britain.
   c. the panic of 1819 and the battle over slavery in Missouri.
   d. the nasty presidential campaign of 1820.

8. The new nationalistic feeling right after the War of 1812 was evident in all of the following *except*

   a. the development of a distinctive national literature.
   b. an increased emphasis on economic independence.
   c. the addition of significant new territory to the United States.
   d. a new pride in the American army and navy.

9. Besides admitting Missouri as a slave state and Maine as a free state, the Missouri Compromise provided that

   a. slavery would not be permitted anywhere in the Louisiana Purchase territory north of the southern boundary of Missouri, except in Missouri itself.
   b. the number of proslavery and antislavery members of the House of Representatives would be kept permanently equal.
   c. the international slave trade would be permanently ended.
   d. slavery would be gradually ended in the District of Columbia.

_____ 10. In the case of *McCulloch* v. *Maryland*, Justice John Marshall held that

    a. the states had the right to regulate commerce within their boundaries.

    b. the federal Bank of the United States was constitutional, and no state had a right to tax it.

    c. the Supreme Court had the right to review the decisions of state supreme courts.

    d. the Supreme Court had the power to determine the constitutionality of federal laws.

_____ 11. The most prominent political figure who shared John Marshall's belief in expanding the power of the federal government at the expense of the states was

    a. James Monroe.

    b. John Calhoun.

    c. Daniel Webster.

    d. Andrew Jackson.

_____ 12. Andrew Jackson's invasion of Florida led to permanent acquisition of that territory after

    a. President Monroe ordered him to seize all Spanish military posts in the area.

    b. the United States declared its rights under the Monroe Doctrine.

    c. Monroe's cabinet endorsed Jackson's action and told him to purchase Florida from Spain.

    d. Secretary of State Adams pressured Spain to cede the area to the United States.

_____ 13. The original impetus for declaring the Monroe Doctrine came from

    a. a British proposal that America join Britain in guaranteeing the independence of the Latin American republics.

    b. the growing British threat to intervene in Latin America.

    c. the American desire to gain new territory in the Caribbean and Central America.

    d. a Russian plan to expand from Alaska into western Canada and Oregon.

_____ 14. As proclaimed by Monroe in his message of 1823, the Monroe Doctrine asserted that

    a. only the United States had a right to intervene to promote democracy in Latin America.

    b. the British and Americans would act together to prevent further Russian expansion on the Pacific coast.

    c. the United States would not tolerate further European intervention or colonization in the Americas.

    d. the United States would support the Greeks in their fight for independence against Turkey.

_____ 15. The immediate effect of the Monroe Doctrine at the time it was issued was

    a. a rise in tension between the United States and the major European powers.

    b. very little.

    c. a close alliance between the United States and the Latin American republics.

    d. a series of clashes between the American and British navies.

C. Identification

Supply the correct identification for each numbered description.

_____ 1. One of the Great Lakes where Oliver H Perry captured a large British fleet

_____ 2. Stirring patriotic song written by Francis Scott Key

3. Famous American frigate that was larger and heavier than most British ships

_____

4. Gathering of prominent New England Federalists who considered secession

_____

5. Two prominent Washington buildings burned by the British in 1814

_____

_____

6. Intellectual magazine that reflected the post-1815 spirit of American nationalism

_____

7. Henry Clay's ambitious nationalistic proposal for tariffs, internal improvements, and expanded manufacturing

_____

8. Somewhat inappropriate term applied to the Monroe administrations, suggesting that this period lacked major conflicts

_____

9. Once-prominent political party that effectively died by 1820

_____

10. Major water transportation route financed and built by New York State after President Madison vetoed federal funding

_____

11. Line designated as the future boundary between free and slave territories under the Missouri Compromise

_____

12. Supreme Court ruling that defended federal power by denying a state the right to tax a federal bank

_____

13. Supreme Court case in which Daniel Webster successfully argued that a state could not change a legal charter once granted

_____

14. Territory occupied jointly by Britain and the United States under the Treaty of 1818

_____

15. A presidential foreign-policy proclamation that might well have been called the "Adams Doctrine" or the "Self-Defense Doctrine"

D. Matching People, Places, and Events

Match the person, place, or event in the left column with the proper description in the right column by inserting the correct letter on the blank line.

___ 1. Stephen Decatur

___ 2. Treaty of Ghent

___ 3. Rush-Bagot agreement

___ 4. Hartford Convention

___ 5. Henry Clay

___ 6. James Monroe

___ 7. Panic of 1819

___ 8. Missouri Compromise

___ 9. John Marshall

A. Admitted one slave and one free state to the Union, and fixed the boundary between slave and free territories

B. Military commander who exceeded his government's instructions during an invasion of Spanish territory

C. British foreign secretary who tried to get Americans to join him in warning other European nations out of Latin America

D. Aristocratic Federalist jurist whose rulings bolstered national power against the states

E. Eloquent spokesman for the "American System" and key architect of the Missouri Compromise

F. Nationalistic secretary of state who promoted American interests against Spain and Britain

G. Area where vulnerable new republics tempted European monarchies to intervene

____ 10. John Quincy Adams

____ 11. Florida

____ 12. Andrew Jackson

____ 13. George Canning

____ 14. Latin America

____ 15. Tsar Alexander I

H. American naval hero of the War of 1812 who said, ". . . our country, right or wrong!"

I. First severe depression since 1790

J. Territory ceded by Spain after Americans invaded and applied diplomatic pressure

K. Gathering of antiwar delegates in New England that ended up being accused of treason

L. President whose personal popularity contributed to the Era of Good Feelings

M. Agreement that simply stopped fighting and left most of the war issues unresolved

N. 1817 agreement that limited American and British naval forces on the Great Lakes

O. Russian ruler whose mediation proposal led to negotiations ending the War of 1812

E. Putting Things in Order

Put the following events in correct order by numbering them from 1 to 6.

____ A battle over extending slavery finally results in two new states and an agreement on how to handle slavery in the territories.

____ A major water route is completed across New York State.

____ Infant American manufacturers successfully press Congress to raise barriers against foreign imports.

____ Rather than follow a British diplomatic lead, President Monroe and Secretary Adams announce a bold new policy for the Western Hemisphere.

____ Spain cedes Florida to the United States.

____ An unpopular war ends in an ambivalent compromise that settles none of the key contested issues.

F. Matching Cause and Effect

Match the historical cause in the left column with the proper effect in the right column by writing the correct letter on the blank line.

Cause

____ 1. American lack of military preparation and poor strategy

____ 2. Oliver H. Perry's and Thomas Macdonough's naval successes

____ 3. Tsar Alexander I's mediation proposal

____ 4. The Hartford Convention

Effect

A. Inspired a new sense of Canadian nationalism

B. Contributed to the death of the Federalist party and the impression that New Englanders were disloyal

C. Produced a series of badly failed attempts to conquer Canada

D. Reduced armaments along the border between the United States and Canada and laid the groundwork for "the longest unfortified boundary in the world"

_____ 5. Canadians' successful defense of their homeland in the War of 1812

_____ 6. The Rush-Bagot agreement

_____ 7. The rising nationalistic economic spirit after the War of 1812

_____ 8. The disappearance of the Federalists and President Monroe's appeals to New England

_____ 9. Overspeculation in western lands

_____ 10. Cheap land and increasing westward migration

_____ 11. The deadlock between North and South over the future of slavery in Missouri

_____ 12. The Missouri Compromise

_____ 13. John Marshall's Supreme Court rulings

_____ 14. The rise of European reactionary powers and the loss of Spain's colonial empire

_____ 15. The Monroe Doctrine

E. Caused the economy to collapse in the panic of 1819

F. Angered Britain and other European nations but had little effect in Latin America

G. Fueled demands in Congress for transportation improvements and the removal of the Native Americans

H. Upheld the power of the federal government against the states

I. Created a temporary one-party system and an "Era of Good Feelings"

J. Produced the Missouri Compromise, which admitted two states and drew a line between slave and free territories

K. Aroused American and British fears of European intervention in Latin America

L. Aroused southern fears for the long-term future of slavery

M. Inspired a new Bank of the United States and the protectionist Tariff of 1816

N. Eventually led to the beginnings of peace negotiations at Ghent

O. Reversed a string of American defeats and prevented a British-Canadian invasion from the north

G. Developing Historical Skills

Categorizing Historical Information

Historical events and information are usually presented in chronological order. But it is often useful to organize them into topical or other categories. The central idea of this chapter is the rise of American nationalism in the period 1815–1824. Among the major subdivisions of this general idea would be the following:

a. Economic nationalism
b. Political nationalism and unity
c. Judicial nationalism
d. Foreign-policy nationalism

Indicate under which of these categories each of the following facts or events from the chapter should be located.

1. Andrew Jackson's invasion of Florida
2. _Dartmouth College_ v. _Woodward_
3. The Tariff of 1816
4. John Quincy Adams's rejection of Canning's proposed British-American statement
5. Clay's American System
6. President Monroe's tour of New England

7. Daniel Webster's speeches
8. The election of 1820

H. Map Mastery

Map Discrimination

Using the maps and charts in Chapter 12, answer the following questions.

1. *The Three U. S. Invasions of 1812/Campaigns of 1813*: Near which two Great Lakes were the major battles related to the American invasions of Canada fought?

2. *Presidential Election of 1812*: What were the only two states that voted in part contrary to the general trend of their section (i.e, North vs. South)?

3. *The Missouri Compromise and Slavery, 1820–1821*: After the Missouri Compromise of 1820, only two organized territories of the United States remained eligible to join the Union as slave states. Which were they?

4. *The Missouri Compromise and Slavery, 1820–1821*: As of 1821, how many slave states had been carved out of the territory of the Louisiana Purchase?

5. *The Missouri Compromise and Slavery, 1820–1821*: After Maine was admitted as a free state in 1820, how many *organized* territories were there north of the line 36° 30'—that is, the border between the slave and free territories?

6. *The Missouri Compromise and Slavery, 1820–1821*: As of 1821, which *five* slave states were north of the line of 36° 30' that was intended to be the future northern limit of slavery?

7. *The U.S.-British Boundary Settlement, 1818:* Under the British-American boundary settlement of 1818, which nation gained the most territory (compared with the natural Missouri River watershed boundary)?

8. *The Southeast, 1810–1819*: Which organized American territory lay immediately north of West Florida at this time?

Map Challenge

Using the map on p. 246, write a brief essay explaining how the Missouri Compromise related both to the *existing* territorial status of slavery and to its possible future expansion to the West. (Recall that the Compromise set 36° 30' as the northern boundary of any future slave territory.)

PART III: Applying What You Have Learned

1. Why was the American military effort generally unsuccessful, especially the numerous attempts to invade Canada?

2. What were the broad consequences of the War of 1812?

3. What were the most important signs of the new American nationalism that developed in the period 1815–1824?

4. How did the forces of nationalism compete with sectional interests in the economic and judicial struggles of the period?

5. What role did the West play in such crucial issues of the period as the tariff, internal improvements, and the expansion of slavery?

6. Discuss the role of Henry Clay, John C. Calhoun, and Daniel Webster in the events and issues of the period 1815–1824. Is it valid to see Clay as spokesman for the West, Webster for the North, and Calhoun for the South?

7. How did American nationalism display itself in foreign policy, particularly in the Florida crisis and in American policy toward Europe and the Western Hemisphere?

8. Why did the issue of admitting Missouri to the Union precipitate a major national crisis? Why did the North and South each agree to the terms of the Missouri Compromise?

9. Why had the Jeffersonian Republicans, by 1815–1824, adopted many of the principles of "loose construction" once held by Hamiltonian Federalists? (See Chapters 6 and 10.) What kinds of strong federal power did the Republicans use, and what kinds were they still reluctant to employ?

13

The Rise of a Mass Democracy, 1824–1840

PART I: Reviewing the Chapter

A. Checklist of Learning Objectives

After mastering this chapter, you should be able to

1. describe and explain the growth of the "New Democracy" in the 1820s.
2. indicate how the "corrupt bargain" of 1824 weakened Adams and set the stage for Jackson's election in 1828.
3. analyze the significance of Jackson's victory in 1828 as a triumph of the "New Democracy."
4. describe the political innovations of the 1830s, including the rise of mass parties, and indicate their significance for American politics and society.
5. describe Jackson's policies toward the southeastern Indian tribes and newly independent Texas.
6. explain the economic and political consequences of the Panic of 1837.
7. assess the positive and negative impact of the new popular democracy.

B. Glossary

To build your social science vocabulary, familiarize yourself with the following terms.

1. **deference** The yielding of opinion to the judgment of someone else. "The deference, apathy, and virtually nonexistent party organizations of the Era of Good Feelings yielded to the boisterous democracy. . . ." (p. 256)
2. **puritanical** Extremely or excessively strict in matters of morals or religion. "The only candidate left was the puritanical Adams. . . ." (p. 258)
3. **mudslinging** Malicious, unscrupulous attacks against an opponent. "Mudslinging reached a disgraceful level. . . ."
4. **spoils** Public offices given as a reward for political support. "Under Jackson the spoils system . . . was introduced on a large scale." (p. 262)
5. **denominations** In American religion, the major branches of Christianity, organized into distinct church structures, e.g., Presbyterians, Baptists, Disciples of Christ, etc. ". . . many denominations sent missionaries into Indian villages." (p. 266)
6. **evangelical** In American religion, those believers and groups, usually Protestant, who emphasizes personal salvation, individual conversion experiences, voluntary commitment, and the authority of Scripture. "The Anti-Masons attracted support from many evangelical Protestant groups. . . ." (p. 271)
7. **hard money** Metal money or coins, as distinguished from paper money. (The term also came to mean reliable or secure money that maintained or increased its purchasing power over time. **Soft money**, or paper money, was assumed to inflate or lose value.) ". . . a decree that required all public lands to be purchased with 'hard' . . . money." (p. 272)

8. **usurpation** The act of seizing, occupying, or enjoying the place, power, or functions of someone without legal right. "Hatred of Jackson and his 'executive usurpation' was its only apparent cement in its formative days." (p. 272)

9. **favorite sons** In American politics, presidential candidates who are nominated by their own state, primarily out of local loyalty. "Their long-shot strategy was instead to run several prominent 'favorite sons' . . . and hope to scatter the vote so that no candidate could win a majority." (p. 273)

10. **machine** A hierarchical political organization, often controlled through patronage or spoils, where professional workers deliver large blocs of voters to preferred candidates. "As a machine-made candidate, he incurred the resentment of many Democrats. . . ." (p. 274)

11. **temperance** Campaigns for voluntary commitment to moderation or total abstinence in the consumption of liquor. (Prohibition involved instead forcible legal bans on the production or consumption of alcohol.) ". . . the Arkansas Indians dubbed him 'Big Drunk.' He subsequently took the pledge of temperance." (p. 276)

12. **populist** A political program or style focused on the common people, and attacking perspectives and policies associated with the well-off, well-born, or well-educated. (The Populist Party was a specific third-party organization of the 1890s.) "The first was the triumph of a populist democratic style." (p. 283)

13. **divine right** The belief that government or rulers are directly established by God. ". . . America was now bowing to the divine right of the people." (p. 283)

PART II: Checking Your Progress

A. True-False

Where the statement is true, mark **T**. Where it is false, mark **F**, and correct it in the space immediately below.

_____ 1. The last election based on the old elitist political system was the four-way presidential campaign of 1824 involving Jackson, Clay, Crawford, and John Quincy Adams.

_____ 2. Henry Clay disproved the charge of a "corrupt bargain" between himself and President Adams by refusing to accept any favors from the administration.

_____ 3. President Adams attempted to uphold strong nationalistic principles in a time of growing support for sectionalism and states' rights.

_____ 4. In his personal lifestyle as well as his policies, Andrew Jackson epitomized the hard-working ordinary frontiersmen in contrast to the wealthy Adams and his supporters.

_____ 5. The election campaign of 1828 was notable for its focus on the issues of the tariff and democracy rather than on personalities and mudslinging.

_____ 6 Jackson's victory in 1828 did represent the triumph of the West and the common people over the older elitist political system.

_____ 7. The Jacksonians put into practice their belief that ordinary citizens were capable of holding almost any public office without particular qualifications.

_____ 8. One consequence of the spoils system was the building of powerful political machines based on jobs and sometimes corrupt rewards distributed to political supporters.

___ 9. The "Tariff of Abominations" was passed over the strong opposition of President Jackson.

___ 10. South Carolina's fierce opposition to the tariff reflected anxiety that enhanced federal power might be turned against the institution of slavery.

___ 11. When the Supreme Court attempted to uphold southeastern Indians' rights, Jackson defied the Supreme Court's rulings and ordered them removed to Oklahoma.

___ 12. Jackson used his veto of the bill to recharter the Bank of the United States to politically mobilize the common people of the West against the financial elite of the East.

___ 13. The Whig party was from the beginning united by its ideological support for states rights and national expansion.

___ 14. American settlers in Texas clashed with the Mexican government over issues of slavery, immigration, and legal rights.

___ 15. William Henry Harrison's background as an ordinary frontiersman born in a log cabin formed the basis for the Whigs' appeal to the common man in 1840.

B. Multiple Choice

Select the best answer and write the proper letter in the space provided.

___ 1. The Jacksonian charge of a "corrupt bargain" to gain John Quincy Adams the presidency arose because

   a. William Crawford threw his electoral votes to Adams in exchange for a seat in the Senate.
   b. Adams was charged with having bribed members of the House to vote for him.
   c. Adams ended his previous opposition to Clay's American System.
   d. Clay was named secretary of state after throwing his support to Adams.

___ 2. Which of the following was *not* among the factors that made John Quincy Adams's presidency a political failure?

   a. Adams's anti-western land and Indian policies.
   b. Adams's involvement with correct machine deals and politicians.
   c. Adams's stubborn and prickly personality.
   d. Adams's support for national roads, a national university, and an astronomical observatory.

___ 3. Andrew Jackson's appeal to the common people arose partly because

   a. Americans finally understood the ideas of the Declaration of Independence.
   b. many citizens were tired of the partisan fights between Republicans and Federalists.
   c. he had risen from the masses and reflected many of their prejudices in his personal attitudes and outlook.
   d. farmer and labor organizations aroused populist opposition to elitist politics.

_____ 4. One political development that illustrated the new popular voice in politics was

    a. the rise of the caucus system of presidential nominations.
    b. the growth of the spoils system as a basis for large political "machines."
    c. the development of extensive speechmaking tours by presidential candidates.
    d. the hostility to the influence of the Masons in national politics.

_____ 5. In the battle over the "Tariff of Abominations,"

    a. New England backed high tariffs while the South demanded lower duties.
    b. both New England and the South opposed the higher tariff rates.
    c. the South fought for higher tariffs while the West sought lower rates.
    d. the South backed higher tariffs while New England sought to lower the rates.

_____ 6. Under the surface of the South's strong opposition to the "Tariff of Abominations" was

    a. a desire to develop its own textile industry.
    b. competition between southern cotton growers and midwestern grain farmers.
    c. a strong preference for British manufactured goods over American-produced goods.
    d. a fear of growing federal power that might interfere with slavery.

_____ 7. Some southeastern Indian tribes like the Cherokees were notable for their

    a. effectiveness in warfare against encroaching whites.
    b. development of effective agricultural, educational, and political institutions.
    c. success in persuading President Jackson to support their cause.
    d. adherence to traditional Native American cultural and religious values.

_____ 8. In promoting his policy of Indian removal, President Andrew Jackson

    a. defied rulings of the U.S. Supreme Court that favored the Cherokees.
    b. admitted that the action would destroy Native American culture and society.
    c. acted against the advice of his cabinet and his military commanders in the Southeast.
    d. hoped to split the Cherokees apart from their allies such as the Creeks and Seminoles.

_____ 9. Jackson's veto of the Bank of the United States recharter bill represented

    a. a bold assertion of presidential power on behalf of western farmers and other debtors.
    b. an attempt to assure bankers and creditors that the federal government had their interests at heart.
    c. a concession to Henry Clay and his National Republican followers.
    d. a gain for sound banking and a financially stable currency system.

_____ 10. One important result of President Jackson's destruction of the Bank of the United States was

    a. a successful economy that could be handed to his successor, Van Buren.
    b. a sounder financial system founded upon thousands of locally controlled banks.
    c. the American banking system's dependence on European investment and control.
    d. the lack of a stable banking system to finance the era of rapid industrialization.

_____ 11. Among the new political developments that appeared in the election of 1832 were

    a. political parties and direct popular voting for president.
    b. newspaper endorsements and public financing of presidential campaigns.
    c. nomination by congressional caucus and voting by the Electoral College.
    d. third-party campaigning, national conventions, and party platforms.

____ 12. In the immediate aftermath of the successful Texas Revolution,

    a. Texas petitioned to join the United States but was refused admission.

    b. Texas joined the United States as a slave state.

    c. Mexico and the United States agreed to a joint protectorate over Texas.

    d. Britain threatened the United States with war over Texas.

____ 13. The Panic of 1837 and subsequent depression were caused by

    a. the stock market collapse and a sharp decline in grain prices.

    b. a lack of new investment in industry and technology.

    c. the threat of war with Mexico over Texas.

    d. over-speculation and Jackson's financial policies.

____ 14. Prominent leaders of the Whig party included

    a. Martin Van Buren and John C. Calhoun.

    b. Henry Clay and Daniel Webster.

    c. Andrew Jackson and William Henry Harrison.

    d. Stephen Austin and Sam Houston.

____ 15. In general, the Whig party tended to favor

    a. individual liberty and states' rights.

    b. the protection of slavery and southern interests.

    c. a strong federal role in both economic and moral issues.

    d. the interests of the working people and farmers against the upper classes.

C. Identification

Supply the correct identification for each numbered description.

_____ 1. New, circus like method of nominating presidential candidates that involved wider participation but usually left effective control in the hands of party bosses

_____ 2. Small, short-lived third political party that originated a new method of nominating presidential candidates in the election campaign of 1831–1832

_____ 3. Contemptuous Jacksonian term for the alleged political deal by which Clay threw his support to Adams in exchange for a high cabinet office

_____ 4. Office to which President Adams appointed Henry Clay

_____ 5. The popular idea that public offices should be handed out on the basis of political support rather than special qualifications

_____ 6. Scornful southern term for the high Tariff of 1828

_____ 7. Theory promoted by John C. Calhoun and other South Carolinians that said states had the right to disregard federal laws to which they objected

_____ 8. The "moneyed monster" that Clay tried to preserve and that Jackson killed with his veto in 1832

_____ 9. Ritualistic secret societies that became the target of a momentarily powerful third party in 1832

_____ 10. Religious believers, originally attracted to the Anti-Masonic party and then to the Whigs, who sought to use political power for moral and religious reform

_____ 11. Any *two* of the southeastern Indian peoples who were removed to Oklahoma

_____

_____ 12. The sorrowful path along which thousands of southeastern Indians were removed to Oklahoma

_____ 13. The nation from which Texas won its independence in 1836

_____ 14. Anti-Jackson political party that generally stood for national community and an activist government

_____ 15. Popular symbols of the bogus but effective campaign the Whigs used to elect "poor-boy" William Henry Harrison in 1840

D. Matching People, Places, and Events

Match the person, place, or event in the left column with the proper description in the right column by inserting the correct letter on the blank line.

___ 1. John C. Calhoun

___ 2. Henry Clay

___ 3. Nicholas Biddle

___ 4. Sequoyah

___ 5. John Quincy Adams

___ 6. Denmark Vesey

___ 7. Stephen Austin

___ 8. Sam Houston

___ 9. Osceola

___ 10. Santa Anna

___ 11. Martin Van Buren

___ 12. Black Hawk

___ 13. William Henry Harrison

___ 14. Whigs

___ 15. Democrats

A. Cherokee leader who devised an alphabet for his people

B. Political party that generally stressed individual liberty, the rights of the common people, and hostility to privilege

C. Seminole leader whose warriors killed fifteen hundred American soldiers in years of guerrilla warfare

D. Former Tennessee governor whose victory at San Jacinto in 1836 won Texas its independence

E. Mexican general and dictator whose large army failed to defeat the Texans

F. Former vice president, leader of South Carolina nullifiers, and bitter enemy of Andrew Jackson

G. Political party that favored a more activist government, high tariffs, internal improvements, and moral reforms

H. Original leader of American settlers in Texas who obtained a huge land grant from the Mexican government

I. Free South Carolina black whose 1822 rebellion raised southern fears about the future of slavery

J. "Old Tippecanoe," who was portrayed by Whig propagandists as a hard-drinking common man of the frontier

K. Jackson's rival for the presidency in 1832, who failed to save the Bank of the United States

L. The "wizard of Albany," whose economically troubled presidency was served in the shadow of Jackson

M. Talented but high-handed bank president who fought a bitter losing battle with the president of the United States

N. Aloof New England statesman whose elitism made him an unpopular leader in the new era of mass democracy

O. Illinois-Wisconsin area Sauk leader who was defeated by American regulars and militia in 1832.

E. Putting Things in Order

Put the following events in correct order by numbering them from 1 to 5.

___ South Carolina threatens "nullification" of federal law and backs down in the face of Andrew Jackson's military threat.

___ A strange four-way election puts an icy New Englander in office amid charges of a "corrupt bargain."

___ A campaign based on hoopla and "log cabins and hard cider slogans" demonstrates that both Whigs and Democrats can effectively play the new mass-party political game.

___ A northern Mexican province successfully revolts and seeks admission to the United States.

___ Despite attempting to follow white patterns of "civilizing," thousands of American Indians are forcibly removed from their homes and driven across the Mississippi River.

F. Matching Cause and Effect

Match the historical cause in the left column with the proper effect in the right column by writing the correct letter on the blank line.

Cause	Effect
___ 1. The growth of American migration into northern Mexico	**A.** Brought many evangelical Christians into politics and showed that others besides Jackson could stir up popular feelings
___ 2. The demand of many whites to acquire Indian land in Georgia and other states	**B.** Provoked protests and threats of nullification from South Carolina
___ 3. The Anti-Masonic Party	**C.** Aroused popular anger and made Jackson's supporters determined to elect him in 1828
___ 4. The failure of any candidate to win an electoral majority in the four-way election of 1824	**D.** Laid the foundations for the spoils system that fueled the new mass political parties
___ 5. The alleged "corrupt bargain" between Adams and Clay for the presidency in 1824	**E.** Threw the bitterly contested election into the U.S. House of Representatives
___ 6. President Adams's strong nationalistic policies	**F.** Laid the basis for a political conflict that resulted in Texas independence
___ 7. The high New England–backed Tariff of 1828	**G.** Caused widespread human suffering and virtually guaranteed Martin Van Buren's defeat in 1840
___ 8. Andrew Jackson's "war" against Nicholas Biddle and his policies	**H.** Fueled the political pressures that led Andrew Jackson to forcibly remove the Cherokees and others
___ 9. Jackson's belief that any ordinary American could hold government office	**I.** Aroused the bitter opposition of westerners and southerners, who were increasingly sectionalist
___ 10. The Panic of 1837	**J.** Got the government out of banking but weakened the American financial system.

G. Developing Historical Skills

Interpreting Political Cartoons and Satire

Political cartoons are an important historical source. Even when they are strongly biased one way or another, they can yield information about political conflicts and contemporary attitudes.

The anti-Jackson cartoon on p. 269 reveals a number of things about how his opponents viewed Jackson. Answer the following questions.

1. What is the fundamental point of the cartoon's attack on the Bank of the United States and its supporters?

2. What visual means does the cartoonist use to develop point?

3. In the pro-Jackson cartoon on p. 270, how is Clay's frustration at Jackson's bank veto portrayed? How is Jackson's successful resistance represented?

4. In the satirical bank note mocking pro-Jackson "pet banks," list at least three distinct *visual* symbols that identify the worthless note with Jackson and his policies.

5. List at least three *verbal* terms or phrases that underscore the supposed fraudulency of Jacksonian banking practices.

H. Map Mastery

Map Discrimination

Using the maps and charts in Chapter 13, answer the following questions.

1. *Election of 1824:* In the election of 1824, how many more electoral votes would Jackson have needed to win a majority and prevent the election from going to the House of Representatives?

2. *Presidential Election of 1828*: In the election of 1828, in which states outside New England did John Quincy Adams win electoral votes?

3. *Presidential Election of 1828*: In the election of 1828, which of the eastern "middle states" did Jackson carry *completely*?

4. *Presidential Election of 1828*: Which two states divided their electoral votes?

5. *The Removal of the Southern Tribes to the West*: Of the five southeastern Indian tribes, which *two* were located wholly within the boundaries of a single state? Which tribe was located in four states?

6. *The Texas Revolution, 1835–1836*: A) When Santa Anna's army entered Texas to attack the Alamo, what two major rivers did it cross? B) When Santa Anna's army moved from the site of its greatest victory to the site of its greatest defeat, what direction did it march?

PART III: Applying What You Have Learned

1. Why was Andrew Jackson such a *personally* powerful embodiment of the new mass democracy in the 1820s and 1830s? Would mass democracy have developed without a popular hero like Jackson?

2. Why did Calhoun and the South see the Tariff of 1828 as such an "abomination" and raise threats of nullification over it?

3. Discuss the attitudes, policies, and events that led to the "Trail of Tears" Indian removal in 1837.

4. What did the two new democratic parties, the Democrats and the Whigs, really stand for? Were they actual ideological opponents, or were their disagreements less important than their shared roots in the new mass democracy?

5. Compare the two-party political system of the 1830s' "New Democracy" with the first two-party system of the early Republic. (See Chapter 10.) In what ways were the two systems similar, and in what ways were they different? Were both parties of the 1830s correct in seeing themselves as heirs of the Jeffersonian Republican tradition rather than the Hamiltonian Federalist tradition?

14

Forging the National Economy, 1790–1860

PART I: Reviewing the Chapter

A. Checklist of Learning Objectives

After mastering this chapter, you should be able to

1. describe the movement and growth of America's population in the early nineteenth century.
2. describe the effects of Irish and German immigration on American society.
3. explain why America was relatively slow to embrace the industrial revolution and the factory.
4. describe the early development of the factory system and Eli Whitney's system of interchangeable parts.
5. indicate the nature of early industrial labor and explain its effects on workers, including women and children.
6. describe the impact of new technology and transportation systems on American business and agriculture.
7. describe the sequence of major transportation and communication systems that developed from 1790 to 1860 and indicate their economic consequences.
8. describe the effects of the market revolution on the American economy, including the new disparities between rich and poor.

B. Glossary

To build your social science vocabulary, familiarize yourself with the following terms.

1. **caste** An exclusive or rigid social distinction based on birth, wealth, occupation, and so forth. "There was freedom from aristocratic caste and state church. . . ." (p. 292)
2. **nativist** One who advocates favoring native-born citizens over aliens or immigrants. "The invasion of this so-called immigrant 'rabble'. . . inflamed the prejudices of American 'nativists.' " (p. 296)
3. **factory** An establishment for the manufacturing of goods, including buildings and substantial machinery. "The factory system gradually spread from England—'the world's workshop'—to other lands." (p. 300)
4. **trademark** A distinguishing symbol or word used by a manufacturer on its goods, usually registered by law to protect against imitators. ". . . unscrupulous Yankee manufacturers . . . learned to stamp their own products with faked English trademarks." (p. 300)
5. **patent** The legal certification of an original invention, product, or process, guaranteeing its holder sole rights to profits from its use or reproduction for a specified period of time. "For the decade ending in 1800, only 306 patents were registered in Washington. . . ." (p. 304)
6. **liability** Legal responsibility for loss or damage. "The principle of limited liability aided the concentration of capital. . . ." (p. 304)

7. **incorporation** The formation of individuals into an organized entity with legally defined privileges and responsibilities. "Laws of 'free incorporation' were first passed in New York in 1848. . . ." (p. 304)

8. **labor union** An organization of workers—usually wage-earning workers—to promote the interests and welfare of its members, often by collective bargaining with employers. "They were forbidden by law to form labor unions. . . ." (p. 304)

9. **strike** An organized work stoppage by employees in order to obtain better wages, working conditions, and so on. "Not surprisingly, only twenty-four recorded strikes occurred before 1835." (p. 304)

10. **capitalist** An individual or group who uses accumulated funds or private property to produce goods for profit in a market. "It made ambitious capitalists out of humble plowmen. . . ." (p. 309)

11. **turnpike** A toll road. "The turnpikes beckoned to the canvas-covered Conestoga wagons. . . ."(p. 310)

12. **posterity** Later descendants or subsequent generations. "He installed a powerful steam engine in a vessel that posterity came to know as the *Clermont*. . . ." (p. 310)

13. **productivity** In economics, the relative capacity to produce goods and services, measured in terms of the number of workers and machines needed to create goods in a certain length of time. "The principle of division of labor . . . spelled productivity and profits. . . ." (p. 317)

14. **barter** The direct exchange of goods and services for one another, without the use of cash or any medium of exchange. "Most families . . . bartered with their neighbors for the few necessities they could not make themselves." (p. 317)

PART II: Checking Your Progress

A. True-False

Where the statement is true, mark **T**. Where it is false, mark **F**, and correct it in the space immediately below.

_____ 1. American frontier life was often plagued by poverty and illness.

_____ 2. The influx of Irish immigrants contributed to America's tolerance of ethnic and religious pluralism.

_____ 3. Most early American manufacturing was concentrated in the South.

_____ 4. The principle of "general incorporation" permitted individual businesspeople to apply for limited-liability corporate charters from the state legislatures.

_____ 5. The early industrial revolution greatly benefited workers by opening up well-paying factory jobs.

_____ 6. Early labor unions made very slow progress, partly because the strike weapon was illegal and ineffective.

_____ 7. The steel plow and mechanical reaper helped turn American farmers from subsistence farming to commercial, market-oriented agriculture.

_____ 8. By 1840, overland highways had proved a more effective form of transportation than canals.

___ 9. The Erie Canal's greatest economic effect was to create strong east-west commercial and industrial links between the Northeast and the West (Midwest).

___ 10. The railroad gained quick acceptance as a more efficient and flexible alternative to waterbound transportation.

___ 11. In the sectional division of labor that developed before the Civil War, the South generally provided raw materials to the Northeast in exchange for manufactured goods, transportation, and commercial services.

___ 12. The growth of a market economy drew most American women off the farms and out of the home into the new factories and mills.

___ 13. By 1850, permanent telegraph lines had been stretched across both the Atlantic Ocean and the North American continent.

___ 14. The advances in manufacturing and transportation decreased the gap between rich and poor in America.

___ 15. The continental American economy provided more opportunity to ordinary workers than existed in the contemporary societies of Europe.

B. Multiple Choice

Select the best answer and write the proper letter in the space provided.

___ 1. The experience of frontier life was especially difficult for

    a. women.
    b. young people.
    c. foreign immigrants.
    d. Roman Catholics.

___ 2. As late as 1850, over one-half of the American population was

    a. foreign-born.
    b. living west of the Mississippi River.
    c. under the age of thirty.
    d. living in cities of over 100,000 people.

___ 3. The primary economic activity in the Rocky Mountain West before the Civil War was

    a. agriculture.
    b. fur-trapping.
    c. mining.
    d. small business trading.

___ 4. Americans came to look on their spectacular western wilderness areas especially as

    a. one of the things that defined and distinguished America as a new nation.
    b. a source of economic exploitation.
    c. a potential attraction for tourists from abroad.
    d. the sacred home of American Indian tribes.

5. The American painter who developed the idea for a national park system was

   a. Samuel F. B. Morse.
   b. Caleb Bingham.
   c. John James Audubon.
   d. George Catlin.

6. The two major sources of European immigration to America in the 1840s and 1850s were

   a. France and Italy.
   b. Germany and France.
   c. Germany and Ireland.
   d. Ireland and Norway.

7. One consequence of the influx of new immigrants was

   a. a decline in the birthrate of native-born Americans.
   b. an upsurge of anti-Catholicism.
   c. a virtual end to westward migration.
   d. a national decline in wage rates.

8. Industrialization was at first slow to arrive in America because

   a. there was a shortage of labor, capital, and consumers.
   b. low tariff rates invited foreign imports.
   c. the country lacked the educational system necessary to develop technology.
   d. the country lacked a patent system to guarantee investors the profits from new machines.

9. The first industry to be shaped by the new factory system of manufacturing was

   a. textiles.
   b. the telegraph.
   c. agriculture.
   d. iron-making.

10. Wages for most American workers rose in the early nineteenth century, except for the most exploited workers like

    a. immigrants and westerners.
    b. textile and transportation workers.
    c. single men and women.
    d. women and children.

11. A major change affecting the American family in the early nineteenth century was

    a. the rise of an organized feminist movement.
    b. the movement of most women into the work force.
    c. increased conflict between parents and children over moral questions.
    d. a decline in the average number of children per household.

12. The first major improvement in the American transportation system came from

    a. canals and railroads.
    b. railroads and clipper ships.
    c. steamboats and highways.
    d. keelboats and Conestoga wagons.

___ 13. The new regional "division of labor" created by improved transportation meant that

    a. the South specialized in cotton, the West in grain and livestock, and the East in manufacturing.

    b. the South specialized in manufacturing, the West in transportation, and the East in grain and livestock.

    c. the South specialized in cotton, the West in manufacturing, and the East in finance.

    d. the South specialized in grain and livestock, the West in cotton, and the East in transportation.

___ 14. The most effective long-term solution to trans-oceanic shipping and travel proved to be

    a. the submarine.

    b. the transatlantic cable.

    c. the clipper ship.

    d. the steamship.

___ 15. One major effect of industrialization was

    a. an increasing economic equality among all citizens.

    b. a strengthening of the family as an economic unit.

    c. an increasingly stable labor force.

    d. a rise in the gap between rich and poor.

C. Identification

Supply the correct identification for each numbered description.

_____ 1. Nation where a potato famine in the 1840s led to a great migration of its people to America

_____ 2. Semisecret Irish organization that became a benevolent society aiding Irish immigrants in America

_____ 3. Liberal German refugees who fled failed democratic revolutions and came to America

_____ 4. Americans who protested and sometimes rioted against Roman Catholic immigrants

_____ 5. The transformation of manufacturing that began in Britain about 1750

_____ 6. Whitney's invention that enhanced cotton production and gave new life to black slavery

_____ 7. Principle that permitted individual investors to risk no more capital in a business venture than their own share of a corporation's stock

_____ 8. Morse's invention that provided instant communication across distance

_____ 9. Common source of early factory labor, often underpaid, whipped, and brutally beaten

_____ 10. Working people's organizations, often considered illegal under early American law

_____ 11. McCormick's invention that vastly increased the productivity of the American grain farmer

_____ 12. The only major highway constructed by the federal government before the Civil War

_____ 13. Fulton's invention that made river transportation a two-way affair

14. "Clinton's Big Ditch" that transformed transportation and economic life across the Great Lakes region from Buffalo to Chicago

15. Beautiful but short-lived American ships, replaced by "tramp steamers"

D. Matching People, Places, and Events

Match the person, place, or event in the left column with the proper description in the right column by inserting the correct letter on the blank line.

____ 1. Samuel Slater

____ 2. Eli Whitney

____ 3. Elias Howe

____ 4. Samuel F.B. Morse

____ 5. Know-Nothings

____ 6. *Commonwealth* v. *Hunt*

____ 7. Cyrus McCormick

____ 8. Robert Fulton

____ 9. Cyrus Field

____ 10. Molly Maguires

____ 11. DeWitt Clinton

A. Inventor of the mechanical reaper that transformed grain growing into a business
B. New York governor who built the Erie Canal
C. Inventor of a machine that revolutionized the ready-made clothing industry
D. Agitators against immigrants and Roman Catholics
E. Wealthy New York manufacturer who laid the first temporary transatlantic cable in 1858
F. Immigrant mechanic who initiated American industrialization by setting up his cotton-spinning factory in 1791
G. Painter turned inventor who developed the first reliable system for instant communication across distance
H. Developer of a "folly" that made rivers two-way streams of transportation
I. Radical, secret Irish labor union of the 1860s and 1870s
J. Yankee mechanical genius who revolutionized cotton production and created the system of interchangeable parts
K. Pioneering Massachusetts Supreme Court decision that declared labor unions legal

E. Putting Things in Order

Put the following events in correct order by numbering them from 1 to 5.

____ First telegraph message—"What hath God wrought?"—is sent from Baltimore to Washington.

____ Industrial revolution begins in Britain.

____ Telegraph lines are stretched across Atlantic Ocean and North American continent.

____ Major water transportation route connects New York City to Lake Erie and points west.

____ Invention of cotton gin and system of interchangeable parts revolutionized southern agriculture and northern industry.

F. Matching Cause and Effect

Match the historical cause in the left column with the proper effect in the right column by writing the correct letter on the blank line.

Cause	Effect
___ 1. The open, rough-and-tumble society of the American West	**A.** Made the fast-growing United States the fourth most populous nation in the Western world
___ 2. Natural population growth and increasing immigration from Ireland and Germany	**B.** Opened the Great Lakes states to rapid economic growth and spurred the development of major cities
___ 3. The poverty and Roman Catholic faith of most Irish immigrants	**C.** Encouraged western farmers to specialize in cash-crop agricultural production for eastern and European markets
___ 4. Eli Whitney's invention of the cotton gin	**D.** Made Americans strongly individualistic and self-reliant
___ 5. The passage of general incorporation and limited-liability laws	**E.** Aroused nativist hostility and occasional riots **F.** Bound the two northern sections together across the mountains and tended to isolate the South
___ 6. The early efforts of labor unions to organize and strike	**G.** Aroused fierce opposition from businesspeople and guardians of law
___ 7. Improved western transportation and the new McCormick reaper	**H.** Enabled businesspeople to create more powerful and effective joint-stock capital ventures
___ 8. The completion of the Erie Canal in 1825	**I.** Transformed southern agriculture and gave new life to slavery
___ 9. The development of a strong east-west rail network	**J.** Weakened many women's economic status and pushed them into a separate "sphere" of home and family
___ 10. The replacement of household production by factory-made, store-bought goods	

G. Developing Historical Skills

Reading a Chart and Bar Graph

Examine the bar graph on p.290 to learn more about the character of the American population from 1790 to 1860.

Answer the following questions.

1. Which decade showed the largest absolute increase in total population?

2. During which decade did the nonwhite population begin to *decrease* as a percentage of the total population?

3. In which census year did the nonwhite population surpass the white population of 1790?

4. Using the bar graph, indicate about how many times larger the total population was in 1860 than it had been in 1820.

H. Map Mastery

Map Discrimination

Using the maps and charts in Chapter 14, answer the following questions.

1. *Cumberland (National) Road and Main Connections*: How many states did the Cumberland Road pass through? (Do not count Missouri.)

2. *Industry and Agriculture, 1860:* Which industry developed near Philadelphia?

3. *Industry and Agriculture, 1860*: If you were a tobacco farmer, in which state would you most likely live?

4. *Principal Canals in 1840*: If you had traveled from Albany, New York, to Evansville, Indiana, which *two* canals and *one* lake would you have traversed?

5. *Principal Canals in 1840*: If you had traveled from Columbia, Pennsylvania, to Cleveland, Ohio, which *two* canals and *one* river would you have traversed?

6. *The Railroad Revolution*: In 1860, how many direct rail lines linked the North and the South west of the Appalachians?

7. *The Railroad Revolution*: Which three Midwestern states had the greatest number of rail lines in 1860?

8. *Main Routes West Before the Civil War*: If you had traveled from Independence, Missouri, to Los Angeles, California, before the Civil War, which major trails would you have traversed?

Map Challenge

Using the maps on pp. 311, 312, and 313, write a brief essay explaining the *economic* importance of the Erie Canal and other canals and railroads for trade between the Northeast and the Northwest.

PART III: Applying What You Have Learned

1. How did changes in the size and character of the population affect American social and economic life from 1790 to 1860?
2. How did the existence of a vast western frontier shape Americans' values and society in the period 1790–1860?
3. What were the effects of the new factory and corporate systems of production on early industrial workers, and how did they respond to these conditions?
4. How did the new transportation systems create a commercially linked national economy and a specialized sectional division of labor?
5. What was the impact of the new economic developments on the role of women in society?
6. In America, early industrialization, westward expansion, and growing sectional tension all occurred at the same time. How was the development of the economy before the Civil War related to both the westward movement and increasing sectional conflict?

15

The Ferment of Reform and
Culture, 1790–1860

PART I: Reviewing the Chapter

A. Checklist of Learning Objectives

After mastering this chapter, you should be able to

1. describe the changes in American religion and their effects on culture and social reform.
2. describe the cause of the most important American reform movements of the period.
3. explain the origins of American feminism and describe its various manifestations.
4. describe the utopian and communitarian experiments of the period.
5. identify the early American achievements in the arts and sciences.
6. analyze the American literary flowering of the early nineteenth century, especially in relation to transcendentalism and other ideas of the time.

B. Glossary

To build your social science vocabulary, familiarize yourself with the following terms.

1. **polygamy** The practice of having two or more spouses at one time. (**Polygyny** refers specifically to two or more wives; **polyandry** to two or more husbands.) "Accusations of polygamy likewise arose and increased in intensity." (p. 323)
2. **theocracy** Literally, rule by God; the term is often applied to a state where religious leaders exercise direct or indirect political authority. ". . . the community became a prosperous frontier theocracy and a cooperative commonwealth." (p. 324)
3. **zealot** One who is carried away by a cause to an extreme or excessive degree. "But less patient zealots came to believe that temptation should be removed by legislation." (p. 330)
4. **utopian** Referring to any place or plan that aims at an ideal social order. "Bolstered by the utopian spirit of the age, various reformers . . . set up more than forty [cooperative] communities. . . ." (p. 333)
5. **communistic** Referring to the theory or practice in which the means of production are owned by the community as a whole. ". . . various reformers . . . set up more than forty communities of a . . . communistic nature." (p. 333)
6. **communitarian** Referring to the belief in or practice of the superiority of community life or values over individual life, but not necessarily the common ownership of material goods. ". . . various reformers . . . set up more than forty communities of a . . . 'communtarian' nature." (p. 333)
7. **free love** The principle or practice of sexual relations unrestricted by law, marriage, or religious constraints. "It practiced free love ('complex marriage'). . . ." (p. 333)
8. **eugenic** Concerning the improvement of the human species through selective breeding or genetic control. "It practiced . . . the eugenic selection of parents to produce superior offspring." (p. 333)

9. **coitus reservatus** The practice of sexual intercourse without the male's release of semen. "It practiced . . . birth control through 'male continence' or *coitus reservatus*." (p. 333)

10. **classical** Concerning the culture of ancient Greece and Rome, or any artistic or cultural values presumed to be based on those enduring ancient principles. "He brought a classical design to his Virginia hilltop home, Monticello. . . ." (p. 338)

11. **mystical** Referring to the belief in the direct apprehension of God or divine mystery, without reliance on reason or human comprehension. "These mystical doctrines of transcendentalism defied precise definition. . . ." (p. 341)

12. **nonconformist** One who refuses to follow established or conventional ideas or habits. "Henry David Thoreau . . . was . . . a poet, a mystic, a transcendentalist, and a nonconformist." (p. 341)

13. **nonviolence** The principle of resolving or engaging in conflict without resort to physical force. "His writings . . . inspired the development of American civil rights leader Martin Luther King, Jr.'s thinking about nonviolence." (p. 341)

14. **urbane** Sophisticated, elegant, cosmopolitan. "Handsome and urbane, he lived a generally serene life. . . ." (p. 342)

15. **providential** Under the care and direction of God or other benevolent natural or supernatural forces. ". . . he lived among cannibals, from whom he providentially escaped uneaten." (p. 344)

PART II: Checking Your Progress

A. True-False

Where the statement is true, mark **T**. Where it is false, mark **F**, and correct it in the space immediately below.

____ 1. The Second Great Awakening reversed the trends toward religious indifference and rationalism of the late eighteenth century.

____ 2. The religious revivals of the Second Great Awakening broke down regional, denominational, and social-class divisions in favor of a common Christianity.

____ 3. The Mormon church migrated to Utah to escape persecution and to establish a tightly organized cooperative social order without persecution.

____ 4. The common public schools aimed at the goal of educating all citizens for participation in democracy, without regard to wealth.

____ 5. Women achieved equality with men in higher education before the Civil War.

____ 6. Many early American reformers were middle-class idealists inspired by evangelical Protestantism.

____ 7. The key role of women in American reform movements was undergirded by a growing "feminization" of the churches that spawned many efforts at social improvement.

____ 8. A major demand put forward by the more advanced women's-rights advocates was women's suffrage.

____ 9. Most early American communal experiments involved attempts to create a perfect society based on brotherly love and communal ownership of property.

____ 10. Early American science was stronger in biology, botany, and geology than it was in basic theoretical science or medicine.

____ 11. The first American national literature written by Irving and Cooper appeared in the immediate aftermath of the American Revolution.

____ 12. Although it rejected most Americans' materialism and focus on practical concerns, transcendentalism strongly reflected American individualism, love of liberty, and hostility to formal institutions and authority.

____ 13. Ralph Waldo Emerson taught the doctrines of simple living and nonviolence, while his friend Henry David Thoreau emphasized self-improvement and the development of American scholarship.

____ 14. The works of Walt Whitman, such as *Leaves of Grass*, revealed his love of democracy, the frontier, and the common people.

____ 15. Most early American imaginative writers and historians came from the Midwest and the South.

B. Multiple Choice

Select the best answer and write the proper letter in the space provided.

____ 1. The tendency toward rationalism and indifference in religion was reversed about 1800 by
   a. the rise of Deism and Unitarianism.
   b. the rise of new groups like the Mormons and Christian Scientists.
   c. the revivalist movement called the Second Great Awakening.
   d. the influx of religiously traditional immigrants.

____ 2. Two denominations that especially gained adherents among the common people of the West and South were
   a. Episcopalians and Unitarians.
   b. Congregationalists and Mormons.
   c. Transcendentalists and Adventists.
   d. Methodists and Baptists.

____ 3. The Second Great Awakening derived its religious strength especially from
   a. intensely organized "prayer groups" of lay believers.
   b. the efficient institutional organization of the major American churches.
   c. the popular preaching of evangelical revivalists in both the West and eastern cities.
   d. the frontier interest in religious pilgrimages and religious art.

____ 4. Evangelical preachers like Charles Grandison Finney linked personal religious conversion to
   a. the construction of large church buildings throughout the Midwest.
   b. the expansion of American political power across the continent.
   c. the Christian reform of social problems.
   d. the organization of effective economic development and industrialization.

5. The term "Burned-Over District" refers to

a. parts of the West where fires were used to clear the land for farming.
b. areas that were fiercely contested by both Baptist and Methodist revivalists.
c. the region of western New York State that experienced especially frequent and intense revivals.
d. the area of Illinois where the Mormon settlements were attacked and destroyed.

6. The major effect of the growing slavery controversy on the churches was

a. a major missionary effort directed at converted African-American slaves.
b. the organization of the churches to lobby for the abolition of slavery.
c. an agreement to keep political issues out of the religious area.
d. the split of Baptists, Methodists, and Presbyterians into separate northern and southern churches.

7. Besides their practice of polygamy, the Mormons aroused hostility from many Americans because of

a. their cooperative economic practices that ran contrary to American economic individualism.
b. their efforts to convert members of other denominations to Mormonism.
c. their populous settlement in Utah , which posed the threat of a breakaway republic in the West.
d. their practice of baptizing in the name of dead ancestors.

8. The major promoter of an effective tax-supported system of public education for all American children was

a. Joseph Smith.
b. Horace Mann.
c. Noah Webster.
d. Susan B. Anthony.

9. Reformer Dorothea Dix worked for the cause of

a. women's right to higher education and voting.
b. international peace.
c. better treatment of the mentally ill.
d. temperance.

10. One cause of women's subordination in nineteenth-century America was

a. the sharp division of labor that separated women at home from men in the workplace.
b. women's attention to causes other than women's rights.
c. the higher ratio of females to males in many communities.
d. the prohibition against women's participation in religious activities.

11. The Seneca Falls Convention launched the modern women's rights movement with its call for

a. equal pay for equal work.
b. an equal rights amendment to the Constitution.
c. equal rights, including the right to vote.
d. access to public education for women.

___ 12. Many of the American utopian experiments of the early nineteenth century focused on

    a. communal economics and alternative sexual arrangements.
    b. temperance and diet reforms.
    c. advanced scientific and technological ways of producing and consuming.
    d. free-enterprise economics and trade.

___ 13. Two leading female imaginative writers who added to New England's literary prominence were

    a. Sarah Orne Jewett and Kate Chopin.
    b. Louisa May Alcott and Emily Dickinson.
    c. Sarah Grimké and Susan B. Anthony.
    d. Harriet Beecher Stowe and Abigail Adams.

___ 14. The Knickerbocker Group of American writers included

    a. Henry David Thoreau, Thomas Jefferson, and Susan B. Anthony.
    b. George Bancroft, Ralph Waldo Emerson, and Herman Melville.
    c. Washington Irving, James Fenimore Cooper, and William Cullen Bryant.
    d. Walt Whitman, Henry Wadsworth Longfellow, and Edgar Allan Poe.

___ 15. The transcendentalist writers such as Emerson, Thoreau, and Fuller stressed the ideas of

    a. inner truth and individual self-reliance.
    b. political community and economic progress.
    c. personal guilt and fear of death.
    d. love of chivalry and return to the medieval past.

C. Identification

Supply the correct identification for each numbered description.

_____ 1. Liberal religious belief, held by many of the Founding Fathers, that stressed rationalism and moral behavior rather than Christian revelation

_____ 2. Religious revival that began on the frontier and swept eastward, stirring an evangelical spirit in many areas of American life

_____ 3. The *two* religious denominations that benefited from the evangelical revivals of the early nineteenth century

_____ 4. Religious group founded by Joseph Smith that eventually established a cooperative commonwealth in Utah

_____ 5. Memorable 1848 meeting in New York where women made an appeal based on the Declaration of Independence

_____ 6. Commune established in New Harmony, Indiana by Scottish industrialist Robert Owen

_____ 7. Intellectual commune in Massachusetts based on "plain living and high thinking"

_____ 8. Thomas Jefferson's stately self-designed home in Virginia that became a model of American architecture

_____ 9. New York literary movement that drew on both regional and national themes

_____ 10. Philosophical and literary movement, centered in New England, that greatly influenced many American writers of the early nineteenth century

_____ 11. The doctrine, promoted by American writer Henry David Thoreau in an essay of the same name, that later influenced Gandhi and Martin Luther King, Jr.

_____ 12. Walt Whitman's shocking collection of emotional poems

_____ 13. A disturbing New England masterpiece about adultery and guilt in the old Puritan era

_____ 14. The great but commercially unsuccessful novel about Captain Ahab's obsessive pursuit of a white whale

_____ 15. The masterpiece of New England writer Louisa May Alcott

D. Matching People, Places, and Events

Match the person, place, or event in the left column with the proper description in the right column by inserting the correct letter on the blank line.

___ 1. Dorothea Dix

___ 2. Brigham Young

___ 3. Elizabeth Cady Stanton

___ 4. Lucretia Mott

___ 5. Emily Dickinson

___ 6. Charles G. Finney

___ 7. Robert Owen

___ 8. John Humphrey Noyes

___ 9. Mary Lyon

___ 10. Louisa May Alcott

___ 11. James Fenimore Cooper

___ 12. Ralph Waldo Emerson

___ 13. Walt Whitman

___ 14. Edgar Allen Poe

___ 15. Herman Melville

A. Leader of a radical New York commune that practiced "complex marriage" and eugenic birth control

B. Bold, unconventional poet who celebrated American democracy

C. The "Mormon Moses" who led persecuted Latter-Day Saints to their promised land in Utah

D. Influential evangelical revivalist of the Second Great Awakening

E. New York writer whose romantic sea tales were more popular than his dark literary masterpiece

F. Pioneering women's educator, founder of Mount Holyoke Seminary in Massachusetts

G. Idealistic Scottish industrialist whose attempt at a communal utopia in America failed

H. Second-rate poet and philosopher, but first-rate promoter of transcendentalist ideals and American culture

I. Eccentric southern-born genius whose tales of mystery, suffering, and the supernatural departed from general American literary trends

J. Quietly determined reformer who substantially improved conditions for the mentally ill

K. Reclusive New England poet who wrote about love, death, and immortality

L. Leading feminist who wrote the "Declaration of Sentiments" in 1848 and pushed for women's suffrage

M. Novelist whose tales of family life helped economically support her own struggling transcendentalist family

N. Path-breaking American novelist who contrasted the natural person of the forest with the values of modern civilization

O. Quaker women's rights advocate who also strongly supported abolition of slavery

E. Putting Things in Order

Put the following events in correct order by numbering them from 1 to 5.

____ A leading New England transcendentalist appeals to American writers and thinkers to turn away from Europe and develop their own literature and culture.

____ A determined reformer appeals to a New England legislature to end the cruel treatment of the insane.

____ A gathering of female reformers in New York declares that the ideas of the Declaration of Independence apply to *both* sexes.

____ Great evangelical religious revival begins in western camp meetings.

____ A visionary New Yorker creates a controversial new religion.

F. Matching Cause and Effect

Match the historical cause in the left column with the proper effect in the right column by writing the correct letter on the blank line.

Cause		Effect	
____	1. The Second Great Awakening	**A.**	Created the first literature genuinely native to America
____	2. The Mormon practice of polygamy	**B.**	Captured in one long poem the exuberant and optimistic spirit of popular American democracy
____	3. Women abolitionists' anger at being ignored by male reformers	**C.**	Caused most utopian experiments to decline or collapse in a few years
____	4. The women's rights movement	**D.**	Inspired writers like Ralph Waldo Emerson, Henry David Thoreau, and Margaret Fuller
____	5. Unrealistic expectations and conflict within perfectionist communes	**E.**	Aroused hostility and scorn in most of the male press and pulpit
____	6. The Knickerbocker and transcendentalist use of new American themes in their writing	**F.**	Made their works little understood in their lifetimes by generally optimistic Americans
____	7. Henry David Thoreau's theory of "civil disobedience"	**G.**	Aroused persecution from morally traditionalist Americans and delayed statehood for Utah
____	8. Walt Whitman's *Leaves of Grass*	**H.**	Inspired a widespread spirit of evangelical reform in many areas of American life
____	9. Herman Melville's and Edgar Allan Poe's concern with evil and suffering	**I.**	Led to expanding the crusade for equal rights to include women
____	10. The Transcendentalist movement	**J.**	Inspired later practitioners of nonviolence like Gandhi and King

G. Developing Historical Skills

Using Primary-Source Documents

Statements from historical contemporaries often reveal fundamental conflicts over values and demonstrate the shock that occurs when new ideas emerge. The quotations form the London *Saturday Review* and from Walt Whitman (p. 342) illustrate such opposing views.

Answer the following questions.

1. What is the London *Saturday Review*'s primary objection to Whitman's poetry?

2. How does Whitman answer such criticisms?

3. How does Whitman's statement reveal the values of individualism and democracy cherished by the emerging American culture?

4. What does the quotation from *Leaves of Grass* in the text (p. 342) indicate about Whitman's typically American view of Europe?

PART III: Applying What You Have Learned

1. What major changes in American religion occurred in the early nineteenth century, and how did they affect American culture and reform?

2. What were the successes and failures of the many American reform movements of the early nineteenth century? Was the failure of some of them (e.g., peace reforms) due to entrenched social conservatism, or to weaknesses in the movements themselves?

3. How did the first American feminists propose altering the condition of women, and what success did they have?

4. Compare the early American achievements in the sciences with those in the arts. Which were the most successful, and why?

5. What were the major concerns of America's greatest imaginative writers in the early nineteenth century? Did those writers fundamentally reflect the deepest values of American culture, or were they at odds with the main currents of American society and politics?

6. In what ways were the movements of American religion, reform, and culture an outgrowth of the American Revolution and American independence, and in what ways did they reflect qualities of American life reaching back to the Puritans?

16

The South and the Slavery Controversy, 1793–1860

PART I: Reviewing the Chapter

A. Checklist of Learning Objectives

After mastering this chapter, you should be able to

1. point out the economic strengths and weaknesses of the "Cotton Kingdom."
2. describe the southern planter aristocracy and identify its strengths and weaknesses.
3. describe the nonslaveholding white majority of the South and explain its relations with both the planter elite and the black slaves.
4. describe the nature of African-American life, both free and slave, before the Civil War.
5. describe the effects of the "peculiar institution" of slavery on both blacks and whites.
6. explain why abolitionism was at first unpopular in the North and describe how it gradually gained strength.
7. describe the fierce southern response to abolitionism and the growing defense of slavery as a "positive good."

B. Glossary

To build your social science vocabulary, familiarize yourself with the following terms.

1. **oligarchy** Rule by a small elite. "Before the Civil War, the South was in some respects not so much a democracy as an oligarchy. . . ." (p. 351)
2. **medievalism** Devotion to the social values, customs, or beliefs thought to be characteristic of the European Middle Ages. "Southern aristocrats . . . strove to perpetuate a type of medievalism that had died out in Europe. . . ." (p. 352)
3. **commission** Fee paid to an agent in a transaction, usually as a percentage of the sale. "They were pained by the heavy outward flow of commissions. . . ." (p. 353)
4. **middlemen** In commerce, those who stand between the producer and the retailer or consumer. "[Southern planters] were pained by the heavy outward flow . . . to northern middlemen, bankers, agents, and shippers." (p. 353)
5. **racism** Belief in the superiority of one race over another or behavior reflecting such a belief. "Thus did the logic of economics join with the illogic of racism in buttressing the slave system." (p. 356)
6. **bankruptcy** Legally, the condition of being declared unable to meet legitimate financial obligations or debts, requiring special supervision by the courts. ". . . families were separated with distressing frequency, usually for economic reasons such as bankruptcy. . . ." (p. 359)
7. **overseer** Someone who governs or directs the work of another. ". . . under the watchful eyes and ready whip-hand of a white overseer or black 'driver.' " (p. 359)
8. **sabotage** Intentional destruction or damage of goods, machines, or productive processes. "They sabotaged expensive equipment. . . ." (p. 362)

9. **fratricidal** Literally, concerning the killing of brothers; the term is often applied to the killing of relatives or countrymen in feuds or civil wars. (The killing of sisters is **sororicide**; of fathers **patricide**; and of mothers **matricide**.) ". . . supported a frightfully costly fratricidal war as the price of emancipation." (p. 366)

10. **barbarism (barbarian)** The condition of being crude, uneducated, or uncivilized. "It was good for the Africans, who were lifted from the barbarism of the jungle. . . ." (p. 366)

PART II: Checking Your Progress

A. True-False

Where the statement is true, mark **T**. Where it is false, mark **F**, and correct it in the space immediately below.

_____ 1. After 1800, the prosperity of both North and South became heavily dependent on growing, manufacturing, and exporting cotton.

_____ 2. The southern planter aristocracy was strongly attracted to medieval cultural ideals.

_____ 3. The growing of cotton on large plantations was economically efficient and agriculturally sound.

_____ 4. Most southern slaveowners owned twenty or more slaves.

_____ 5. In 1860, three-fourths of all white southerners owned no slaves at all.

_____ 6. Poor whites supported slavery because it made them feel racially superior and because they hoped someday to be able to buy slaves.

_____ 7. The one group of southern whites who opposed slavery consisted of those who lived in mountain areas far from plantations and from blacks.

_____ 8. Free blacks enjoyed considerable status and wealth in both the North and the South before the Civil War.

_____ 9. Slaveowners generally treated their black slaves as a valuable economic investment.

_____ 10. Slavery almost completely destroyed the black family.

_____ 11. American slaves used many small methods of resistance to demonstrate their hatred of slavery and their yearning for freedom.

_____ 12. Abolitionists like William Lloyd Garrison quickly attained great popularity in the North.

_____ 13. While moralistic white abolitionists like Garrison refused to become involved in politics, practical black abolitionists like Douglass looked for a way to abolish slavery through political action.

_____ 14. After about 1830, the South no longer tolerated even moderate pro-abolitionist discussion.

_____ 15. Southern whites increasingly argued that their slaves were happier and better off than northern wage earners.

B. Multiple Choice

Select the best answer and write the proper letter in the space provided.

_____ 1. The primary market for southern cotton production was

    a. the North.
    b. France.
    c. Latin America.
    d. Britain.

_____ 2. The invention that transformed the southern cotton economy was

    a. the sewing machine.
    b. the mechanical cotton-picker.
    c. the cotton gin.
    d. the steamboat.

_____ 3. A large portion of the profits from cotton growing went to

    a. northern traders and European manufacturers.
    b. southern and northern slave traders.
    c. southern textile industrialists.
    d. midwestern farmers and cattlemen.

_____ 4. Among the economic consequences of the South's cotton economy was

    a. increasing immigration of laborers from Europe.
    b. a dependence on the North for trade and manufacturing.
    c. a stable system of credit and finance.
    d. a relatively equal distribution of property and wealth.

_____ 5. Most southern slaveowners held

    a. over a hundred slaves.
    b. over fifty slaves.
    c. fewer than ten slaves.
    d. only one slave.

_____ 6. Even though they owned no slaves, most southern whites supported the slave system because

    a. they were bribed by the planter class.
    b. they enjoyed the economic benefits of slavery.
    c. they felt racially superior to blacks and hoped to be able to buy slaves.
    d. they disliked the northern abolitionists.

7. The only group of white southerners who strongly opposed slavery and the slaveowners were

    a. poor southern whites.
    b. urban merchants and manufacturers.
    c. religious leaders.
    d. Appalachian mountain whites.

8. The condition of the 500,000 or so free blacks was

    a. considerably better in the North than in the South.
    b. notably improving in the decades before the Civil War.
    c. as bad or worse in the North than in the South.
    d. politically threatened but economically secure.

9. Most of the growth in the African-American slave population before 1860 came from

    a. the illegal importation of slaves from Africa.
    b. the re-enslavement of formerly free blacks.
    c. natural reproduction.
    d. the incorporation into the United States of new slave territories.

10. Most slaveowners treated their slaves as

    a. objects to be beaten and brutalized as often as possible.
    b. economically profitable investments.
    c. members of their extended family.
    d. potential converts to evangelical Christianity..

11. The African-American family under slavery was

    a. generally stable and mutually supportive.
    b. almost nonexistent.
    c. largely female-dominated.
    d. seldom able to raise children to adulthood.

12. Most of the early abolitionists were motivated by

    a. a desire to create an independent black republic in Africa.
    b. anger at the negative economic consequences of slavery.
    c. religious feeling against the "sin" of slavery.
    d. a philosophical commitment to racial integration.

13. The most prominent black abolitionist leader was

    a. Sojourner Truth.
    b. David Walker.
    c. William Lloyd Garrison.
    d. Frederick Douglass.

14. After 1830, most southerners came to look on slavery as

    a. a curse on their region.
    b. a necessary evil.
    c. a positive good.
    d. a threat to their social ideals.

___ 15. By the 1850s, most northerners could be described as

    a. opposed to slavery but also hostile to immediate abolitionists.
    b. fervently in favor of immediate abolition.
    c. sympathetic to white southern arguments in defense of slavery.
    d. eager to let the slaveholding South break apart the Union.

C. Identification

Supply the correct identification for each numbered description.

_____ 1. Term for the South that emphasized its economic dependence on a single staple product

_____ 2. Prosouthern New England textile owners who were economically tied to the southern "lords of the lash"

_____ 3. British novelist whose romantic vision of a feudal society made him highly popular in the South

_____ 4. The poor, vulnerable group that was the object of prejudice in the North and despised as a "third race" in the South

_____ 5. Theodore Dwight Weld's powerful antislavery book

_____ 6. The area of the South where most slaves were held, stretching from South Carolina across to Louisiana

_____ 7. Organization founded in 1817 to send blacks back to Africa

_____ 8. The group of theology students, led by Theodore Dwight Weld, who were expelled for abolitionist activity and later became leading preachers of the antislavery gospel

_____ 9. William Lloyd Garrison's fervent abolitionist newspaper that preached an immediate end to slavery

_____ 10. Garrisonian abolitionist organization, founded in 1833, that included the eloquent Wendell Phillips among its leaders

_____ 11. Strict rule passed by prosouthern Congressmen in 1836 to prohibit all discussion of slavery in the House of Representatives

_____ 12. Northern antislavery politicians, like Abraham Lincoln, who rejected radical abolitionism but sought to prohibit the expansion of slavery in the western territories

D. Matching People, Places, and Events

Match the person, place, or event in the left column with the proper description in the right column by inserting the correct letter on the blank line.

___ 1. Sir Walter Scott   **A.** Wealthy New York abolitionist merchant whose home was demolished by a mob in 1834

___ 2. Harriet Beecher Stowe   **B.** Visionary black preacher whose bloody slave rebellion in 1831 tightened the reins of slavery in the South

___ 3. Nat Turner   **C.** Midwestern institution whose president expelled eighteen students for organizing a debate on slavery

___ 4. Liberia   **D.** New York free black woman who fought for emancipation and women's rights

___ 5. Theodore Dwight Weld   **E.** Leading radical abolitionist who burned the Constitution as "a covenant with death and an agreement with hell"

_____ 6. Lewis Tappan

_____ 7. Lane Theological Seminary

_____ 8. William Lloyd Garrison

_____ 9. David Walker

_____ 10. Sojourner Truth

_____ 11. Martin Delany

_____ 12. Frederick Douglass

_____ 13. Virginia legislature

_____ 14. John Quincy Adams

_____ 15. Elijah Lovejoy

F. Author of an abolitionist novel that portrayed the separation of slave families by auction

G. Site of the last major southern debate over slavery and emancipation, in 1831–1832

H. English novelist whose romantic medievalism encouraged the semifeudal ideals of the southern planter aristocracy

I. Black abolitionist who visited West Africa in 1859 to examine sites where African-Americans might relocate

J. Former president who fought for the right to discuss slavery in Congress

K. Illinois editor whose death at the hands of a mob made him an abolitionist martyr

L. West African republic founded in 1822 by freed blacks from the United States

M. Escaped slave and great black abolitionist who fought to end slavery through political action

N. Black abolitionist writer who called for a bloody end to slavery in an appeal of 1829

O. Leader of the "Lane Rebels" who wrote the powerful antislavery work _American Slavery As It Is_

E. Putting Things in Order

Put the following events in correct order by numbering them from 1 to 5.

_____ The last slaves to be legally imported from Africa enter the United States.

_____ A radical abolitionist editor is murdered, and so becomes a martyr to the antislavery cause.

_____ A radical abolitionist newspaper and a slave rebellion spread fear through the South.

_____ A new invention increases the efficiency of cotton production, laying the basis for the vast Cotton Kingdom.

_____ A group of seminary students expelled for their abolitionist views spread the antislavery gospel far and wide.

F. Matching Cause and Effect

Match the historical cause in the left column with the proper effect in the right column by writing the correct letter on the blank line.

	Cause		Effect
_____	1. Whitney's cotton gin and southern frontier expansionism	**A.**	Often resulted in the cruel separation of black families
_____	2. Excessive soil cultivation and financial speculation	**B.**	Kept poor, nonslaveholding whites committed to a system that actually harmed them
_____	3. Belief in white superiority and the hope of owning slaves	**C.**	Aroused deep fears of rebellion and ended rational discussion of slavery in the South
_____	4. The selling of slaves at auctions	**D.**	Made abolitionists personally unpopular but convinced many Northerners that slavery was a threat to American freedom

_____ 5. The slaves' love of freedom and hatred of their condition

_____ 6. The religious fervor of the Second Great Awakening

_____ 7. Politically minded abolitionists like Frederick Douglass

_____ 8. Garrison's *Liberator* and Nat Turner's bloody slave rebellion

_____ 9. White southern defenses of slavery as a "positive good"

_____ 10. The constant abolitionist agitation in the North

E. Caused slaves to work slowly, steal from their masters, and frequently run away

F. Stirred a fervent abolitionist commitment to fight the "sin" of slavery

G. Turned the South into a booming one-crop economy where "cotton was king"

H. Opposed Garrison and organized the Liberty party and the Free Soil party

I. Created dangerous weaknesses beneath the surface prosperity of the southern cotton economy

J. Widened the moral and political gap between the white South and the rest of the Western world

G. Developing Historical Skills

Visual Images and Slavery

The bitter controversy over slavery is reflected in the visual images (drawings, prints, photographs) of the "peculiar institution." Some images present slavery from an abolitionist viewpoint, as a moral horror. Others depict it in benign or even favorable terms. Examine eight of the illustrations in this chapter on pp. 351, 352, 357, 358, 359, 360, 363, and 367 answer the following questions.

1. Which four images depict negative features of the slave system? What visual details emphasize the mistreatment of the slaves?

2. Which three images present slavery in relatively positive terms? What visual details show slavery in a favorable light?

3. The photograph on p. 359 seems neither directly "proslavery" nor "antislavery." How might supporters or opponents of slavery each interpret this image of a slave nanny with a white child?

H. Map Mastery

Map Discrimination

Using the maps and charts in Chapter 16, answer the following questions.

1. *Southern Cotton Production, 1860*: Which six states contained nearly all the major cotton-production areas of the South in 1860?

2. *Slaveowning Families, 1850*: Approximately how many slaveowning families owned fifty or more slaves?

3. *Distribution of Slaves, 1820*: Which five states contained a substantial number of slave-majority counties in 1820?

4. *Distribution of Slaves, 1860*: List the six slaveholding states, not counting Texas and Florida, that contained the most counties with less than 10 percent slaves in 1860.

Map Challenge

Using the maps on pp. 354 and 355, write a brief essay explaining the relation between the areas of cotton production and the areas with the heaviest concentration of slaves in 1820 and 1860. Include some discussion of why Virginia and the Carolinas had substantial areas with more than 50 percent slaves but almost no major cotton-production areas.

PART III: Applying What You Have Learned

1. Describe the complex structure of southern society. What role did plantation owners, small slaveholders, independent white farmers, poor whites, free blacks, and black slaves each have in the southern social order?

2. Compare the attitudes and practices regarding slavery and race relations in the North and the South. Explain the common statement that southerners liked blacks as individuals but despised the race, while northerners claimed to like blacks as a race but disliked individuals. (p. 357)

3. How did the reliance on cotton production and slavery affect the South economically, socially, and morally, and how did this reliance affect its relations with the North?

4. How did slavery affect the lives of African-Americans in both the South and the North?

5. A large majority of Americans, both North and South, strongly rejected radical abolitionism. Why, then, did abolitionism and antislavery come to shape American politics in the 1840s and 1850s?

6. In what ways did slavery make the South a fundamentally different kind of society from the North? Could the South ever have abolished slavery gradually on its own, as the North did after the American Revolution? (See Chapter 9.) Why or why not?

17

Manifest Destiny and Its Legacy, 1841–1848

PART I: Reviewing the Chapter

A. Checklist of Learning Objectives

After mastering this chapter, you should be able to

1. explain the spirit of "Manifest Destiny" that inspired American expansionism in the 1840s.
2. indicate how American anti-British feeling led to various conflicts over debts, Maine, Canadian rebellion, Texas, and Oregon.
3. explain why the movement to annex Texas gained new momentum and why the issue aroused such controversy.
4. indicate how the issues of Oregon and Texas became central in the election of 1844 and why Polk's victory was seen as a mandate for "Manifest Destiny."
5. describe how the issues of California and the Texas boundary created conflict and war with Mexico.
6. describe how the dramatic American victory in the Mexican War led to the breathtaking territorial acquisition of the whole Southwest.
7. describe the consequences of the Mexican War, especially its effect on the slavery question.

B. Glossary

To build your social science vocabulary, familiarize yourself with the following terms.

1. **caucus** An unofficial organization or consultation of like-minded people to plan a political course or advance their cause, often within some larger body. " . . . the stiff-necked Virginian was formally expelled from his party by a caucus of Whig congressmen. . . ." (p. 372)
2. **royalty** The share of the proceeds from work paid to an inventor, author, composer, and so on. ". . . they were being denied rich royalties by the absence of an American copyright law." (p. 373)
3. **default** To fail to pay a loan or interest due. ". . . several states defaulted on their bonds. . . ." (p. 373)
4. **repudiate** To refuse to accept responsibility for paying a bill or debt. "When . . . several states . . . repudiated [their bonds] openly, honest English citizens assailed Yankee trickery." (p. 373)
5. **protectorate** The relation of a strong nation to a weak one under its control and protection. ". . . Texas was driven to open negotiations . . . in the hope of securing the defensive shield of a protectorate." (p. 374)
6. **colossus** Anything of extraordinary size and power. "Such a republic would check the southward surge of the American colossus. . . ." (p. 374)
7. **resolution** In government, a formal statement of policy or judgment by a legislature, but requiring no legal statute. "He therefore arranged for annexation by a joint resolution." (p. 375)

8. **intrigue** A plot or scheme formed by secret, underhanded means. ". . . the Lone Star Republic had become a danger spot, inviting foreign intrigue that menaced the American people." (p. 375)

9. **parallel** In geography, the imaginary lines parallel to the earth's equator, marking latitude. (There are 360 degrees of latitude on the globe.) " . . . the United States had sought to divide the vast domain at the forty-ninth parallel." (p. 376)

10. **deadlock** To completely block or stop action as a consequence of the mutual pressure of equal and opposed forces. "The Democrats, meeting later in the same city, seemed hopelessly deadlocked." (p. 377)

11. **dark horse** In politics, a candidate with little apparent support who unexpectedly wins a nomination or election. "Polk may have been a dark horse, but he was hardly an unknown or decrepit nag." (p. 377)

12. **mandate** In politics, the belief that an official has been issued a clear charge by the electorate to pursue some particular policy goal. "Land-hungry Democrats . . . proclaimed that they had received a mandate from the voters to take Texas." (p. 378)

13. **platform** The campaign document stating a party's or candidate's position on the issues, and upon which they "stand" for election. "Polk . . . had no intention of insisting on the . . . pledge of his own platform." (p. 379)

14. **no-man's-land** A territory to which neither of two disputing parties has clear claim and where they may meet as combatants. ". . . Polk was careful to keep American troops out of virtually all of the explosive no-man's-land between the Nueces and the Rio Grande. . . ." (p. 381)

15. **indemnity** A repayment for loss or damage inflicted. "Victors rarely pay an indemnity. . . ." (p. 385)

PART II: Checking Your Progress

A. True-False

Where the statement is true, mark **T**. Where it is false, mark **F**, and correct it in the space immediately below.

____ 1. After President Harrison's death, Vice President John Tyler carried on the strong Whig policies of leaders like Clay and Webster.

____ 2. By the 1840s, the bitter memories of two Anglo-American wars had disappeared, putting an end to major British-American conflicts.

____ 3. The "Aroostook War" over the Maine boundary was settled by a territorial compromise in the Webster-Ashburton Treaty.

____ 4. A primary motive driving Americans to annex Texas was fear that the Lone Star Republic would become an ally or protectorate of Britain.

____ 5. Because the two-thirds vote necessary for a treaty of annexation could not be obtained in the Senate, Texas was annexed by a simple majority resolution of both houses of Congress.

____ 6. In the dispute with Britain over Oregon, the United States repeatedly demanded control of the whole territory as far north as "fifty-four forty."

____ 7. In the election of 1844, Clay lost to Polk partly because he tried to straddle the Texas annexation issue and thus lost antislavery support.

____ 8. Polk's victory in 1844 was interpreted as a mandate for Manifest Destiny and led directly to the annexation of Texas and a favorable settlement of the Oregon dispute.

____ 9. The Polk administration aimed to seize California by force and made no effort at peaceful purchase of the territory.

____ 10. The immediate cause of the Mexican War was an attempt by Mexico to reconquer Texas.

____ 11. Polk's primary objective in fighting the Mexican War was to obtain California.

____ 12. The overwhelming American military victory over Mexico led some Americans to call for the United States to take over all of Mexico.

____ 13. The Treaty of Guadalupe Hidalgo gave the United States a small slice of present-day southern New Mexico and Arizona.

____ 14. The outcome of the Mexican War became a source of continuing bad feeling between the United States and much of Latin America.

____ 15. The Wilmot Proviso prohibiting slavery in territory acquired from Mexico helped shove the slavery issue out of sight.

B. Multiple Choice

Select the best answer and write the proper letter in the space provided.

____ 1. The conflict between President Tyler and Whig leaders like Henry Clay took place over issues of
   a. slavery and expansion.
   b. banking and tariff policy.
   c. foreign policy.
   d. agriculture and transportation policy.

____ 2. Among the major sources of the tension between Britain and the United States in the 1840s was
   a. American involvement in Canadian rebellions and border disputes.
   b. British support for American abolitionists.
   c. American anger at British default on canal and railroad loans.
   d. American intervention in the British West Indies.

____ 3. The "Aroostook War" involved
   a. a battle between American and French fishermen over Newfoundland fishing rights.
   b. a battle between American and Canadian lumberjacks over the northern Maine boundary.
   c. a battle between British and American sailors over impressment.
   d. a battle between Americans and Mexicans over the western boundary of Louisiana.

4. During the early 1840s, Texas maintained its independence by

    a. waging a constant war against Mexico.
    b. refusing to sign treaties with any outside powers.
    c. relying on the military power of the United States.
    d. establishing friendly relations with Britain and other European powers.

5. Which of the following was *not* among the reasons why Britain strongly supported an independent Texas?

    a. Britain was interested in eventually incorporating Texas into the British empire.
    b. British abolitionists hoped to make Texas an antislavery bastion.
    c. British manufacturers looked to Texas as a way to reduce their dependence on American cotton.
    d. Britain planned to use Texas as a check on American southward expansion.

6. Texas was finally admitted to the Union in 1844 as a result of

    a. the Mexican War.
    b. the Texans' willingness to abandon slavery.
    c. President Tyler's interpretation of the election of 1844 as a "mandate" to acquire Texas.
    d. a compromise agreement with Britain.

7. "Manifest Destiny" represented the widespread American belief that

    a. Americans were destined to uphold democracy and freedom.
    b. there would inevitably be a civil war over slavery some time in the future.
    c. Mexico was destined to be acquired by the United States.
    d. God had destined the United States to expand across the whole North American continent.

8. Britain eventually lost out in the contest for the disputed Oregon territory because

    a. the rapidly growing number of American settlers overwhelmed the small British population.
    b. the British recognized the greater validity of American legal claims on the territory.
    c. superior American naval forces made the British position in the region untenable.
    d. an international arbitration commission ruled in favor of the American claims.

9. Henry Clay lost the election of 1844 to James Polk because

    a. his attempt to straddle the Texas annexation issue lost him votes to the antislavery Liberty party in New York.
    b. his strong stand for expansion in Texas and Oregon raised fears of war with Britain.
    c. he supported lower tariffs and an independent Treasury system.
    d. he lacked experience in presidential politics.

10. The final result of the British-American conflict over the Oregon country in 1844–1846 was

    a. an American success in winning the goal of a boundary at "fifty-four forty."
    b. an agreement to continue the joint occupation of Oregon for twenty years more.
    c. a compromise agreement on a border at the forty-ninth parallel.
    d. an outbreak of war between the two nations.

____ 11. The immediate cause of the Mexican War was

    a. American refusal to pay Mexican claims for damage to its citizens.

    b. Mexican refusal to sell California and a dispute over the Texas boundary.

    c. Mexican support for the antislavery movement in Texas.

    d. American determination to establish democracy in northern Mexico.

____ 12. The phrase "spot resolutions" refers to

    a. President Polk's message asking Congress to declare war on Mexico "on the spot."

    b. the amendment introduced after the Mexican War declaring that not one new spot of land be opened to slavery.

    c. Congressman Abraham Lincoln's resolution demanding to know the exact spot of American soil where American blood had supposedly been shed.

    d. the congressional act determining which spots of Mexican land should be ceded to the United States.

____ 13. The main American military campaign that finally captured Mexico City was commanded by

    a. General Stephen W. Kearny.

    b. Captain John C. Frémont.

    c. General Zachary Taylor.

    d. General Winfield Scott.

____ 14. The Treaty of Guadalupe Hidalgo ending the Mexican War provided for

    a. a return to the status quo that had existed before the war.

    b. the eventual American acquisition of all of Mexico.

    c. American acquisition of about half of Mexico and payment of several million dollars in compensation.

    d. the acquisition of California and joint U.S.-Mexican control of Arizona and New Mexico.

____ 15. The major domestic consequence of the Mexican War was

    a. the decline of the Democratic party.

    b. a sharp revival of the issue of slavery.

    c. a large influx of Hispanic immigrants into the southern United States.

    d. a significant increase in taxes to pay the costs of the war.

C. Identification

Supply the correct identification for each numbered description.

_____ 1. British colony where Americans regularly aided anti-government rebels

_____ 2. State where "Aroostook War" was fought over a disputed boundary with Canada

_____ 3. Nation that strongly backed independence for Texas, hoping to turn it into an economic asset and antislavery bastion

_____ 4. Antislavery Whigs who opposed both the Texas annexation and the Mexican War on moral grounds

_____ 5. Act of both houses of Congress by which Texas was annexed

_____ 6. Northern boundary of Oregon territory jointly occupied with Britain, advocated by Democratic party and others as the desired line of American expansion

_____ 7. Two-thousand-mile-long path along which thousands of Americans journeyed to the Willamette Valley in the 1840s

_____ 8. the widespread American belief that God had ordained the United States to occupy all the territory of North America

_____ 9. Small antislavery party that took enough votes from Henry Clay to cost him the election of 1844

_____ 10. Final compromise line that settled the Oregon boundary dispute in 1846

_____ 11. Rich Mexican province that Polk tried to buy and Mexico refused to sell

_____ 12. River that Mexico claimed as the Texas-Mexico boundary, crossed by Taylor's troops in 1846

_____ 13. Resolutions offered by Congressman Abraham Lincoln demanding to know the precise location where Mexicans had allegedly shed American blood on "American" soil

_____ 14. Treaty ending Mexican War and granting vast territories to the United States

_____ 15. Controversial amendment, which passed the House but not the Senate, stipulating that slavery should be forbidden in territory acquired from Mexico

D. Matching People, Places, and Events

Match the person, place, or event in the left column with the proper description in the right column by inserting the correct letter on the blank line.

___ 1. John Tyler

___ 2. Henry Clay

___ 3. Aroostook War

___ 4. Daniel Webster

___ 5. Texas

___ 6. Oregon

___ 7. James K. Polk

___ 8. John C. Fremont

___ 9. Abraham Lincoln

___ 10. Rio Grande

___ 11. Zachary Taylor

___ 12. Winfield Scott

___ 13. Santa Anna

A. Congressional author of the "spot resolutions" criticizing the Mexican War

B. "Old Fuss and Feathers," whose conquest of Mexico City brought U.S. victory in the Mexican War

C. Leader of Senate Whigs and unsuccessful presidential candidate against Polk in 1844

D. Long-winded American diplomat who negotiated the Treaty of Guadalupe Hidalgo

E. Whig leader and secretary who negotiated an end to Maine boundary dispute in 1842

F. Claimed by United States as southern boundary of Texas

G. Dashing explorer/adventurer who led the overthrow of Mexican rule in California after war broke out

H. Clash between Canadians and Americans over disputed timber country

I. Mexican military leader who failed to stop humiliating American invasion of his country

J. Independent nation that was the object of British, Mexican, and French scheming in the early 1840s

K. American military hero who invaded northern Mexico from Texas in 1846–1847

L. Congressional author of resolution forbidding slavery in territory acquired from Mexico

M. Dark-horse presidential winner in 1844 who effectively carried out ambitious expansionist campaign plans

____ 14. Nicholas Trist

____ 15. David Wilmot

N. Northwestern territory in dispute between Britain and United States, subject of "Manifest Destiny" rhetoric in 1844

O. Leader elected vice president on the Whig ticket who spent most of his presidency in bitter feuds with his fellow Whigs

E. Putting Things in Order

Put the following events in correct order by numbering them from 1 to 5.

____ United States ends a long courtship by incorporating an independent republic that had once been part of Mexico.

____ The first American president to die in office is succeeded by his controversial vice president.

____ A treaty adding vast territory to the United States is hastily pushed through the Senate.

____ American and Mexican troops clash in disputed border territory, leading to a controversial declaration of war.

____ An ambitious "dark horse" wins an election against an opponent trapped by the Texas annexation issue.

F. Matching Cause and Effect

Match the historical cause in the left column with the proper effect in the right column by writing the correct letter on the blank line.

Cause	Effect
____ 1. Tyler's refusal to carry out his own Whig party's policies	**A.** Thwarted a growing movement calling for the United States to annex all of Mexico
____ 2. Strong American hostility to Britain	**B.** Enabled the United States to take vast territories in the Treaty of Guadalupe Hidalgo
____ 3. British support for the Texas Republic	**C.** Helped lead to a controversial confrontation with Mexico along the Texas border
____ 4. Rapidly growing American settlement in Oregon	**D.** Increased American determination to annex Texas
____ 5. The upsurge of Manifest Destiny in the 1840s	**E.** Split the Whigs and caused the entire cabinet except Webster to resign
____ 6. Clay's unsuccessful attempts to straddle the Texas issue	**F.** Heated up the slavery controversy between North and South
____ 7. Polk's frustration at Mexico's refusal to sell California	**G.** Sparked bitter feuds over Canadian rebels, the boundaries of Maine and Oregon, and other issues
____ 8. The overwhelming American military victory over Mexico	**H.** Turned antislavery voters to the Liberty party and helped elect the expansionist Polk
____ 9. The rapid Senate ratification of the Treaty of Guadalupe Hidalgo	**I.** Created widespread popular support for Polk's expansionist policies on Texas, Oregon, and California
____ 10. The Wilmot Proviso	**J.** Strengthened American claims to the Columbia River country and made Britain more willing to compromise

G. Developing Historical Skills

Reading Maps for Routes

Historical maps often include the routes taken in connection with particular events. The map of the *Major Campaigns of the Mexican War* (p. 382) includes a number of such routes.
Answer the following questions.

1. Near what Mexican port city did both General Taylor and General Scott pass?

2. From which city (and battle site) did American forces move both west to California and south toward Buena Vista?

3. According to the map, where did American naval forces come from? Where did they go during the course of the war? Where were they involved in battles?

4. Across what territories did Kearny and Frémont pass during the war? In which significant battles did each of them take part?

H. Map Mastery

Map Discrimination

Using the maps and charts in Chapter 17, answer the following questions.

1. *Maine Boundary Settlement, 1842*: The Webster-Ashburton Treaty line settled the boundary between the American state of Maine and which two Canadian provinces?

2. *The Oregon Controversy, 1846*: The part of the Oregon Country that was in dispute between the United States and Britain lay between what two boundaries?

3. *The Oregon Controversy, 1846*: How many degrees and minutes (°, ') of latitude were there between the northern and southern boundaries of the *whole* Oregon Country?

4. *Major Campaigns of the Mexican War*: Stephen Kearny's invasion route from Fort Leavenworth to Los Angeles led him across what three rivers?

5. *Major Campaigns of the Mexican War*: Name any three of the cities within present-day Mexico that were occupied by the armies of generals Taylor or Scott.

Map Challenge

Using the map of *Major Campaigns of the Mexican War* on p. 382, write a brief essay explaining the relation between the movement of American military forces during the war and the *political* issues of the Mexican War.

PART III: Applying What You Have Learned

1. What led to the rise of the spirit of "Manifest Destiny" in the 1840s, and how did that spirit show itself in the American expansionism of the decade?
2. How did rivalry with Britain affect the American decision to annex Texas, the Oregon dispute, and other lesser controversies of the period?
3. Most Americans believed that expansion across North America was their "destiny." Was expansion actually inevitable? What forces might have stopped it? How would American history have changed if, say, the Mexican War had not occurred?
4. Why did the crucial election of 1844 come to be fought over expansionism, and how did Polk exercise his "mandate" for expansion in his attempt to obtain California?
5. What were the causes and consequences of the Mexican War?
6. How was the "Manifest Destiny" of the 1840s—particularly the expansion into Texas and Mexico—related to the sectional conflict over slavery?

18

Renewing the Sectional
Struggle, 1848–1854

PART I: Reviewing the Chapter

A. Checklist of Learning Objectives

After mastering this chapter, you should be able to

1. explain how the issue of slavery in the territories acquired from Mexico disrupted American politics from 1848 to 1850.

2. point out the major terms of the Compromise of 1850 and indicate how this agreement attempted to deal with the issue of slavery.

3. indicate how the Whig party disintegrated and disappeared because of its divisions over slavery.

4. describe how the Pierce administration engaged in various prosouthern overseas and expansionist ventures.

5. describe Douglas's Kansas-Nebraska Act and explain why it stirred the sectional controversy to new heights.

B. Glossary

To build your social science vocabulary, familiarize yourself with the following terms.

1. **self-determination** In politics, the right of a people to assert its own national identity or form of government without outside influence. "The public liked it because it accorded with the democratic tradition of self-determination." (p. 391)

2. **homestead** A family home or farm with buildings and land sufficient for survival. ". . . they broadened their appeal . . . by urging free government homesteads for settlers." (p. 391)

3. **vigilante** Concerning groups that claim to punish crime and maintain order without legal authority to do so. ". . . violence was only partly discouraged by rough vigilante justice." (p. 393)

4. **sanctuary** A place of refuge or protection, where people are safe from punishment by the law. ". . . scores of . . . runaway slaves . . . were spirited . . . to the free-soil sanctuary of Canada." (p. 395)

5. **fugitive** A person who flees from danger or prosecution. ". . . southerners were demanding a new and more stringent fugitive-slave law." (p. 395)

6. **topography** The precise surface features and details of a place—for example, rivers, bridges, hills—in relation to one another. "The good Lord had decreed—through climate, topography, and geography—that a plantation economy . . . could not profitably exist in the Mexican Cession territory. . . ." (p. 396)

7. **mundane** Belonging to this world, as opposed to the spiritual world. "Seward argued earnestly that Christian legislators must obey God's moral law as well as mundane human law." (p. 397)

8. **statecraft** The art of government leadership. "The Whigs . . . missed a splendid opportunity to capitalize on their record in statecraft." (p. 401)

9. **isthmian (isthmus)** Concerning a narrow strip of land connecting two larger bodies of land. "... neither America nor Britain would fortify or secure exclusive control over any future isthmian water-way." (p. 402)

10. **filibustering (filibuster)** Adventurers who conduct a private war against a foreign country. "During 1850–1851 two 'filibustering' expeditions descended upon Cuba." (p. 403) (In a different meaning, the term also refers to deliberately prolonging speechmaking in order to block legislation.)

11. **mikado** A title of the Japanese emperor used by foreigners. "The mikado's empire, after some disagreeable experiences with the European world. ..." (p. 403)

12. **cloak-and-dagger** Concerning the activities of spies or undercover agents, especially involving elaborate deceptions. "An incredible cloak-and-dagger episode followed." (p. 404)

13. **manifesto** A proclamation or document aggressively asserting a controversial position or advocating a daring course of action. " ... rose in an outburst of wrath against this 'manifesto of brigands.'" (p. 404)

14. **booster** One who promotes a person or enterprise, especially in a highly enthusiastic way. "An ardent booster for the West, he longed to ... stretch a line of settlements across the continent." (p. 405)

15. **truce** A temporary suspension of warfare by agreement of the hostile parties. "This bold step Douglas was prepared to take, even at the risk of shattering the uneasy truce patched up by the Great Compromise of 1850." (p. 406)

PART II: Checking Your Progress

A. True-False

Where the statement is true, mark **T**. Where it is false, mark **F**, and correct it in the space immediately below.

____ 1. Democratic politicians and others attempted to avoid the issue of slavery in the territories by saying it should be left to "popular sovereignty."

____ 2. The Free Soil party consisted of a small, unified band of radical abolitionists.

____ 3. The California gold rush of 1849 diverted the nation's attention from slavery.

____ 4. Southerners demanded a more effective fugitive-slave law to stop the "Underground Railroad" from running escaped slaves to Canada.

____ 5. In the Senate debate of 1850, Calhoun spoke for compromise, while Clay and Webster each defended his own section's interests.

____ 6. In the key provisions of the Compromise of 1850, New Mexico and Utah were admitted as slave states, while California was left open to popular sovereignty.

____ 7. The provision of the Compromise of 1850 that aroused the fiercest northern opposition was the Fugitive Slave Law.

____ 8. The greatest political winner in the Compromise of 1850 was the South.

____ 9. The Whig Party disappeared because its northern and southern wings were too deeply split over the Fugitive Slave Law and other sectional issues.

____ 10. The Pierce administration's expansionist efforts in Central America, Cuba, and the Gadsden Purchase were basically designed to serve southern proslavery interests.

____ 11. The Gadsden Purchase resulted in a general national agreement to build the transcontinental railroad along the southern route.

____ 12. Douglas's Kansas-Nebraska Act was intended to organize western territories so that a transcontinental railroad could be built along a northern route.

____ 13. Both southerners and northerners alike refused to accept Douglas's plan to repeal the Missouri Compromise.

____ 14. The Kansas-Nebraska Act wrecked the Compromise of 1850 and created deep divisions within the Democratic Party.

____ 15. The Republican Party was initially organized as a northern protest against Douglas's Kansas-Nebraska Act.

B. Multiple Choice

Select the best answer and write the proper letter in the space provided.

____ 1. "Popular sovereignty" was the idea that
   a. the government of each new territory should be elected by the people.
   b. the American public should vote on whether to admit states with or without slavery.
   c. the people of a territory should determine for themselves whether or not to permit slavery.
   d. the United States should assume popular control of the territory acquired from Mexico.

____ 2. In the election of 1848, the response of the Whig and Democratic parties to the rising controversy over slavery was
   a. a strong proslavery stance by the Democrats and a strong antislavery stance by the Whigs.
   b. platforms stressing both parties' clear differences with the antislavery Free Soil party.
   c. an attempt to ignore the issue.
   d. to free each individual candidate to take his own stand on the issue.

____ 3. Quick formation of an effective government in California was essential because of
   a. the desire of antislavery forces to gain a new state for their cause.
   b. the threat that Mexico would reconquer the territory.
   c. the need to have a government capable of building a transcontinental railroad.
   d. the very large and unruly population drawn into the state by the discovery of gold.

____ 4. The proposed admission of California directly into the Union was dangerously controversial because
   a. the territory was in a condition of complete lawlessness and anarchy.
   b. the Mexicans were threatening renewed warfare if California joined the Union.
   c. California's admission as a free state would destroy the equal balance of slave and free states in the U.S. Senate.
   d. there was a growing movement to declare California an independent nation.

5. The existence of the "underground railroad" added to southern demands for

   a. the stationing of armed police and troops along the Ohio River and the Mason-Dixon line to capture runaways.
   b. the death penalty for abolitionists.
   c. a stricter federal Fugitive Slave Law.
   d. the enslavement of free blacks in the South.

6. Among the notable advocates of compromise in the controversy over slavery in 1850 were

   a. William Seward and Zachary Taylor.
   b. Henry Clay and Daniel Webster.
   c. John C. Calhoun and Abraham Lincoln.
   d. Stephen Douglas and Harriet Tubman.

7. During the debate over the Compromise of 1850, northern antislavery forces were particularly outraged by what they considered the "betrayal" of Senator

   a. Stephen A. Douglas.
   b. Daniel Webster.
   c. William Seward.
   d. John C. Calhoun.

8. Under the terms of the Compromise of 1850,

   a. California was admitted to the Union as a free state, and slavery in Utah and New Mexico territories would be left up to popular sovereignty.
   b. California was admitted as a free state, and Utah and New Mexico as slave states.
   c. California, Utah, and New Mexico were kept as territories but with slavery prohibited.
   d. New Mexico and Texas were admitted as slave states and Utah and California as free states.

9. The final battle to gain passage of the Compromise of 1850 was substantially aided by

   a. the conversion of William Seward to the idea of compromise.
   b. the death of President Taylor and the succession of President Fillmore.
   c. the removal of the proposed Fugitive Slave Law from the compromise bill.
   d. the agreement to rely on popular sovereignty to resolve the future of slavery in California.

10. The greatest winner in the Compromise of 1850 was

    a. the North.
    b. the South.
    c. neither the North nor the South.
    d. the border states.

11. One of the primary effects of the Fugitive Slave Law passed as part of the Compromise of 1850 was

    a. an end to slave escapes and the Underground Railroad.
    b. the extension of the underground railroad into Canada.
    c. a sharp rise in northern antislavery feeling.
    d. an increase in violent slave rebellions.

12. The conflict over slavery after the election of 1852 led shortly to

    a. the death of the Whig party.
    b. the death of the Democratic party.
    c. the death of the Republican party.
    d. the rise of the Free Soil party.

13. Southerners seeking to expand the territory of slavery were especially interested in acquiring

    a. Canada and Alaska.
    b. Venezuela and Colombia.
    c. Nicaragua and Cuba.
    d. Hawaii and Japan.

14. The primary goal of Commodore Matthew Perry's treaty with Japan in 1854 was

    a. establishing a balance of power in East Asia.
    b. opening Japan to American trade.
    c. guaranteeing the territorial integrity of China.
    d. establishing American naval bases in Hawaii and Okinawa.

15. Northerners especially resented Douglas's Kansas-Nebraska Act because

    a. it aimed to build a transcontinental railroad along the southern route.
    b. it would make him the leading Democratic candidate for the presidency.
    c. it repealed the Missouri Compromise prohibiting slavery in northern territories.
    d. it would bring Kansas into the Union as a slave state.

C. Identification

Supply the correct identification for each numbered description.

_____ 1. Hotheaded southern agitators who pushed for southern interests and favored secession from the Union

_____ 2. The doctrine that the issue of slavery should be decided by the residents of a territory themselves, not by the federal government

_____ 3. The boundary line between slave and free states in the East, originally the southern border of Pennsylvania

_____ 4. The informal network that conducted runaway slaves from the South to Canada

_____ 5. Senator William Seward's doctrine that slavery should be excluded from the territories as contrary to a divine moral law standing above even the Constitution

_____ 6. The provision of the Compromise of 1850 that comforted southern slave-catchers and aroused the wrath of northern abolitionists

_____ 7. Third-party entry in the election of 1848 that opposed slavery expansion and prepared the way for the Republican Party

_____ 8. A series of agreements between North and South that temporarily dampened the slavery controversy and led to a short-lived era of national good feelings

_____ 9. Political party that fell apart and disappeared after losing the election of 1852

_____ 10. An agreement between Britain and America concerning any future Central American canal

_____ 11. A top-secret dispatch, drawn up by American diplomats in Europe, that detailed a plan for seizing Cuba from Spain

_____ 12. Southwestern territory acquired by the Pierce administration to facilitate a southern transcontinental railroad

_____ 13. The sectional agreement of 1820, repealed by the Kansas-Nebraska Act

_____ 14. The political party that was deeply divided by Douglas's Kansas-Nebraska Act

_____ 15. A new political party organized as a protest against the Kansas-Nebraska Act

D. Matching People, Places, and Events

Match the person, place, or event in the left column with the proper description in the right column by inserting the correct letter on the blank line.

___ 1. Lewis Cass

___ 2. Zachary Taylor

___ 3. California

___ 4. District of Columbia

___ 5. Harriet Tubman

___ 6. Daniel Webster

___ 7. William Seward

___ 8. Utah and New Mexico

___ 9. Franklin Pierce

___ 10. Winfield Scott

___ 11. Nicaragua

___ 12. Matthew Perry

___ 13. Cuba

___ 14. Kansas and Nebraska

___ 15. Stephen A. Douglas

A. American naval commander who opened Japan to the West in 1854

B. Democratic presidential candidate in 1848, original proponent of the idea of "popular sovereignty"

C. Weak Democratic president whose pro-southern cabinet pushed aggressive expansionist schemes

D. Famous "conductor" on the Underground Railroad who rescued more than three hundred slaves from bondage

E. Illinois politician who helped smooth over sectional conflict in 1850 but then reignited it in 1854

F. Central American nation desired by proslavery expansionists in the 1850s

G. Military hero of the Mexican War who became the Whigs' last presidential candidate in 1852

H. Whig president who nearly destroyed the Compromise of 1850 before he died in office

I. Rich Spanish colony coveted by American proslavery expansionists in the 1850s

J. Place where the slave trade was ended by the Compromise of 1850

K. Organized as territories under Douglas's controversial law of 1854 that left their decision on slavery up to popular sovereignty

L. New York senator who argued that the expansion of slavery was forbidden by a "higher law"

M. Organized as territories under the Compromise of 1850, with their decision about slavery left up to popular sovereignty

N. Northern spokesman whose support for the Compromise of 1850 earned him the hatred of abolitionists

O. Acquired from Mexico in 1848 and admitted as a free state in 1850 without ever having been a territory

E. Putting Things in Order

Put the following events in correct order by numbering them from 1 to 5.

____ A series of delicate agreements between the North and South temporarily smoothes over the slavery conflict.

____ A Mexican War hero is elected president, as the issue of how a deal with slavery in the territory acquired from Mexico arouses national controversy.

____ A spectacular growth of settlement in the far West creates demand for admission of a new free state and agitates the slavery controversy.

____ Stephen A. Douglas's scheme to build a transcontinental railroad leads to repeal of the Missouri Compromise, which reopens the slavery controversy and spurs the formation of a new party.

____ The Pierce administration acquires a small Mexican territory to encourage a southern route for the transcontinental railroad.

F. Matching Cause and Effect

Match the historical cause in the left column with the proper effect in the right column by writing the correct letter on the blank line.

Cause		**Effect**
____ 1. The evasion of the slavery issue by Whigs and Democrats in 1848	**A.**	Was the predecessor of the antislavery Republican Party
____ 2. The California gold rush	**B.**	Fell apart after the leaking of the Ostend Manifesto
____ 3. The Underground Railroad	**C.**	Caused a tremendous northern protest and the birth of the Republican party
____ 4. The Free Soil Party	**D.**	Made the issue of slavery in the Mexican Cession areas more urgent
____ 5. The Compromise of 1850	**E.**	Created a short-lived national mood of optimism and reconciliation
____ 6. The Fugitive Slave Law	**F.**	Heightened competition between southern and northern railroad promoters over the choice of a transcontinental route
____ 7. The Pierce administration's schemes to acquire Cuba	**G.**	Led to the formation of the new Free-Soil antislavery party
____ 8. The Gadsden Purchase	**H.**	Aroused active northern resistance to legal enforcement and prompted attempts at nullification in Massachusetts
____ 9. Stephen Douglas's indifference to slavery and desire for a northern railroad route	**I.**	Led to the passage of the Kansas-Nebraska Act, without regard for the consequences
____ 10. The Kansas-Nebraska Act	**J.**	Aroused southern demands for an effective fugitive-slave law

G. Developing Historical Skills

Understanding Cause and Effect

It is often crucial to understand how certain historical forces or events cause other historical events or developments. In the pairs of historical events listed below, designated (A) and (B), indicate which was the cause and which was the effect. Then indicate in a brief sentence how the cause led to the effect.

1. (A) The acquisition of California   (B) The Mexican War

2. (A) The entry of California into the Union (B) The California gold rush

3. (A) The death of President Zachary Taylor   (B) The passage of the Compromise of 1850

4. (A) Northern aid to fugitive slaves (B) The passage of the Fugitive Slave Law

5. (A) The disappearance of the Whig party   (B) The election of 1852

6. (A) The Compromise of 1850   (B) Southern "filibuster" ventures

7. (A) The Gadsden Purchase   (B) The southern plan for a transcontinental railroad

8. (A) Douglas's plan for a transcontinental railroad   (B) The Kansas-Nebraska Act

9. (A) The Ostend Manifesto (B) The end of Pierce administration schemes to acquire Cuba

10. (A) The rise of the Republican party   (B) The Kansas-Nebraska Act

H. Map Mastery

Map Discrimination

Using the maps and charts in Chapter 18, answer the following questions.

1. *Texas and the Disputed Area Before the Compromise of 1850:* A large territory claimed by Texas was taken from it in the Compromise of 1850, and parts of it were later incorporated into *five* other states. Which were they?

2. *Slavery After the Compromise of 1850:* Under the Compromise of 1850, which *free* state was partially located south of the line 36°30' (the southern border of Missouri), which had been established by the Missouri Compromise as the border between slave and free territories?

3. *Slavery After the Compromise of 1850:* Under the Compromise of 1850, which territory located *north* of 36°30' *could* have adopted slavery if it had chosen to do so?

4. *Slavery After the Compromise of 1850:* After 1850, how many organized territories prohibited slavery? Identify them.

5. *Central American c. 1850:* In Central America, British influence extended along the Atlantic coasts of which two nations?

6. *Central America c. 1850:* In the 1850s, the territory of the future Panama Canal was part of which South American country?

7. *The Gadsden Purchase, 1853:* The proposed southern transcontinental railroad was supposed to run through which two Texas cities?

8. *Kansas and Nebraska, 1854:* The proposed *northern* transcontinental railroad was supposed to run through which territory organized by Stephen Douglas's act of 1854?

9. *The Legal Status of Slavery, from the Revolution to the Civil War:* In 1854, what was the status of slavery in the only state that bordered on the Kansas Territory?

10. *The Legal Status of Slavery, from the Revolution to the Civil War*: Under the Kansas-Nebraska Act, how far north could slavery have extended had it been implemented in Nebraska territory?

Map Challenge

Using the map of *The Legal Status of Slavery, from the Revolution to the Civil War*, write a brief essay in which you describe how the Missouri Compromise, the Compromise of 1850, and the Kansas-Nebraska Act each affected the legal status of slavery in various territories.

PART III: Applying What You Have Learned

1. What urgent issues created the crisis leading up to the Compromise of 1850?
2. What was the effect of the morally powerful slavery debate on American political parties? What caused the demise of the Whig Party, and the rise of the Free Soil and Republican parties?
3. How did the Compromise of 1850 attempt to deal with the most difficult issues concerning slavery? Was the Compromise a "success?" By what standard?
4. Why were proslavery southerners so eager to push for further expansion in Nicaragua, Cuba, and elsewhere in the 1850s?
5. What were the causes and consequences of the Kansas-Nebraska Act?
6. How similar was the Compromise of 1850 to the Missouri Compromise of 1820? (See Chapter 13.) How did each sectional compromise affect the balance of power between North and South? Why could sectional issues be compromised in 1820 and 1850, but not in 1854?

19

Drifting Toward Disunion, 1854–1861

PART I: Reviewing the Chapter

A. Checklist of Learning Objectives

After mastering this chapter, you should be able to

1. relate the sequence of major crises that led from the Kansas-Nebraska Act to secession.
2. explain how and why "bleeding Kansas" became a dress rehearsal for the Civil War.
3. trace the growing power of the Republican party in the 1850s and the increasing divisions and helplessness of the Democrats.
4. explain how the Dred Scott decision and Brown's Harpers Ferry raid deepened sectional antagonism.
5. trace the rise of Lincoln as the leading exponent of the Republican doctrine of no expansion of slavery.
6. analyze the complex election of 1860 in relation to the sectional crisis.
7. describe the movement toward secession, the formation of the Confederacy, and the failure of the last compromise effort.

B. Glossary

To build your social science vocabulary, familiarize yourself with the following terms.

1. **puppet government** A government set up and controlled by outside forces. "The slavery supporters triumphed and then set up their own puppet government at Shawnee Mission." (p. 413)
2. **bigoted** Blindly or narrowly intolerant. ". . . the allegation . . . alienated many bigoted Know-Nothings. . . ." (p. 416)
3. **public domain** Land or other things belonging to the whole nation, controlled by the federal government. "Financial distress . . . gave a new vigor to the demand for free farms of 160 acres from the public domain." (p. 419)
4. **bandwagon** In politics, a movement or candidacy that gains rapid momentum because of people's purported desire to join a successful cause. "After mounting the Republican bandwagon, he emerged as one of the foremost politicians and orators of the Northwest." (p. 420)
5. **apportionment** The allotment or distribution of legislative representatives in districts according to population. (**re-apportionment** occurs after each census according to growth or loss of population.) "Yet thanks to inequitable apportionment, the districts carried by Douglas supporters represented a smaller population. . . ." (p. 422)
6. **splintering** Concerning the small political groups left after a larger group has divided or broken apart. "But Douglas . . . hurt his own chances . . . while further splitting his splintering party." (p. 422)
7. **affidavit** A sworn, written testimony, usually attested to by a notary public or legal officer. "His presumed insanity was supported by affidavits from seventeen friends and relatives. . . ." (p. 422)

8. **martyr** One who is tortured or killed for adherence to a belief. ". . . Ralph Waldo Emerson compared the new martyr-hero with Jesus." (p. 424)

9. **border state** The northernmost slave states contested by North and South; during the Civil War the four border states (Maryland, Delaware, Kentucky, and Missouri) remained within the Union, though they contained many Confederate sympathizers and volunteers. " . . . a man of moderate views from the border state of Kentucky." (p. 425)

10. **vassalage** The service and homage given by a feudal subordinate to an overlord; by extension, any similar arrangement between political figures or entities. ". . . secession [w]as a golden opportunity to cast aside their generations of 'vassalage' to the North." (p. 431)

PART II: Checking Your Progress

A. True-False

Where the statement is true, mark **T**. Where it is false, mark **F**, and correct it in the space immediately below.

____ 1. Harriet Beecher Stowe's *Uncle Tom's Cabin* proved to be the most influential publication in arousing the northern and European publics against the evils of slavery.

____ 2. Prosouthern Kansas pioneers brought numerous slaves with them in order to guarantee that Kansas would not become a free state.

____ 3. The violence in Kansas was provoked by both radical abolitionists and militant proslavery forces.

____ 4. By opposing the proslavery Lecompton Constitution in Kansas, Senator Stephen A. Douglas was able to unite the Democratic party.

____ 5. Both South Carolina and Massachusetts defiantly reelected the principal figures in the Brooks-Sumner beating incident.

____ 6. Although the Republican candidate lost to Buchanan, the election of 1856 demonstrated the growing power of the new antislavery party.

____ 7. The Dred Scott decision upheld the doctrine of popular sovereignty that the people of each territory should determine whether or not to permit slavery.

____ 8. Republicans considered the Supreme Court's *Dred Scott* decision invalid and vowed to defy it.

____ 9. In the Lincoln-Douglas debates, Lincoln's criticisms forced Douglas to back away from his support for popular sovereignty.

____ 10. John Brown's raid at Harpers Ferry failed to set off a slave uprising but succeeded in inflaming passions in both North and South.

____ 11. Northern Democrats walked out of the Democratic party in 1860 when southerners nominated Stephen A. Douglas for president.

____ 12. The election of 1860 was really two campaigns, Lincoln versus Douglas in the North and Bell versus Breckinridge in the South.

_____ 13. Lincoln won a solid majority of the popular vote but only a minority in the Electoral College.

_____ 14. Seven states seceded and formed the Confederate States of America during the "lame-duck" period between Lincoln's election and his inauguration.

_____ 15. Lincoln made a strong effort to get the South to accept the Crittenden Compromise in order to avoid a civil war.

B. Multiple Choice

Select the best answer and write the proper letter in the space provided.

_____ 1. Harriet Beecher Stowe's *Uncle Tom's Cabin*

    a. greatly strengthened northern antislavery feeling.
    b. argued that nonslaveholding whites suffered the most from slavery.
    c. increased the desire for sectional compromise on the issue of slavery.
    d. was based on Stowe's long personal experience with slavery in the Deep South.

_____ 2. Hinton R. Helper's *The Impending Crisis of the South* contended that

    a. slavery violated the essential principles of the U.S. Constitution.
    b. slavery was contrary to the religious values held by most Americans.
    c. slavery did great harm to the poor whites of the South.
    d. slavery violated the human rights of African-Americans.

_____ 3. The conflict over slavery in Kansas

    a. came about because the first settlers brought substantial numbers of slaves to the territory.
    b. was resolved by the Crittenden Compromise.
    c. was temporarily resolved by the Compromise of 1850.
    d. was greatly escalated by abolitionist-funded settlers and proslavery "border ruffians" from Missouri.

_____ 4. As presented to Congress, the Lecompton Constitution provided for

    a. the admission of Kansas as a free state.
    b. a statewide referendum on slavery to be held after Kansas's admission to the Union.
    c. a prohibition against either New England or Missouri involvement in Kansas politics.
    d. the admission of Kansas as a slave state.

_____ 5. The fanatical abolitionist John Brown made his first entry into violent antislavery politics by

    a. killing five proslavery settlers at Pottawatomie Creek, Kansas.
    b. organizing a slave rebellion in Missouri.
    c. leading an armed raid on the federal arsenal at Harpers Ferry, Virginia.
    d. organizing an armed militia of blacks and whites to conduct escaped slaves to Canada.

6. The Sumner-Brooks affair revealed

   a. that antislavery northerners were as willing to turn to violence as proslavery southerners.
   b. that violent disagreements about slavery were being felt in the halls of Congress.
   c. that neither northerners nor southerners were yet ready to tolerate political violence over slavery.
   d. how loyalty to section was beginning to supersede loyalty to political party.

7. The election of 1856 was most noteworthy for

   a. the Democrats' surprising loss of the White House.
   b. the support immigrants and Catholics gave to the American Party.
   c. the dramatic rise of the Republican party.
   d. the absence of the slavery issue from the campaign.

8. In the *Dred Scott* decision, the Supreme Court

   a. avoided controversy by ruling that the slave Dred Scott had no right to sue in federal court.
   b. ruled that the Kansas-Nebraska Act was unconstitutional.
   c. ruled that Congress could not prohibit slavery in the territories because slaves were private property.
   d. ruled that slaves could sue in federal court only if their masters permitted them to do so.

9. The panic of 1857 encouraged the South to believe that

   a. its economy was fundamentally stronger than that of the North.
   b. it ought to take new steps to develop its own banking and manufacturing institutions.
   c. it would be wise to support the Homestead Act.
   d. its economic future was closely tied to that of the North.

10. A key issue in the Lincoln-Douglas debates was

    a. whether secession from the Union was legal.
    b. whether the people of a territory could prohibit slavery in light of the *Dred Scott* decision.
    c. whether Illinois should continue to prohibit slavery.
    d. whether Kansas should be admitted to the Union as a slave or a free state.

11. Southerners were particularly enraged by the John Brown affair because

    a. so many slaves had joined the insurrection.
    b. they believed Brown's violent abolitionist sentiments were shared by the whole North.
    c. Brown had expressed his contempt for the southern way of life.
    d. Brown escaped punishment by pleading insanity.

12. In the campaign of 1860, the Democratic Party

    a. tried to unite around the compromise "popular sovereignty" views of Stephen A. Douglas.
    b. campaigned on a platform of restoring the compromises of 1820 and 1850.
    c. split in two, with each faction nominating its own presidential candidate.
    d. threatened to support secession if the sectionally-based Republicans won the election.

13. Lincoln won the presidency

    a. with an electoral majority derived only from the North.

    b. with a majority of both the electoral and the popular vote.

    c. primarily because of the divisions in the Democratic party.

    d. with an electoral majority evenly derived from all sections of the nation.

14. Within two months after the election of Lincoln,

    a. Northerners were mobilizing for a civil war.

    b. seven southern states had seceded and formed the Confederate States of America.

    c. all the slaveholding states had held conventions and passed secessionist resolutions.

    d. President Buchanan appealed for troops to put down the secessionist rebellion.

15. Lincoln rejected the proposed Crittenden Compromise because

    a. it did not address the issue of the future of slavery.

    b. it permitted the further extension of slavery north of the line of 36° 30'.

    c. it represented a further extension of Douglas's popular sovereignty idea.

    d. the Supreme Court would probably have ruled it unconstitutional.

C. Identification

Supply the correct identification for each numbered description.

1. A powerful, personal novel that altered the course of American politics

2. A book by a southern writer that argued that slavery especially oppressed poor whites

3. Rifles paid for by New England abolitionists and brought to Kansas by anti-slavery pioneers

4. Term that described the prairie territory where a small-scale civil war erupted in 1856

5. Tricky proslavery document designed to bring Kansas into the Union but blocked by Stephen A. Douglas

6. Anti-immigrant party headed by former President Fillmore that competed with Republicans and Democrats in the election of 1856

7. Controversial Supreme Court ruling that blacks had no civil or human rights and that Congress could not prohibit slavery in the territories

8. Sharp economic decline that increased northern demands for a high tariff and convinced southerners that the North was economically vulnerable

9. Thoughtful political discussions during an Illinois Senate campaign that sharply defined national issues concerning slavery

10. Newly formed middle-of-the-road party of elderly politicians that sought compromise in 1860, but carried only three border states

11. First state to secede from the Union in December 1860

12. A new nation that proclaimed its independence in Montgomery, Alabama, in 1861

_____ 13. A last-ditch plan to save the Union by providing guarantees for slavery in the territories

_____ 14. Four-way race for the presidency that resulted in the election of a sectional minority president

_____ 15. Period between Lincoln's election and his inauguration, during which the ineffectual President Buchanan remained in office

D. Matching People, Places, and Events

Match the person, place, or event in the left column with the proper description in the right column by inserting the correct letter on the blank line.

___ 1. Harriet Beecher Stowe

___ 2. Hinton R. Helper

___ 3. New England Emigrant Aid Company

___ 4. John Brown

___ 5. James Buchanan

___ 6. Charles Sumner

___ 7. Preston Brooks

___ 8. John C. Frémont

___ 9. Dred Scott

___ 10. Harpers Ferry, Virginia

___ 11. Stephen A. Douglas

___ 12. Pottawatomie Creek, Kansas

___ 13. John C. Breckenridge

___ 14. Montgomery, Alabama

___ 15. Jefferson Davis

A. Southern congressman whose bloody attack on a northern senator fueled sectional hatred

B. Leading northern Democrat whose presidential hopes fell victim to the conflict over slavery

C. Black slave whose unsuccessful attempt to win his freedom deepened the sectional controversy

D. Former United States senator who in 1861 became the president of what called itself a new nation

E. "The little woman who wrote the book that made this great war" (the Civil War)

F. Fanatical and bloody-minded abolitionist martyr admired in the North and hated in the South

G. Southern-born author whose book attacking slavery's effects on whites aroused northern opinion

H. Scene of militant abolitionist John Brown's massacre of proslavery men in 1856

I. Site where seven seceding states united to declare their independence from the United States

J. Romantic western hero and the first Republican candidate for president

K. Abolitionist senator whose verbal attack on the South provoked a physical assault that severely injured him

L. Site of a federal arsenal where a militant abolitionist attempted to start a slave rebellion

M. Buchanan's vice president, nominated for president by breakaway southern Democrats in 1860

N. Weak Democratic president whose manipulation by proslavery forces divided his own party

O. Abolitionist group that sent settlers and "Beecher's Bibles" to oppose slavery in Kansas

E. Putting Things in Order

Put the following events in correct order by numbering them from 1 to 6.

___ A black slave's attempt to win freedom produces a controversial Supreme Court decision.

___ A newly organized territory becomes a bloody battleground between proslavery and antislavery forces.

____ The hanging of a fanatically violent abolitionist makes him a martyr in the North and a hated symbol in the South.

____ A "black Republican" whose minority sectional victory in a presidential election provokes southern secession.

____ The fictional tale of a black slave's vicious treatment by the cruel Simon Legree touches millions of northern hearts and creates stronger opposition to slavery.

____ A group of states calling itself a new southern nation declares its independence and chooses its first president.

F.   Matching Cause and Effect

Match the historical cause in the left column with the proper effect in the right column by writing the correct letter on the blank line.

Cause	Effect
____ 1. H. B. Stowe's *Uncle Tom's Cabin*	**A.** Moved South Carolina to declare immediate secession from the Union
____ 2. The exercise of "popular sovereignty" in Kansas	**B.** Shattered one of the last links between the sections and almost guaranteed Lincoln's victory in 1860
____ 3. Buchanan's support for the pro-slavery Lecompton Constitution	**C.** Convinced southerners that the North generally supported murder and slave rebellion
____ 4. The Dred Scott case	**D.** Made Lincoln a leading national Republican figure and hurt Douglas's presidential chances
____ 5. The 1858 Illinois senate race	
____ 6. John Brown's raid on Harpers Ferry	**E.** Ended the last hopes of a peaceable sectional settlement and an end to secession
____ 7. The splitting of the Democratic party in 1860	**F.** Paralyzed the North while the southern secessionist movement gained momentum
____ 8. The election of Lincoln as president	**G.** Infuriated Republicans and made them determined to defy the Supreme Court
____ 9. The "lame-duck" period and Buchanan's indecisiveness	**H.** Offended Senator Douglas and divided the Democratic party
____ 10. Lincoln's rejection of the Crittenden Compromise	**I.** Persuaded millions of northerners and Europeans that slavery was evil and should be eliminated
	J. Led to a "mini" prairie civil war between proslavery and antislavery factions

G.   Developing Historical Skills

Interpreting Primary-Source Documents

In order properly to interpret primary-source documents in history, two skills are essential: first, the ability to read closely and carefully for the intended meaning; and second, the ability to understand the historical context and possible implications of a text or statement.

The small, boxed samples of primary documents in this chapter demonstrate these principles. The questions below will help you practice the skills of textual interpretation by asking you to read the documents very carefully for meaning and to consider some of their implications.

1. Lincoln's statement from the Lincoln-Douglas debate (p. 421).

   a. In what ways does Lincoln claim that blacks are *equal* to whites, and in what ways does he claim that whites are *superior*?

   b. What do the first two sentences tell you about the *reason* Lincoln is making a distinction between equality of natural rights and complete equality of the races?

2. John Brown's letter before his hanging (p. 423).

   a. What does Brown mean when he writes that "I am worth inconceivably more to hang than for any other purpose. . . ."?

   b. What does Brown's statement imply about how abolitionists might make use of Brown's impending death?

3. Greeley's New York *Tribune* editorial (p. 437).

   a. What two arguments does Greeley use for letting the seceding states "go in peace?"

   b. The editorial was written three days after Lincoln's election. What fear is motivating Greeley?

4. Letter of South Carolina Senator Hammond (p. 429).

   a. What does the letter suggest will be the federal government's response to secession?

   b. Why did the attitude reflected in the letter make efforts like the Crittenden Compromise fail?

5. London *Times* editorial (p. 431).

   a. What is the editorial's view of the relation between the southern states and the United States government?

   b. What position does it appear the London *Times* would advocate the British government take regarding the American Civil War?

6. Harriet Beecher Stowe's *Uncle Tom's Cabin* (pp. 411 and 412).

   a. What details in Stowe's account of Tom's last morning in the cabin before the sale of his family might especially appeal to female readers?

   b. How does Stowe characterize the black slave Tom and his wife Chloe?

   c. What details in the excerpts in *Examining the Evidence* (p. 411) and on p. 412 show Stowe's explicit appeal to the religious sentiments of her readers?

H. Map Mastery

Map Discrimination

Using the maps and charts in Chapter 19, answer the following questions.

1. *Presidential Election of 1856*: In the presidential election of 1856, how many electoral votes did Buchanan get from the free states? (See map of *The Legal Status of Slavery*, Chapter 17, for free and slave states.)

2. *Presidential Election of 1856; Presidential Election of 1860 (electoral vote by state)*: Which four states carried by Democrat Buchanan in 1856 were also carried completely by Republican Lincoln in 1860?

3. *Presidential Election of 1860 (showing popular vote by county):* Using this map of the presidential voting by counties in 1860, indicate which five states gave Douglas his strongest support.

4. *Presidential Election of 1860 (showing popular vote by county):* In which five states did Bell receive his strongest support?

5. *Presidential Election of 1860 (showing popular vote by county)*: Which Border State was the most closely divided among Douglas, Bell, and Breckenridge?

6. *Presidential Election of 1860 (showing popular vote by county)*: Which state was the only one divided among Lincoln, Douglas, and Breckenridge?

7. *Presidential Election of 1860 (showing vote by county)*: In which six northern states did Lincoln carry every single country?

8. *Southern Opposition to Secession, 1860–1861*: In which four future Confederate states was the *opposition* to secession strongest?

9. *Southern Opposition to Secession, 1860–1861*: In which three states did every single county for which returns are available support secession?

10. *Southern Opposition to Secession, 1860–1861*: In which two states were many county conventions divided about secession?

Map Challenge

Using the electoral maps of *The Presidential Election of 1856* and *The Presidential Election of 1860,* write a brief essay in which you describe what political changes enabled the Republicans to turn defeat in 1856 into victory in 1860.

PART III: Applying What You Have Learned

1. How did each of the crisis events of the 1850s help lead toward the Civil War?
2. What role did violence play in increasing the sectional conflict?
3. How did the political developments of the period work to fragment the Democratic party and benefit the Republicans?
4. Explain the crucial role of Stephen A. Douglas in the political events of the 1850s. Why did Douglas's attempts to shove aside the conflict over slavery fail?
5. Could the Crittenden Compromise or some other proposal have prevented or at least postponed the Civil War? Why was compromise successful in 1820 and 1850 but not 1860?
6. How did the North and the South each view the various events of the 1850s? Why were their views so different?

20

Girding for War: The North and the South, 1861–1865

PART I: Reviewing the Chapter

A. Checklist of Learning Objectives

After mastering this chapter, you should be able to

1. explain how the firing on Fort Sumter and Lincoln's call for troops galvanized both sides for war.
2. describe the crucial early struggle for the Border States.
3. indicate the strengths and weaknesses of both sides as they went to war.
4. describe the diplomatic struggle for the sympathies of the European powers.
5. compare Lincoln's and Davis's political leadership during the war.
6. describe the curtailment of civil liberties and the mobilization of military manpower during the war.
7. analyze the economic and social consequences of the war for both sides.

B. Glossary

To build your social science vocabulary, familiarize yourself with the following terms.

1. **balance of power** The distribution of political or military strength among several nations so that no one of them becomes too strong or dangerous . "They could gleefully transplant to America their ancient concept of the balance of power." (p. 435)
2. **moral suasion** The effort to move others to a particular course of action through appeals to moral values and beliefs, without the use of enticements or force. "In dealing with the Border States, President Lincoln did not rely solely on moral suasion. . . ." (p. 437)
3. **martial law** The imposition of military rule above or in place of civil authority during times of war and emergency. "In Maryland he declared martial law where needed. . . ." (p. 437)
4. **ultimatum** A final proposal or demand, as by one nation to another, that if rejected, will likely lead to war. "The London Foreign Office prepared an ultimatum. . . ." (p. 442)
5. **loophole(d)** Characterized by small exceptions or conditions that enable escape from the general rule or principle. "These vessels were not warships within the meaning of the loopholed British law. . . ." (p. 442)
6. **squadron** A special unit of warships assigned to a particular naval task. ". . . they probably would have sunk the blockading squadrons. . . ." (p. 443)
7. **arbitration** The settlement of a dispute by putting the mandatory decision in the hands of a third, neutral party. (**Mediation** is using the services of a third party to promote negotiations and suggest solutions, but without the power of mandatory decision-making.) "It agreed in 1871 to submit the *Alabama* dispute to arbitration. . . ." (p. 443)
8. **appropriation** A sum of money or property legally authorized to be spent for a specific purpose. "He directed the secretary of the treasury to advance $2 million without appropriation. . . ." (p. 445)

9. **habeas corpus** In law, a judicial order requiring that a prisoner be brought before a court at a specified time and place in order to determine the legality of the imprisonment (literally, "produce the body.") "He suspended the precious privilege of the writ of habeas corpus. . . ." (p. 445)

10. **arbitrary** Governed by indeterminate preference or whim rather than by settled principle or law. "Jefferson Davis was less able than Lincoln to exercise arbitrary power. . . ." (p. 445)

11. **quota** The proportion or share of a larger number of things that a smaller group is assigned to contribute. ". . . with each state assigned a quota based on population." (p. 445)

12. **greenback** United States paper currency, especially that printed before the establishment of the Federal Reserve System. "Greenbacks thus fluctuated with the fortunes of Union arms. . . ." (p. 447)

13. **bond** In finance, an interest-bearing certificate issued by a government or business that guarantees repayment to the purchaser on a specified date at a predetermined rate of interest. ". . . the Treasury was forced to market its bonds through the private banking house of Jay Cooke and Company. . . ." (p. 447)

14. **graft** The corrupt acquisition of funds, through outright theft or embezzling or through questionably legal methods like kickbacks or insider trading. "But graft was more flagrant in the North than in the South. . . ." (p. 448)

15. **profiteer** One who takes advantage of a shortage of supply to charge excessively high prices and thus reap large profits. "One profiteer reluctantly admitted that his profits were 'painfully large.' " (p. 448)

PART II: Checking Your Progress

A. True-False

Where the statement is true, mark **T**. Where it is false, mark **F**, and correct it in the space immediately below.

_____ 1. Lincoln successfully prevented any more states from seceding after his inauguration.

_____ 2. In order to appease the Border States, Lincoln first insisted that the North was fighting only to preserve the Union and not to abolish slavery.

_____ 3. The South's advantage in the Civil War was that it only had to stalemate the war on its own territory, while the North had to fight a war of conquest against a hostile population.

_____ 4. The North generally had superior military leadership, while the South struggled to find successful commanders for its armies.

_____ 5. In the long run, Northern economic and population advantages effectively wore down Southern resistance.

_____ 6. The South's chances for independence when the war began were actually quite good.

_____ 7. Although officially neutral, Britain sometimes engaged in acts that in effect aided the South.

_____ 8. Northern pressure forced the British to stop the *Alabama* from raiding Union shipping.

_____ 9. The Civil War–related crisis in U.S.-British relations threatened to expand into a war over Canada.

____ 10. Once the Civil War was over, the threat of U.S. intervention forced Napoleon III of France to withdraw his support of Maximilian in Mexico.

____ 11. The Civil War draft reflected the North's commitment to fighting a war based on the principle of equal treatment of citizens from all economic conditions.

____ 12. Lincoln's temporary violations of civil liberties were strongly opposed by Congress.

____ 13. The North effectively financed its Civil War effort through an income tax, higher tariffs, and the sale of federal government bonds.

____ 14. The South in effect used severe inflation as a means of financing its war effort.

____ 15. The Northern civilian economy was severely damaged by the war effort.

B. Multiple Choice

Select the best answer and write the proper letter in the space provided.

____ 1. Lincoln's plan for the besieged federal forces in Fort Sumter was
   a. to order the soldiers there to attack the surrounding Confederate army.
   b. to send about 3,000 soldiers and marines to reinforce the fort.
   c. to make a symbolic show of support and then withdraw the forces.
   d. to provision the garrison but not to reinforce it.

____ 2. The firing on Fort Sumter had the effect of
   a. pushing ten other states to join South Carolina in seceding from the Union.
   b. causing Lincoln to declare a war to free the slaves.
   c. strengthening many Northerners' view that the South should be allowed to secede.
   d. arousing Northern support for a war to put down the South's "rebellion."

____ 3. Among the states that joined the Confederacy only after Lincoln's call for troops were
   a. Florida, Louisiana, and Texas.
   b. Virginia, Arkansas, and Tennessee.
   c. Missouri, Maryland, and Delaware.
   d. South Carolina, North Carolina, and Mississippi.

____ 4. Lincoln at first declared that the war was being fought
   a. only to save the Union and not to free the slaves.
   b. in order to end slavery only in the Border States.
   c. in order to restore the Missouri Compromise.
   d. only to punish South Carolina for firing on Fort Sumter.

____ 5. Which of the following was *not* among the Border States?
   a. Missouri
   b. Kentucky
   c. Oklahoma
   d. Maryland

6. The term "Butternut region" refers to

   a. the mountain areas of the South that remained loyal to the Union.
   b. the areas of southern Ohio, Indiana, and Illinois that opposed an antislavery war.
   c. the areas of the upper Midwest that supplied a large portion of the committed Union volunteers.
   d. the areas of southern Pennsylvania and New York that supported the war but hated the draft.

7. In the Indian Territory (Oklahoma), most of the "Five Civilized Tribes"

   a. supported the Confederacy.
   b. supported a war for the Union but not a war against slavery.
   c. sent many young warriors to fight for the Union cause.
   d. tried to stay neutral in the "white man's war."

8. Among the potential advantages the Confederacy possessed at the beginning of the civil War was

   a. a stronger and more balanced economy.
   b. a stronger navy.
   c. better-trained officers and soldiers.
   d. a larger reserve of manpower.

9. Among the potential advantages the Union possessed at the beginning of the Civil War was

   a. better preparation of its ordinary soldiers for military life.
   b. a continuing influx of immigrant manpower from Europe.
   c. more highly educated and experienced generals.
   d. the ability to fight a primarily defensive war.

10. The response to the Civil War in Europe was

    a. almost unanimous support for the North.
    b. support for the South among the upper classes and for the North among the working classes.
    c. almost unanimous support for the South.
    d. support for the South in France and Spain and for the North in Britain and Germany.

11. The South's weapon of "King Cotton" failed to draw Britain into the war on the side of the Confederacy because

    a. the British discovered that they could substitute flax and wool for cotton.
    b. the British were able to grow sufficient cotton in their own land.
    c. the British found sufficient cotton from previous stockpiles and from other sources like Egypt and India.
    d. the threat of war with France distracted British attention for several years.

12. The success of the Confederate raider *Alabama* highlighted the issue of

    a. Northern inferiority on the high seas.
    b. Britain's un-neutral policy of allowing Confederate ships to be built in its naval yards.
    c. the British navy's ability to break the Union blockade of Southern ports.
    d. the superiority of Confederate ironclad ships over the Union's wooden vessels.

___ 13. Lincoln argued that his assertion of executive power and suspension of certain civil liberties was justified because

    a. it was necessary to set aside small provisions of the Constitution in order to save the Union.

    b. the South had committed even larger violations of the Constitution.

    c. during wartime a president has unlimited power over the civilian population.

    d. he had indicated that he would take such steps during his campaign for the presidency.

___ 14. Many of the new millionaires who emerged in the North during the Civil War

    a. committed their personal fortunes to the Union cause.

    b. made their fortunes by providing poorly made "shoddy" goods to the Union armies.

    c. made their highest profits by selling captured cotton to British textile manufacturers.

    d. earned public distrust by secretly advocating a negotiated settlement with the Confederacy.

___ 15. Women made particular advances during the Civil War by

    a. advocating the right to vote for both African-Americans and women.

    b. entering industrial employment and providing medical aid for soldiers on both sides.

    c. pushing for women to take up noncombatant roles in the military.

    d. upholding the feminine ideals of peace and reconciliation.

C. Identification

Supply the correct identification for each numbered description.

_____ 1. Four Border States where secession failed but slavery still survived

_____

_____

_____

_____ 2. The effective Northern effort to strangle the Southern economy and de-throne "King Cotton"

_____ 3. A ship from which two Confederate diplomats were removed, creating a major crisis between London and Washington

_____ 4. Vessel built in Britain that wreaked havoc on Northern shipping until it was finally sunk in 1864

_____ 5. Ironclad warships that were kept out of Confederate hands by Minister Adams's stern protests to the British government

_____ 6. Provision established by Congress in 1863, after volunteers ran out, that provoked violent protests in Northern cities

_____ 7. Slippery Northern men who collected fees for enlisting in the Union army and then deserted

_____ 8. Medical occupation that gained new status and employment opportunities because of women's Civil War service

_____ 9. Financial arrangement set up by the federal government to sell government bonds and stabilize the currency

10. Scornful term for Northern manufacturers who made quick fortunes out of selling cheaply made shoes and other inadequate goods to the U.S. Army

11. Civil liberty that was suspended by Lincoln in defiance of the Constitution and the Supreme Court's chief justice

12. Organization developed to provide medical supplies and assistance to Union armies in the field

D.   Matching People, Places, and Events

Match the person, place, or event in the left column with the proper description in the right column by inserting the correct letter on the blank line.

____ 1. Napoleon III

____ 2. Charles Francis Adams

____ 3. Canada

____ 4. Maximilian

____ 5. New York City

____ 6. Britain

____ 7. Abraham Lincoln

____ 8. Jefferson Davis

____ 9. Elizabeth Blackwell

____ 10. Clara Barton

A.   American envoy whose shrewd diplomacy helped keep Britain neutral during the Civil War

B.   An Old World aristocrat, manipulated as a puppet in Mexico, who was shot when his puppet-master deserted him

C.   An inexperienced leader in war but a genius at inspiring and directing his nation's cause

D.   Leader whose conflict with states' rights advocates and rigid personality harmed his ability to mobilize and direct his nation's war effort

E.   Nation whose upper classes hoped for a Confederate victory, while its working classes sympathized with the antislavery North

F.   Slippery French dictator who ignored the Monroe Doctrine by intervening in Mexican politics

G.   Site of cross-border raids and plots by Southern agents and anti-British Americans during the Civil War.

H.   Helped transform nursing into a respected profession during the Civil War

I.   Scene of the largest Northern antidraft riot in 1863

J.   First woman physician, organizer of the United States Sanitary Commission

E.   Putting Things in Order

Put the following events in correct order by numbering them from 1 to 5.

____ Enactment of military draft causes major riot in New York City.

____ Napoleon III's puppet emperor is removed from power in Mexico under threat of American intervention.

____ The firing on Fort Sumter unifies the North and leads to Lincoln's call for troops.

____ The *Alabama* escapes from a British port and begins wreaking havoc on Northern shipping.

____ Charles Francis Adams's successful diplomacy prevents the Confederacy from obtaining two Laird ram warships.

F. Matching Cause and Effect

Match the historical cause in the left column with the proper effect in the right column by writing the correct letter on the blank line.

Cause	Effect

Cause

____ 1. South Carolina's assault on Fort Sumter

____ 2. Lincoln's first call for troops to suppress the "rebellion"

____ 3. Lincoln's careful use of moral suasion, politics, and military force

____ 4. The large Northern human-resources advantage

____ 5. The North's naval blockade and industrial superiority

____ 6. The British aristocracy's sympathy with the South

____ 7. American minister C. F. Adams's diplomacy

____ 8. Grant's victory at Vicksburg

____ 9. The class-biased unfairness of the Civil War draft

____ 10. Lincoln's belief that the Civil War emergency required drastic action

Effect

A. Split the South in two and opened the way for Sherman's invasion of Georgia

B. Enabled Northern generals to wear down Southern armies, even at the cost of many lives

C. Unified the North and made it determined to preserve the Union by military force

D. Eventually gave the Union a crucial economic advantage over the mostly agricultural South

E. Deterred the British and French from recognizing and aiding the Confederacy

F. Caused four more Upper South states to secede and join the Confederacy

G. Kept the Border States in the Union

H. Led the British government toward actions that aided the Confederacy and angered the Union

I. Led to riots by underprivileged Northern whites, especially Irish-Americans

J. Led to temporary infringements on civil liberties and Congress's constitutional powers

G. Developing Historical Skills

Interpreting Tables

Tables convey a great deal of data, often numerical, in concise form. Properly interpreted, they can effectively aid historical understanding.

The following questions will help you interpret some of the tables in this chapter.

1. *Manufacturing by Sections, 1860* (p. 439).

   a. Compare the *number* of manufacturing establishments in the South and New England. Now compare the amount of invested capital, the number of laborers, and the product value of these same two sections. What do you conclude about the character of the manufacturing establishments in the South and New England?

   b. Approximately how many laborers were employed in the average Southern manufacturing establishment? About how many in the average New England establishment? How many in the average establishment in the middle states?

2. *Immigration to United States, 1860–1866* (p. 440)).

    a. From which country did immigration decline rather sharply at the end as well as at the beginning of the Civil War?

    b. From which country did immigration rise most sharply after the end of the Civil War?

    c. From which country did the coming of the Civil War evidently cause the sharpest decline in immigration?

    d. How was immigration affected by the first year of the Civil War? How was it affected by the second year of war? By the third? How long did it take for immigration from each country to return to its prewar level?

3. *Number of Men in Uniform at Date Given* (p. 446)).

    a. In what period did the absolute difference in military manpower between the two sides increase most dramatically?

    b. What was the approximate manpower ratio of Union to Confederate forces on each of the following dates: July 1861, March 1862, January 1863, January 1865?

    c. What happened to the military manpower ratio in the last two years of the war?

PART III: Applying What You Have Learned

1. How did the Civil War change from a limited war to preserve the Union into a "total war" to abolish slavery?

2. What political factors affected Lincoln's approach to the goals and conduct of the war? Why was he a more successful political leader than Jefferson Davis?

3. How did careful Union diplomacy manage the Civil War crisis with Britain and end British flirtations with the Confederacy?

4. How did the North and the South each handle their economic and human resources needs? Why were the economic consequences of the war so different for the two sides?

5. What changes did the Civil War bring about in civilian society, North and South? How did it particularly affect women?

6. Some historians have called the Civil War "the Second American Revolution." What was "revolutionary" about the political, social, and economic conduct of the war?

21

The Furnace of Civil War, 1861–1865

PART I: Reviewing the Chapter

A. Checklist of Learning Objectives

After mastering this chapter, you should be able to

1. describe the failure of the North to gain its expected early victory in 1861.
2. explain the significance of Antietam and the Northern turn to a "total war" against slavery.
3. describe the role that African-Americans played during the war.
4. describe the military significance of the battles of Gettysburg in the East and Vicksburg in the West.
5. describe the political struggle between Lincoln's "Union party" and the antiwar Copperheads.
6. describe the end of the war and list its final consequences.

B. Glossary

To build your social science vocabulary, familiarize yourself with the following terms.

1. **intelligence** In military affairs or diplomacy, specific information about an adversary's forces, deployments, production, and so on. "He consistently but erroneously believed that the enemy outnumbered him, partly because . . . his intelligence reports were unreliable." (p. 453)
2. **reconnaissance** Operations designed specifically to observe and ferret out pertinent information about an adversary. ". . . 'Jeb' Stuart's cavalry rode completely around his army on reconnaissance." (p. 454)
3. **proclamation** An official announcement or publicly declared order. "Thus, the Emancipation Proclamation was stronger on proclamation than emancipation." (p. 459)
4. **flank** The side of an army, where it is vulnerable to attack. "Lee . . . sent 'Stonewall' Jackson to attack the Union flank." (p. 462)
5. **court-martial** A military court or a trial held in such a court under military law. "Resigning from the army to avoid a court-martial for drunkenness, he failed at various business ventures. . . ." (p. 464)
6. **garrison** A military fortress, or the troops stationed at such a fortress, usually designed for defense or occupation of a territory. "Vicksburg at length surrendered . . . , with the garrison reduced to eating mules and rats." (p. 465)
7. **morale** The condition of courage, confidence, and willingness to endure hardship. "One of his major purposes was . . . to weaken the morale of the men at the front by waging war on their homes." (p. 467)
8. **pillaging** Plundering, looting, destroying property by violence. ". . . his army . . . engaged in an orgy of pillaging." (p. 467)
9. **tribunal** An agency or institution (sometimes but not necessarily a court) constituted to render judgments and assign punishment. "But he was convicted by a military tribunal in 1863 for treasonable utterances. . . ." (p. 469)

10. **running mate** In American politics, the candidate for the lesser of two offices when they are decided together—for example, the U.S. vice presidency. "Lincoln's running mate was ex-tailor Andrew Johnson. . . ." (p. 469)

PART II: Checking Your Progress

A. True-False

Where the statement is true, mark **T**. Where it is false, mark **F**, and correct it in the space immediately below.

_____ 1. The First Battle of Bull Run was the turning point of the Civil War because it convinced the South the war would be long and difficult.

_____ 2. The Emancipation Proclamation was more important for its political effects on the North and Europe than for actually freeing large numbers of slaves.

_____ 3. The Union's first military breakthroughs came on the eastern front in Maryland and Virginia.

_____ 4. The Battle of Antietam was a turning point of the war because it prevented British and French recognition of the Confederacy.

_____ 5. Lincoln's decision to make the war a fight against slavery was widely popular in the North.

_____ 6. The use of black soldiers in the Union Army proved militarily ineffective.

_____ 7. Lee's invasion of Pennsylvania in 1863 was intended to encourage the Northern peace movement and promote foreign intervention.

_____ 8. The Northern victories at Vicksburg and Gettysburg effectively spelled doom for the Confederacy.

_____ 9. In the final year of the conflict, Grant and Sherman waged a "total war" that was immensely destructive of Southern lives and property.

_____ 10. The Northern Democrats were deeply divided between those who backed the war and those who favored peace negotiations with the South.

_____ 11. The formation of a temporary "Union party" in 1864 was a device used by Lincoln to gain the support of prowar Democrats.

_____ 12. As a popular war leader, Lincoln received whole-hearted support within the Republican Party and in the nation as a whole.

_____ 13. The South's last hope was that the victory of a "Peace Democrat" in the election of 1864 would enable it to achieve its political goal of independence.

_____ 14. Most Southerners eventually came to see Lincoln's assassination as a tragedy for them.

Name_____ Section_____ Date_____

_____ 15. The Civil War failed to settle the central issues of slavery, states' rights, and secession that caused the war.

B. Multiple Choice

Select the best answer and write the proper letter in the space provided.

_____ 1. One effect of the first Battle of Bull Run was

    a. to convince the North that victory would not be difficult.
    b. to increase the South's already dangerous overconfidence.
    c. to demonstrate the superiority of Southern volunteer soldiers over Northern draftees.
    d. to cause a wave of new Southern enlistments in the army.

_____ 2. The primary weakness of General George McClellan as a military commander was

    a. his inability to gain the support of his troops.
    b. his tendency to rush into battle with inadequate plans and preparation.
    c. his lack of confidence in his own abilities.
    d. his excessive caution and reluctance to use his troops in battle.

_____ 3. After the unsuccessful Peninsula Campaign, Lincoln and the Union turned to

    a. a new strategy based on "total war" against the Confederacy.
    b. a new strategy based on an invasion through the mountains of western Virginia and Tennessee.
    c. a pattern of defensive warfare designed to protect Washington, D.C.
    d. a reliance on the navy rather than the army to win the war.

_____ 4. The Union blockade of Confederate ports was

    a. initially leaky but eventually effective.
    b. challenged by the powerful navies of Britain and France.
    c. immediately effective in capturing Confederate blockade-running ships.
    d. largely ineffective in shutting off the sale of Confederate cotton in Europe.

_____ 5. Antietam was one of the crucial battles of the Civil War because

    a. it ended any possibility of Confederate invasion of the North.
    b. it was the last chance for the Confederates to win a major battle.
    c. it fundamentally undermined Confederate morale.
    d. it prevented British and French recognition of the Confederacy.

_____ 6. Officially, the Emancipation Proclamation freed only

    a. slaves who had fled their masters and joined the Union Army.
    b. slaves under control of the rebellious Confederate states.
    c. slaves in the Border States and in areas under Union Army control.
    d. slaves in Washington, D.C.

7. The political effects of the Emancipation Proclamation were

   a. to bolster public support for the war and the Republican party.
   b. to strengthen the North's moral cause but weaken the Lincoln administration in the Border States and parts of the North.
   c. to turn the Democratic party from support of the war toward favoring recognition of the Confederacy.
   d. to weaken support for the Union among British and French public opinion.

8. The thousands of black soldiers in the Union Army

   a. added a powerful new weapon to the antislavery dimension of the Union cause.
   b. were prevented from participating in combat.
   c. seldom fought effectively in battle.
   d. saw action in the very first days of the war.

9. Lee's goals in invading the North in the summer of 1863 were

   a. to capture major Northern cities like Philadelphia and Pittsburgh.
   b. to deflect attention from "Stonewall" Jackson's movements against Washington.
   c. to strengthen the Northern peace movement and encourage foreign intervention in the war.
   d. to cut off Northern supply lines and damage the Union's economic foundations.

10. Grant's capture of Vicksburg was especially important because

    a. it quelled Northern peace agitation and cut off the Confederate trade route across the Mississippi.
    b. it ended the threat of a Confederate invasion of southern Illinois and Indiana.
    c. it blocked the French army in Mexico from moving to aid the Confederacy.
    d. it destroyed Southern naval power.

11. The "Copperheads" were

    a. Northern Democrats who opposed the Union war effort.
    b. Republicans who opposed the Lincoln administration.
    c. Democrats who backed the Union but opposed a war against slavery.
    d. radical Republicans who advocated a war to destroy slavery and punish the South.

12. Andrew Johnson, Lincoln's vice presidential running mate in 1864, was

    a. a Copperhead.
    b. a War Democrat.
    c. a conservative Republican.
    d. a radical Republican.

13. Lincoln's election victory in 1864 was sealed by Union military successes at

    a. Gettysburg, Antietam, and Vicksburg.
    b. The Wilderness, Lookout Mountain, and Appomattox.
    c. Bull Run, the Peninsula, and Fredericksburg.
    d. Mobile, Atlanta, and the Shenandoah Valley.

___ 14. Sherman's march "from Atlanta to the sea" was especially notable for

    a. its tactical brilliance against Confederate cavalry forces.

    b. its effective use of public relations to turn Southern sympathies against the Confederacy.

    c. its brutal use of "total war" tactics of destruction and pillaging against Southern civilian populations.

    d. its impact in inspiring Northern public opinion to turn against slavery.

___ 15. As the Democratic party nominee in 1864, General George McClellan

    a. denounced Lincoln as a traitor and called for an immediate end to the war.

    b. repudiated the Copperhead platform that called for a negotiated settlement with the Confederacy.

    c. indicated that if elected president he would take personal command of all Union armies.

    d. called for waging a "total war" against the civilian population to the South.

C. Identification

Supply the correct identification for each numbered description.

_____ 1. First major battle of the Civil War, in which untrained Northern troops and civilian picnickers fled back to Washington

_____ 2. McClellan's disastrously unsuccessful attempt to end the war quickly by a back-door conquest of Richmond

_____ 3. Key battle of 1862 that forestalled European intervention to aid the Confederacy and led to the Emancipation Proclamation

_____ 4. Document that proclaimed a war against slavery and guaranteed a fight to the finish

_____ 5. General U.S. Grant's nickname, taken from his military demand to the enemy at Fort Donelson and elsewhere

_____ 6. Crucial Confederate fortress on the Mississippi whose fall to Grant in 1863 cut the South in two

_____ 7. Pennsylvania battle that ended Lee's last hopes of achieving victory through an invasion of the North

_____ 8. Mississippi site where black soldiers were massacred after their surrender

_____ 9. Northern Democrats who opposed the Civil War and sympathized with the South

_____ 10. Edward Everett Hale's story of treason and banishment, inspired by the wartime banishing of Copperhead Clement Vallandigham

_____ 11. Georgia city captured and burned by Sherman just before the election of 1864

_____ 12. The temporary 1864 coalition of Republicans and War Democrats that backed Lincoln's re-election

_____ 13. Washington site where Lincoln was assassinated by Booth on April 14, 1865

_____ 14. Virginia site where Lee surrendered to Grant in April 1865

_____ 15. Romantic name given to the Southern fight for independence, indicating nobility despite defeat

D. Matching People, Places, and Events

Match the person, place, or event in the left column with the proper description in the right column by inserting the correct letter on the blank line.

____ 1. Bull Run

____ 2. George McClellan

____ 3. Robert E. Lee

____ 4. Antietam

____ 5. "Stonewall" Jackson

____ 6. George Pickett

____ 7. Ulysses S. Grant

____ 8. Gettysburg

____ 9. Vicksburg

____ 10. William T. Sherman

____ 11. Clement Vallandigham

____ 12. Salmon P. Chase

____ 13. The Wilderness

____ 14. Andrew Johnson

____ 15. John Wilkes Booth

A. Daring Southern commander killed at the Battle of Chancellorsville

B. Southern officer whose failed charge at Gettysburg marked "the high water mark of the Confederacy"

C. Ruthless Northern general who waged a march through Georgia

D. Fortress whose capture split the Confederacy in two

E. Site where Lee's last major invasion of the North was turned back

F. Gentlemanly top commander of the Confederate army

G. Site of one of Grant's bloody battles with the Confederates near Richmond in 1864

H. Crucial battle in Maryland that staved off European recognition of the Confederacy

I. Ambitious secretary of the treasury who wanted to replace Lincoln as president in 1864

J. Fanatical actor whose act of violence actually harmed the South

K. Union commander who first made his mark with victories in the West.

L. Southern War Democrat who ran as Lincoln's "Union party" vice-presidential candidate in 1864

M. Notorious Copperhead, convicted of treason, who ran for governor of Ohio while exiled to Canada.

N. Union general who repudiated his party's Copperhead platform and polled 45 percent of the popular vote in 1864

O. Site of Union defeat in very early battle of the war

E. Putting Things in Order

Put the following events in correct order by numbering them from 1 to 5.

____ Within one week, two decisive battles in Mississippi and Pennsylvania almost ensure the Confederacy's eventual defeat.

____ Defeat in a battle near Washington, D.C., ends Union military complacency.

____ A militarily indecisive battle in Maryland enables Lincoln to declare that the Civil War has become a war on slavery.

____ The Civil War ends with the defeated army granted generous terms of surrender.

____ In both Georgia and Virginia, determined Northern generals wage bloody and destructive "total war" against a weakened but still-resisting South.

F. Matching Cause and Effect

Match the historical cause in the left column with the proper effect in the right column by writing the correct letter on the blank line.

Cause

____ 1. Political dissent by Copperheads and jealous Republicans

____ 2. A series of Union military victories in late 1864

____ 3. The assassination of Lincoln

____ 4. Grant's Tennessee and Mississippi River campaigns

____ 5. The Battle of Bull Run

____ 6. The Battle of Antietam

____ 7. The Battle of Gettysburg

____ 8. Grant's final brutal campaign in Virginia

____ 9. The Emancipation Proclamation

____ 10. The growing Union manpower shortage in 1863

Effect

A. Enabled Lincoln to issue the Emancipation Proclamation and blocked British and French intervention

B. Split the South in two and opened the way for Sherman's invasion of Georgia

C. Deprived the nation of experienced leadership during Reconstruction

D. Made it difficult for Lincoln to prosecute the war effectively

E. Helped lead to the enlistment of black fighting men in the Union Army

F. Ended the South's effort to win the war by aggressive invasion

G. Guaranteed that the South would fight to the end to try to save slavery.

H. Forced Lee to surrender at Appomattox

I. Led some Southerners to believe they would win an easy victory

J. Ensured Lincoln's reelection and ended the South's last hope of achieving independence by political means

G. Developing Historical Skills

Interpreting Painting

Paintings may depict historical subjects and in the process convey information about an artist's interpretation of an event, a problem, or a whole society. Answer these questions about the Winslow Homer painting *Prisoners from the Front*. (p. 474)

____ 1. Study the clothing carefully. Who is in what kind of uniform, and who is not? What is the artist suggesting about the economic and military condition of the two sides? What is suggested about the condition of civilians in the two sections?

____ 2. Describe the posture and facial expressions of the five main figures. What kind of attitude does each suggest?

___ 3. Look at the weapons in the painting, and at the distance between the Northern officer and the Confederates. What does Homer seem to be suggesting about the relations between the sections after the war?

H. Map Mastery

Map Discrimination

Using the maps and charts in Chapter 21, answer the following questions.

1. *Main Thrusts, 1861–1865*: Which two states of the Southeast saw little of the major fighting of the Civil War?

2. *Emancipation in the South:* In which four states were the slaves *all* freed by state action—without any federal involvement?

3. *Emancipation in the South*: Which two states kept slavery until it was finally abolished by the Thirteenth Amendment to the Constitution?

4. *The Mississippi River and Tennessee, 1862–1863*: On what three rivers were the major Confederate strategic points that Grant successfully assaulted in 1862–1863?

5. *Sherman's March, 1864–1865:* What major secessionist South Carolina city was *not* in the direct path of Sherman's army in 1864–1865?

6. *Grant's Virginia Campaign, 1864–1865:* What major battle of Grant's final campaign was fought very close to the Confederate capital city?

Map Challenge

Using the maps in this chapter, write a brief essay explaining Union military strategy in the Civil War.

Part III: Applying What You Have Learned

1. How did the military stalemate of 1861–1862 affect both sides in the Civil War?
2. What were the primary military strategies of each side, and how did each side attempt to carry them out?
3. Why was Lincoln so slow to declare the Civil War as a fight against slavery? Was he wise to move slowly, or could an early Emancipation Proclamation have undermined the Union cause?
4. What role did African-Americans, both slave and free, play in the Civil War?
5. What were the key military and political turning points of the war? Why did the South hold onto hopes of winning its goals as late as 1864 and even early 1865?
6. Were the costs of the Civil War worth the results to the nation as a whole? What issues were settled by the war, and what new problems were created?

22

The Ordeal of Reconstruction,
1865–1877

PART I: Reviewing the Chapter

A. Checklist of Learning Objectives

After mastering this chapter, you should be able to

1. define the major problems facing the South and the nation after the Civil War.
2. describe the responses of both whites and African-Americans to the end of slavery.
3. analyze the differences between the presidential and congressional approaches to Reconstruction.
4. explain how the blunders of President Johnson and the white South opened the door to more radical congressional Reconstruction policies.
5. describe the actual effects of congressional Reconstruction in the South.
6. indicate how militant white opposition gradually undermined the Republican attempt to empower Southern blacks.
7. explain why the radical Republicans impeached Johnson but failed to convict him.
8. explain the legacy of Reconstruction, and assess its successes and failures.

B. Glossary

To build your social science vocabulary, familiarize yourself with the following terms.

1. **treason** The crime of betrayal of one's country, involving some overt act violating an oath of allegiance or providing illegal aid to a foreign state. In the United States, treason is the only crime specified in the Constitution. "What should be done with the captured Confederate ringleaders, all of whom were liable to charges of treason?" (p. 477)
2. **civil disabilities** Legally imposed restrictions of a person's civil rights or liberties. "But Congress did not remove all remaining civil disabilities until thirty years later. . . ." (p. 478)
3. **legalistically** In accord with the exact letter of the law, sometimes with the intention of thwarting its broad intent. "Some planters resisted emancipation more legalistically. . . ." (p. 479)
4. **mutual aid societies** Nonprofit organizations designed to provide their members with financial and social benefits, often including medical aid, life insurance, funeral costs, and disaster relief. "These churches . . . gave rise to other benevolent, fraternal, and mutual aid societies." (p. 480)
5. **confiscation (confiscated)** Legal government seizure of private property without compensation. ". . . the bureau was authorized to settle former slaves on forty-acre tracts confiscated from the Confederates. . . ." (p. 481)
6. **pocket veto** The presidential act of blocking a Congressionally passed law not by direct veto but by simply refusing to sign it at the end of a session. (A president can pocket-veto a bill within ten days of a session's end or after.) "Lincoln 'pocket-vetoed' this bill by refusing to sign it after Congress had adjourned." (p. 483)
7. **lease** To enter into a contract by which one party gives another use of land, buildings, or other property for a fixed time and fee. ". . . some [codes] even barred blacks from renting or leasing land." (p. 484)

8. **chain gang** A group of prisoners chained together while engaged in forced labor. "A black could be punished for 'idleness' by being sentenced to work on a chain gang." (p. 484)

9. **sharecrop** An agricultural system in which a tenant receives land, tools, and seed on credit and pledges in return a share of the crop to the creditor. ". . . former slaves slipped into the status of sharecropper farmers. . . ." (p. 484)

10. **peonage** A system in which debtors are held in servitude, to labor for their creditors. "Luckless sharecroppers gradually sank into a morass of virtual peonage. . . ." (p. 484)

11. **scalawag** A white Southerner who supported Republican Reconstruction after the Civil War. "The so-called scalawags were Southerners, often former Unionists and Whigs." (p. 492)

12. **carpetbagger** A Northern politician who came south to exploit the unsettled conditions after the Civil War; hence, any politician who relocates for political advantage. "The carpet-baggers, on the other hand, were supposedly sleazy Northerners. . . ." (p. 492)

13. **felony** A major crime for which severe penalties are exacted under the law. "The crimes of the Reconstruction governments were no more outrageous than the scams and felonies being perpetrated in the North at the same time. . . ." (p. 493)

14. **terror (terrorist)** Using violence or the threat of violence in order to create intense fear in the attempt to promote some political policy or objectives. "Such tomfoolery and terror proved partially effective." (p. 493)

15. **president pro tempore** In the United States Senate, the officer who presides in the absence of the vice president. "Under existing law, the president pro tempore of the Senate . . . would then become president." (p. 495)

PART II: Checking Your Progress

A. True-False

Where the statement is true, mark **T**. Where it is false, mark **F**, and correct it in the space immediately below.

____ 1. The South was economically devastated by the Civil War.

____ 2. Military defeat in the Civil War brought white Southerners to accept the reality of Northern political domination.

____ 3. The newly freed slaves often used their liberty to travel or seek lost loved ones.

____ 4. The focus of black community life after emancipation became the black church.

____ 5. Lincoln's "10 percent" Reconstruction plan was designed to return the Southern states to the Union quickly and with few restrictions.

____ 6. Southerners at first feared Andrew Johnson because he had been one of the few elite planters who backed Lincoln.

____ 7. The cause of black education was greatly advanced by white Northern female teachers who came South after the Civil War.

____ 8. The enactment of the Black Codes in the south strengthened those who supported a moderate approach to Reconstruction.

____ 9. Congressional Republicans demanded that the Southern states ratify the Fourteenth Amendment in order to be readmitted to the Union.

_____ 10. Radical Republicans succeeded in their goal of redistributing land to the former slaves.

_____ 11. During Reconstruction, blacks controlled most of the Southern state legislatures.

_____ 12. The Republican Reconstruction legislature enacted educational and other reforms in Southern state government.

_____ 13. The Ku Klux Klan largely failed in its goal of intimidating blacks and preventing them from voting.

_____ 14. Johnson's impeachment was essentially an act of political vindictiveness by radical Republicans.

_____ 15. The moderate Republican plan for Reconstruction might have succeeded if the Ku Klux Klan had been suppressed.

B. Multiple Choice

Select the best answer and write the proper letter in the space provided.

_____ 1. After emancipation, many blacks traveled in order to

    a. return to Africa or the West Indies.
    b. seek a better life in Northern cities.
    c. find lost family members or seek new economic opportunities.
    d. track down and punish cruel overseers.

_____ 2. The Freedmen's Bureau was originally established to provide

    a. land and supplies for black farmers.
    b. labor registration.
    c. food, clothes, and education for emancipated slaves.
    d. political training in citizenship for black voters.

_____ 3. Lincoln's original plan for Reconstruction in 1863 was that a state could be re-integrated into the Union when

    a. it repealed its original secession act and took its soldiers out of the Confederate Army.
    b. 10 percent of its voters took an oath of allegiance to the Union and pledged to abide by emancipation.
    c. it formally adopted a plan guaranteeing black political and economic rights.
    d. it ratified the Fourteenth and Fifteenth Amendments to the Constitution.

_____ 4. The Black Codes passed by many of the Southern state governments in 1865 aimed to

    a. provide economic assistance to get former slaves started as sharecroppers.
    b. ensure a stable and subservient labor force under white control.
    c. permit blacks to vote if they met certain educational or economic standards.
    d. gradually force blacks to leave the South.

5. The congressional elections of 1866 resulted in

   a. a victory for Johnson and his pro-Southern Reconstruction plan.
   b. a further political stalemate between the Republicans in Congress and Johnson.
   c. a decisive defeat for Johnson and a veto-proof Republican Congress.
   d. a gain for Northern Democrats and their moderate compromise plan for Reconstruction.

6. In contrast to radical Republicans, moderate Republicans generally

   a. favored states' rights and opposed direct federal involvement in individuals' lives.
   b. favored the use of federal power to alter the Southern economic system.
   c. favored emancipation but opposed the Fourteenth Amendment.
   d. favored returning the Southern states to the Union without significant Reconstruction.

7. Besides putting the South under the rule of federal soldiers, the Military Reconstruction Act of 1867 required that

   a. Southern states give blacks the vote as a condition of readmittance to the Union.
   b. blacks and carpetbaggers be given control of Southern legislatures.
   c. former slaves be given land and education at federal expense.
   d. former Confederate officials and military officers be tried for treason.

8. The Fourteenth amendment provided for

   a. an end to slavery.
   b. permanent disfranchisement of all Confederate officials.
   c. full citizenship and civil rights for former slaves.
   d. voting rights for women.

9. The Fifteenth Amendment provided for

   a. readmitting Southern states to the Union.
   b. full citizenship and civil rights for former slaves.
   c. voting rights for former slaves.
   d. voting rights for women.

10. Women's-rights leaders opposed the Fourteenth and Fifteenth Amendments because

   a. they objected to racial integration in the women's movement.
   b. the amendments granted citizenship and voting rights to black and white men but not to women.
   c. they favored passage of the Equal Rights Amendment first.
   d. most of them were Democrats who would be hurt by the amendments.

11. The right to vote encouraged southern black men to

   a. form a third political party as an alternative to the Democrats and Republicans.
   b. seek an apology and reparations for slavery.
   c. organize the Union League as a vehicle for political empowerment and self-defense.
   d. organize large-scale migrations out of the South to the West.

12. The radical Reconstruction regimes in the Southern states

   a. took away white Southerners' civil rights and voting rights.
   b. consisted almost entirely of blacks.
   c. included white Northerners, white Southerners, and blacks.
   d. eliminated the public education systems in most Southern states.

____ 13. Most of the Northern "carpetbaggers" were actually

    a. former Union soldiers, businessmen, or professionals.
    b. undercover agents of the federal government.
    c. former Southern Whigs and Unionists who had opposed the Confederacy.
    d. Northern teachers and missionaries who wanted to aid the freedmen.

____ 14. The radical Republicans' impeachment of President Andrew Johnson resulted in

    a. Johnson's acceptance of the radicals' Reconstruction plan.
    b. a failure to convict and remove Johnson by a margin of only one vote.
    c. Johnson's conviction on the charge of violating the Tenure of Office Act.
    d. Johnson's resignation and appointment of Ulysses Grant as his successor.

____ 15. The skeptical public finally accepted Seward's purchase of Alaska because

    a. there were rumors of extensive oil deposits in the territory.
    b. it was considered strategically vital to American defense.
    c. it would provide a new frontier safety valve after the settling of the West.
    d. Russia had been the only great power friendly to the Union during the Civil War.

C. Identification

Supply the correct identification for each numbered description.

_____ 1. Common term for the blacks newly liberated from slavery

_____ 2. Federal agency that greatly assisted blacks educationally but failed in other aid efforts

_____ 3. The largest African-American denomination (church) after slavery

_____ 4. Lincoln's 1863 program for a rapid Reconstruction of the South

_____ 5. The constitutional amendment freeing all slaves

_____ 6. The harsh Southern state laws of 1865 that limited black rights and imposed restrictions to ensure a stable black labor supply

_____ 7. The constitutional amendment granting civil rights to freed slaves and barring former Confederates from office

_____ 8. Republican Reconstructionists who favored a more rapid restoration of Southern state governments and opposed radical plans for drastic economic transformation of the South

_____ 9. Republican Reconstructionists who favored keeping the South out of the federal government until a complete social and economic revolution was accomplished in the region

_____ 10. The black political organization that promoted self-help and defense of political rights

_____ 11. Supreme Court ruling that military tribunals could not try civilians when the civil courts were open

_____ 12. Derogatory term for white Southerners who cooperated with the Republican Reconstruction governments

13. Derogatory term for Northerners who came to the South during Reconstruction and sometimes took part in Republican state governments

14. Constitutional amendment guaranteeing blacks the right to vote

15. "Seward's Folly," acquired in 1867 from Russia

D. Matching People, Places, and Events

Match the person, place, or event in the left column with the proper description in the right column by inserting the correct letter on the blank line.

_____ 1. Exodusters

_____ 2. Oliver O. Howard

_____ 3. Andrew Johnson

_____ 4. Abraham Lincoln

_____ 5. Civil Rights Bill of 1866

_____ 6. Charles Sumner

_____ 7. Thaddeus Stevens

_____ 8. Military Reconstruction Act of 1867

_____ 9. Hiram Revels

_____ 10. Ku Klux Klan

_____ 11. Force Acts of 1870 and 1871

_____ 12. Tenure of Office Act

_____ 13. Union League

_____ 14. Benjamin Wade

_____ 15. William Seward

A. A constitutionally questionable law whose violation by President Johnson formed the basis for his impeachment

B. The first congressional attempt to guarantee black rights in the South, passed over Johnson's veto

C. Born a poor white southerner, he became the white South's champion against radical Reconstruction

D. Secretary of state who arranged an initially unpopular but valuable land deal in 1867

E. Laws designed to stamp out Ku Klux Klan terrorism in the South

F. Black Republican senator from Mississippi during Reconstruction

G. Secret organization that intimidated blacks and worked to restore white supremacy

H. Blacks who left the South for Kansas and elsewhere during Reconstruction

I. Congressional law that imposed military rule on the South and demanded harsh conditions for readmission of the seceded states

J. Beaten in the Senate chamber before the Civil War, he became the leader of Senate Republican radicals during Reconstruction

K. Problack general who led an agency that tried to assist the freedmen

L. Leading Black political organization during Reconstruction

M. Author of the moderate "10 percent" Reconstruction plan that ran into congressional opposition

N. The president pro tempore of the Senate who hoped to become president of the United States after Johnson's impeachment conviction.

O. Leader of radical Republicans in the House of Representatives

E.   Putting Things in Order

Put the following events in correct order by numbering them from 1 to 5.

_____   Constitution is amended to guarantee former slaves the right to vote.

_____   Lincoln announces a plan to rapidly restore southern states to the Union.

_____   Northern troops are finally withdrawn from the South, and Southern state governments are reconstituted without federal constraint.

_____   An unpopular antiradical president escapes conviction and removal from office by one vote.

_____   Johnson's attempt to restore the South to the Union is overturned because of congressional hostility to ex-Confederates and southern passage of the Black Codes.

F.   Matching Cause and Effect

Match the historical cause in the left column with the proper effect in the right column by writing the correct letter on the blank line.

Cause	Effect
_____ 1. The South's military defeat in the Civil War	**A.** Provoked a politically motivated trial to remove the president from office
_____ 2. The Freedmen's Bureau	**B.** Intimidated black voters and tried to keep blacks "in their place"
_____ 3. The Black Codes of 1865	**C.** Prompted Republicans to refuse to seat Southern delegations in Congress
_____ 4. The election of ex-Confederates to Congress in 1865	**D.** Destroyed the southern economy but strengthened Southern hatred of "yankees"
_____ 5. Johnson's "swing around the circle" in the election of 1866	**E.** Successfully educated former slaves but failed to provide much other assistance to them
_____ 6. Military Reconstruction and the Fourteenth and Fifteenth Amendments	**F.** Forced all the Southern states to establish governments that upheld black voting and other civil rights
_____ 7. The "radical" Southern state Reconstruction governments	**G.** Embittered white Southerners while doing little to really help blacks
_____ 8. The Ku Klux Klan	**H.** Engaged in some corruption but also enacted many valuable social reforms
_____ 9. The radical Republicans' hatred of Johnson	**I.** Weakened support for mild Reconstruction policies and helped elect overwhelming Republican majorities to Congress
_____ 10. The whole Reconstruction era	**J.** Imposed slaverylike restrictions on blacks and angered the North

G. Developing Historical Skills

Interpreting Photographs and Drawings

Answer the following questions about the photographs and drawings in this chapter.

1. *The Faculty of a Freedmen's Bureau School near Norfolk, Virginia* (p. 481)

   What is the ratio of black to white teachers on the freedmen's school staff? Who appears to be the principal of the school? Where are the black teachers positioned in the photograph? Might this suggest anything about the relations between white and black teachers in the school?

2. *A Family of Sharecroppers at the End of the Civil War* (photograph, p. 485)

   What physical details suggest the poverty of these former slaves? How would you characterize the attitudes of the people in the photograph?

3. *Freedmen Voting, Richmond, Virginia, 1871* (drawing, p. 482)

   What appears to be the economic status of the new black voters portrayed here? How does their condition differ from that of the voting officials, black and white? What does the drawing suggest about the power of the newly enfranchised freedmen?

Part III: Applying What You Have Learned

1. What were the major problems facing the South and the nation after the Civil War? How did Reconstruction address them, or fail to do so?

2. How did freed blacks react to the end of slavery? How did both Southern and Northern whites react?

3. How did the white South's intransigence and President Johnson's political bungling open the way for the congressional Republican program of military Reconstruction?

4. What was the purpose of congressional Reconstruction, and what were its actual effects in the South?

5. What did the attempt at black political empowerment achieve? Why did it finally fail? Could it have succeeded with a stronger Northern political will behind it?

6. Why did Reconstruction apparently fail so badly? Was the failure primarily one of immediate political circumstances, or was it more deeply rooted in the history of American sectional and race relations?

23

Politics in the Gilded Age,
1869–1896

PART I: Reviewing the Chapter

A. Checklist of Learning Objectives

After mastering this chapter, you should be able to

1. describe the political corruption of the Grant administration and the various efforts to clean up politics in the Gilded Age.
2. describe the economic slump of the 1870s and the growing conflict between "hard-money" and "soft-money" advocates.
3. explain the intense political activity of the Gilded age, despite the low quality of political leadership and the agreement of the two parties on most issues.
4. indicate how the disputed Hayes-Tilden election of 1876 led to the Compromise of 1877 and the end of Reconstruction.
5. describe how the end of Reconstruction led to the loss of black rights and the imposition of the Jim Crow system of segregation in the South.
6. explain the growth of class and ethnic conflict during the 1870s and after.
7. describe the sharp personal and partisan clashes between Grover Cleveland and his Republican opponents.
8. show how the rise of the Populists and the depression of the 1890s stirred growing social protests and class conflict.

B. Glossary

To build your social science vocabulary, familiarize yourself with the following terms.

1. **coalition** A temporary alliance of political factions or parties for some specific purpose. "The Republicans, now freed from the Union party coalition of war days, enthusiastically nominated Grant. . . ." (p. 503)
2. **corner** To gain exclusive control of a commodity in order to fix its price. "The crafty pair concocted a plot in 1869 to corner the gold market." (p. 503)
3. **censure** An official statement of condemnation passed by a legislative body against one of its members or some other official of government. While severe, a censure itself stops short of penalties or **expulsion**, which is removal from office. "A newspaper exposé and congressional investigation led to formal censure of two congressmen. . . ." (p. 504)
4. **amnesty** A general pardon for offenses or crimes against a government. "The Republican Congress in 1872 passed a general amnesty act. . . ." (p. 506)
5. **civil service** Referring to regular employment by government according to a standardized system of job descriptions, merit qualifications, pay, and promotion, as distinct from **political appointees** who receive positions based on affiliation and party loyalty. "Congress also moved to reduce high Civil War tariffs and to fumigate the Grant administration with mild civil service reform." (p. 506)

6. **unsecured loans** Money loaned without identification of collateral (existing assets) to be forfeited in case the borrower defaults on the loan. "The Freedman's Savings and Trust Company had made unsecured loans to several companies that went under." (p. 506)

7. **contraction** In finance, reducing the available supply of money, thus tending to raise interest rates and lower prices. "Coupled with the reduction of greenbacks, this policy was called 'contraction.'" (p. 507)

8. **deflation (ary)** An increase in the value of money in relation to available goods, causing prices to fall. **Inflation**, a decrease in the value of money in relation to goods, causes prices to rise. "It had a noticeable deflationary effect—the amount of money per capita in circulation actually *decreased* . . . ." (p. 507)

9. **fraternal organization** A society of men drawn together for social purposes and sometimes to pursue other common goals. ". . . the Grand Army of the Republic [was] a politically potent fraternal organization of several hundred thousand Union veterans of the Civil War." (p. 507)

10. **consensus** Common or unanimous opinion. "How can this apparent paradox of political consensus and partisan fervor be explained?" (p. 507)

11. **kickback** The return of a portion of the money received in a sale or contract, often secretly or illegally, in exchange for favors. "The lifeblood of both parties was patronage—disbursing jobs by the bucketful in return for votes, kickbacks, and party service." (p. 507)

12. **lien** A legal claim by a lender or another party on a borrower's property as a guarantee against repayment, and prohibiting any sale of the property. ". . . storekeepers extended credit to small farmers for food and supplies and in return took a lien on their harvest." (p. 510)

13. **assassination** Politically motivated murder of a public figure. ". . . he asked all those who had benefited politically by the assassination to contribute to his defense fund." (p. 514)

14. **laissez-faire** The doctrine of noninterference, especially by the government, in matters of economics or business (literally, "leave alone"). "[The new president was] a staunch apostle of the hands-off creed of laissez-faire. . . ." (p. 518)

15. **pork barrel** In American politics, government appropriations for political purposes, especially projects designed to please a legislator's local constituency. "One [way to reduce the surplus] was to squander it on pensions and 'pork-barrel' bills. . . ." (p. 519)

PART II: Checking Your Progress

A. True-False

Where the statement is true, mark **T**. Where it is false, mark **F**, and correct it in the space immediately below.

F 1. Ulysses Grant's status as a military hero enabled him to become a successful president who stood above partisan politics.

T 2. The scandals of the Grant administration included bribes and corrupt dealings reaching to the cabinet and the vice president of the United States.

F 3. The Liberal Republican movement's political skilled enabled it to clean up the corruption of the Grant administration.

T 4. The severe economic downturn of the 1870s caused business failures, labor conflict, and battles over currency.

F 5. The close, fiercely contested elections of the Gilded Age reflected the deep divisions between Republicans and Democrats over national issues.

T   6. The battles between the "Stalwart" and "Half-Breed" Republican factions were mainly over who would get patronage and spoils.

F   7. The disputed Hayes-Tilden election was settled by a political deal in which Democrats got the presidency and Republicans got economic and political concessions.

T   8. The Compromise of 1877 purchased political peace between North and South by sacrificing southern blacks and removing federal troops in the South.

T   9. The sharecropping and tenant farming systems forced many Southern blacks into permanent economic debt and dependency.

T   10. Western hostility to Chinese immigrants arose in part because the Chinese provided a source of cheap labor that competed with white workers.

T   11. By reducing politicians' use of patronage, the new civil-service system inadvertently made them more dependent on big campaign contributors.

F   12. The Cleveland-Blaine campaign of 1884 was conducted primarily as a debate about the issues of taxes and the tariff.

T   13. The Republican party in the post–Civil War era relied heavily on the political support of veterans' groups, to which it gave substantial pension benefits in return.

T   14. The Populist party's attempt to form a coalition of farmers and workers failed partly because of the racial division between poor whites and blacks in the South.

F   15. Cleveland effectively addressed the depression of the 1890s by compromising with pro-silver money advocates.

B. Multiple Choice

Select the best answer and write the proper letter in the space provided.

B   1. Financiers Jim Fisk and Jay Gould tried to involve the Grant administration in a corrupt scheme to

    a. skim funds from the Bureau of Indian Affairs.
    b. sell "watered" railroad stock at high prices.
    c. corner the gold market.
    d. bribe congressmen in exchange for federal land grants.

C   2. Boss Tweed's widespread corruption was finally brought to a halt by

    a. federal prosecutors who uncovered the theft.
    b. outraged citizens who rebelled against the waste of public money.
    c. the journalistic exposés of *The New York Times* and cartoonist Thomas Nast.
    d. Tweed's political opponents in New York City.

B

3. The Credit Mobilier scandal involved

    a. the abuse of federal credit intended for urban development.
    b. railroad corporation fraud and the subsequent bribery of congressmen.
    c. Secretary of War Belknap's fraudulent sale of contracts to supply Indian reservations.
    d. the attempt of insiders to gain control of New York's gold and stock markets.

B

4. Grant's greatest failing in the scandals that plagued his administration was

    a. his refusal to turn over evidence to congressional investigators.
    b. his toleration of corruption and his loyalty to crooked friends.
    c. his acceptance of behind-the-scenes payments for performing his duties as president.
    d. his use of large amounts of "dirty" money in his political campaigns.

C

5. The depression of the 1870s led to increasing demands for

    a. inflation of the money supply by issuing more paper or silver currency.
    b. federal programs to create jobs for the unemployed.
    c. restoration of sound money by backing all paper currency with gold.
    d. stronger regulation of the banking system.

D

6. The political system of the "Gilded Age" was generally characterized by

    a. "split-ticket" voting, low voter turnout, and single-issue special-interest groups.
    b. strong party loyalties, low voter turnout, and deep ideological differences.
    c. "third-party" movements, high voter turnout and strong disagreement on foreign-policy issues.
    d. strong party loyalties, high voter turnout, and few disagreements on national issues.

B

7. The primary goal for which all factions in both political parties contended during the Gilded Age was

    a. racial justice.
    b. a sound financial and banking system.
    c. patronage.
    d. a more assertive American foreign policy.

A

8. The key tradeoff featured in the Compromise of 1877,

    a. Republicans got the presidency in exchange for the final removal of federal troops from the South.
    b. Democrats got the presidency in exchange for federal guarantees of black civil rights.
    c. Republicans got the presidency in exchange for Democratic control of the cabinet.
    d. Democrats got the presidency in exchange for increased immigration quotas from Ireland.

A

9. Which of the following was *not* among the changes that affected African-Americans in the South after federal troops were withdrawn in the Compromise of 1877?

    a. the forced relocation of black farmers to the Kansas and Oklahoma "dust bowl."
    b. the imposition of literacy requirements and poll taxes to prevent black voting.
    c. the development of the tenant farming and share-cropping systems.
    d. the introduction of legal systems of racial segregation.

B   10. The Supreme Court's ruling in *Plessy* v. *Ferguson* upholding "separate but equal" public facilities in effect legalized

    a. southern blacks' loss of voting rights.

    b. the system of unequal segregation between the races.

    c. the program of separate black and white economic development endorsed by Booker T. Washington.

    d. the rights to "equal protection of the law" guaranteed by the Fourteenth Amendment.

D   11. The great railroad strike of 1877 revealed

    a. the growing strength of American labor unions.

    b. the refusal of the U.S. federal government to intervene in private labor disputes.

    c. the ability of American workers to cooperate across ethnic and racial lines.

    d. the growing threat of class warfare in response to the economic depression of the mid-1870s.

B   12. The final result of the widespread anti-Chinese agitation in the West was

    a. a program to encourage Chinese students to enroll in American colleges and universities.

    b. a Congressional law to prohibit any further Chinese immigration.

    c. the stripping of citizenship even from native-born Chinese-Americans.

    d. legal segregation of all Chinese into "Chinatown" districts in San Francisco and elsewhere.

B   13. President James Garfield was assassinated by

    a. a fanatically anti-Republican Confederate veteran.

    b. a mentally unstable disappointed office seeker.

    c. an anticapitalist immigrant anarchist.

    d. a corrupt gangster under federal criminal indictment.

A   14. In its first years, the Populist Party advocated, among other things

    a. free silver, a graduated income tax, and government ownership of the railroads, telegraph, and telephone.

    b. higher tariffs and federally sponsored unemployment insurance and pensions.

    c. tighter restriction on black economic, social, and political rights.

    d. a Homestead Act to permit farmers and unemployed workers to obtain free federal land in the West.

D   15. Grover Cleveland stirred a furious storm of protest when, in response to the extreme financial crisis of the 1890s, he

    a. lowered tariffs to permit an influx of cheaper foreign goods into the country.

    b. signed a bill introducing a federal income tax that cut into workers' wages.

    c. pushed the Federal Reserve Board into sharply raising interest rates.

    d. borrowed $65 million dollars from J.P. Morgan and other bankers in order to save the monetary gold standard.

C. Identification

Supply the correct identification for each numbered description.

_____ 1. The symbol of the Republican political tactic of attacking Democrats with reminders of the Civil War

_____ 2. Corrupt construction company whose bribes and payoffs to congressmen and others created a major Grant administration scandal

_____ 3. Short-lived third party of 1872 that attempted to curb Grant administration corruption

_____ 4. Precious metal that "soft-money" advocates demanded be coined again to compensate for the "Crime of '73"

_____ 5. "Soft-money" third party that polled over a million votes and elected fourteen congressmen in 1878 by advocating inflation

_____ 6. Mark Twain's sarcastic name for the post–Civil War era, which emphasized its atmosphere of greed and corruption

_____ 7. Civil War Union veterans' organization that became a potent political bulwark of the Republican party in the late nineteenth century

_____ 8. Republican party faction led by Senator Roscoe Conkling that opposed all attempts at civil-service reform

_____ 9. Republican party faction led by Senator James G. Blaine that paid lip service to government reform while still battling for patronage and spoils

_____ 10. The complex political agreement between Republicans and Democrats that resolved the bitterly disputed election of 1876

_____ 11. Asian immigrant group that experienced discrimination on the West Coast

_____ 12. System of choosing federal employees on the basis of merit rather than patronage introduced by the Pendleton Act of 1883

_____ 13. Sky-high Republican tariff of 1890 that caused widespread anger among farmers in the Midwest and the South.

_____ 14. Insurgent political party that gained widespread support among farmers in the 1890s

_____ 15. Notorious clause in southern voting laws that exempted from literacy tests and poll taxes anyone whose ancestors had voted in 1860, thereby excluding blacks

D. Matching People, Places, and Events

Match the person, place, or event in the left column with the proper description in the right column by inserting the correct letter on the blank line.

___ 1. Ulysses S. Grant

___ 2. Jim Fisk

___ 3. Boss Tweed

___ 4. Horace Greeley

A. Heavyweight New York political boss whose widespread fraud landed him in jail in 1871

B. Bold and unprincipled financier whose plot to corner the U.S. gold market nearly succeeded in 1869

C. Winner of the contested 1876 election who presided over the end of Reconstruction and a sharp economic downturn

D. Great military leader whose presidency foundered in corruption and political ineptitude

_____ 5. Jay Cooke

_____ 6. Denis Kearney

_____ 7. Tom Watson

_____ 8. Roscoe Conkling

_____ 9. James G. Blaine

_____ 10. Rutherford B. Hayes

_____ 11. James Garfield

_____ 12. Jim Crow

_____ 13. Grover Cleveland

_____ 14. William Jennings Bryan

_____ 15. J. P. Morgan

E. Term for the racial segregation laws imposed in the 1890s

F. Eloquent young Congressman from Nebraska who became the most prominent advocate of "free silver" in the early 1890s.

G. President whose assassination after only a few months in office spurred the passage of a civil-service law

H. Irish-born leader of the anti-Chinese movement in California

I. Radical Populist leader whose early success turned sour, and who then became a vicious racist

J. Wealthy New York financier whose bank collapse in 1873 set off an economic depression

K. Imperious New York senator and leader of the "Stalwart" faction of Republicans

L. First Democratic president since the Civil War; defender of _laissez-faire_ economics and low tariffs

M. Enormously wealthy banker whose secret bailout of the federal government in 1895 aroused fierce public anger

N. Colorful, eccentric newspaper editor who carried the Liberal Republican and Democratic banners against Grant in 1872

O. Charming but corrupt "Half-Breed" Republican senator and presidential nominee in 1884

E. Putting Things in Order

Put the following events in correct order by numbering them from 1 to 5.

_4_ A bitterly disputed presidential election is resolved by a complex political deal that ends Reconstruction in the South.

_1_ Two unscrupulous financiers use corrupt means to manipulate New York gold markets and the U.S. Treasury.

_5_ A major economic depression causes widespread social unrest and the rise of the Populist Party as a vehicle of protest.

_3_ Grant administration scandals split the Republican party, but Grant overcomes the inept opposition to win reelection.

_2_ Monetary deflation and the high McKinley Tariff lead to growing agitation for "free silver" by Congressman William Jennings Bryan and others.

F. Matching Cause and Effect

Match the historical cause in the left column with the proper effect in the right column by writing the correct letter on the blank line.

Cause

_____ 1. Favor-seeking business-people and corrupt politicians

_____ 2. _The New York Times_ and cartoonist Thomas Nast

Effect

A. Created fierce partisan competition and high voter turnouts, even though the parties agreed on most national issues

B. Caused anti-Chinese violence and restrictions against Chinese immigration

___   3.   Upright Republicans' disgust with Grant administration scandals

___   4.   The economic crash of the mid-1870s

___   5.   Local cultural, moral, and religious differences

___   6.   The Compromise of 1877 that settled the disputed Hayes-Tilden election

___   7.   White workers' resentment of Chinese labor competition

___   8.   Public shock at Garfield's assassination by Guiteau

___   9.   The 1890s depression and the drain of gold from the federal treasury

___   10.   The inability of Populist leaders to overcome divisions between white and black farmers

C.   Led to the formation of the Liberal Republican party in 1872

D.   Induced Grover Cleveland to negotiate a secret loan from J. P. Morgan's banking syndicate

E.   Forced Boss Tweed out of power and into jail

F.   Helped ensure passage of the Pendleton Act

G.   Caused numerous scandals during President Grant's administration

H.   Led to failure of the third party revolt in the South and a growing racial backlash

I.   Caused unemployment, railroad strikes, and a demand for "cheap money"

J.   Led to the withdrawal of troops from the South and the virtual end of federal efforts to protect black rights there

G. Developing Historical Skills

Historical Fact and Historical Explanation

Historians uncover a great deal of information about the past, but often that information takes on significance only when it is analyzed and interpreted. In this chapter, many facts about the presidents and elections of the Gilded Age are presented: for example, the very close elections in 1876, 1884, 1888, and 1892; the large voter turnouts; and the lack of significant issues in most elections.

These facts take on larger meaning, however, when we examine the *reasons* for them. Reread the section "Pallid Politics in the Gilded Age" (pp. 507–508) and answer each of the following questions in a sentence or two.

1.   What *fundamental* difference between the two parties made partisan politics so fiercely contested in the Glided Age?

2.   Why did this underlying difference *not* lead to differences over issues at the national level?

3.   Why were so many of the elections extremely close, no matter who the candidates were?

4. Why was winning each election so very important to both parties, even though there was little disagreement on issues?

H. Map Mastery

Map Discrimination

Using the maps and charts in Chapter 23, answer the following questions.

1. *Hayes-Tilden Disputed Election of 1876*: In the controversial Hayes-Tilden election of 1876, how many *undisputed* electoral votes did Republican Hayes win in the former Confederate states?

2. *Hayes-Tilden Disputed Election of 1876*: Democrat Tilden carried four states in the North—states that did not have slavery before 1865. Which were they?

3. *Growth of Classified Civil Service*: The *percentage* of offices classified under civil service was approximately how many times greater under President McKinley than under President Arthur: two, three, four, five, or ten?

4. *Presidential Election of 1884*: Which of the following states gained the most electoral votes between 1876 and 1884: New York, Indiana, Missouri, or Texas?

5. *Presidential Election of 1884*: How many states that were carried by Republican Hayes in 1876 were carried by Democrat Cleveland in 1884?

Map Challenge

Using the election map on p. 508 and the account of the Compromise of 1877 in the text (pp. 508–509), discuss the election of 1876 in relation to both Reconstruction and the political balance of the Gilded Age. Include some analysis of the reasons why this was the last time for nearly a century that the states in the Deep South voted Republican.

PART III: Applying What You Have Learned

1. What made politics in the Gilded Age extremely popular—with over 80 percent voter participation—yet so often corrupt and unconcerned with issues?
2. What caused the end of the Reconstruction? What did the North and South each gain from the Compromise of 1877?
3. What were the results of the Compromise of 1877 for race relations? How were the political, economic, and social conditions of southern African-Americans interrelated?
4. What caused the rise of the "money issue" in American politics? What were the backers of "greenback" and silver money trying to achieve?
5. What were the causes and political results of the rise of agrarian protest in the 1880s and 1890s? Why were the Populists' attempts to form a coalition of white and black farmers and industrial workers ultimately unsuccessful?
6. In what ways did the political conflicts of the Gilded Age still reflect the aftermath of the Civil War and Reconstruction? (See Chapter 22.) To what extent did the political leaders of the time address issues of race and sectional conflict, and to what extent did they merely shove them under the rug?

24

Industry Comes of Age, 1865–1900

PART I: Reviewing the Chapter

A. Checklist of Learning Objectives

After mastering this chapter, you should be able to

1. explain how the transcontinental railroad network provided the basis for the great post–Civil War industrial transformation.

2. identify the abuses in the railroad industry and discuss how these led to the first efforts at industrial regulation by the federal government.

3. describe how the economy came to be dominated by giant "trusts," such as those headed by Carnegie and Rockefeller in the steel and oil industries.

4. discuss the growing class conflict caused by industrial growth and combination, and the early efforts to alleviate it.

5. explain why the South was generally excluded from industrial development and fell into a "third world" economic dependency.

6. analyze the social changes brought by industrialization, particularly the altered position of working men and women.

7. explain the failures of the Knights of Labor and the modest success of the American Federation of Labor.

B. Glossary

To build your social science vocabulary, familiarize yourself with the following terms.

1. **pool** In business, an agreement to divide a given market in order to avoid competition. "The earliest form of combination was the 'pool'. . . . " (p. 535)

2. **rebate** A return of a portion of the amount paid for goods or services. "Other rail barons granted secret rebates. . . ." (p. 535)

3. **free enterprise** An economic system that permits unrestricted entrepreneurial business activity; capitalism. "Dedicated to free enterprise . . . , they cherished a traditionally keen pride in progress." (p. 535)

4. **regulatory commission** In American government, any of the agencies established to control a special sphere of business or other activity; members are usually appointed by the president and confirmed by Congress. "It heralded the arrival of a series of independent regulatory commissions in the next century. . . ." (p. 536)

5. **trust** A combination of corporations, usually in the same industry, in which stockholders trade their stock to a central board in exchange for trust certificates. (By extension, the term cam to be applied to any large, semi-monopolistic business.) "He perfected a device for controlling bothersome rivals—the 'trust.' " (p. 538)

6. **syndicate** An association of financiers organized to carry out projects requiring very large amounts of capital. "His prescribed remedy was to . . . ensure future harmony by placing officers of his own banking syndicate on their various boards of directors." (p. 538)

7. **patrician** Characterized by noble or high social standing. "An arrogant class of 'new rich' was now elbowing aside the patrician families. . . ." (p. 542)

8. **plutocracy** Government by the wealthy. "Plutocracy . . . took its stand firmly on the Constitution." (p. 542)

9. **Third World** Term developed during the Cold War for the non-Western (first world) and noncommunist (second world) nations of the world, most of them formerly under colonial rule and still economically poor and dependent. "The net effect was to keep the South in a kind of 'Third World' servitude to the Northeast. . . ." (p. 544)

10. **socialist (socialism)** Political belief in promoting social and economic equality through the ownership and control of the major means of production by the whole community rather than by individuals or corporations. "Some of it was envious, but much of it rose from the small and increasingly vocal group of socialists. . . ." (p. 548)

11. **radical** One who believes in fundamental change in the political, economic, or social system. ". . . much of [this criticism] rose from . . . socialists and other radicals, many of whom were recent European immigrants." (p. 548)

12. **lockout** The refusal by an employer to allow employees to work unless they agree to his or her terms. "Employers could lock their doors against rebellious workers—a process called the 'lockout'. . . ." (p. 549)

13. **yellow dog contract** A labor contract in which an employee must agree not to join a union as a condition of holding the job. "[Employers] could compel them to sign 'ironclad oaths' or 'yellow dog contracts'. . . ." (p. 549)

14. **cooperative** An organization for producing, marketing, or consuming goods in which the members share the benefits. ". . . they campaigned for . . . producers' cooperatives. . . ."

15. **anarchist (anarchism)** Political belief that all organized, coercive government is wrong in principle, and that society should be organized solely on the basis of free cooperation. (Some anarchists practiced violence against the state, while others were nonviolent pacifists.) "Eight anarchists were rounded up, although nobody proved that they had anything to do directly with the bomb." (p. 551)

PART II: Checking Your Progress

A. True-False

Where the statement is true, mark **T**. Where it is false, mark **F**, and correct it in the space immediately below.

T 1. Private railroad companies built the transcontinental rail lines by raising their own capital funds without the assistance of the federal government.

T 2. The rapid expansion of the railroad industry was often accompanied by rapid mergers, bankruptcies, and reorganizations.

T 3. The railroads created an integrated national market, stimulated the growth in cities, and encouraged European immigration.

F 4. Railroad owners were generally fair and honest in their dealings with shippers, the government, and the public.

___F___ 5. The early, weak federal efforts at railroad regulation did bring some order and stability to industrial competition.

___T___ 6. The Rockefeller oil company technique of "horizontal integration" involved combining into one organization all the phases of manufacturing from the raw material to the customer.

___T___ 7. Rockefeller, Morgan, and others organized monopolistic trusts and "interlocking directorates" in order to consolidate business and eliminate cutthroat competition.

___T___ 8. Corporations effectively used the Fourteenth Amendment and sympathetic court rulings to prevent much effective government regulations of their activities.

___F___ 9. The pro-industry ideology of the "New South" enabled that region to make rapid economic gains by 1900.

___T___ 10. Two new inventions that brought large numbers of women into the workplace were the typewriter and the telephone.

___F___ 11. Industrialization generally gave the industrial wage earner greater status and control over his or her own life.

___T___ 12. The impact of new machines and mass immigration held down wages and gave employers advantages in their dealings with labor.

___T___ 13. The Knights of Labor organized skilled and unskilled workers, blacks and whites, women and men.

___T___ 14. The Knights of Labor were severely hurt by the Haymarket Square episode, even though they had no connection with the bombing.

___F___ 15. The American Federation of Labor tried hard but failed to organize unskilled workers, women, and blacks.

B. Multiple Choice

Select the best answer and write the proper letter in the space provided.

___B___ 1. The federal government contributed to the building of the national rail network by

    a. importing substantial numbers of Chinese immigrants to build the railroads.
    b. providing free grants of federal land to the railroad companies.
    c. building and operating the first transcontinental rail lines.
    d. transporting the mail and other federal shipments over the rail lines.

___D___ 2. The most efficient and public-minded of the early railroad-building industrialists was

    a. Collis P. Huntington.
    b. Leland Stanford.
    c. Cornelius Vanderbilt.
    d. James J. Hill.

B 3. The railroad most significantly stimulated American industrialization by

    a. opening up the West to settlement.
    b. creating a single national market for raw materials and consumer goods.
    c. eliminating the inefficient canal system.
    d. inspiring greater federal investment in technical research and development.

D 4. The railroad barons aroused considerable public opposition by practices such as

    a. forcing Indians off their traditional hunting grounds.
    b. refusing to pay their employees decent wages.
    c. refusing to build railroad lines in less settled areas.
    d. stock watering and bribery of public officials.

C 5. The railroads affected even the organization of time in the United States by

    a. introducing regularly scheduled departures and arrivals on railroad timetables.
    b. introducing the concept of daylight savings time.
    c. introducing four standard time zones across the country.
    d. turning travel that had once taken days into a matter of hours.

C 6. The first important federal law aimed at regulating American industry was

    a. the Federal Communications Act.
    b. the Pure Food and Drug Act.
    c. the Interstate Commerce Act.
    d. the Federal Trade Commission.

B 7. Financier J. P. Morgan exercised his economic power most effectively by

    a. developing "horizontal integration" in the oil industry.
    b. lending money to the federal government.
    c. consolidating rival industries through "interlocking directorates."
    d. serving as the middleman between American industrialists and foreign governments.

D 8. Two late-nineteenth-century technological inventions that especially drew women out of the home and into the workforce were

    a. the railroad and the telegraph.
    b. the electric light and the phonograph.
    c. the cash register and the stock ticker.
    d. the typewriter and the telephone.

D 9. Andrew Carnegie's industrial system of "vertical integration" involved

    a. the construction of large, vertical steel factories in Pittsburgh and elsewhere.
    b. the cooperation between manufacturers like Andrew Carnegie and financiers like J. P. Morgan.
    c. the integration of diverse immigrant ethnic groups into the steel industry labor force.
    d. the combination of all phases of the steel industry from mining to manufacturing into a single organization.

A   10. The large trusts like Standard Oil and Swift and Armour justified their economic domination of their industries by claiming that

   a. they were fundamentally concerned with serving the public interest over private profit.
   b. only large-scale methods of production and distribution could provide superior products at low prices.
   c. competition among many small firms was contrary to the law of economics.
   d. only large American corporations could compete with huge British and German international companies.

B   11. The oil industry first thrived in the late 1880s by producing

   a. natural gas and heating oil for home heating purposes.
   b. kerosene for oil lamps.
   c. gasoline for automobiles.
   d. heavy-duty diesel fuel for the railroads and industry.

D   12. Andrew Carnegie's "Gospel of Wealth" proclaimed his belief that

   a. wealth was God's reward for hard work, while poverty resulted from laziness and immorality.
   b. churches needed to take a stronger stand on the economic issues of the day.
   c. faith in capitalism and progress should take the place once reserved for religion.
   d. those who acquired great wealth were morally responsible to use it for the public good.

A   13. The attempt to create an industrialized "New South" in the late nineteenth century generally failed because

   a. the South was discriminated against and held down as a supplier of raw materials to northern industry.
   b. southerners were too bitter at the Union to pursue national goals.
   c. continued political violence made the South an unattractive place for investment.
   d. there was little demand for southern products like textiles and cigarettes.

C   14. For American workers, industrialization generally meant

   a. a steady, long-term decline in wages and the standard of living.
   b. an opportunity to create small businesses that might eventually produce large profits.
   c. a long-term rise in the standard of living but a loss of independence and control of work.
   d. a stronger sense of identification with their jobs and employers.

B   15. In contrast to the Knights of Labor, the American Federation of Labor advocated

   a. uniting both skilled and unskilled workers into a single large union.
   b. concentrating on improving wages and hours and avoiding general social reform.
   c. working for black and female labor interests as well as those of white men.
   d. using secrecy and violence against employers.

C. Identification

Supply the correct identification for each numbered description.

_____ 1. Federally owned acreage granted to the railroad companies in order to encourage the building of rail lines

_____ 2. The original transcontinental railroad, commissioned by Congress, which built its rail line west from Omaha

_____ 3. The California-based railroad company, headed by Leland Stanford, that employed Chinese laborers in building lines across the mountains

_____ 4. The northernmost of the transcontinental railroad lines, organized by economically wise and public-spirited industrialist James J. Hill

_____ 5. Dishonest device by which railroad promoters artificially inflated the price of their stocks and bonds

_____ 6. Supreme Court case of 1886 that prevented states from regulating railroads or other forms of interstate commerce

_____ 7. Federal regulatory agency often used by rail companies to stabilize the industry and prevent ruinous competition

_____ 8. Late-nineteenth-century invention that revolutionized communication and created a large new industry that relied heavily on female workers

_____ 9. First of the great industrial trusts, organized through a principle of "horizontal integration" that ruthlessly incorporated or destroyed competitors

_____ 10. The first billion-dollar American corporation, organized when J. P. Morgan bought out Andrew Carnegie

_____ 11. Term that identified southern promoters' belief in a technologically advanced industrial South

_____ 12. Black labor organization that briefly flourished in the late 1860s

_____ 13. Secret, ritualistic labor organization that enrolled many skilled and unskilled workers but collapsed suddenly after the Haymarket Square bombing

_____ 14. Skilled labor organizations, such as those of carpenters and printers, that were most successful in conducting strikes and raising wages

_____ 15. The conservative labor group that successfully organized a minority of American workers but left others out

D. Matching People, Places, and Events

Match the person, place, or event in the left column with the proper description in the right column by inserting the correct letter on the blank line.

___ 1. Leland Stanford

___ 2. Russell Conwell

___ 3. James J. Hill

A. Inventive genius of industrialization who worked on devices such as the electric light, the phonograph, and the motion picture

B. The only businessperson in America wealthy enough to buy out Andrew Carnegie and organize the United States Steel Corporation

___	4. Cornelius Vanderbilt	**C.**	Illinois governor who pardoned the Haymarket anarchists
		D.	Southern newspaper editor who tirelessly promoted industrialization as the salvation of the economically backward South
___	5. Charles Dana Gibson		
___	6. Alexander Graham Bell	**E.**	Aggressive energy-industry monopolist who used tough means to build a trust based on "horizontal integration"
		F.	Magazine illustrator who created a romantic image of the new, independent woman
___	7. Thomas Edison		
		G.	Aggressive eastern railroad builder and consolidator who scorned the law as an obstacle to his enterprise
___	8. Andrew Carnegie		
___	9. John D. Rockefeller	**H.**	Pro-business clergyman whose "Acres of Diamonds" speeches criticized the poor
___	10. J. Pierpont Morgan	**I.**	Scottish immigrant who organized a vast new industry on the principle of "vertical integration"
___	11. Henry Grady	**J.**	Former California governor and organizer of the Central Pacific Railroad
___	12. Terence V. Powderly	**K.**	Organizer of a conservative craft-union group and advocate of "more" wages for skilled workers
___	13. Haymarket Square	**L.**	Eloquent leader of a secretive labor organization that made substantial gains in the 1880s before it suddenly collapsed
___	14. John P. Altgeld	**M.**	Public-spirited railroad builder who assisted farmers in the northern areas served by his rail lines
___	15. Samuel Gompers	**N.**	Site of a bombing, during a labor demonstration, that aroused public hysteria against strikes
		O.	Former teacher of the deaf whose invention created an entire new industry

E. Putting Things in Order

Put the following events in correct order by numbering them from 1 to 5.

___ J. P. Morgan buys out Andrew Carnegie to form the first billion-dollar U.S. corporation.

___ The first federal law regulating railroads is passed.

___ The killing of policemen during a labor demonstration results in the execution of radical anarchists and the decline of the Knights of Labor.

___ A teacher of the deaf invents a machine that greatly eases communication across distance.

___ A golden spike is driven, fulfilling the dream of linking the nation by rail.

F. Matching Cause and Effect

Match the historical cause in the left column with the proper effect in the right column by writing the correct letter on the blank line.

	Cause		**Effect**
___	1. Federal land grants and subsidies	**A.**	Eliminated competition and created monopolistic "trusts" in many industries
___	2. The building of a transcontinental rail network	**B.**	Fostered growing class divisions and public demands for restraints on corporate trusts
		C.	Created a strong but narrowly based union organization

3. Corrupt financial dealings and political manipulations by the railroads

4. New developments in steel making, oil refining, and communication

5. The ruthless competitive techniques of Rockefeller and other industrialists

6. The growing concentration of wealth and power in the new corporate "plutocracy"

7. The North's use of discriminatory price practices against the South

8. The growing mechanization and depersonalization of factory work

9. The Haymarket Square bombing

10. The American Federation of Labor's concentration on skilled craft workers

D. Stimulated the growth of a huge unified national market for American manufactured goods

E. Created a public demand for railroad regulation, such as the Interstate Commerce Act

F. Often made laborers feel powerless and vulnerable to their well-off corporate employers

G. Helped destroy the Knights of Labor and increased public fear of labor agitation

H. Laid the technological basis for huge new industries and spectacular economic growth

I. Encouraged the railroads to build their lines across the North American continent

J. Kept the South in economic dependency as a poverty-stricken supplier of farm products and raw materials to the Northeast

G. Developing Historical Skills

Interpreting Historical Paintings and Photographs

Historical paintings, lithographs, and photographs not only convey substantive information; they can also tell us how an artist or photographer viewed and understood the society and events of his or her day. Examine the photographs and painting indicated below and answer the following questions about them.

1. Examine the working people in the images on pp. 542, 544, 546, and 547. What is the relationship of the workers in each image to their workplace? What is their relation to one another? What does each of the photos reveal about the nature of industrial labor?

2. Examine the painting of "The Strike" by Robert Koehler on p.550. Where is the scene taking place? What is the relationship between the place of work and the scene in the painting? What has likely happened to bring the workers to this scene?

3. Analyze the clothing of all the figures in the Koehler painting. What does it tell you about the economic and social condition of the various people?

4. Two main conversations seem to be taking place in the foreground of the painting. What might each be about? What is the artist suggesting by presenting *both* conversations?

PART III: Applying What You Have Learned

1. What was the impact of the transcontinental rail system on the American economy and society in the late nineteenth century?

2. How did the huge industrial trusts develop in industries such as steel and oil, and what was their effect on the economy?

3. What early efforts were made to control the new corporate industrial giants, and how effective were these efforts?

4. What was the effect of the new industrial revolution on American laborers, and how did various labor organizations attempt to respond to the new conditions?

5. Compare the impact of the new industrialization on the North and the South. Why was the "New South" more a slogan than a reality?

6. William Graham Sumner said that the wealth and luxury enjoyed by millionaires was justifiable as a "good bargain for society." Based on the industrialists' role in the late 1800s, support or criticize Sumner's assertion.

7. How did the industrial transformation after the Civil War compare with the earlier phase of American economic development? (See Chapter 14.) Why were the economic developments of 1865–1900 often seen as a threat to American democracy, whereas those of 1815–1860 were not?

25

America Moves to the City, 1865–1900

PART I: Reviewing the Chapter

A. Checklist of Learning Objectives

After mastering this chapter, you should be able to

1. describe the new industrial city and its impact on American society.
2. describe the "New Immigration" and explain why it aroused opposition from many native-born Americans.
3. discuss the efforts of social reformers and churches to aid the New Immigrants and alleviate urban problems.
4. analyze the changes in American religious life in the late nineteenth century.
5. explain the changes in American education from elementary to the college level.
6. describe the literary and cultural life of the period, including the widespread trend towards "realism."
7. explain the growing national debates about morality in the late nineteenth century, particularly in relation to the changing roles of women and the family.

B. Glossary

To build your social science vocabulary, familiarize yourself with the following terms.

1. **megalopolis** An extensive, heavily populated area, containing several dense urban centers. ". . . gave way to the immense and impersonal megalopolis. . . ." (p. 558)
2. **tenement** A multidwelling building, often poor or overcrowded. "The cities . . . harbored . . . towering skyscrapers and stinking tenements." (p. 560)
3. **affluence** An abundance of wealth. "These leafy 'bedroom communities' eventually ringed the brick-and-concrete cities with a greenbelt of affluence." (p. 560)
4. **despotism** Government by an absolute or tyrannical ruler. ". . . people had grown accustomed to cringing before despotism." (p. 561)
5. **parochial** Concerning a religious parish or small district. (By extension, the term is used, often negatively, to refer to narrow or local perspectives as distinct from broad or cosmopolitan outlooks.) "Catholics expanded their parochial-school system. . . ." (p. 565)
6. **sweatshop** A factory where employees are forced to work long hours under difficult conditions for meager wages. "The women of Hull House successfully lobbied in 1893 for an Illinois antisweatshop law that protected women workers. . . ." (p. 568)
7. **pauper** A poor person, often one who lives on tax-supported charity. "The first restrictive law . . . banged the gate in the faces of paupers. . . ." (p. 570)
8. **convert** A person who turns from one religion or set of beliefs to another. "A fertile field for converts was found in America's harried, nerve-racked, and urbanized civilization. . . ." (p. 572)

9. **Fundamentalist** A conservative Protestant who rejects religious modernism and adheres to a strict and literal interpretation of Christian doctrine and Scriptures. "Conservatives, or 'Fundamentalists,' stood firmly on the Scripture. . . ." (p. 572)

10. **agnostic** One who believes that there can be no human knowledge of any God or gods. "The . . . skeptic . . . lectured widely on 'Some Mistakes of Moses' and 'Why I Am an Agnostic.'" (p. 573)

11. **behavioral psychology** The branch of psychology that examines human action, often considering it more important than mental or inward states. "His [work] helped to establish the modern discipline of behavioral psychology." (p. 576)

12. **syndicated** In journalism, material that is sold by an organization for publication in several newspapers. "Bare-knuckle editorials were, to an increasing degree, being supplanted by feature articles and non-controversial syndicated material." (p. 577)

13. **tycoon** A wealthy businessperson, especially one who openly displays power and position. "Two new journalistic tycoons emerged." (p. 577)

14. **feminist (feminism)** One who promotes complete political, social, and economic equality of opportunity for women. " . . . in 1898 they heard the voice of a major feminist prophet." (p. 583)

15. **prohibition** Forbidding by law the manufacture, sale, or consumption of liquor. (**Temperance** is the voluntary abstention from liquor consumption.) "Statewide prohibition . . . was sweeping new states into the 'dry' column." (p. 586)

PART II: Checking Your Progress

A. True-False

Where the statement is true, mark **T**. Where it is false, mark **F**, and correct it in the space immediately below.

T   1. Rapid and uncontrolled growth made American cities places of both exciting opportunity and severe social problems.

F   2. After 1880, most immigrants to America came from northern and western Europe.

T   3. Most of the New Immigrants who arrived in America were escaping from the slums and poverty of European cities.

T   4. Female social workers established settlement houses to aid struggling immigrants and promote social reform.

T   5. Many native-born Americans considered the New Immigrants a threat to American democracy and Anglo-Saxon purity.

T   6. Two religions that gained strength in the United States from the New Immigrants were Roman Catholicism and Judaism.

F   7. The growth of Darwinian science contributed to the turn towards religious belief in the late nineteenth century.

F   8. In the late nineteenth century, secondary (high school) education was increasingly carried on by private schools.

F   9. Booker T. Washington believed that blacks should try to achieve social equality with whites but not economic equality.

T   10. American higher education depended on both public "land-grant" funding and private donations for its financial support.

T   11. Urban newspapers often promoted a sensational "yellow journalism" that emphasized sex and scandal rather that politics or social reform.

F   12. Post–Civil War writers like Mark Twain and William Dean Howells turned from social realism toward fantasy and science fiction in their novels.

T   13. There was growing tension in the late nineteenth century between women's traditionally defined "sphere" of family and home and the social and cultural changes of the era.

T   14. The new urban environment generally weakened the family but offered new opportunities for women to achieve social and economic independence.

T   15. Voices like Victoria Woodhull, Kate Chopin, and Charlotte Perkins Gilman signaled women's growing dissatisfaction with Victorian ideas about sex and gender roles.

B. Multiple Choice

Select the best answer and write the proper letter in the space provided.

C   1. The new cities' glittering consumer economy was symbolized especially by the rise of

     a. separate districts for retail merchants.
     b. fine restaurants and food shops.
     c. large, elegant department stores.
     d. large, carefully constructed urban parks.

D   2. One of the most difficult new problems generated by the rise of cities and the urban American life-style was

     a. dealing with horses and other animals in crowded urban settings.
     b. developing means of communication in densely populated city centers.
     c. disposing of large quantities of consumer-generated waste material.
     d. finding effective methods of high-rise construction for limited urban space.

C   3. Two new technical developments of the late nineteenth century that contributed to the spectacular growth of American cities were

     a. the telegraph and the railroads.
     b. the compressor and the internal combustion engine.
     c. the electric trolley and the skyscraper.
     d. the oil furnace and the air conditioner.

D   4. Countries from which many of the "New Immigrants" came included

     a. Sweden and Great Britain.
     b. Germany and Ireland.
     c. Poland and Italy.
     d. China and Japan.

D   5. Among the factors driving millions of European peasants from their homeland to America were

    a. American food imports and religious persecution.
    b. The rise of European nation-states and the decline of the Catholic Church.
    c. the rise of communist and fascist regimes.
    d. major international wars among the European great powers.

B   6. Besides providing direct services to immigrants, the reformers of Hull House worked for general goals like

    a. the secret ballot and direct election of senators.
    b. antisweatshop laws to protect women and child laborers.
    c. social security and unemployment compensation.
    d. conservation and federal aid to municipal governments.

D   7. The one immigrant group that was totally banned from America after 1882 as a result of nativist agitation was the

    a. Irish.
    b. Greeks.
    c. Africans.
    d. Chinese.

D   8. Two religious groups that grew most dramatically because of the "New Immigration" were

    a. Methodists and Baptists.
    b. Christian Scientists and the Salvation Army.
    c. Episcopalians and Unitarians.
    d. Jews and Roman Catholics.

A   9. The phrase "social Gospel" refers to

    a. the fact that many people were turning to God seeking solutions to social conflicts.
    b. the decline in traditional religious beliefs in the late nineteenth century.
    c. the efforts of some Christian reformers to apply their religious beliefs to new social problems.
    d. the conflict between socialists and traditional religious believers.

B   10. Besides aiding immigrants and promoting social reforms, settlement houses like Jane Addams's Hull House demonstrated that

    a. it was almost impossible to bring about real economic reform in the cities.
    b. the cities offered new challenges and opportunities for women.
    c. women could not bring about successful social change without the vote.
    d. labor was unsympathetic to middle-class reform efforts.

B   11. Traditional American Protestant religion received a substantial blow from

    a. the psychological ideas of William James.
    b. the theological ideas of the Fundamentalists.
    c. the chemical theories of Charles Eliot.
    d. the biological ideas of Charles Darwin.

B 12. Unlike Booker T. Washington, W. E. B. Du Bois advocated
    a. economic opportunity for blacks.
    b. integration and social equality for blacks.
    c. practical as well as theoretical education for blacks.
    d. that blacks remain in the South rather than move north.

A 13. In the late nineteenth century, American colleges and universities benefited especially from
    a. federal and state "land-grant" assistance and the private philanthropy of wealthy donors.
    b. the growing involvement of the churches in higher education.
    c. the fact that a college degree was becoming a prerequisite for employment in industry.
    d. the growth of federal grants and loans to college students.

A 14. American social reformers like Henry George and Edward Bellamy advocated
    a. utopian reforms to end poverty and eliminate class conflict.
    b. an end to racial prejudice and segregation.
    c. the resettlement of the urban poor on free western homesteads.
    d. a transformation of the traditional family through communal living arrangements.

D 15. Authors like Mark Twain, Stephen Crane, and Jack London turned American literature toward a greater concern with
    a. close observation and contemplation of nature.
    b. postmodernism and deconstruction of traditional narratives.
    c. fantasy and romance.
    d. social realism and contemporary problems.

C. Identification

Supply the correct identification for each numbered description.

_____ 1. High-rise urban buildings that provided barrackslike housing for urban slum dwellers

_____ 2. Term for the post-1880 newcomers who came to America primarily from southern and eastern Europe

_____ 3. Immigrants who came to America to earn money for a time and then returned to their native land

_____ 4. The religious doctrines preached by those who believed the churches should directly address economic and social problems

_____ 5. Settlement house in the Chicago slums that became a model for women's involvement in urban social reform

_____ 6. Profession established by Jane Addams and others that opened new opportunities for women while engaging urban problems

_____ 7. Nativist organization that attacked "New Immigrants" and Roman Catholicism in the 1880s and 1890s

_____ 8. The church that became the largest American religious group, mainly as a result of the "New Immigration"

9. Black educational institution founded by Booker T. Washington to provide training in agriculture and crafts

_____ 10. Organization founded by W. E. B. Du Bois and others to advance black social and economic equality

_____ 11. Henry George's best-selling book that advocated social reform through the imposition of a "single tax" on land

_____ 12. Federal law promoted by a self-appointed morality crusader and used to prosecute moral and sexual dissidents

_____ 13. Charlotte Perkins Gilman's book urging women to enter the work force and advocating cooperative kitchens and child-care centers

_____ 14. Organization formed by Elizabeth Cady Stanton and others to promote the vote for women

_____ 15. Women's organization founded by reformer Frances Willard and others to oppose alcohol consumption

D. Matching People, Places, and Events

Match the person, place, or event in the left column with the proper description in the right column by inserting the correct letter on the blank line.

____ 1. Louis Sullivan

____ 2. Walter Rauschenbusch

____ 3. Jane Addams

____ 4. Dwight L. Moody

____ 5. Mary Baker Eddy

____ 6. Booker T. Washington

____ 7. W. E. B. Du Bois

____ 8. William James

____ 9. Henry George

____ 10. Emily Dickinson

____ 11. Mark Twain

____ 12. Victoria Woodhull

____ 13. Anthony Comstock

____ 14. Charlotte Perkins Gilman

A. Controversial reformer whose book *Progress and Poverty* advocated solving problems of economic inequality by a tax on land

B. Midwestern-born writer and lecturer who created a new style of American literature based on social realism and humor

C. American painter whose sensitive portrayals made her one of the prominent new impressionists

D. Author and founder of a popular new religion based on principles of spiritual healing

E. Leading Protestant advocate of the "social gospel" who tried to make Christianity relevant to urban and industrial problems

F. Former slave who promoted industrial education and economic opportunity but not social equality for blacks

G. Harvard scholar who made original contributions to modern psychology and philosophy

H. Radical feminist propagandist whose eloquent attacks on conventional social morality shocked many Americans in the 1870s

I. Brilliant feminist writer who advocated cooperative cooking and child-care arrangements to promote women's economic independence and equality

J. Leading social reformer who lived with the poor in the slums and pioneered new forms of activism for women

K. Vigorous nineteenth-century crusader for sexual "purity" who used federal law to enforce his moral views

_____ 15. Mary Cassatt

L. Harvard-educated scholar and advocate of full black social and economic equality through the leadership of a "talented tenth"

M. Chicago-based architect whose high-rise innovation allowed more people to crowd into limited urban space

N. Popular evangelical preacher who brought the tradition of old-time revivalism to the industrial city

O. Gifted but isolated New England poet, the bulk of whose works were not published until after her death

E. Putting Things in Order

Put the following events in correct order by numbering them from 1 to 5.

_____ Well-educated young midwesterner moves to Chicago slums and creates a vital center of social reform and activism.

_____ Introduction of a new form of high-rise slum housing drastically increases the overcrowding of the urban poor.

_____ Nativist organization is formed to limit the "New Immigration" and attack Roman Catholicism.

_____ The formation of a new national organization signals growing strength for the women's suffrage movement.

_____ A western territory becomes the first U.S. government to grant full voting rights to women.

F. Matching Cause and Effect

Match the historical cause in the left column with the proper effect in the right column by writing the correct letter on the blank line.

Cause

_____ 1. New industrial jobs and urban excitement

_____ 2. Uncontrolled rapid growth and the "New Immigration" from Europe

_____ 3. Cheap American grain exports to Europe

_____ 4. The cultural strangeness and poverty of southern and eastern European immigrants

_____ 5. Social gospel ministers and settlement-house workers

_____ 6. Darwinian science and growing urban materialism

Effect

A. Encouraged the mass urban public's taste for scandal and sensation

B. Created intense poverty and other problems in the crowded urban slums

C. Weakened the religious influence in American society and created divisions within the churches

D. Led women and men to delay marriage and have fewer children

E. Helped uproot European peasants from their ancestral lands and sent them seeking new opportunities in America and elsewhere

F. Supported the substantial improvements in American undergraduate and graduate education in the late nineteenth century

_____ 7. Government land grants and private philanthropy

_____ 8. Popular newspapers and "yellow journalism"

_____ 9. Changes in moral and sexual attitudes

_____ 10. The difficulties of family life in the industrial city

G. Lured millions of rural Americans off the farms and into the cities

H. Assisted immigrants and other slum dwellers and pricked middle-class consciences about urban problems

I. Provoked sharp hostility from some native-born Americans and organized labor groups

J. Created sharp divisions about the "new morality" and issues such as divorce

G. Developing Historical Skills

Interpreting a Line Graph

A line graph is another visual way to convey information. It is often used to present notable historical changes occurring over substantial periods of time. Study the line graph on p.561 and answer the following questions.

1. There are five major "peaks" of immigration, and four major "valleys." What factors helped cause each of the periods of heavy immigration? What helped cause each of the sharp declines?

2. About how long did each of the first four periods of major immigration last? About how long did each of the four "valleys" last? How long has the current (to 1997) phase of rising or steady immigration lasted?

3. During what five-year period was there the sharpest rise in immigration? What five-year period saw the sharpest fall?

4. In about what *three* years did approximately 800,000 immigrants enter the United States? In about what *seven* years did approximately 200,000 immigrants enter the United States?

5. Approximately how many fewer immigrants came in 1920 than in 1914? About how many more immigrants came in 1990 than in 1950?

PART III: Applying What You Have Learned

1. What new opportunities did the cities create for Americans?
2. What new social problems did urbanization create? How did Americans respond to these problems?
3. How did the "New Immigration" differ from the "Old Immigration," and how did Americans respond to it?
4. How was American religion affected by the urban transformation, the New Immigration, and cultural and intellectual changes?
5. How did American social criticism, imaginative writing, and art all relate to the urban industrial changes of the late nineteenth century?
6. How and why did women assume a larger place in American society at this time? (Compare their status in this period with that of the pre–Civil War period described in Chapter 16.) How were changes in their condition related to changes in both the family and the larger social order?

26

The Great West and the Agricultural Revolution, 1865–1896

PART I: Reviewing the Chapter

A. Checklist of Learning Objectives

After mastering this chapter, you should be able to

1. describe the nature of the cultural conflicts and battles that accompanied the white American migration into the Great Plains and the Far West.
2. explain the development of federal policy towards Native Americans in the late nineteenth century.
3. analyze the brief flowering and decline of the cattle and mining frontiers.
4. explain the impact of the closing of the frontier, and the long-term significance of the frontier for American history.
5. describe the revolutionary changes in farming on the Great Plains.
6. describe the economic forces that drove farmers into debt, and describe how the Grange, the Farmers' Alliances, and the Populist Party organized to protest their oppression.

B. Glossary

To build your social science vocabulary, familiarize yourself with the following terms.

1. **nomadic (nomad)** A way of life characterized by frequent movement from place to place for economic sustenance. ". . . the Sioux transformed themselves from foot-traveling, crop-growing villagers to wide-ranging nomadic traders. . . ." (p. 591)
2. **immunity** Freedom or exemption from some imposition. ". . . [the] militia massacred . . . four hundred Indians who apparently thought they had been promised immunity." (p. 593)
3. **reservation** Public lands designated for use by Indians. "The vanquished Indians were finally ghettoized on reservations. . . ." (p. 595)
4. **ward** Someone considered incompetent to manage his or her own affairs and therefore placed under the legal guardianship of another person or group. ". . . there [they had] to eke out a sullen existence as wards of the government." (p. 595)
5. **probationary** Concerning a period of testing or trial, after which a decision is made based on performance. "The probationary period was later extended. . . ." (p. 597)
6. **folklore** The common traditions and stories of a people. "These bowlegged Knights of the Saddle . . . became part of American folklore." (p. 602)
7. **irrigation** Watering land artificially, through canals, pipes, or other means. ". . . irrigation projects . . . caused the 'Great American Desert' to bloom. . . ." (p. 604)
8. **meridian** In geography, any of the imaginary lines of longitude running north and south on the globe. ". . . settlers . . . rashly pushed . . . beyond the 100th meridian. . . ." (p. 604)

9. **contiguous** Joined together by common borders, "Only Oklahoma, New Mexico, and Arizona remained to be lifted into statehood from contiguous territory on the mainland of North America." (p. 606)

10. **safety valve** Anything, such as the American frontier, that allegedly serves as a necessary outlet for built-up pressure, energy, and so on. "But the 'safety-valve' theory does have some validity." (p. 607)

11. **loan shark** A person who lends money at an exorbitant or illegal rate of interest. "The [farmers] . . . cried out in despair against the loan sharks. . . ." (p. 610)

12. **serfdom** The feudal condition of being permanently bound to land owned by someone else. ". . . the farmers were about to sink into a status suggesting Old World serfdom." (p. 610)

13. **mumbo jumbo** Mysterious and unintelligible words or behavior. "Kelley, a Mason, even found farmers receptive to his mumbo jumbo of passwords and secret rituals. . . ." (p. 611)

14. **prophet** A person believed to speak with divine power or special gifts, sometimes including predicting the future (hence any specially talented or eloquent advocate of a cause). "Numerous fiery prophets leapt forward to trumpet the Populist cause." (p. 613)

15. **citadel** A fortress occupying a commanding height. " . . . join hands with urban workers, and mount a successful attack on the northeastern citadels of power." (p. 614)

PART II: Checking Your Progress

A. True-False

Where the statement is true, mark **T**. Where it is false, mark **F**, and correct it in the space immediately below.

T 1. Cultural conflicts and population loss to disease weakened the Plains Indians' ability to resist white encroachment onto their lands.

T 2. The Plains Indians were rather quickly and easily defeated by the U.S. Army.

T 3. A crucial factor in defeating the Indians was the destruction of the buffalo, a vital source of food and other supplies.

T 4. Humanitarian reformers respected the Indians' traditional culture and tried to preserve their tribal way of life.

T 5. Individual gold and silver miners proved unable to compete with large mining corporations and trained engineers.

F 6. During the peak years of the Long Drive, the cattlemen's prosperity depended on driving large beef herds great distances to railroad terminal points.

T 7. More families acquired land under the Homestead Act than from the states and private owners.

T 8. Although very few city dwellers ever migrated west to take up farming, the frontier "safety valve" did have some positive effects on eastern workers.

T 9. The farmers who settled the Great Plains were usually single-crop producers dependent on unstable distant markets for their livelihoods.

F   10. The greatest problem facing the farmers was inflation in the prices of machinery and supplies they had to buy.

T   11. A fundamental problem of the Farmers' Alliance was their inability to overcome the racial division between white and black farmers in the South.

T   12. The economic crisis of the 1890s strengthened the Populists' belief that farmers and industrial workers should form an alliance against economic and political oppression.

F   13. Republican political manager Mark Hanna struggled to raise enough funds to combat William Jennings Bryan's pro-silver campaign.

T   14. Bryan's populist campaign failed partly because he was unable to persuade enough urban workers to join his essentially rural-based cause.

T   15. McKinley's victory in 1896 ushered in an era marked by Republican domination, weakened party organization, and the fading of the money issue in American politics.

B. Multiple Choice

Select the best answer and write the proper letter in the space provided.

A   1. Western Indians offered strong resistance to white expansion through their effective use of
- a. artillery and infantry tactics.
- b. their alliance with remaining Mexican resisters in the West.
- c. nighttime and winter campaigning.
- (d.) repeating rifles and horses.

B   2. Intertribal warfare among Plains Indians increased in the late nineteenth century because of
- a. the attempt of the Chippewas to gain dominance over all other groups.
- b. the confining of several different groups within a single reservation.
- (c.) growing competition for the rapidly dwindling hunting grounds.
- d. the rise of the "Ghost Dance" among some Indian groups.

A   3. The federal government's attempt to confine Indians to certain areas through formal treaties was largely ineffective because
- a. the nomadic Plains Indians largely rejected the idea of formal authority and defined territory.
- b. Congress refused to ratify treaties signed with the Indians.
- c. the treaties made no effective provisions for enforcement.
- d. the largest tribe, the Sioux, refused to sign any treaties with the whites.

C   4. The warfare that led up to the Battle of the Little Big Horn was set off by
- a. white intrusion into the previously reserved Indian territory of Oklahoma.
- b. Indian attacks on the transcontinental railroad construction crews.
- c. white intrusions after the discovery of gold in the sacred Black Hills.
- d. a conflict over the interpretation of the second Treaty of Fort Laramie.

B 5. Indian resistance was finally subdued because

    a. most of the effective Indian leadership was bought off.
    b. the coming of the railroad led to the destruction of the buffalo and the Indians' way of life.
    c. most Indians lost the will to resist.
    d. the army developed effective techniques of guerrilla warfare.

A 6. The federal government attempted to force Indians away from their traditional values and customs by

    a. instructing them in white farming methods.
    (b.) creating a network of children's boarding schools and white "field matrons."
    c. establishing scholarships for Indian students at white colleges.
    d. developing programs of bilingual education in reservation schools.

D 7. Both the mining and cattle frontiers saw

    a. an increase of ethnic and class conflict.
    b. a loss of economic viability after an initial boom.
    c. a turn from large-scale investment to the individual entrepreneur.
    d. a movement from individual operations to large-scale corporate businesses.

A 8. The problem of developing agriculture in the arid West was solved most successfully through

    a. concentrating agriculture in the more fertile mountain valleys.
    b. the use of small-scale family farms rather than large "bonanza" farms.
    (c.) the use of irrigation from dammed western rivers.
    d. the turn to desert crops like olives and dates.

C 9. The "safety valve" theory of the frontier holds that

    a. Americans were able to divert the most violent elements of the population to the West.
    b. the conflict between farmers and ranchers was relieved by the Homestead Act.
    c. unemployed city dwellers could move west and thus relieve labor conflict in the East.
    d. political movements such as the Populists provided relief for the most serious grievances of western farmers.

D 10. Which one of these factors did *not* make the trans-Mississippi West a unique part of the America frontier experience?

    a. the large numbers of Indians, Hispanics, and Asian-Americans in the region
    (b.) the problem of applying new technologies in a hostile wilderness
    c. the scale and severity of environmental challenges in an arid environment
    d. the large role of the federal government in economic and social development

D 11. By the 1880s, most western farmers faced hard times because

    a. free land was no longer available under the Homestead Act.
    b. they were unable to increase grain production to keep up with demand.
    c. they were being strangled by excessive federal regulation of agriculture.
    d. they were forced to sell their grain at low prices in a depressed world market.

B 12. Which of the following was *not* among the political goals advocated by the Populist Party in the 1890s?

    a. nationalizing the railroad, telegraph, and telephone
    b. creation of a national system of unemployment insurance and old-age pensions
    c. a graduated income tax
    d. free and unlimited coinage of silver money

A 13. The U.S. government's response to the Pullman strike aroused great anger from organized labor because

    a. it seemed to represent "government by injunction" designed to destroy labor unions.
    b. it broke apart the growing alliance between urban workers and farmers.
    c. it undermined efforts to organize federal workers like those in the postal service.
    d. it turned their most effective leader, Eugene V. Debs, into a cautious conservative.

A 14. William Jennings Bryan gained the Democratic nomination in 1896 because he strongly advocated

    a. unlimited coinage of silver in order to inflate currency.
    b. higher tariffs in order to protect the American farmer.
    c. government ownership of the railroads and the telegraph system.
    d. a coalition between white and black farmers in the South and Midwest.

C 15. McKinley defeated Bryan primarily because he was able to win the support of

    a. white southern farmers.
    b. eastern wage earners and city dwellers.
    c. urban and rural blacks.
    d. former Populists and Greenback Laborites.

C. Identification

Supply the correct identification for each numbered description.

_____ 1. Major northern Plains Indian nation that fought and eventually lost a bitter war against the U.S. Army, 1876–1877

_____ 2. Southwestern Indian tribe led by Geronimo that carried out some of the last fighting against white conquest

_____ 3. Generally poor areas where vanquished Indians were eventually confined under federal control

_____ 4. Indian religious movement, originating out of the sacred Sun Dance that the federal government attempted to stamp out in 1890

_____ 5. Federal law that attempted to dissolve tribal landholding and establish Indians as individual farmers

_____ 6. Huge silver and gold deposit that brought wealth and statehood to Nevada

_____ 7. General term for the herding of cattle from the grassy plains to the railroad terminals of Kansas, Nebraska, and Wyoming

_____ 8. Federal law that offered generous land opportunities to poorer farmers but also provided the unscrupulous with opportunities for hoaxes and fraud

_____ 9. Improved type of fencing that enabled farmers to enclose land on the treeless plains

_____ 10. Former "Indian Territory" where "sooners" tried to get the jump on "boomers" when it was opened for settlement in 1889

_____ 11. Third political party that emerged in the 1890s to express rural grievances and mount major attacks on the Democrats and Republicans

_____ 12. Popular pamphlet written by William Hope Harvey that portrayed pro-silver arguments triumphing over the traditional views of bankers and economics professors.

_____ 13. Bitter labor conflict in Chicago that brought federal intervention and the jailing of union leader Eugene V. Debs

_____ 14. Spectacular convention speech by a young pro-silver advocate that brought him the Democratic presidential nomination in 1896

_____ 15. Popular term for those who favored the "status quo" in metal money and opposed the pro-silver Bryanites in 1896

D. Matching People, Places, and Events

Match the person, place, or event in the left column with the proper description in the right column by inserting the correct letter on the blank line.

____ 1. Sand Creek, Colorado

____ 2. Little Big Horn

____ 3. Sitting Bull

____ 4. Chief Joseph

____ 5. Geronimo

____ 6. Helen Hunt Jackson

____ 7. John Wesley Powell

____ 8. William Hope Harvey

____ 9. Eugene V. Debs

____ 10. James B. Weaver

____ 11. Mary E. Lease

____ 12. Mark Hanna

A. Ohio industrialist and organizer of McKinley's victory over Bryan in the election of 1896

B. Leader of the Nez Percé tribe who conducted a brilliant but unsuccessful military campaign in 1877

C. Author of the popular pro-silver pamphlet "Coin's Financial School"

D. Former Civil War general and Granger who ran as the Greenback Labor party candidate for president in 1880

E. Leader of the Sioux during wars of 1876–1877

F. Explorer and geologist who warned that traditional agriculture could not succeed west of the 100th meridian

G. Leader of the Apaches of Arizona in their warfare with the whites

H. Site of Indian massacre by militia forces in 1864

I. Massachusetts writer whose books aroused sympathy for the plight of the Native Americans

J. Site of major U.S. Army defeat in the Sioux War of 1876–1877

K. Railway union leader who converted to socialism while serving jail time during the Pullman strike

L. Eloquent Kansas Populist who urged farmers to "raise less corn and more hell"

E. Putting Things in Order

Put the following events in correct order by numbering them from 1 to 5.

____ A sharp economic depression leads to a major railroad strike and the intervention of federal troops in Chicago.

____ The violation of agreements with the Dakota Sioux leads to a major Indian war and a military disaster for the U.S. cavalry.

____ A federal law grants 160 acres of land to farmers at token prices, thus encouraging the rapid settlement of the Great West.

____ The U.S. Census Bureau declares that there is no longer a clear line of frontier settlement, ending a formative chapter of American history.

____ Despite a fervent campaign by their charismatic young champion, pro-silver Democrats lose a pivotal election to "Gold Bug" Republicans.

F. Matching Cause and Effect

Match the historical cause in the left column with the proper effect in the right column by writing the correct letter on the blank line.

Cause	Effect
____ 1. The encroachment of white settlement and the violation of treaties with Indians	**A.** Caused widespread protests and strikes like the one against the Pullman Company in Chicago
____ 2. Railroad building, disease, and the destruction of the buffalo	**B.** Threatened the two-party domination of American politics by the Republicans and Democrats
____ 3. Reformers' attempts to make Native Americans conform to white ways	**C.** Created new psychological and economic problems for a nation accustomed to a boundlessly open West
____ 4. The coming of big-business mining and stock-raising to the West	**D.** Ended the romantic, colorful era of the miners' and the cattlemen's frontier
____ 5. "Dry farming," barbed wire, and irrigation	**E.** Decimated Indian populations and hastened their defeat at the hands of advancing whites
____ 6. The passing of the frontier of 1890	**F.** Effectively ended the free-silver agitation and the domination of the money question in American politics
____ 7. The growing economic specialization of western farmers	**G.** Made settlers vulnerable to vast industrial and market forces beyond their control
____ 8. The rise of the Populist Party in the early 1890s	**H.** Made it possible to farm the dry, treeless areas of the Great Plains and the West
____ 9. The economic depression that began in 1893	**I.** Further undermined Native Americans' traditional tribal culture and morale
____ 10. The return of prosperity after 1897 and new gold discoveries in Alaska, South Africa, and elsewhere	**J.** Led to nearly constant warfare with Plains Indians from 1868 to about 1890

G. Developing Historical Skills

Comparing Election Maps

Comparing maps of two consecutive elections enables you to see what political changes have occurred in a relatively brief historical period. The election map on p. 628 shows the vote by county; the one on p. 637 shows the vote by state. Keep that difference in mind as you answer the following questions.

1. Six western states had significant votes for the Populist Weaver in 1892. Who carried them in 1896?

2. List six states where Democrat Cleveland had strong support in 1892 that turned around and voted Republican in 1896. In which region were most such states located?

3. List five states that stayed solidly Republican in both 1892 and 1896, and five states that stayed solidly Democratic. In which regions were each of these groups of "solid" states located?

4. In 1892, nine midwestern and western states had substantial concentrations of Populist voters. In the election of 1896, how many of those nine states went Democratic, and how many went Republican?

H. Map Mastery

Map Discrimination

Using the maps and charts in Chapter 26, answer the following questions.

1. In the election of 1892, which three western states had no counties that backed the Populist party?

2. Which four southern states had the most Populist support in the election of 1892 (that is, at least three counties that went Populist)?

3. In the election of 1896, how many electoral votes did McKinley win from states west of the Mississippi River?

4. How many electoral votes did McKinley win in the southern states of the old Confederacy?

Map Challenge

Using the maps of *American Agriculture in 1900* (p. 609) and *Presidential Election of 1896* (p. 620), discuss why the relationship between the Populist and pro-silver movements and the patterns of American agriculture. Include in your analysis some analysis of those Midwestern agricultural states that did may have been influenced by Populism but did not vote for Bryan in 1896.

PART III: Applying What You Have Learned

1. How did whites finally overcome resistance of the Plains Indians, and what happened to the Indians after their resistance ceased?

2. What social, ethnic, environmental, and economic factors made the trans-Mississippi West a unique region among the successive American frontiers?

3. What were the actual effects of the frontier on American society at different stages of its development? What was valuable in Frederick Jackson Turner's "frontier thesis," despite its being discredited by subsequent historians?

4. How did the forces of economic class conflict and race figure into the farmer and labor revolt of the 1880s and 1890s? Was there ever any chance that a bi-racial coalition of farmers could have succeeded not only in economic change but in overcoming the South's racial divisions?
   Were race relations actually worse after the Populist revolt failed?

5. Were the Populist and pro-silver movements of the 1880s and 1890s essentially backward-looking protests by a passing rural America, or were they, despite their immediate political failure, genuine prophetic voices raising central critical questions about democracy and economic justice in the new corporate industrial America?

6. What were the major issues in the crucial campaign of 1896? Why did McKinley win, and what were the long-term effects of his victory?

7. Some historians have seen Bryan as the political heir of Jefferson and Jackson, and McKinley as the political heir of Hamilton and the Whigs. Are such connections valid? Why or why not? (See Chapters 10, 12, and 13.)

27

The Path of Empire,
1890–1899

PART I: Reviewing the Chapter

A. Checklist of Learning Objectives

After mastering this chapter, you should be able to

1. explain why the United States suddenly abandoned its isolationism and turned outward at the end of the nineteenth century.
2. indicate how the Venezuelan and Hawaiian affairs expressed the new American assertiveness as well as American ambivalence about foreign involvements.
3. describe how America became involved with Cuba and explain why a reluctant President McKinley was forced to go to war with Spain.
4. state the unintended consequences of Dewey's victory at Manila Bay.
5. describe the easy American military conquest of Cuba and Puerto Rico.
6. explain McKinley's decision to keep the Philippines and list the opposing arguments in the debate about imperialism.
7. analyze the long-term consequences and significance of the Spanish-American War.

B. Glossary

To build your social science vocabulary, familiarize yourself with the following terms.

1. **concession** A privilege granted by a government to another government, private company, or individual. ". . . Japan, Germany, and Russia all extorted concessions from the anemic Chinese Empire." (p. 624)
2. **nation-state** The modern form of political organization in which the government coincides exactly with a single national territory and population having a distinctive culture, language, history, and so on. "If America was to survive in the competition of modern nation-states, perhaps it, too, would have to become an imperial power." (p. 624)
3. **reciprocity** An exchange of equal privileges between two governments. "America's grip was further tightened in 1875 by a commercial reciprocity agreement. . . ." (p. 627)
4. **scorched-earth policy** The policy of burning and destroying all the property in a given area so as to deny it to an enemy. "Driven to desperation, the insurgents now adopted a scorched-earth policy." (p. 628)
5. **reconcentration** The policy of forcibly removing a population to confined areas in order to deny support to enemy forces. " He undertook to crush the rebellion by herding many civilians into barbed-wire reconcentration camps." (p. 629)
6. **jingoist** Aggressively patriotic and warlike. ". . . Cleveland—an antijingoist and anti-imperialist—refused to budge." (p. 629)
7. **atrocity** A specific act of extreme cruelty. "Where atrocity stories did not exist, they were invented." (p. 629)

8. **proviso** An article or clause in a statute, treaty, or contract establishing a particular stipulation or condition affecting the whole document. "This proviso proclaimed . . . that when the United States had overthrown Spanish misrule, it would give the Cubans their freedom. . . ." (p. 631)

9. **archipelago** A large group of islands within a limited area. "An impression spread that America needed the archipelago. . . ." (p. 633)

10. **hostage** A person or thing forcibly held in order to obtain certain goals or agreements. "Hereafter these distant islands were to be . . . a kind of indefensible hostage given to Japan." (p. 642)

PART II: Checking Your Progress

A. True-False

Where the statement is true, mark **T**. Where it is false, mark **F**, and correct it in the space immediately below.

F 1. The American government was deeply involved in the key international developments of the 1870s and 1880s.

T 2. Alfred T. Mahan argued in his book that ~~the conquest of colonies~~ *Control of the Sea* necessary to provide raw ~~materials and markets~~ was the key to world history.

T 3. The South American boundary dispute over Guyana in 1895–1896 nearly resulted in a U.S. war with ~~Venezuela~~.

T 4. The ~~Venezuelan~~ *Britain* boundary dispute was resolved when the United States backed away because of its growing conflict with Germany.

T 5. President Cleveland refused to annex Hawaii because he believed that the white America planters there had unjustly deposed Hawaii's Queen Liliuokalani.

T 6. Americans first became involved in Cuba because they sympathized with the Cubans' revolt against imperialist Spain.

F 7. The Hearst press worked to promote a peaceful, negotiated settlement involving Cuban self-government under Spanish rule.

T 8. President McKinley tried to resist the pressure for war with Spain coming from ~~business-people and Wall Street financiers~~ *the press*.

F 9. Admiral Dewey's squadron attacked Spanish forces in the Philippines because of secret orders give by Assistant Navy Secretary Theodore Roosevelt.

T 10. American forces received assistance in capturing Manila by native Filipinos who were rebelling against Spain.

T 11. The American military conquest of Cuba was *in* efficient but ~~very~~ *not* costly in battlefield casualties.

F 12. President McKinley declared that religion played a role in his decision to keep the Philippines.

T 13. The treaty to annex the Philippines was approved by a wide margin in the Senate.

F   14. The Supreme Court decided in the insular cases that American constitutional law and the bill of rights applied to the people under American rule in Puerto Rico and the Philippines.

T   15. The Spanish-American War made the United States a full-fledged power in East Asia.

B.   Multiple Choice

Select the best answer and write the proper letter in the space provided.

B   1. Alfred Thayer Mahan promoted American overseas expansion by

   a.   developing a lurid "yellow press" that stimulated popular excitement.
   b.   arguing that sea power was the key to world domination.
   c.   provoking naval incidents with Germany and Britain in the Pacific.
   d.   arguing that the Monroe Doctrine implied American control of Latin America.

A   2. Which of the following was *not* among the factors propelling America toward overseas expansion in the 1890s?

   a.   the desire to expand overseas agricultural and manufacturing exports
   b.   the "yellow press" of Joseph Pulitzer and William Randolph Hearst
   c.   the need to find new African and Asian sources of raw materials for American industry
   d.   the ideologies of Anglo-Saxon superiority and social Darwinism

A   3. The final result of the Venezuela-Guiana crisis with Britain was

   a.   a series of battles between British and American naval forces.
   b.   the intervention of the German kaiser in Latin America.
   c.   American colonial control of Guiana.
   d.   British retreat and growing American-British friendship.

A   4. President Grover Cleveland refused to annex Hawaii because

   a.   white planters had illegally overthrown Queen Liliuokalani against the wishes of most native Hawaiians.
   b.   there was no precedent for the United States to acquire territory except by purchase.
   c.   the Germans and the British threatened possible war.
   d.   he knew the public disapproved and the Senate would not ratify a treaty of annexation.

C   5. Americans first became concerned with the situation in Cuba because

   a.   Spanish control of Cuba violated the Monroe Doctrine.
   b.   imperialists and business leaders were looking to acquire colonial territory for the United States.
   c.   Americans sympathized with Cuban rebels in their fight for freedom from Spanish rule.
   d.   the Battleship *Maine* exploded in Havana harbor.

D   6. Even before the sinking of the Maine, the American public's indignation at Spain had been whipped into a frenzy by

   a.   Spanish Catholics' persecution of the Protestant minority in Cuba.
   b.   Spain's aggressive battleship-building program.
   c.   William Randolph Hearst's sensational newspaper accounts of Spanish atrocities in Cuba.
   d.   the Spanish government's brutal treatment of American sailors on leave in Havana.

_B_ 7. Even after the *Maine* exploded, the United States was slow to declare war on Cuba because

    a. the public was reluctant to get into a war.
    b. President McKinley was reluctant to get into a war.
    c. the Cubans did not want Americans to intervene in their affairs.
    d. there was no clear evidence that the Spanish had really blown up the *Maine*.

_B_ 8. As soon as the U.S. declared war on Spain, Commodore George Dewey sailed to the Philippine Islands because

    a. that was the best place to strike a blow for a free Cuba.
    b. he had been ordered to do so by Assistant Navy Secretary Theodore Roosevelt.
    c. the American navy happened to be on a tour of East Asian ports.
    d. he was invited to do so by Philippine nationalists.

_C_ 9. Emilio Aguinaldo was

    a. the leader of Cuban insurgents against Spanish rule.
    b. the leader of Filipino insurgents against Spanish rule.
    c. the commander of the Spanish navy in the Battle of Manila Bay.
    d. the first native Hawaiian to become governor of the islands after the American takeover.

_D_ 10. The largest cause of American deaths in Cuba was

    a. the direct-charge tactics of Theodore Roosevelt's Rough Riders.
    b. the effective artillery bombardments of the Spanish navy.
    c. armed clashes with Cuban rebels and civilians.
    d. bad food, disease, and unsanitary conditions.

_A_ 11. In addition to Cuba, American forces successfully seized the Spanish-owned Caribbean colony of

    a. Puerto Rico.
    b. the Virgin Islands.
    c. the Dominican Republic.
    d. Guam.

_B_ 12. President William McKinley based his decision to make the Philippines an American colony on

    a. the belief in white Anglo-Saxon superiority to the Asian Filipinos.
    b. a combination of religious piety and material economic interests.
    c. the belief that the Philippines would be the first step toward an American empire in China.
    d. the strong agitation for empire coming from the Hearst and Pulitzer yellow press.

_C_ 13. Among prominent Americans who opposed annexation of the Philippines were

    a. Leonard Wood and Walter Reed.
    b. William Randolph Hearst and Theodore Roosevelt.
    c. Mark Twain and William James.
    d. Mark Hanna and "Czar" Thomas Reed.

A   14. Pro-imperialist Americans argued that the Philippines should be seized because of

    a. patriotism and economic opportunities.

    b. the Monroe Doctrine and national security.

    c. the Declaration of Independence and the wishes of the Philippine people.

    d. overpopulation and the need to acquire new land for American settlers.

D   15. The Platt Amendment provided that

    a. the people of Puerto Rico were citizens of the United States.

    b. the United States would eventually grant independence to the Philippines and Puerto Rico.

    c. no European power could establish new bases or colonies in the Pacific.

    d. the United States had the right to intervene with troops and maintain military bases in Cuba.

C. Identification

Supply the correct identification for each numbered description.

_____ 1. Book written by a Protestant minister that proclaimed the superiority of Anglo-Saxon civilization

_____ 2. Remote Pacific site of a naval clash between the United States and Germany in 1889

_____ 3. South American nation that nearly came to blows with the United States in 1892 over an incident involving the deaths of American sailors

_____ 4. The principle of American foreign policy invoked by Secretary of State Olney to justify American intervention in the Venezuelan boundary dispute

_____ 5. Valuable naval base acquired by the United States from the Hawaiian government in 1887

_____ 6. Term for the sensationalistic and jingoistic prowar journalism practiced by W. R. Hearst and Joseph Pulitzer

_____ 7. American battleship sent on a "friendly" visit to Cuba that ended in disaster and war

_____ 8. Amendment to the declaration of war with Spain that stated the United States would grant Cubans their independence after the war

_____ 9. Site of the dramatic American naval victory that led to U.S. acquisition of rich, Spanish-owned Pacific islands

_____ 10. Colorful volunteer regiment of the Spanish-American War led by a militarily inexperienced but politically influential colonel

_____ 11. The Caribbean island conquered from Spain in 1898 that became an important American colony

_____ 12. Group that battled against American colonization of the Philippines, which included such influential citizens as Mark Twain and Andrew Carnegie

_____ 13. Supreme Court cases of 1901 that determined that the U.S. Constitution and bill of rights did not apply in colonial territories under the American flag

14. American-imposed restriction written into the constitution of Cuba that guaranteed American naval bases on the island and declared that the United States had the right to intervene in Cuba

_____ 15. Deadly tropical disease conquered during the Spanish-American War by Dr. Walter Reed and other American medical researchers

D. Matching People, Places, and Events

Match the person, place, or event in the left column with the proper description in the right column by inserting the correct letter on the blank line.

___ 1. Josiah Strong

___ 2. Alfred Thayer Mahan

___ 3. Richard Olney

___ 4. Queen Liliuokalani

___ 5. Grover Cleveland

___ 6. "Butcher" Weyler

___ 7. William R. Hearst

___ 8. William McKinley

___ 9. George E. Dewey

___ 10. Theodore Roosevelt

___ 11. Emilio Aguinaldo

___ 12. Leonard Wood

___ 13. William James

___ 14. William Jennings Bryan

___ 15. Walter Reed

A. Imperialist advocate, aggressive assistant navy secretary, Rough Rider

B. Harvard philosopher and one of the leading anti-imperialists opposing U.S. acquisition of the Philippines

C. Spanish general whose brutal tactics against Cuban rebels outraged American public opinion

D. Native Hawaiian ruler overthrown in a revolution led by white planters and aided by U.S. troops

E. Commander in Spanish-American War who organized the efficient American military government of Cuba

F. American naval officer who wrote influential books emphasizing sea power and advocating a big navy

G. Naval commander whose spectacular May Day victory in 1898 opened the doors to American imperialism in Asia

H. Vigorous promoter of sensationalistic anti-Spanish propaganda and eager advocate of imperialistic war

I. American doctor who led the medical efforts to conquer yellow fever during U.S. occupation of Cuba

J. American clergyman who preached Anglo-Saxon superiority and called for stronger U.S. missionary effort overseas

K. Belligerent U.S. secretary of state who used the Monroe Doctrine to pressure Britain in the Venezuelan boundary crisis

L. President who initially opposed war with Spain but eventually supported U.S. acquisition of the Philippines

M. Leading Democratic politician whose intervention narrowly tipped the Senate vote in favor of acquiring the Philippines in 1899

N. American president who refused to annex Hawaii on the grounds that the native ruler had been unjustly deposed

O. Leader of the Filipino insurgents who aided Americans in defeating Spain and taking Manila

E. Putting Things in Order

Put the following events in correct order by numbering them from 1 to 5.

____ American rebels in Hawaii seek annexation by the United States, but the American president turns them down.

____ A battleship explosion arouses fury in America and leads the nation into a "splendid little war" with Spain.

____ A South American boundary dispute leads to aggressive American assertion of the Monroe Doctrine against Britain.

____ Americans grant Cuba self-government but retain naval bases and the right to intervene.

____ The U.S. Senate narrowly approves a treaty giving the United States a major colony off the coast of Asia.

F. Matching Cause and Effect

Match the historical cause in the left column with the proper effect in the right column by writing the correct letter on the blank line.

Cause	Effect
____ 1. Economic expansion, the yellow press, and competition with other powers	**A.** Enabled America's unprepared military forces to gain quick and easy victories
____ 2. The Venezuelan boundary dispute	**B.** Created an emotional and irresistible public demand for war with Spain
____ 3. The white planter revolt against Queen Liliuokalani	**C.** Strengthened the Monroe Doctrine and made Britain more willing to accommodate U.S. interests
____ 4. The Cuban revolt against Spain	**D.** Led to the surprising U.S. victory over Spain at Manila Bay
____ 5. The *Maine* explosion	**E.** Set off the first debate about the wisdom and rightness of American overseas imperialism
____ 6. Theodore Roosevelt's secret orders to Commodore Dewey	**F.** Turned America away from isolationism and toward international involvements in the 1890s
____ 7. The confusion and weakness of Spain's army and navy	**G.** Aroused strong sympathy from most Americans
____ 8. McKinley's decision to keep the Philippines	**H.** Enhanced American national pride and made the United States an international power in East Asia
____ 9. W. J. Bryan's last-minute support for the treaty acquiring the Philippines	**I.** Set off a bitter debate about imperialism in the Senate and the country
____ 10. The Spanish-American War	**J.** Tipped a narrow Senate vote in favor of imperialist acquisition of the Philippines

G. Map Mastery

Map Discrimination

Using the maps and charts in Chapter 27, answer the following questions.

1. *The Venezuela-British Guiana Boundary Dispute*: In the Venezuelan boundary conflict, which nation—Britain or Venezuela—gained more of the disputed territory in the final settlement?

2. *The Pacific*: What two prime naval harbors did the United States acquire in (a) Samoa and (b) Hawaii?

3. *Dewey's Route in the Philippines, 1898*: Manila Bay lies off the coast of which island of the Philippine archipelago?

4. *The Cuban Campaign, 1898*: Which of the two battles fought by Rough Riders—San Juan Hill and El Caney—occurred nearer Santiago Harbor?

5. *The Cuban Campaign, 1898*: Which of the two Spanish-owned Caribbean islands conquered by the United States in 1898 was farthest from Florida?

Map Challenge

Using the map of *The Pacific* on p. 627, discuss the exact geographical relation of each of America's new Pacific colonies—Samoa, Hawaii, the Philippines—to (a) the United States mainland and (b) China and Japan. Which of the colonies was most strategically important to America's position in the Pacific, which least, and which was most vulnerable? Why?

PART III: Applying What You Have Learned

1. What were the causes and signs of America's sudden turn toward international involvement at the end of the nineteenth century?

2. How did the United States get into the Spanish-American War over the initial objections of President McKinley?

3. What role did the press and public opinion play in the origin, conduct, and results of the Spanish-American War?

4. What were the key arguments for and against U. S. imperialism?

5. What were some of the short-term and long-term results of American acquisition of the Philippines and Puerto Rico?

6. How was U. S. overseas imperialism in 1898 similar to and different from earlier American expansion across North America, or "Manifest Destiny"? (See especially Chapter 13.) Was this "new imperialism" a fundamental departure from America's traditions, or simply a further extension of "westward migration"?

28

America on the World Stage, 1899–1909

PART I: Reviewing the Chapter

A. Checklist of Learning Objectives

After mastering this chapter, you should be able to

1. describe the Filipino rebellion against U.S. rule and the war to suppress it.
2. explain the U.S. "Open Door" policy in China.
3. discuss the significance of the "proimperialist" Republican victory in 1900 and the rise of Theodore Roosevelt as a strong advocate of American power in international affairs.
4. describe the aggressive steps Roosevelt took to build a canal in Panama and explain why his "corollary" to the Monroe Doctrine aroused such controversy.
5. discuss Roosevelt's other diplomatic achievements, particularly in relation to Japan.

B. Glossary

To build your social science vocabulary, familiarize yourself with the following terms.

1. **Americanization** The process of assimilating American character, manner, ideals, culture, and so on. "The Filipinos, who hated compulsory Americanization, preferred liberty." (p. 648)
2. **sphere of influence** In international affairs, the territory where a powerful state exercises the dominant control over weaker states or territories. ". . . they began to tear away valuable lease-holds and economic spheres of influence from the Manchu government." (p. 648)
3. **partition** In politics, the act of dividing a weaker territory or government among several more powerful states. "Defenseless China was spared partition during these troubled years." (p. 649)
4. **blue blood** Person descended from nobility or aristocracy. "What manner of man was Theodore Roosevelt, the red-blooded blue blood?" (p. 653)
5. **bellicose** Disposed to fight or go to war. "Incurably boyish and bellicose, Roosevelt loved to fight. . . ." (p. 654)
6. **preparedness** The accumulation of sufficient armed forces and matériel to go to war. "[Roosevelt was] an ardent champion of military and naval preparedness. . . ." (p. 654)
7. **corollary** A secondary inference or deduction from a main proposition that is taken as established or proven. "Roosevelt therefore devised a devious policy of 'preventive intervention,' better known as the Roosevelt Corollary of the Monroe Doctrine." (p. 657)
8. **dictum** An authoritative edict or assertion. "Roosevelt's corollary . . . bore only a strained relation to the original dictum of 1823." (p. 657)
9. **preemptive** The prior appropriation of land or other goods, in order to prevent their appropriation by others. "Yet in its own right the corollary had considerable merit as a preemptive stroke." (p. 658)
10. **indemnity** A payment assessed to compensate for an injury or unwarranted action. "The Japanese presented stern demands for a huge indemnity." (p. 659)

PART II: Checking Your Progress

A. True-False

Where the statement is true, mark **T**. Where it is false, mark **F**, and correct it in the space immediately below.

T   1. The Filipino insurrection against U.S. rule was larger and more costly in lives than the Spanish-American War.

F   2. John Hay's Open Door notes effectively saved China from foreign intervention and partition.

T

F   3. The McKinley-Roosevelt victory in 1900 over the anti-imperialist campaign of William Jennings Bryan was interpreted as a public mandate for American imperialism.

F   4. Theodore Roosevelt believed that America and its president should exercise restraint in international involvements.

T   5. Roosevelt encouraged and assisted the Panamanian revolution against Colombia in 1903.

F   6. Roosevelt took strong action to acquire canal rights in Panama because there was no alternative route for a Central American canal.

T   7. The Roosevelt corollary to the Monroe Doctrine stated that only the United States had the right to intervene in Latin American nations' affairs.

F

T   8. Roosevelt's negotiation to bring about a peace treaty between Russia and Japan earned the United States the ~~gratitude~~ of both nations.

          hostility

T   9. The Japanese crisis of 1906 forced President Roosevelt to intervene in the policies of the San Francisco School Board.

T   10. The "Gentlemen's Agreement" and the Root-Takahira agreement demonstrated Roosevelt's eagerness to avoid a major conflict with Japan.

B. Multiple Choice

Select the best answer and write the proper letter in the space provided.

C   1. The most immediate consequence of American acquisition of the Philippines was

     a. the establishment of Manila as a crucial American defense post in East Asia.
     b. an agreement between Americans and Filipinos to move toward Philippine independence.
     c. a guerrilla war between the United States and Filipino rebels.
     d. threats by Japan to seize the Philippines from American control.

C   2. In the Open Door notes, Secretary of State John Hay called on all the imperial powers to

     a. guarantee American control of the Philippines.
     b. reduce the arms race in China and the Pacific.
     c. respect Chinese rights and permit economic competition in their spheres of influence.
     d. grant the United States an equal share in the colonization of China.

B 3. The Boxer Rebellion marked a sharp departure for American foreign policy because

    a. the United States had previously backed anti-imperialist nationalist forces in China.

    b. the United States had never before sent military forces to intervene on the East Asian mainland.

    c. it involved the United States in military cooperation with Japan.

    d. it contradicted the policies spelled out in Secretary Hay's Open Door notes.

D 4. Theodore Roosevelt was nominated as President McKinley's vice-presidential running mate in 1900 because

    a. his exploits in the Spanish-American War had made him a national hero.

    b. the midwestern McKinley needed an easterner to balance the ticket.

    c. McKinley wanted to take advantage of Roosevelt's military experience in the Spanish-American War.

    d. local political bosses in New York wanted to get Roosevelt out of the state.

A 5. In the election of 1900, Democrat William Jennings Bryan declared that the key issue was

    a. American imperialism in the Philippines.

    b. Republican mismanagement of the economy.

    c. American foreign policy toward China.

    d. social reform in both cities and agricultural areas.

C 6. As president, Theodore Roosevelt gained political strength especially through

    a. his careful use of traditional diplomacy.

    b. his willingness to follow Congress's lead in domestic policy.

    c. his personal popularity with the public and his belief in direct action.

    d. his ability to subordinate his own personality to that of his cabinet.

B 7. Besides Panama, the primary alternative site for a Central American canal was

    a. Cuba.

    b. Nicaragua.

    c. Mexico.

    d. Colombia.

B 8. Roosevelt overcame Colombia's refusal to approve a canal treaty by

    a. increasing the amount of money the United States was willing to pay for a canal zone.

    b. encouraging Panamanian rebels to revolt and declare independence from Colombia.

    c. looking for another canal site elsewhere in Central America.

    d. seeking mediation of the dispute by other Latin American nations.

D 9. The Roosevelt corollary to the Monroe Doctrine declared that

    a. no European powers could intervene in or colonize Latin America.

    b. the United States had a right to build, maintain, and defend the Panama Canal.

    c. the United States would take no more colonial territory in Latin America.

    d. the United States had the right to intervene in Latin American countries to maintain financial and political order.

_b_ 10. Roosevelt's policies in Panama and elsewhere in Latin America led to

    a. a Good Neighbor policy between the United States and its "little brothers" in Latin America.

    b. resentment and hostility toward American intervention in Latin America.

    c. growing tension between the United States and Germany over influence in the region.

    d. anti-Roosevelt feeling among the Hispanic population in the United States.

_c_ 11. Theodore Roosevelt's slogan that stated his essential foreign policy principle was

    a. "Open covenants openly arrived at."

    b. "Millions for defense but not one cent for tribute."

    c. "Speak softly and carry a big stick."

    d. "Democracy and Liberty in a New World Order."

_b_ 12. Roosevelt mediated the Portsmouth Treaty to settle the war between

    a. Britain and Japan.

    b. Russia and Japan.

    c. China and Japan.

    d. Spain and North Africa.

_c_ 13. The diplomatic crisis between the United States and Japan in 1906 was caused by

    a. confrontations between the American and Japan navies.

    b. American refusal to recognize Japanese spheres of influence in China.

    c. the San Francisco School Board's segregation of Japanese immigrant children.

    d. American prohibition of all immigration from Japan.

_b_ 14. The Gentlemen's Agreement" between the United States and Japan provided that

    a. the Americans and Japanese would each guarantee the other's rights in China.

    b. the San Francisco schools would integrated in exchange for Japan putting and end to Japanese immigration to America.

    c. Japan would recognize American control of the Philippines in exchange for American acceptance of Japan's domination of Manchuria and Korea.

    d. Japanese immigrants would be able to work in the United States but not become citizens.

_A_ 15. Roosevelt's "Great White Fleet" essentially served as

    a. a support force for the Roosevelt corollary to the Monroe Doctrine.

    (b.) a demonstration of American naval power in East Asia.

    c. a sign that America would intervene in China if necessary.

    d. a means of providing relief shipment of food to famine victims in Latin America and Asia.

C. Identification

Supply the correct identification for each numbered description.

_____ 1. John Hay's clever diplomatic efforts to preserve Chinese territorial integrity and maintain American access to China

_____ 2. Antiforeign Chinese revolt of 1900 that brought military intervention by Western troops, including Americans

_____ 3. Proverbial symbol of Roosevelt's belief that presidents should engage in diplomacy but also maintain a strong military readiness to back up their policy

_____ 4. Diplomatic agreement of 1901 that permitted the United States to build and fortify a Central American canal alone, without British involvement

_____ 5. Nation whose senate in 1902 refused to ratify a treaty permitting the United States to build a canal across its territory

_____ 6. Agreement between the United States and the revolutionary government of Panama granting America the right to build a canal

_____ 7. Questionable extension of a traditional American policy; declared an American right to intervene in Latin American nations under certain circumstances

_____ 8. War concluded by Roosevelt-mediated treaty that earned TR the Nobel Peace Prize but caused much ill will toward America from the two signatories

_____ 9. Diplomatic understanding of 1907–1908 that ended a Japanese-American crisis over treatment of Japanese immigrants to the U.S.

_____ 10. Large U.S. naval force sent on a peaceful but highly visible voyage to Japan and elsewhere in 1907

D. Matching People, Places, and Events

Match the person, place, or event in the left column with the proper description in the right column by inserting the correct letter on the blank line.

___ 1. Emilio Aguinaldo

___ 2. John Hay

___ 3. William Jennings Bryan

___ 4. Theodore Roosevelt

___ 5. Philippe Bunau-Varilla

___ 6. Thomas Platt

___ 7. George Washington Goethals

___ 8. Portsmouth, New Hampshire

___ 9. San Francisco, California

___ 10. Algeciras, Spain

A. American engineer who organized the building of the Panama Canal

B. Site of a Roosevelt-mediated international conference on Morocco

C. Place where a local school board's attempt to segregate Japanese children created an international incident

D. American secretary of state who attempted to preserve Chinese independence and protect American interests in China

E. Site of Roosevelt-sponsored negotiations that ended the Russo-Japanese War

F. Scheming French engineer who helped stage a revolution in Panama and then became the new country's "instant" foreign minister

G. Filipino leader of a guerilla war against American rule from 1899 to 1901

H. Diplomat, moralizer, wielder of the big stick, "a combination of St. Paul and St. Vitus"

I. Politician who successfully schemed to get TR out of New York and off to Washington

J. Candidate who waged an unsuccessful presidential campaign on the issue of American imperialism in the Philippines

E. Putting Things in Order

Put the following events in correct order by numbering them from 1 to 5.

_____ TR mediates a peace treaty between two combatants in the Far East.

_____ A Chinese uprising against foreigners brings American troops to Beijing (Peking).

_____ "That damn cowboy" becomes president of the United States after an assassination.

_____ A school-spawned crisis provokes the end of Japanese immigration to America and a flurry of diplomacy to smooth relations between U.S. and Japan.

_____ Questionable Roosevelt actions in Central America help create a new republic and pave the way for a U.S.-built canal.

F. Matching Cause and Effect

Match the historical cause in the left column with the proper effect in the right column by writing the correct letter on the blank line.

Cause	Effect
_____ 1. The Filipino rebellion against the United States	**A.** Led to John Hay's energetic and clever Open Door diplomacy
_____ 2. The threat of European partition of China	**B.** Paved the way for the Root-Takahira agreement between the United States and Japan
_____ 3. The Boxer Rebellion	**C.** Sent TR to the vice presidency and from there to the White House
_____ 4. Boss Platt's desire to get Roosevelt out of New York	**D.** Convinced the San Francisco School Board to allow Japanese children into the city's schools
_____ 5. The Colombian Senate's refusal to ratify a canal treaty	**E.** Led to a costly, dirty war that shocked and dismayed Americans
_____ 6. The "Roosevelt corollary" to the Monroe Doctrine and U.S. intervention in Cuba and the Dominican Republic	**F.** Resulted in a pro-American and procanal revolution that declared an independent Panama
_____ 7. The Russo-Japanese War	**G.** Sent waves of new Japanese immigrants into California
_____ 8. West Coast fear of the "yellow peril" of Japanese immigration	**H.** Brought a foreign expedition into China and forced China to pay an indemnity to the United States
_____ 9. Roosevelt's intervention in the San Francisco School Board crisis	**I.** Created strong anti-American feeling in Latin America
_____ 10. The Great White Fleet's visit to Japan	**J.** Prompted the San Francisco school segregation crisis of 1906

G. Developing Historical Skills

Main Ideas and Supporting Evidence

Historical writing, like many other kinds of writing, develops a main idea with supporting detailed evidence. Each of the five statements below is the main idea of one section of Chapter 28. For each main idea in these headed subsections, list three factual details from the text that support it.

1. *"Little Brown Brothers" in the Philippines* (pp.646–648)

   Assuming control of the Philippines caused terrible military and political conflict between the American government and the Filipinos.

2. *TR: Brandisher of the Big Stick* (pp. 653–655)

   Theodore Roosevelt was a very energetic and able politician who overcame all kinds of obstacles.

3. *Uncle Sam Creates Puppet Panama* (pp. 655–656)

   Frustrated by Colombian opposition, Theodore Roosevelt encouraged a group of Panamanians to stage a revolution and pave the way for an American canal.

4. *TR's Perversion of the Monroe Doctrine* (pp. 657–658)

   Roosevelt's "corollary" to the Monroe Doctrine distorted traditional American policy, aroused Latin American resentment, and led to frequent American interventions in the region.

5. *Roosevelt on the World Stage* (pp. 658–659)

   Roosevelt successfully resolved the Russo-Japanese War, but at some cost to American relations with the two countries.

PART III: Applying What You Have Learned

1. What were the effects of America's new East Asian involvement in both the Philippines and China in 1899–1901?
2. What were the essential principles of Theodore Roosevelt's foreign policy, and how did he apply them to specific situations?
3. How did Roosevelt's policies in Latin America demonstrate American power in the region, and why did they arouse opposition from Latin Americans?
4. What were the central issues in America's relations with China and Japan? How did Roosevelt handle tense relations with Japan?
5. What were the strengths and weaknesses of Theodore Roosevelt's aggressive foreign policy? What were the benefits of TR's activism and what were its drawbacks?
6. The text states that the Roosevelt corollary to the Monroe Doctrine distorted the original policy statement of 1823. How did it do so? (See Chapter 10.) Compare the circumstances and purposes of the two policies.

29

Progressivism and the Republican Roosevelt, 1901–1912

PART I: Reviewing the Chapter

A. Checklist of Learning Objectives

After mastering this chapter, you should be able to

1. discuss the origins and nature of the progressive movement.
2. describe how the early progressive movement developed its roots at the city and state level.
3. identify the critical role that women played in progressive social reform.
4. tell how President Roosevelt began applying progressive principles to the national economy.
5. explain why Taft's policies offended progressives, including Roosevelt.
6. describe how Roosevelt led a progressive revolt against Taft that openly divided the Republican party.

B. Glossary

To build your social science vocabulary, familiarize yourself with the following terms.

1. **progressive** In politics, one who believes in continuing social advancement, improvement, or reform. "The new crusaders, who called themselves 'progressives,' waged war on many evils. . . ." (p. 664)
2. **conspicuous consumption** The theory, developed by economist Thorstein Veblen, that much spending by the affluent occurs primarily to display wealth and status to others rather than from enjoyment of the goods or services. " . . . a savage attack on 'predatory wealth' and 'conspicuous consumption.'" (p. 665)
3. **direct primary** In politics, the nomination of a party's candidates for office through a special election of that party's voters. "These ardent reformers pushed for direct primary elections. . . ." (p. 667)
4. **initiative** In politics, the procedure whereby voters can, through petition, present proposed legislation directly to the electorate. "They favored the 'initiative' so that voters could directly propose legislation. . . ." (p. 667)
5. **referendum** The submission of a law, proposed or already in effect, to a direct vote of the electorate. "Progressives also agitated for the 'referendum.'" (p. 667)
6. **recall** In politics, a procedure for removing an official from office through popular election or other means. "The 'recall' would enable the voters to remove faithless elected officials. . . ." (p. 667)
7. **city manager** An administrator appointed by the city council or other elected body to manage affairs, supposedly in a nonpartisan or professional way. "Other communities adopted the city-manager system. . . ." (p. 669)

8. **red-light district** A section of a city where prostitution is officially or unofficially tolerated. ". . . wide-open prostitution (vice-at-a-price) . . . flourished in red-light districts. . . ." (p. 669)

9. **franchise** In government, a special privilege or license granted to a company or group to perform a specific function. "Public-spirited city-dwellers also moved to halt the corrupt sale of franchises for streetcars. . . ." (p. 669)

10. **bureaucracy (bureaucrat)** The management of government or business through departments and subdivisions manned by a system of officials (bureaucrats) following defined rules and processes. (The term is often though not necessarily disparaging.) "These wedges into the federal bureaucracy, however small, gave female reformers a national stage. . . ." (p. 670)

11. **workers' (workmen's) compensation** Insurance, provided either by government or employers or both, providing benefits to employees suffering work-related injury or disability. ". . . by 1917 thirty states had put workers' compensation laws on the books. . . ." (p. 672)

12. **reclamation** The process of bringing or restoring wasteland to productive use. "Settlers repaid the cost of reclamation. . . ." (p. 676)

13. **collectivism** A political or social system in which individuals are subordinated to mass organization and direction. "He strenuously sought the middle road between unbridled individualism and paternalistic collectivism." (p. 683)

14. **insubordination** Deliberate disobedience to proper authority. ". . . Taft dismissed Pinchot on the narrow grounds of insubordination. . . ." (p. 685)

PART II: Checking Your Progress

A. True-False

Where the statement is true, mark **T**. Where it is false, mark **F**, and correct it in the space immediately below.

F 1. The progressive movement believed that social and economic problems should be solved at the community level without involvement by the federal government.

T 2. Muckraking journalists, social-gospel ministers, and women reformers all aroused Americans' concern about economic and social problems.

F 3. The leading progressive reformers were primarily immigrants and urban industrial workers.

T 4. Many female progressives saw the task of improving life in factories and slums as an extension of their traditional roles as wives and mothers.

F 5. President Theodore Roosevelt ended the anthracite coal strike by threatening to use federal troops to ~~break the miners' union.~~ *seize their mines*

T 6. Roosevelt promoted stronger federal legislation to regulate the railroads and other major industries.

F 7. Roosevelt believed that all the monopolistic corporate trusts should be broken up and competition restored among smaller businesses.

F T 8. Upton Sinclair's novel *The Jungle* was intended to arouse consumers' concern about ~~unsanitary practices in the meat industry.~~ *plight of meat-packing workers*

T 9. Conservation policies like land reclamation and forest preservation were probably Theodore Roosevelt's most popular and enduring presidential achievement.

T 10. Defenders of nature became divided between fervent "preservationists" who wanted to stop all human intrusions and more moderate "conservationists."

I 11. Roosevelt effectively used the power of the presidency and the federal government to tame unrestricted capitalism while preserving the basic foundations of American business.

F 12. Taft's "dollar diplomacy" was a successful attempt to mobilize American business to support U.S. foreign policy in East Asia and Latin America.

if T 13. Progressive Republicans became angry with President Taft because he began to form alliances with Democrats and Socialists. Of his tariff + conservation policies

T 14. The Ballinger-Pinchot conservation controversy pushed Taft into alliance with the Republican "Old Guard" against the pro-Roosevelt progressives.

T 15. President Taft used his control of the Republican party machinery to deny Roosevelt the nomination in 1912.

B. Multiple Choice

Select the best answer and write the proper letter in the space provided.

C 1. The primary emphasis of the progressive movement was on
   a. freeing individuals and business from federal control.
   b. protecting farmers and small business from corporate power.
   c. strengthening government as an instrument of social betterment.
   d. organizing workers into a unified and class-conscious political party.

A 2. Prominent among those who aroused the progressive movement by stirring the public's sense of concern were
   a. socialists, social gospelers, women, and muckraking journalists.
   b. union leaders, machine politicians, immigrant spokespeople, and engineers.
   c. bankers, advertising people, congressmen, and scientists.
   d. athletes, entertainers, filmmakers, and musicians.

C 3. Which of the following was *not* among the targets of muckraking journalistic exposés?
   a. urban politics and government
   b. the oil, insurance, and railroad industries
   c. the U.S. Army and Navy
   d. child labor and the "white slave" traffic in women

C 4. Most progressives were
   a. poor farmers.
   b. urban workers.
   c. urban middle-class people.
   d. wealthy people.

D   5. Among the political reforms sought by the progressives were

     a. an end to political parties, political conventions, and the Supreme Court's right to judicial review of legislation.
     b. an Equal Rights Amendment, federal financing of elections, and restrictions on negative campaigning.
     c. civil-service reform, racial integration, and free silver.
     d. initiative and referendum, direct election of senators, and women's suffrage.

B   6. The states where progressivism first gained great influence were

     a. Massachusetts, Maine, and New Hampshire.
     b. Wisconsin, Oregon, and California.
     c. Michigan, Kansas, and Nevada.
     d. New York, Florida, and Texas.

A   7. The Supreme Court case of *Muller v. Oregon* was seen as a victory for both progressivism and women's rights because

     a. it upheld the constitutionality of laws granting special protection to women in the workplace.
     b. it held that women should receive "equal pay for equal work."
     c. it upheld workplace safety regulations to prevent disasters like the Triangle Shirtwaist fire.
     d. it opened almost all categories of the new industrial employment to women.

C   8. Roosevelt ended the Pennsylvania coal strike by

     a. urging labor and management to negotiate a settlement.
     b. passing federal legislation legalizing unions.
     c. forcing mediation by threatening to seize the coal mines and operate them with federal troops.
     d. declaring a national state of emergency and ordering the miners back to work.

B   9. The Roosevelt-backed Elkins Act and Hepburn Act were aimed at

     a. better protection for industrial workers.
     b. more effective regulation of the railroad industry.
     c. protection for consumers of beef and produce.
     d. breaking up the Standard Oil monopoly.

A   10. The controversy over the Hetch Hetchy Valley in Yosemite National Park revealed

     a. a philosophical disagreement between wilderness "preservationists" and more moderate "conservationists."
     b. President Roosevelt's hostility toward creating any more national parks.
     c. a political conflict between the lumber industry and conservationists.
     d. a split between urban California's need for water and environmentalists' concerns to preserve free-flowing streams..

D   11. Two areas where Roosevelt's progressivism made its substantial headway were

     a. agricultural and mining legislation.
     b. stock-market and securities legislation.
     c. immigration and racial legislation.
     d. consumer and conservation legislation.

B 1̸2. Roosevelt was blamed for the "Panic of 1907" because

    (a.) his "boat-rocking tactics" had allegedly unsettled industry.
    b. his policies of regulating and protecting industrial workers had caused a depression.
    c. his inability to establish a stable monetary policy led to a wall street crash.
    d. the public wanted him to run again for president in 1908.

A 13. As a result of his successful campaign in 1908, William Howard Taft was expected to

    a. continue and extend Roosevelt's progressive policies.
    b. forge a coalition with William Jennings Bryan and the Democrats.
    c. emphasize foreign policy instead of Roosevelt's domestic reforms.
    d. turn away from Roosevelt and toward the conservative wing of the Republican party.

A 1̸4. Progressive Republicans grew disillusioned with Taft primarily over the issues of

    a. dollar diplomacy and military intervention in the Caribbean and Central America.
    b. labor union rights and women's concerns.
    (c.) trust-busting, tariffs, and conservation.
    d. regulation of the banking and railroad industries.

C 15. Roosevelt finally decided to break with the Republicans and form a third party because

    a. he had always regarded the Republican party as too conservative.
    b. he could no longer stand to be in the same party with Taft.
    c. Taft used his control of the Republican convention to deny Roosevelt the nomination.
    d. Roosevelt believed that he would have a better chance of winning the presidency as a third-party candidate.

C. Identification

Supply the correct identification for each numbered description.

_____ 1. A largely middle-class movement that aimed to use the power of government to correct the economic and social problems of industrialism

_____ 2. Popular journalists who used publicity to expose corruption and attack abuses of power in business and government

_____ 3. Progressive proposal to allow voters to bypass state legislatures and propose legislation themselves

_____ 4. Progressive device that would enable voters to remove corrupt or ineffective officials from office

_____ 5. Roosevelt's policy of having the federal government promote the public interest by dealing evenhandedly with both labor and business

_____ 6. Effective railroad-regulation law of 1906 that greatly strengthened the Interstate Commerce Commission

_____ 7. Disastrous industrial fire of 1911 that spurred workmen's compensation laws and some state regulation of wages and hours in New York

_____ 8. Upton Sinclair's novel that inspired proconsumer federal laws regulating meat, food, and drugs

_____ 9. Powerful women's reform organization led by Frances Willard

_____ 10. Brief but sharp economic downturn of 1907, blamed by conservatives on the supposedly dangerous president

_____ 11. Generally unsuccessful Taft foreign policy in which government attempted to encourage overseas business ventures

_____ 12. Powerful corporation broken up by a Taft-initiated antitrust suit in 1911

D. Matching People, Places, and Events

Match the person, place, or event in the left column with the proper description in the right column by inserting the correct letter on the blank line.

____ 1. Jacob Riis

____ 2. Lincoln Steffens

____ 3. Ida Tarbell

____ 4. Seventeenth Amendment

____ 5. Robert La Follette

____ 6. Triangle Shirtwaist Company fire

____ 7. Anthracite coal strike

____ 8. Meat Inspection Act of 1906

____ 9. *Muller* v. *Oregon*

____ 10. William Howard Taft

____ 11. *Lochner* v. *New York*

____ 12. Gifford Pinchot

A. Politically inept inheritor of the Roosevelt legacy who ended up allied to the reactionary Republican "Old Guard"

B. Case that upheld protective legislation on the grounds of women's supposed physical weakness

C. New York City disaster that underscored urban workers' need for government protection

D. The most influential of the state-level progressive governors and a presidential aspirant in 1912

E. Author of *How the Other Half Lives,* a shocking description of the New York slums

F. Leading muckraking journalist whose articles documented the Standard Oil Company's abuse of power

G. Proconservation federal official whose dismissal by Taft angered Roosevelt progressives

H. Dangerous labor conflict resolved by Rooseveltian negotiation and threats against business people

I. Early muckraker who exposed the political corruption in many American cities

J. Progressive law aimed at curbing practices like those exposed in Upton Sinclair's *The Jungle*

K. Progressive measure that required U.S. senators to be elected directly by the people rather than by state legislatures

L. Supreme court ruling that overturned a progressive law mandating a ten-hour workday

E. Putting Things in Order

Put the following events in correct order by numbering them from 1 to 5.

____ A former president opposes his handpicked successor for the Republican presidential nomination.

____ Sensational journalistic accounts of corruption and abuse of power in politics and business spur the progressive movement.

____ A progressive forestry official feuds with Taft's secretary of the interior, deepening the division within the Republican party.

____ A novelistic account of Chicago's meat-packing industry sparks new federal laws to protect consumers.

_____ A brief but sharp financial crisis leads to conservative criticism of Roosevelt's progressive policies.

F. Matching Cause and Effect

Match the historical cause in the left column with the proper effect in the right column by writing the correct letter on the blank line.

	Cause		Effect
_____	1. Old-time Populists, muckraking journalists, social-gospel ministers, and European socialist immigrants	A.	Ended the era of uncontrolled exploitation of nature and involved the federal government in preserving natural resources
_____	2. Progressive concern about political corruption	B.	Led to reforms like the initiative, referendum, and direct election of senators
_____	3. Governors like Robert La Follette	C.	Forced a compromise settlement of a strike that threatened the national well-being
_____	4. Roosevelt's threat to seize the anthracite coal mines	D.	Outraged consumers and led to the Meat Inspection Act and the Pure Food and Drug Act
_____	5. Settlement Houses and women's clubs	E.	Laid the basis for a third-party crusade in the election of 1912
_____	6. Upton Sinclair's *The Jungle*	F.	Incensed pro-Roosevelt progressives and increased their attacks on the Republican "Old Guard"
_____	7. Roosevelt's personal interest in conservation	G.	Led the way in using universities and regulatory agencies to pursue progressive goals
_____	8. Taft's political mishandling of tariff and conservation policies	H.	Made Taft's dollar-diplomacy policy a failure
_____	9. Russia's and Japan's hostility to an American role in China	I.	Provided the pioneering forces who laid the foundations for the Progressive movement.
_____	10. Roosevelt's feeling that he was cheated out of the Republican nomination by the Taft machine	J.	Served as the launching pads for widespread female involvement in progressive reforms

G. Developing Historical Skills

Classifying Historical Information

Often a broad historical movement, such as progressivism, can best be understood by breaking it down into various component parts. Among the varieties of progressive reform discussed in this chapter are (A) political progressivism, (B) economic or industrial progressivism, (C) consumer progressivism, and (D) environmental progressivism.

Put each of the following progressive acts, policies, or court cases into one of those categories by writing in the correct letter.

____ 1. The Newlands Act of 1902

____ 2. The ten-hour law for bakers

____ 3. The movement for women's suffrage

____ 4. The anthracite coal strike of 1902

____ 5. Direct election of senators

____ 6. The Meat Inspection Act of 1906

____ 7. The Pure Food and Drug Act

____ 8. Initiative, referendum, and recall

____ 9. *Muller* v. *Oregon*

____ 10. The Hepburn Act of 1906

____ 11. Yosemite and Grand Canyon National Parks

____ 12. Workmen's compensation laws

PART III: Applying What You Have Learned

1. What caused the progressive movement, and how did it get under way?
2. What did the progressive movement accomplish at the local, state, and national levels?
3. What made women such central forces in the progressive crusade? What specific backgrounds and ideologies did they bring to the public arena? What were the strengths and limitations of the progressive emphasis on providing special protection to children and women?
4. Discuss Roosevelt's support for conservation and consumer protection. Why were these among the most successful progressive achievements?
5. What caused the Taft-Roosevelt split, and how did it reflect the growing division between "Old Guard" and "progressive" Republicans?
6. How was progressivism a response to the development of the new urban and industrial order in American? (See Chapters 24 and 25.)

30

Wilsonian Progressivism at Home and Abroad, 1912–1916

PART I: Reviewing the Chapter

A. Checklist of Learning Objectives

After mastering this chapter, you should be able to

1. discuss the key issues of the pivotal 1912 election and the basic principles of Wilsonian progressivism.
2. describe how Wilson successfully reformed the "triple wall of privilege."
3. state the basic features of Wilson's foreign policy and explain how they drew him into intervention in Latin America.
4. describe America's response to World War I and explain the increasingly sharp conflict over America's policies toward Germany.
5. explain how domestic and foreign controversies played into Wilson's narrow victory over Hughes in 1916.

B. Glossary

To build your social science vocabulary, familiarize yourself with the following terms.

1. **entrepreneurship** The process whereby an individual initiates a business at some risk in order to expand it and thereby earn a profit. "Wilson's New Freedom, by contrast, favored small enterprise, entrepreneurship, and the free functioning of . . . markets." (p. 688)
2. **self-determination** In politics, the right of a people to shape its own national identity and form of government, without outside coercion or influence. ". . . [the Confederacy] . . . partly inspired his ideal of self-determination for people of other countries." (p. 690)
3. **piety** Devotion to religious duty and practices. ". . Wilson was reared in an atmosphere of fervent piety." (p. 690)
4. **graduated income tax** A tax on income in which the taxation rates grow progressively higher for those with higher income. "Congress enacted a graduated income tax. . . ." (p. 691)
5. **levy** A forcible tax or other imposition. ". . . [the] income tax [began] with a modest levy on income over $3,000. . . ." (p. 691)
6. **inelasticity** The inability to expand or contract rapidly. "[The] most serious shortcoming [of the country's financial structure] was the inelasticity of the currency." (p. 691)
7. **commercial paper** Any business document having monetary or exchangeable value. "The . . . paper money [was] backed by commercial paper. . . ." (p. 692)
8. **promissory note** A written pledge to pay a certain person a specified sum of money at a certain time. "The . . . paper money [was] backed by commercial paper, such as promissory notes of business people." (p. 692)

9. **Magna Carta** The "Great Charter" of England, which feudal nobles of England forced King John I to sign in 1215. As the first written guarantee of certain traditional rights, such as trial by a jury of peers, against arbitrary royal power, it served as a model for later assertions of Anglo-Saxon liberties. "Union leader Samuel Gompers hailed the [Clayton] act as the Magna Carta of labor. . . ." (p. 692)

10. **agricultural extension** The system of providing services and advice to farmers through dispersed local agents. "Other laws benefited rural American by providing for . . . the establishment of agricultural extension work in the state colleges." (p. 693)

11. **enclave** A small territory surrounded by foreign or hostile territory. "Though often segregated in Spanish-speaking enclaves, they helped to create a unique borderland culture. . . ." (p. 695)

12. **gringo** Contemptuous Latin American term for North Americans. "Challenging Carranza's authority while also punishing the gringos. . . ." (p. 696)

13. **censor** An official who examines publications, mail, literature, and so forth in order to remove or prohibit the distribution of material deemed dangerous or offensive. "Their censors sheared away war stories harmful to the Allies . . . ." (p. 697)

14. **torpedo** To launch from a submarine or airplane a self-propelled underwater explosive designed to detonate on impact. ". . . the British passenger liner *Lusitania* was torpedoed and sank. . . ." (p. 699)

15. **draft** In politics, to choose an individual to run for office without that person's prior solicitation of the nomination. (A *military* draft, or conscription, legally compels individuals into the armed services.) "Instead, they drafted Supreme Court Justice Charles Evans Hughes, a cold intellectual who had achieved a solid record as governor of New York." (p. 701)

PART II: Checking Your Progress

A. True-False

Where the statement is true, mark **T**. Where it is false, mark **F**, and correct it in the space immediately below.

T   1. Wilson won the election of 1912 largely because the Republican party split in two.

F   2. In the 1912 campaign, Wilson's "New Freedom" favored a socially activist government and preserving large regulated trusts, while Roosevelt's "New Nationalist" favored small enterprise and breaking up a big business by antitrust action.

T   3. Wilson believed that the president should provide national leadership by appealing directly to the people.

T   4. Wilson successfully used his popular appeal to push through progressive reforms of the tariff, monetary systems, and trusts.

F   T   5. Wilson's policies were unfair to blacks. Wilson's progressive outlook showed itself clearly in his attempt to improve the conditions and treatment of blacks.

T   6. Wilson attempted to reverse the big-stick and dollar-diplomacy foreign policies of Roosevelt and Taft, especially in Latin America.

F   T   7. Wilson consistently refused to send American troops to intervene in the Caribbean.

T   8. In his policy toward the revolutionary Mexican government of Huerta, Wilson attempted to walk a middle line between recognition and intervention.

I   9. The mediation of three Latin American nations saved Wilson from a full-scale war with Mexico.

F   10. General Pershing's expedition into Mexico was an attempt to bring the pro-American faction of Mexican revolutionaries to power.

F   11. In the early days of World War I, more Americans sympathized with Germany than with Britain.

T F   12. The American economy benefited greatly from supplying goods to the Allies.

F T   13. After the *Lusitania's* sinking, the Midwest and West favored war with Germany, while the East generally favored attempts at negotiation.

T F   14. After the sinking of the *Sussex*, Wilson successfully pressured Germany into stopping submarine attacks against neutral shipping.

T   15. In the 1916 campaign, Wilson ran on the slogan "He Kept Us Out of War," while his opponent Hughes tried to straddle the issue of a possible war with Germany.

B. Multiple Choice

Select the best answer and write the proper letter in the space provided.

D   1. The basic contrast between the two progressive candidates, Roosevelt and Wilson, was that

    a. Roosevelt wanted genuine political and social reforms, while Wilson wanted only to end obvious corruption.
    b. Roosevelt wanted to promote free enterprise and competition, while Wilson wanted the federal government to regulate the economy and promote social welfare.
    c. Roosevelt wanted the federal government to regulate the economy and promote social welfare, while Wilson wanted to restore economic competition and social equality.
    d. Roosevelt wanted to focus on issues of jobs and economic growth, while Wilson wanted social legislation to protect women, children, and city-dwellers.

B   2. Wilson won the election of 1912 primarily because

    a. his policies were more popular with the public.
    b. Taft and Roosevelt split the former Republican vote.
    c. the Socialists took nearly a million votes from Roosevelt.
    d. he was able to win over many of the Roosevelt supporters to his cause.

C   3. Wilson's primary weakness as a politician was

    a. his lack of skill in public speaking.
    b. his inability to grasp the complexity of governmental issues.
    c. his tendency to be inflexible and refuse to compromise.
    d. his lack of overarching political ideals.

_B_ 4. The "triple wall of privilege" that Wilson set out to reform consisted of

    a. farmers, shippers, and the military.
    b. the tariffs, the banks, and the trusts.
    c. the universities, private dining clubs, and political bosses.
    d. congressional leaders, lobbyists, and lawyers.

_D_ 5. During the Wilson administration, Congress exercised the authority granted by the newly enacted Sixteenth Amendment to pass

    a. prohibition of liquor.
    b. women's suffrage.
    c. voting rights for blacks.
    d. a federal income tax.

_A_ 6. The new regulatory agency created by the Wilson administration in 1914 that attacked monopolies, false advertising, and consumer fraud was

    a. the Federal Trade Commission.
    b. the Interstate Commerce Commission.
    c. the Federal Reserve System.
    d. the Consumer Products Safety Commission.

_B_ 7. While it attacked business monopolies, the Clayton Anti-Trust Act exempted from anti-trust prosecution

    a. industries essential to national defense.
    b. agricultural and labor organizations.
    c. the oil and steel industries.
    d. professional organizations of doctors and lawyers.

_C_ 8. Wilson effectively reformed the banking and financial system by

    a. establishing a third Bank of the United States to issue and regulate the currency.
    b. taking the United States off the gold standard.
    c. establishing a publicly controlled Federal Reserve Board with regional banks under bankers' control.
    d. transferring authority to regulate banking and currency to the states and the private sector.

_B_ 9. Wilson's progressive measures substantially aided all of the following groups _except_

    a. workers.
    b. blacks.
    c. farmers.
    d. children.

_B_ 10. Wilson's initial attitude toward the Mexican revolutionary government was

    a. a refusal to recognize the legitimacy of General Huerta's regime.
    b. a willingness to intervene with troops on behalf of threatened American business interests.
    c. strong support and provision of economic assistance to the Huerta regime.
    d. an attempt to mobilize other Latin American governments to help oust Huerta.

C   11. The threatened war between the United States and Mexico in 1914 was avoided by the mediation of the ABC powers, which consisted of

    a. Australia, Britain, and Canada.
    b. Antigua, Brazil, and Cuba.
    c. Argentina, Brazil, and Chile.
    d. the Association of British Commonwealth nations.

A   12. General Pershing's expedition into Mexico was sent in direct response to

    a. the refusal of Huerta to abandon power.
    b. the threat of German intervention in Mexico.
    c. the arrest of American sailors in the Mexican port of Tampico.
    d. the killing of American citizens in New Mexico by "Pancho" Villa.

B   13. The sympathy of a majority of Americans for the Allies and against Germany was especially conditioned by

    a. British bribes and payoffs to American journalists.
    b. the Germans' involvement in overseas imperialism.
    c. the German invasion of neutral Belgium.
    d. the British refusal to use poison gas in warfare.

D   14. After the *Lusitania, Arabic,* and *Sussex* sinkings, Wilson successfully pressured the German government to

    a. end the use of the submarine against British warships.
    b. end its attempt to blockade the British Isles.
    c. publish warnings to all Americans considering traveling on unarmed ships.
    d. cease from sinking neutral merchant and passenger ships without warning.

D   15. Wilson's most effective slogan in the campaign of 1916 was

    a. "The full dinner pail."
    b. "Free and unlimited coinage of silver in the ratio of sixteen to one."
    c. "A war to make the world safe for democracy."
    d. "He kept us out of war."

C. Identification

Supply the correct identification for each numbered description.

_____ 1. Four-footed symbol of Roosevelt's Progressive third party in 1912

_____ 2. A fourth political party, led by a former labor union leader, that garnered nearly a million votes in 1912

_____ 3. Wilson's political philosophy of restoring democracy through trust-busting and economic competition

_____ 4. A twelve-member agency appointed by the president to oversee the banking system under a new federal law of 1913

_____ 5. New presidentially appointed regulatory commission designed to prevent monopoly and guard against unethical trade practices

_____ 6. Wilsonian law that tried to curb business monopoly while permitting labor and agricultural organizations

_____ 7. Wilsonian reform law that established an eight-hour day for railroad workers

_____ 8. Troubled Caribbean island nation where a president's murder led Wilson to send in the marines and assume American control of the police and finances

_____ 9. Term for the three Latin American nations whose mediation prevented war between the United States and Mexico in 1914

_____ 10. World War I alliance headed by Germany and Austria-Hungary

_____ 11. The coalition of powers—led by Britain, France, and Russia—that opposed Germany and its partners in World War I

_____ 12. New underwater weapon that threatened neutral shipping and seemed to violate all traditional norms of international law

_____ 13. Large British passenger liner whose sinking in 1915 prompted some Americans to call for war against Germany

_____ 14. Germany's carefully conditional agreement in 1916 not to sink passenger and merchant vessels without warning

_____ 15. Key electoral state where a tiny majority for Wilson tipped the balance against Hughes in 1916

D. Matching People, Places, and Events

Match the person, place, or event in the left column with the proper description in the right column by inserting the correct letter on the blank line.

___ 1. Thomas Woodrow Wilson

___ 2. Theodore Roosevelt

___ 3. Samuel Gompers

___ 4. Louis D. Brandeis

___ 5. Virgin Islands

___ 6. General Huerta

___ 7. Venustiano Carranza

___ 8. Tampico and Vera Cruz

___ 9. "Pancho" Villa

___ 10. John J. Pershing

___ 11. Belgium

___ 12. Serbia

___ 13. Kaiser Wilhelm II

___ 14. Haiti

A. Small European nation in which an Austro-Hungarian heir was killed, leading to the outbreak of World War I

B. Mexican revolutionary whose assaults on American citizens and territory provoked a U.S. expedition into Mexico

C. Ports where clashes between Mexicans and American military forces nearly led to war in 1914

D. Caribbean territory purchased by the United States from Denmark in 1917

E. Narrowly unsuccessful presidential candidate who tried to straddle both sides of the fence regarding American policy toward Germany

F. Small European nation whose neutrality was violated by Germany in the early days of World War I

G. Commander of the American military expedition into Mexico in 1916–1917

H. Southern-born intellectual who pursued strong moral goals in politics and the presidency

I. Leading progressive reformer and the first Jew named to the U.S. Supreme Court

J. Caribbean nation where Wilson sent American marines in 1915

K. Energetic progressive and vigorous nationalist who refused to wage another third-party campaign in 1916

L. Labor leader who hailed the Clayton Anti-Trust Act as the "Magna Carta of labor"

M. Second revolutionary Mexican president, who took aid from the United States but strongly resisted American military intervention in his country

___ 15. Charles Evans Hughes   **N.** Autocratic ruler who symbolized ruthlessness and arrogance to many pro-Allied Americans

         O. Mexican revolutionary whose bloody regime Wilson refused to recognize and nearly ended up fighting

E. Putting Things in Order

Put the following events in correct order by numbering them from 1 to 5.

___ Wilson extracts a dangerously conditional German agreement to halt submarine warfare.

___ Wilson's superb leadership pushes major reforms of the tariff and monetary system through Congress.

___ The bull moose and the elephant are both electorally defeated by a donkey bearing the banner of "New Freedom."

___ The heavy loss of American lives to German submarines nearly leads the United States into war with Germany.

___ Despite efforts to avoid involvement in the Mexican revolution, Wilson's occupation of a Mexican port raises the threat of war.

F. Matching Cause and Effect

Match the historical cause in the left column with the proper effect in the right column by writing the correct letter on the blank line.

___ 1. The split between Taft and Roosevelt

___ 2. Wilson's presidential appeals to the public over the heads of Congress

___ 3. The Federal Reserve Act

___ 4. Conservative justices of the Supreme Court

___ 5. Political turmoil in Haiti and Santo Domingo (Dominican Republic)

___ 6. The Mexican revolution

___ 7. "Pancho" Villa's raid on Columbus, New Mexico

___ 8. America's close cultural and economic ties with Britain

___ 9. Germany's sinking of the *Lusitania, Arabic,* and *Sussex*

___ 10. Wilson's apparent success in keeping America at peace through diplomacy

A. Caused most Americans to sympathize with the Allies rather than the Central Powers

B. Helped push through sweeping reforms of the tariff and the banking system in 1913

C. Enabled the Democrats to win a narrow presidential victory in the election of 1916

D. Allowed Wilson to win a minority victory in the election of 1912

E. Declared unconstitutional progressive Wilsonian measures dealing with labor unions and child labor

F. Caused President Wilson and other outraged Americans to demand an end to unrestricted submarine warfare

G. Created constant political instability south of the border and undermined Wilson's hopes for better U.S. relations with Latin America

H. Was the immediate provocation for General Pershing's punitive expedition into Mexico

I. Finally established an effective national banking system and a flexible money supply

J. Caused Wilson to send in U.S. marines to restore order and supervise finances

G. Developing Historical Skills

Understanding Documents in Context

Historical documents cannot usually be understood in isolation. Awareness of the circumstances and conditions under which they were written is essential to comprehending their importance. The text reproduces on p. 701 the advertisement with notice from the German government that appeared in the New York *Herald* on May 1, 1915, six days before the *Lusitania* was sunk. Read the ad carefully, and reread text pp. 698–703 to understand and evaluate the context in which the warning appeared. Then answer the following questions.

1. What was the *policy* of the German government regarding submarine use at the time the ad was taken out?

2. Why might the German government be particularly concerned about warning American passengers thinking of traveling on a British liner? How would the notice be useful even if some Americans did travel on the ship?

3. What fact about the *Lusitania*'s cargo did the German government know that it did not put into the warning?

4. Why were many Americans outraged about the *Lusitania* sinking despite the warning?

PART III: Applying What You Have Learned

1. What were the essential qualities of Wilson's presidential leadership, and how did he display them in 1913–1914?
2. What were the results of Wilson's great reform assault on the "triple wall of privilege"—the tariff, the banks, and the trusts?
3. How was Wilson's foreign policy an attempt to expand idealistic progressive principles from the domestic to the international arena? Why did Wilson's progressive democratic idealism lead to the kind of U.S. interventions he professed to dislike?
4. What were the causes and consequences of U.S. entanglement with Mexico in the wake of the Mexican Revolution? Could the U.S. have avoided involvement in Mexican affairs?
5. Why was it so difficult for Wilson to maintain America's neutrality from 1914–1916?
6. How did Wilson's foreign policy differ from that of the other great progressive president, Theodore Roosevelt? (See Chapter 29.) Which president was more effective in foreign policy and why?

31

The War to End War,
1917–1918

PART I: Reviewing the Chapter

A. Checklist of Learning Objectives

After mastering this chapter, you should be able to

1. explain what caused America to enter World War I.
2. describe how Wilsonian idealism turned the war into an ideological crusade that inspired fervor and overwhelmed dissent.
3. discuss the mobilization of America for war.
4. explain the consequences of World War I for labor, women, and African-Americans.
5. describe America's economic and military role in the war.
6. analyze Wilson's attempt to forge a peace based on his Fourteen Points and explain why developments at home and abroad forced him to compromise.
7. discuss the opposition of Lodge and others to Wilson's League and show how Wilson's refusal to compromise doomed the Treaty of Versailles.

B. Glossary

To build your social science vocabulary, familiarize yourself with the following terms.

1. **isolationism** In American diplomacy, the traditional belief that the United States should refrain from involvement in overseas politics, alliances, or wars, and confine its national security interest to its own borders (sometimes along with the Caribbean and Central America). **Internationalism** or **Wilsonianism** is the contrasting belief that America's national security requires involvement and sometimes diplomatic or military alliances overseas. "But their obstruction was a powerful reminder of the continuing strength of American isolationism." (p. 706)
2. **collective security** In international affairs, reliance on a group of nations or an international organization as protection against aggressors, rather than on national self-defense alone. " . . . an international organization that Wilson dreamed would provide a system of collective security." (p. 707)
3. **mobilization** The organization of a nation and its armed forces for war. "Creel typified American war mobilization. . . ." (p. 708)
4. **pardon** The official release of a person from punishment for a crime. ". . . presidential pardons were rather freely granted. . . ." (p. 709)
5. **ration** A fixed allowance of food or other scarce commodity. "He deliberately rejected issuing ration cards. . . ." (p. 713)
6. **conscientious objector** A person who refuses to participate in war on grounds of conscience or belief. ". . . about 4,000 conscientious objectors were excused." (p. 715)
7. **Bolshevik** The radical majority faction of the Russian Socialist party that seized power in the October 1917 revolution; they later took the name *Communist*. (Bolshevik is the Russian word

for "majority;" their rivals for power were **Mensheviks**, or minority.) "The Bolsheviks long resented these 'capitalistic' interventions. . . ." (p. 716)

8. **salient** A portion of a battle line that extends forward into enemy territory. ". . . nine American divisions . . . joined four French divisions to push the Germans from the St. Mihiel salient. . . ." (p. 717)

9. **parliamentary** Concerning political systems in which the government is constituted from the controlling party's members in the legislative assembly. "Unlike all the parliamentary statesmen at the table, [Wilson] did not command a legislative majority at home." (p. 719)

10. **protectorate** In international affairs, a weaker or smaller country held to be under the guidance or protection of a major power; the arrangement is a weaker form of imperialism or colonialism. (A **colony** is a territory owned outright by a more powerful nation.) ". . . preventing any vengeful parceling out of the former colonies and protectorates of the vanquished powers." (p. 720)

11. **trustee** A nation that holds the territory of a former colony as the conditional agent of an international body under defined terms. "The victors would . . . receive the conquered territory . . . only as trustees of the League of Nations." (p. 720)

12. **mandate** Under the League of Nations (1919–1939), a specific commission that authorized a trustee to administer a former colonial territory. "Japan was conceded the strategic Pacific islands under a League of Nations mandate. . . ." (p. 720)

13. **self-determination** The Wilsonian doctrine that each people should have the right to freely choose its own political affiliation and national future, e.g., independence or incorporation into another nation. "Faced with fierce Wilsonian opposition to this violation of self-determination. . . ." (p. 721)

14. **reservation** A portion of a deed, contract, or treaty that places conditions or restrictions on the general obligations. ". . . he finally came up with fourteen formal reservations. . . ." (p. 723)

15. **demagogue** A politician who arouses fervor by appealing to the lowest emotions of a mass audience, such as fear, hatred, and greed. " . . . a debacle that played into the hands of the German demagogue Adolf Hitler." (p. 725)

PART II: Checking Your Progress

A. True-False

Where the statement is true, mark **T**. Where it is false, mark **F**, and correct it in the space immediately below.

____ 1. Germany responded to Wilson's call for "peace without victory" by proposing a temporary armistice.

____ 2. Wilson's proclamation of the war as a crusade to end all war and spread democracy around the world inspired intense ideological enthusiasm among Americans.

____ 3. Among Wilson's Fourteen Points were freedom of the seas, national self-determination for minorities, and an international organization to secure peace.

____ 4. The Committee on Public Information used an aroused American patriotism more than formal laws and censorship to promote the war cause.

____ 5. The primary targets of prosecution under the Espionage and Sedition Acts were German and Austrian agents in the United States.

____ 6. Even during the war mobilization, Americans were extremely reluctant to grant the federal government extensive powers over the economy.

    7. Despite bitter and sometimes violent strikes, American labor made economic and organizational gains as a result of World War I.

    8. War-inspired black migration into northern cities led to major racial riots in 1917–1919.

    9. The passage of the Nineteenth Amendment granting women's suffrage guaranteed the permanence of women's wartime economic gains.

    10. American troops actually played only a small role in the Allies' final victory.

    11. Before he would negotiate an armistice, President Wilson insisted that the Germans overthrow Kaiser Wilhelm II.

    12. Wilson's skillful handling of Republican political opposition strengthened his hand at the Paris Peace Conference.

    13. Other Allied leaders forced Wilson to make serious compromises in his Fourteen Points in order to keep the League of Nations in the Treaty of Versailles.

    14. Wilson's unwillingness to compromise and accept Republican reservations to the Treaty of Versailles sent the whole treaty down to defeat.

    15. In the election of 1920, Republican Harding supported the League of Nations while Democrat Cox tried to evade the issue.

B. Multiple Choice

Select the best answer and write the proper letter in the space provided.

    1. The immediate cause of American entry into World War I was

        a. German support for a possible Mexican invasion of the southwestern United States.
        b. Germany's resumption of unrestricted submarine warfare.
        c. the German defeat of France.
        d. desire of American munitions makers for large profits.

    2. Wilson aroused the somewhat divided American people to fervent support of the war by

        a. seizing control of the means of communication and demanding national unity.
        b. declaring the German people to be immoral Huns and barbarians.
        c. proclaiming an ideological war to end war and make the world safe for democracy.
        d. proclaiming the war a religious crusade.

    3. The capstone "Fourteenth Point" of Wilson's declaration of war aims called for

        a. the establishment of parliamentary democracies throughout Europe.
        b. guarantees of basic human rights for all people in the world.
        c. an international organization to guarantee collective security.
        d. freedom of travel without restrictions.

4. The purpose of George Creel's Committee on Public Information was

    a. to develop information on American wartime industrial production.

    b. to whip up public support for the war and promote anti-German propaganda.

    c. to develop counterintelligence information on German spies and saboteurs in the United States.

    d. to recruit volunteers for the armed forces.

5. The two key laws aimed at enforcing loyalty and suppressing antiwar dissent were

    a. the War Mobilization Act and the National Defense Act.

    b. the Selective Service Act and the Public Information Act.

    c. the Eighteenth Amendment and the Anti-German Language Act.

    d. the Espionage Act and the Sedition Act.

6. Among the primary victims of the prowar propaganda campaign to enforce loyalty were

    a. German-Americans and socialists.

    b. Russian-Americans and communists.

    c. Mexican-Americans and immigrants.

    d. African-Americans and feminists.

7. Among the political changes the war helped bring about was

    a. a constitutional amendment granting women the right to vote.

    b. a law granting labor unions the right to strike.

    c. a constitutional amendment guaranteeing African-Americans the right to travel freely.

    d. a constitutional amendment prohibiting child labor.

8. Particularly violent strikes erupted during and after World War I in the

    a. shipping and railroad industries.

    b. mining and steel industries.

    c. textile and clothing manufacturing industries.

    d. factories employing women war workers.

9. During World War I, African-American military men served primarily in

    a. segregated, non-combat support units.

    b. the navy and the coast guard.

    c. the most dangerous trenches in northern France.

    d. in northern cities where their presence did not threaten the system of segregation.

10. A major difference between the World War I Selective Service Act and the Civil War draft was that

    a. in World War I women as well as men were drafted.

    b. in World War I it was not possible to purchase an exemption or to hire a substitute.

    c. in World War I draftees were sent immediately into front line combat.

    d. in World War I draftees received the same training as professional soldiers.

11. American soldiers were especially needed in France in the spring of 1918 because

    a. the Allied invasion of Germany was faltering short of its goal.

    b. Britain had moved many of its soldiers from the western front to Russia.

    c. a renewed German offensive was threatening to break through to Paris.

    d. the Russians were threatening to enter the war on the Germans' side.

_____ 12. Most of the military supplies for General Pershing's expeditionary force came from

    a. America's European allies.
    b. factories in the United States.
    c. captured German matériel.
    d. Britain's colonies in Africa.

_____ 13. Wilson blundered when choosing the American peace delegation by failing to

    a. have a set of clear diplomatic goals.
    b. include any Republicans in the delegation.
    c. consult with his key Allies, Britain and France.
    d. include experts who would understand the intricate politics of Europe.

_____ 14. The European powers and Japan weakened Wilson at the peace conference by

    a. refusing to support his proposed League of Nations.
    b. supporting the Republicans who were criticizing Wilson at home.
    c. demanding continuing American aid and involvement in European affairs.
    d. forcing him to compromise his ideals on matters of self-determination and punishment of Germany.

_____ 15. Wilson bore considerable responsibility for the failure of the United States to join the League of Nations because

    a. he linked the League too closely to European politics.
    b. he ordered Democratic senators to defeat the pro-League treaty with the Lodge reservations.
    c. he failed to take the case for the League to the American public.
    d. he had agreed that America would pay most of the cost of the League.

C. Identification

Supply the correct identification for each numbered description.

_____ 1. Wilson's appeal to all the belligerents in January 1917, just before the Germans resumed submarine warfare

_____ 2. Message that contained a German proposal to Mexico for an anti-American alliance

_____ 3. Wilson's idealistic statement of American war aims in January 1918 that inspired the Allies and demoralized their enemies

_____ 4. American government propaganda agency that aroused zeal for Wilson's ideals and whipped up hatred for the kaiser

_____ 5. Radical antiwar labor union whose members were prosecuted under the Espionage and Sedition Act

_____ 6. Weak federal agency designed to organize and coordinate U.S. industrial production for the war effort

_____ 7. Constitutional provision endorsed by Wilson as a war measure whose ratification achieved a long-sought goal for American women

_____ 8. Treasury Department bond-selling drives that raised about $21 billion to finance the American war effort

_____ 9. The nations that dominated the Paris Peace Conference—namely, Britain, France, Italy, and the United States

_____ 10. Wilson's proposed international body that constituted the key provision of the Versailles treaty

_____ 11. Controversial peace agreement that compromised many of Wilson's Fourteen Points but retained his League

_____ 12. Senatorial committee whose chairman used delaying tactics and hostile testimony to develop opposition to Wilson's treaty and League of Nations

_____ 13. A hard core of isolationist senators who bitterly opposed any sort of league; also called the "Battalion of Death"

_____ 14. Amendments to the proposed Treaty of Versailles, sponsored by Wilson's hated senatorial opponent, that attempted to guarantee America's sovereign rights in relation to the League of Nations

_____ 15. Wilson's belief that the presidential election of 1920 should constitute a direct popular vote on the League of Nations

D. Matching People, Places, and Events

Match the person, place, or event in the left column with the proper description in the right column by inserting the correct letter on the blank line.

___ 1. George Creel	**A.** Inspirational leader of the Western world in wartime who later stumbled as a peacemaker
___ 2. Eugene V. Debs	**B.** Senatorial leader of the isolationist "irreconcilables" who absolutely opposed all American involvement in Europe.
___ 3. Bernard Baruch	**C.** Climactic final battle of World War I
___ 4. Herbert Hoover	**D.** The "tiger" of France, whose drive for security forced Wilson to compromise at Versailles
___ 5. John J. Pershing	**E.** Head of the American propaganda agency that mobilized public opinion for World War I
___ 6. Alice Paul	**F.** Folksy Ohio senator whose 1920 presidential victory ended the last hopes for U.S. participation in the League of Nations
___ 7. Meuse-Argonne	**G.** Hated leader of America's enemy in World War I
___ 8. Kaiser Wilhelm II	**H.** Head of the Food Administration who pioneered successful voluntary mobilization methods
___ 9. Woodrow Wilson	**I.** Leader of the pacifist National Women's Party who opposed U.S. involvement in World War I
___ 10. Henry Cabot Lodge	**J.** Site where state police killed 39 striking miners and their families in 1917
___ 11. Georges Clemenceau	**K.** Commander of the overseas American Expeditionary Force in World War I
	L. Site of one of the largest World War I-era race riots.
___ 12. William Borah	**M.** Wilson's great senatorial antagonist who fought to keep America out of the League of Nations
___ 13. Ludlow, Colorado	**N.** Head of the War Industries Board, which attempted to impose some order on U.S. war production
___ 14. East St. Louis, Illinois	**O.** Socialist leader who won nearly a million votes as a presidential candidate while in federal prison for antiwar activities
___ 15. Warren G. Harding	

Name_____ Section_____ Date_____

E. Putting Things in Order

Put the following events in correct order by numbering them from 1 to 5.

____ Germany's resumption of submarine warfare forces the United States onto a declaration of war.

____ The Senate's final defeat of the Versailles treaty and a Republican election victory end Wilson's last hopes for American entry into the League of Nations.

____ The United States takes the first hesitant steps toward preparedness in the event of war.

____ The effectiveness of American combat troops in crucial battles helps bring about an Allied victory in World War I.

____ Wilson struggles with other Allied leaders in Paris to hammer out a peace treaty and organize the postwar world.

F. Matching Cause and Effect

Match the historical cause in the left column with the proper effect in the right column by writing the correct letter on the blank line.

Cause	Effect
____ 1. Germany's resumption of unrestricted submarine warfare	**A.** Led to major racial violence in Chicago and East St. Louis, Illinois
____ 2. Wilson's Fourteen Points	**B.** Forced Democrats to vote against a modified treaty and killed American participation in the League of Nations
____ 3. The wartime atmosphere of emotional patriotism and fear	**C.** Stopped the final German offensive and turned the tide toward Allied victory
____ 4. Women's labor in wartime factories	**D.** Allowed domestic disillusionment and opposition to the treaty and League to build strength
____ 5. The migration of African-Americans to northern cities	**E.** Finally pushed the United States into World War I
____ 6. American troops' entry into combat in the spring and summer of 1918	**F.** Weakened the president's position during the peacemaking process
____ 7. Wilson's political blunders in the fall of 1918	**G.** Caused harsh attacks on German-Americans and other Americans who opposed the war
____ 8. The strong diplomatic demands of France, Italy, and Japan	**H.** Lifted Allied and American spirits and demoralized Germany and its allies
____ 9. Senator Lodge's tactics of delaying and proposing reservations in the Versailles treaty	**I.** Forced Wilson to compromise his Fourteen Points in order to keep the League as part of the peace treaty
____ 10. Wilson's refusal to accept any reservations supported by Lodge	**J.** Helped pass the Nineteenth Amendment but did not really change society's emphasis on the maternal role

G. Developing Historical Skills

Analyzing Visual Propaganda

This exercise involves analyzing visual propaganda designed to make emotional appeals on behalf of a cause. In this case, the propaganda was designed to enlist the American public's support for the war effort against Germany. The kinds of propaganda used on behalf of a cause can tell the historian a great deal about what issues were perceived to be at stake and what public values were being appealed to.

Answer the following questions about the cartoons and drawings in this chapter.

1. *Anti-German Propaganda* (p. 708): How do the words and image of this poster work together to persuade an American audience to buy liberty loans? Besides the specific message, what general portrait of Germany, the war, and America's reasons for fighting are conveyed?

2. *A Universal Draft, 1917*: How do the visual and verbal symbols in this cartoon convey the combination of invitation and threat implied in the War Department's 1918 wartime manpower rules? How would you characterize the depiction of "Uncle Sam's" mood here?

3. *Food for Thought* (p. 713): How does this poster visually make the connection between the patriotic war effort and gardens"? What specific words or phrases create the link between women's food-growing effort and military service on fields of combat? What specific appeal is this image making to women?

PART III: Applying What You Have Learned

1. What caused American entry into World War I, and how did Wilson turn the war into an ideological crusade?

2. Did World War I substantially alter American society and culture (e.g., ethnic, class, gender, and race relations), or were its effects primarily an "affair of the mind," i.e., altering American ideas and world views?

3. What was America's military and ideological contribution to the Allied victory?

4. How were the goals of the war presented to the American public? What does the text mean when it says that the war and Wilson's ideals may have been "oversold?" (p. 708)

5. How was Wilson forced to compromise during the peace negotiations, and why did America in the end refuse to ratify the treaty and join the League of Nations?

6. Apart from such immediate factors as the Lodge-Wilson antagonism, what general features of earlier American history worked against American involvement in European affairs and participation in the League of Nations?

32

American Life in the "Roaring Twenties," 1919–1929

PART I: Reviewing the Chapter

A. Checklist of Learning Objectives

After mastering this chapter, you should be able to

1. analyze the movement toward social conservatism following World War I.
2. describe the cultural conflicts over such issues as prohibition and evolution.
3. discuss the rise of the mass-consumption economy, led by the automobile industry.
4. describe the cultural revolution brought about by radio, films, and changing sexual standards.
5. explain how new ideas and values were reflected and promoted in the American literary renaissance of the 1920s.
6. explain how the era's cultural changes affected women and African-Americans.

B. Glossary

To build your social science vocabulary, familiarize yourself with the following terms.

1. **syndicalism** A theory or movement that advocates bringing all economic and political power into the hands of labor unions by means of strikes. ". . . a number of legislatures . . . passed criminal syndicalism laws." (p. 729)
2. **Bible Belt** The region of the American South, extending roughly from North Carolina west to Oklahoma and Texas, where Protestant Fundamentalism and belief in literal interpretation of the Bible have traditionally been strongest. ". . . the Klan spread with astonishing rapidity, especially in the Midwest and the 'Bible Belt' South." (p. 730)
3. **provincial** Narrow and limited; isolated from cosmopolitan influences. "Isolationist America of the 1920s, ingrown and provincial, had little use for the immigrants. . . ." (p. 730)
4. **racketeer** A person who obtains money illegally by fraud, bootlegging, gambling, or threats of violence. "Racketeers even invaded the ranks of local labor unions. . . ." (pp. 736–737)
5. **underworld** Those who live outside society's laws, by vice or crime. ". . . the annual 'take' of the underworld was estimated to be from $12 billion to $18 billion. . . ." (p. 737)
6. **credit** In business, the arrangement of purchasing goods or services immediately but making the payment at a later date. "Buying on credit was another innovative feature of the postwar economy." (p. 739)
7. **installment plan** A credit system by which goods already acquired are paid for in a series of payments at specified intervals. ". . . encouraged by tempting installment-plan buying, countless Americans with shallow purses acquired the habit of riding as they paid." (p. 741)
8. **magnate** An influential person in a large-scale enterprise. ". . . an outraged public forced the screen magnates to set up their own rigorous code of censorship." (pp. 744–745)

9. **repression** In psychology, the forcing of instincts or ideas painful to the conscious mind into the unconscious, where they continue to exercise influence. "The Viennese physician appeared to argue that sexual repression was responsible for a variety of nervous and emotional ills." (p. 746)

10. **charismatic** Concerning the personal magnetism or appeal of a leader for his or her followers; literally, "gift of grace." "Harlem in the 1920s also spawned a charismatic political leader, Marcus Garvey." (p. 748)

11. **functionalism** The theory that a plan or design should be derived from practical purpose. "Architecture also married itself to the new materialism and functionalism." (p. 750)

12. **surtax** A special tax, usually involving a raised rate on an already existing tax. ". . . Congress . . . abolish[ed] the surtax, the income tax, and estate taxes." (p. 752)

PART II: Checking Your Progress

A. True-False

Where the statement is true, mark **T**. Where it is false, mark **F**, and correct it in the space immediately below.

___ 1. The "red scare" of 1919–1920 led the U.S. government to threaten military assault on the Communist government of Russia.

___ 2. The Sacco-Vanzetti case aroused liberal and radical protest because of alleged prejudice by the judge and jury against the atheistic immigrant defendants.

___ 3. The Ku Klux Klan of the 1920s was strongest in the East and the West.

___ 4. The Immigration Act of 1924 reflected nativist prejudice against the new immigrants from southern and eastern Europe.

___ 5. The Eighteenth Amendment and the Volstead Act were frequently violated, especially by big-city dwellers and immigrants.

___ 6. The Scopes trial verdict acquitted biology teacher Scopes and overturned the Tennessee law prohibiting the teaching of evolution in the schools.

___ 7. The 1920s saw a shift from heavy industrial production toward a mass-consumption economy.

___ 8. Henry Ford's great economic achievement was the production of a cheap, reliable, mass-produced automobile.

___ 9. The automobile's large social and cultural effects in such areas as family life and gender relations were comparable to its economic importance.

___ 10. The radio and film industries initially emphasized non-commercial and public service uses of the mass media.

___ 11. The 1920s saw attempts to restore stricter standards of sexual behavior, especially for women.

_____ 12. Jazz was initially pioneered by blacks but was eventually taken up and promoted by whites.

_____ 13. The center of black literacy and cultural achievement in the 1920s was Atlanta, Georgia.

_____ 14. The most prominent writers of the 1920s upheld the moral virtues of small-town American life against the critical attitudes and moral questioning of the big cities.

_____ 15. The real estate and stock market booms of the 1920s included large elements of speculation and excessive credit risk.

B. Multiple Choice

Select the best answer and write the proper letter in the space provided.

_____ 1. The "red scare" of the early 1920s was initially set off by

   a. the Sacco-Vanzetti case.
   b. the rise of the radical Industrial Workers of the World.
   c. the Bolshevik revolution in Russia.
   d. an influx of radical immigrants.

_____ 2. Besides attacking minorities like Catholics, blacks, and Jews, the Ku Klux Klan of the 1920s opposed contemporary cultural and social changes such as

   a. evolution and birth control.
   b. prohibition and higher education.
   c. automobiles and airplanes.
   d. patriotism and immigration restriction.

_____ 3. The quota system established for immigration in the 1920s was based partly on the idea that

   a. America could accept the refugees created by war and revolution in Europe.
   b. immigrants from northern and western Europe were superior to those from southern and eastern Europe.
   c. immigration from Europe would be largely replaced by immigration from Asia.
   d. priority in immigration would be based on family relations, profession, and education.

_____ 4. The concentration of many American ethnic groups in separate neighborhoods with their own distinct institutions, cultures, and values meant that

   a. English was no longer the dominant language in the United States.
   b. the United States was intolerant of ethnic differences.
   c. Catholics and Jews had a political base from which to gain the presidency.
   d. it was almost impossible to organize the American working class across ethnic and religious lines.

_____ 5. One clear result of prohibition was

   a. a rise in criminal organizations that supplied illegal liquor.
   b. an improvement in family relations and the general moral tone of society.
   c. a turn from alcohol to other forms of substance abuse.
   d. the rise of voluntary self-help organizations like Alcoholics Anonymous.

6. The American city where gangsterism flourished most blatantly in the 1920s was

    a. New York City.
    b. Harlem.
    c. Chicago.
    d. New Orleans.

7. The essential issue in the Scopes trial was whether

    a. scientists ought to be allowed to investigate the biological origins of humanity.
    b. the teachings of Darwin could be reconciled with those of religion.
    c. Darwinian evolutionary science could be taught in the public schools.
    d. Fundamentalist Protestantism could be taught in the public schools.

8. The most highly acclaimed industrial innovator of the new mass-production economy was

    a. Babe Ruth.
    b. Bruce Barton.
    c. Ransom E. Olds.
    d. Henry Ford.

9. Two major American industries that benefited economically from the widespread use of the automobile were

    a. plastics and synthetic fibers.
    b. rubber and petroleum.
    c. textiles and leather.
    d. electronics and aluminum.

10. One of the primary *social* effects of the new automobile age was

    a. a weakening of traditional family ties between parents and youth.
    b. a strengthening of intergenerational ties among parents, children, and grandchildren.
    c. a tightening of restrictions on women.
    d. a closing of the gap between the working class and the wealthy.

11. Radio and the movies both had the cultural effect of

    a. increasing Americans' interest in history and literature.
    b. increasing mass standardization and weakening traditional forms of culture.
    c. undermining the tendency of industry toward big business and mass production.
    d. encouraging creativity and cultural independence among the people.

12. In the 1920s, the major changes pursued by American women were

    a. voting rights and political equality.
    b. economic equality and equal pay for equal work.
    c. social reform and family welfare.
    d. cultural freedom and expanded sexual experience.

13. The primary achievement of Marcus Garvey's Universal Negro Improvement Association was

    a. its promotion of black jazz and blues.
    b. its positive impact on black racial pride.
    c. its economic development program in Harlem.
    d. its transportation of numerous blacks to Liberia.

____ 14. The literary figure who promoted many new writers of the 1920s in his magazine, *The American Mercury*, was

    a. H. L. Mencken.
    b. W. C. Handy.
    c. F. Scott Fitzgerald.
    d. Henry Adams.

____ 15. Many of the prominent new writers of the 1920s were

    a. fascinated by their historical roots in old New England.
    b. disgusted with European domination of American culture.
    c. interested especially in nature and social reform.
    d. highly critical of traditional American "Puritanism" and small-town life.

C. Identification

Supply the correct identification for each numbered description.

_____ 1. The movement of 1919–1920, spawned by fear of Bolshevik revolution, that resulted in the arrest and deportation of many political radicals

_____ 2. Hooded defenders of Anglo-Saxon and "Protestant" values against immigrants, Catholics, and Jews

_____ 3. Restrictive legislation of 1924 that reduced the number of newcomers to the United States and discriminated against immigrants from southern and eastern Europe

_____ 4. New constitutional provision, popular in the Midwest and South, that encouraged lawbreaking and gangsterism in big cities

_____ 5. Term for area of the South where traditional evangelical and Fundamentalist religion remained strong

_____ 6. Legal battle over teaching evolution that pitted modern science against Fundamentalist religion

_____ 7. New industry spawned by the mass-consumption economy that encouraged still more consumption

_____ 8. Henry Ford's cheap, mass-produced automobile

_____ 9. Invented in 1903 and first used primarily for stunts and mail carrying

_____ 10. One of the few new consumer products of the 1920s that encouraged people to stay at home rather than pulling them away from home and family

_____ 11. Feminist Margaret Sanger's cause that contributed to changing sexual behaviors, especially for women

_____ 12. Syncopated style of music created by blacks that attained national popularity in the 1920s

_____ 13. Marcus Garvey's self-help organization that proposed leading blacks to Africa.

_____ 14. H. L. Mencken's monthly magazine that led the literary attack on traditional moral values, the middle class, and "Puritanism"

_____ 15. The New York institution in which continuously rising prices and profits were fueled by speculation in the 1920s

D. Matching People, Places, and Events

Match the person, place, or event in the left column with the proper description in the right column by inserting the correct letter on the blank line.

___ 1. A. Mitchell Palmer

___ 2. Nicola Sacco and Bartolomeo Vanzetti

___ 3. Al Capone

___ 4. John Dewey

___ 5. William Jennings Bryan

___ 6. Henry Ford

___ 7. Bruce Barton

___ 8. Langston Hughes

___ 9. Charles A. Lindbergh

___ 10. Marcus Garvey

___ 11. Sigmund Freud

___ 12. H. L. Mencken

___ 13. F. Scott Fitzgerald

___ 14. Ernest Hemingway

___ 15. Andrew Mellon

A. The "Poet Laureate" of Harlem and author of *The Weary Blues*

B. Innovative writer whose novels reflected the disillusionment of many Americans with propaganda and patriotic idealism

C. Italian-American anarchists whose trial and execution aroused widespread protest

D. Mechanical genius and organizer of the mass-produced automobile industry

E. U.S. attorney general who rounded up thousands of alleged Bolsheviks in the red scare of 1919–1920

F. Baltimore writer who criticized the supposedly narrow and hypocritical values of American society

G. Top gangster of the 1920s, eventually convicted of income-tax evasion

H. Former presidential candidate who led the fight against evolution at the 1925 Scopes trial

I. U. S. treasury secretary who attempted to promote business investment by reducing taxes on the rich

J. A leader of the advertising industry and author of a new interpretation on Christ in *The Man Nobody Knows*

K. Viennese psychologist whose writings were interpreted by Americans as a call for sexual liberation and gratification

L. Leading American philosopher and proponent of "progressive education"

M. Humble aviation pioneer who became a cultural hero of the 1920s

N. Minnesota-born writer whose novels were especially popular with young people in the 1920s

O. Jamaican-born leader who enhanced African-American pride despite his failed migration plans

E. Putting Things in Order

Put the following events in correct order by numbering them from 1 to 5.

___ The trial of a Tennessee high-school biology teacher symbolizes a national conflict over values of religion and science.

___ Fear of the Bolshevik revolution sparks a crusade against radicals and Communists in America.

___ A modest young man becomes a national hero by accomplishing a bold feat of aviation.

___ Two Italian immigrants are convicted of murder and robbery, provoking charges of prejudice against the judge and jury.

___ A new immigration law tightens up earlier emergency restrictions and imposes discriminatory quotas against the "New Immigrants."

F. Matching Cause and Effect

Match the historical cause in the left column with the proper effect in the right column by writing the correct letter on the blank line.

Cause	Effect
___ 1. American fear of Bolshevism	**A.** Caused the rise of the Ku Klux Klan and the imposition of immigration restrictions
___ 2. Nativist American fear of immigrants and Catholics	**B.** Caused many influential writers of the 1920s to criticize traditional values and search for new moral standards
___ 3. Prohibition	**C.** Caused the red scare and the deportation of foreign radicals
___ 4. The automobile industry	**D.** Enabled many ordinary citizens to join in a speculative Wall Street boom
___ 5. The radio	**E.** Stimulated highway construction, petroleum production, and other related industries
___ 6. Rising prosperity, new technologies, and the ideas of Sigmund Freud	**F.** Helped stimulate mass attention to sports and entertainment while spreading the reach of advertising
___ 7. Resentment against conventional small-town morality	**G.** Reduced the tax burden on the wealthy and contributed to the stock-market boom
___ 8. The economic boom of the 1920s	**H.** Greatly raised the incomes and living standards of many Americans
___ 9. The ability to buy stocks with only a small down payment	**I.** Created a new atmosphere of sexual frankness and liberation, especially among the young
___ 10. Andrew Mellon's tax policies	**J.** Helped spawn "bootlegging" and large-scale organized crime

G. Developing Historical Skills

Understanding Cultural Developments in Historical Context

The first part of this chapter describes the major social and economic changes of the 1920s. The second part describes the cultural developments that also occurred in the 1920s. Since the artists, writers, and others who produced the culture and ideas of the period were living amidst these very same social changes, your knowledge of the historical context can help you understand why they created the kind of works they did.

Answer the following questions.

1. In what ways were the "movies," for all their glamour, similar to the automobile industry as developed by Henry Ford?

2. How did new technological and economic innovations like the automobile (pp. 739–742) and social changes like urbanization help bring about the cultural liberation of women?

3. In what ways did the novels of F. Scott Fitzgerald (pp. 749–750)) or musical developments like jazz (p. 746–747) especially appeal to people living amid the social and economic changes of the 1920s? Did these cultural developments simply mirror existing politics and society, or were they in some ways a challenge to them?

4. Why were writers like H. L. Mencken, Sinclair Lewis, and Sherwood Anderson so harshly critical of American rural and small-town life in their work? Why would writers with such attitudes have been unlikely to succeed in any period before the 1920s?

PART III: Applying What You Have Learned

1. How and why did America turn toward domestic isolation and social conservatism in the 1920s?
2. How was the diverse American "melting pot" affected by the political and cultural changes of the 1920s? (Include both white ethnic groups and blacks in your discussion.)
3. How did some of the events of the 1920s reflect national conflicts over social, cultural, and religious values?
4. How did the automobile and other new products create a mass-consumption economy in the 1920s?
5. How did the new films, literature, and music of the 1920s affect Americans' values in areas of religion, sexuality, and family life? Were African-American cultural developments fundamentally different, or were they part of the *same* cultural movement?
6. In what ways were the twenties a social and cultural reaction against the progressive idealism that held sway before and during World War I? (See Chapters 29, 30, and 31.)

33

The Politics of Boom
and Bust, 1920–1932

PART I: Reviewing the Chapter

A. Checklist of Learning Objectives

After mastering this chapter, you should be able to

1. analyze the domestic political conservatism and economic prosperity of the 1920s.
2. explain the Republican administrations' policies of isolationism, disarmament, and high-tariff protectionism.
3. compare the easygoing corruption of the Harding administration with the straight-laced uprightness of his successor Coolidge.
4. describe the international economic tangle of loans, war debts, and reparations, and indicate how the United States dealt with it.
5. discuss how Hoover went from being a symbol of twenties business success to a symbol of depression failure.
6. explain how the stock-market crash set off the deep and prolonged Great Depression.
7. indicate how Hoover's response to the depression was a combination of old-time individualism and the new view of federal responsibility for the economy.

B. Glossary

To build your social science vocabulary, familiarize yourself with the following terms.

1. **nationalization** Ownership of the major means of production by the national or federal government. ". . . wartime government operation of the lines might lead to nationalization." (p. 755)
2. **dreadnought** A heavily armored battleship with large batteries of twelve-inch guns. ". . . Secretary Hughes startled the delegates . . . with a comprehensive, concrete plan for . . . scrapping some of the huge dreadnoughts. . . ." (p. 757)
3. **accomplice** An associate or partner of a criminal who shares some degree of guilt. ". . . he and his accomplices looted the government to the tune of about $200 million. . . ." (p. 759)
4. **reparations** Compensation by a defeated nation for damage done to civilians and their property during a war. "Overshadowing all other foreign-policy problems . . . was . . . a complicated tangle of private loans, Allied war debt, and German reparations payments." (p. 763)
5. **pump-priming** In economics, the spending or lending of a small amount of funds in order to stimulate a larger flow of economic activity. " 'Pump-priming' loans by the RFC were no doubt of widespread benefit. . . ." (p. 772)

PART II: Checking Your Progress

A. True-False

Where the statement is true, mark **T**. Where it is false, mark **F**, and correct it in the space immediately below.

____ 1. The most corrupt members of Harding's cabinet were the secretaries of state and the treasury.

____ 2. The Republican administrations of the 1920s believed in strict enforcement of antitrust laws to maintain strong business competition.

____ 3. The Republican administrations of the 1920s pursued their isolationist approach to national security by engaging in a large military buildup.

____ 4. The high tariff policies of the 1920s enhanced American prosperity but hindered Europe's economic recovery from World War I.

____ 5. Calvin Coolidge's image of honesty and thrift helped restore public confidence in the government after the Harding administration scandals.

____ 6. Farmers looked unsuccessfully to the federal government to help relieve their severe economic troubles in the 1920s.

____ 7. The main sources of support for liberal third-party presidential candidate Robert La Follette in 1924 were urban workers and social reformers.

____ 8. The main exception to America's isolationist foreign policy in the 1920s was continuing U.S. armed intervention in the Caribbean and Central America.

____ 9. Britain and France did not begin to repay their war debts to the United States until the Dawes plan provided American loans to Germany.

____ 10. In the election of 1928, Democratic nominee Al Smith's urban, Catholic, and "wet" background cost him support from traditionally Democratic southern voters.

____ 11. The Hawley-Smoot Tariff strengthened the trend toward expanded international trade and economic cooperation.

____ 12. The American economic collapse of the Great Depression was the most severe suffered by any major industrial nation in the 1930s.

____ 13. The depression was caused partly by over-expansion of credit and excessive consumer debt.

____ 14. Throughout his term, Hoover consistently followed his belief that the federal government should play no role in providing economic relief and assisting the recovery from the depression.

____ 15. The Reconstruction Finance Corporation provided federal loans to business and governmental institutions but no aid to individuals.

B. Multiple Choice

Select the best answer and write the proper letter in the space provided.

1. As president, Warren G. Harding proved to be

    a. thoughtful and ambitious but rather impractical.
    b. an able administrator and diplomat but a poor politician.
    c. politically competent and concerned for the welfare of ordinary people.
    d. weak-willed and tolerant of corruption among his friends.

2. The general policy of the federal government toward industry in the early 1920s was

    a. a weakening of federal regulation and encouragement of trade associations.
    b. an emphasis on federal regulation rather than state and local controls.
    c. an emphasis on vigorous antitrust enforcement rather than on regulation.
    d a turn toward direct federal control of key industries like the railroads.

3. Two groups who suffered severe political setbacks in the immediate post–World War I environment were

    a. Protestants and Jews.
    b. organized labor and blacks.
    c. small businesses and farmers.
    d. women and city dwellers.

4. Two terms that describe the Harding and Coolidge administrations' approach to foreign policy are

    a. internationalism and moralism.
    b. interventionism and militarism.
    c. isolationism and disarmament.
    d. balance of power and alliance-seeking.

5. The proposed ratio of "5-5-3" in the Washington Disarmament Conference of 1921–1922 referred to

    a. the allowable ratio of American, British, and Japanese troops in China.
    b. the respective number of votes Britain, France, and the United States would have in the League of Nations.
    c. the allowable ratio of battleships and carriers among the United States, Britain, and Japan.
    d. the number of nations from Europe, the Americas, and Asia, respectively, that would have to ratify the treaties before they went into effect..

6. The very high tariff rates of the 1920s had the economic effect of

    a. stimulating the formation of common markets among the major industrial nations.
    b. causing severe deflation in the United States and Europe.
    c. turning American trade away from Europe and toward Asia.
    d. causing the Europeans to erect their own tariff barriers and thus severely reduce international trade.

7. The central scandal of Teapot Dome involved members of Harding's cabinet who

    a. sold spoiled foodstuffs to the army and navy.
    b. took bribes for leasing federal oil lands.
    c. violated prohibition by tolerating gangster liquor deals.
    d. stuffed ballot boxes and played dirty tricks on campaign opponents.

8. The one major group that experienced hard economic times amidst the general prosperity of the 1920s was

   a. small business.
   b. farmers.
   c. bankers and stock brokers.
   d. the middle class.

9. Besides deep divisions within the Democratic party, the elections of 1924 revealed

   a. Coolidge's inability to attain Harding's level of popularity.
   b. the weakness of profarmer and prolabor Progressive reform..
   c. the turn of the solid South from the Democrats to the Republicans.
   d. The rise of liberalism within the Democratic party.

10. The international economic crisis caused by unpaid war reparations and loans was partially resolved by

    a. private American bank loans to Germany.
    b. forgiving the loans and reparations.
    c. the creation of a new international economic system by the League of Nations.
    d. the rise of Mussolini and Hitler.

11. Al Smith's Roman Catholicism and opposition to prohibition hurt him especially

    a. in the South.
    b. among ethnic voters.
    c. among African-Americans.
    d. among women voters.

12. The election of Hoover over Smith in 1928 seemed to represent a victory of

    a. northern industrial values over southern agrarianism.
    b. small business over the ideas of big government and big business.
    c. ethnic and cultural diversity over traditional Anglo-Saxon values.
    d. big business and efficiency over urban and Catholic values.

13. One important cause of the great stock market crash of 1929 was

    a. overexpansion of production and credit beyond the ability to pay for them.
    b. a "tight" money policy that made it difficult to obtain loans.
    c. the lack of tariff protection for American markets from foreign competitors.
    d. excessive government regulation of business.

14. The sky-high Hawley-Smoot Tariff of 1930 had the economic effect of

    a. providing valuable protection for hard-pressed American manufacturers.
    b. lowering the value of American currency in international money markets.
    c. crippling international trade and deepening the depression.
    d. forcing foreign governments to negotiate fairer trade agreements.

15. The federal agency that Hoover established to provide "pump-priming" loans to business was the

    a. Tennessee Valley Authority.
    b. Bonus Expeditionary Force.
    c. Reconstruction Finance Corporation.
    d. American Legion.

C. Identification

Supply the correct identification for each numbered description.

_____ 1. Poker-playing cronies from Harding's native state who contributed to the morally loose atmosphere in his administration

_____ 2. Supreme Court ruling that removed workplace protection and invalidated a minimum wage for women

_____ 3. World War I veterans' group that promoted patriotism and economic benefits for former servicemen

_____ 4. Agreement emerging from the Washington Disarmament Conference that reduced naval strength and established a ratio of warships among the major shipbuilding powers

_____ 5. Toothless international agreement of 1928 that pledged nations to outlaw war

_____ 6. Naval oil reserve in Wyoming that gave its name to one of the major Harding administration scandals

_____ 7. Farm proposal of the 1920s, passed by Congress but vetoed by the president, that provided for the federal government to buy farm surpluses and sell them abroad

_____ 8. American-sponsored arrangement for rescheduling German reparations payments that only temporarily eased the international debt tangle of the 1920s

_____ 9. Southern Democrats who turned against their party's "wet," Catholic nominee and voted for the Republican in 1938

_____ 10. Sky-high tariff bill of 1930 that deepened the depression and caused international financial chaos

_____ 11. The climactic day of the October 1929 Wall Street stock-market crash

_____ 12. Depression shantytowns, named after the president whom many blamed for their financial distress

_____ 13. Hoover-sponsored federal agency that provided loans to hard-pressed banks and businesses after 1932

_____ 14. Encampment of unemployed veterans who were driven out of Washington by General Douglas MacArthur's forces in 1932

_____ 15. The Chinese province invaded and overrun by the Japanese army in 1932

D. Matching People, Places, and Events

Match the person, place, or event in the left column with the proper description in the right column by inserting the correct letter on the blank line.

___ 1. Warren G. Harding

___ 2. Charles Evans Hughes

___ 3. Andrew Mellon

___ 4. Henry Sinclair

___ 5. John Davis

A. The worst single event of the great stock market crash of 1929

B. Extremely high tariff act that killed international trade and deepened the Great Depression

C. The "Happy Warrior" who attracted votes in the cities but lost them in the South

D. Harding's interior secretary, convicted of taking bribes for leases on federal oil reserves

___ 6. Albert B. Fall

___ 7. Harry Daugherty

___ 8. Calvin Coolidge

___ 9. Robert La Follette

___ 10. Herbert Hoover

___ 11. Al Smith

___ 12. Black Tuesday

___ 13. Hawley-Smoot Bill

___ 14. Douglas MacArthur

___ 15. Henry Stimson

E. Weak, compromise Democratic candidate in 1924

F. U.S. attorney general and a member of Harding's corrupt "Ohio Gang" who was forced to resign in administration scandals

G. Strong-minded leader of Harding's cabinet and initiator of major naval agreements

H. Wealthy industrialist and conservative secretary of the treasury in the 1920s

I. Weak-willed president whose easygoing ways opened the door to widespread corruption in his administration

J. Hoover's secretary of state, who sought sanctions against Japan for its aggression in Manchuria

K. Secretary of commerce through much of the 1920s whose reputation for economic genius became a casualty of the Great Depression

L. Leader of a liberal third-party insurgency who attracted little support outside the farm belt

M. Wealthy oilman who bribed cabinet officials in the Teapot Dome scandal

N. Commander of the troops who forcefully ousted the "army" of unemployed veterans from Washington in 1932

O. Tight-lipped Vermonter who promoted frugality and pro-business policies during his presidency

E. Putting Things in Order

Put the following events in correct order by numbering them from 1 to 5.

___ Amid economic collapse, Congress raises tariff barriers to new heights and thereby deepens the depression.

___ An American-sponsored plan to ease German reparations payments provides a temporarily successful approach to the international war-debt tangle.

___ An American-sponsored international conference surprisingly reduces naval armaments and stabilizes Far Eastern power relations.

___ The prosperous economic bubble of the 1920s suddenly bursts, setting off a sustained period of hardship.

___ A large number of corrupt dealings and scandals become public knowledge just as the president who presided over them is replaced by his impeccably honest successor.

F. Matching Cause and Effect

Match the historical cause in the left column with the proper effect in the right column by writing the correct letter on the blank line.

Cause

___ 1. Republican probusiness policies

___ 2. American concern about the arms race and the danger of war

Effect

A. Led to a Republican landslide in the election of 1928

B. Weakened labor unions and prevented the enforcement of progressive antitrust legislation

___ 3. The high-tariff Fordney-McCumber Law of 1922

___ 4. The loose moral atmosphere of Harding's Washington

___ 5. The improved farm efficiency and production of the 1920s

___ 6. America's demand for completerepayment of the Allies' war debt

___ 7. Hoover's media campaign and Smith's political liabilities

___ 8. The stock-market crash

___ 9. Domestic overexpansion of production and dried-up international trade

___ 10. Hoover's limited efforts at federally sponsored relief and recovery

C. Plunged the United States into the worst economic depression in its history

D. Drove crop prices down and created a rural economic depression

E. Led to the successful Washington Disarmament Conference and the Five Power Naval Agreement of 1922

F. Encouraged numerous federal officials to engage in corrupt dealings

G. Helped cause the stock-market crash and deepen the Great Depression

H. Failed to end the depression but did prevent more serious economic suffering

I. Sustained American prosperity but pushed Europe into economic protectionism and turmoil

J. Aroused British and French anger and toughened their demands for German war reparations

G. Developing Historical Skills

Reading Diagrams

Sometimes a schematic drawing or diagram can help explain a complicated historical process in a simpler way than words. The international financial tangle of the 1920s is an exceptionally complicated affair, but examining the diagram on p. 764 makes it much easier to understand.

Answer the following questions.

1. What two roles did Americans play in the process?

2. What economic relationship did Great Britain and France have with Germany?

3. To whom did Britain owe war debts? To whom did France owe war debts?

4. Why was credit from American bankers so essential to all the European powers? Can you explain what happened when that credit was suddenly cut off after the stock-market crash of 1929?

PART III: Applying What You Have Learned

1. What basic economic and political policies were pursued by the conservative Republican administrations of the 1920s?

2. What were the effects of America's international economic and political isolationism in the 1920s?

3. What weakness existed beneath the surface of the general 1920s prosperity, and how did these weaknesses help cause the Great Depression?

4. Why were liberal or "progressive" politics so weak in the 1920s? Discuss the strengths and weaknesses of La Follette and Smith as challengers to the Republicans in 1924 and 1928.

5. The three Republican presidents of the 1920s are usually lumped together as essentially identical in outlook. Is it right to see them that way, or were the personal or political differences between them at all significant?

6. What were the effects of the Great Depression on the American people, and how did President Hoover attempt to balance his belief in "rugged individualism" with the economic necessities of the time? Why do historians today tend to see Hoover as a more tragic figure than people of the time, who bitterly denounced him?

7. How did some of the economic policies of the 1920s and 1930s help cause and deepen the depression?

34

The Great Depression and the New Deal, 1933–1938

PART I: Reviewing the Chapter

A. Checklist of Learning Objectives

After mastering this chapter, you should be able to

1. describe the rise of Franklin Roosevelt to the presidency in 1932.
2. explain how the early New Deal pursued the "three Rs" of relief, recovery, and reform.
3. describe the New Deal's effect on labor and labor organizations.
4. discuss the early New Deal's efforts to organize business and agriculture in the NRA and the AAA and indicate what replaced those programs after they were declared unconstitutional.
5. describe the Supreme Court's hostility to many New Deal programs and explain why FDR's "Court-packing" plan failed.
6. explain the political coalition that Roosevelt mobilized on behalf of the New Deal and the Democratic Party.
7. discuss the changes the New Deal underwent in the late thirties and explain the growing opposition to it.
8. analyze the arguments presented by both critics and defenders of the New Deal.

B. Glossary

To build your social science vocabulary, familiarize yourself with the following terms.

1. **dispossessed** The economically deprived. ". . . she . . . emerged as a champion of the dispossessed. . . ." (p. 778)
2. **rubber-stamp** To approve a plan or law quickly or routinely, without examination. ". . . it was ready to rubber-stamp bills drafted by White House advisors. . . ." (p. 781)
3. **blank-check** Referring to permission to use an unlimited amount of money or authority. ". . . Congress gave the president extraordinary blank-check powers. . . ." (p. 781)
4. **foreign exchange** The transfer of credits or accounts between the citizens or financial institutions of different nations. "The new law clothed the president with power to regulate banking transactions and foreign exchange. . . ." (p. 782)
5. **hoarding** Secretly storing up quantities of goods or money. "Roosevelt moved swiftly . . . to protect the melting gold reserve and to prevent panicky hoarding." (p. 783)
6. **boondoggling** Engaging in trivial or useless work; any enterprise characterized by such work. "Tens of thousands of jobless were employed at . . . make-work tasks, which were dubbed 'boondoggling.' " (p. 785)
7. **Fascist (Fascism)** A political system or philosophy that advocates a mass-based party dictatorship, extreme nationalism, racism, and the glorification of war. "Fear of Long's becoming a fascist dictator ended. . . ." (p. 786)

8. **parity** Equivalence in monetary value under different conditions; specifically, in the United States, the price for farm products that would give them the same purchasing power as in the period 1909–1914. ". . . this agency was to establish 'parity prices' for basic commodities." (p. 788)

9. **holding company** A company that owns, and usually controls, the stocks and securities of another company. "New Dealers . . . directed their fire at public utility holding companies. . . ." (p. 791)

10. **collective bargaining** Bargaining between an employer and his or her organized work force over hours, wages, and other conditions of employment. "The NRA blue eagles, with their call for collective bargaining, had been a godsend. . . ." (p. 795)

11. **jurisdictional** Concerning the proper sphere in which authority may be exercised. ". . . bitter and annoying jurisdictional feuding involving strikes continued. . . ." (p. 797)

12. **checks and balances** In American politics, the interlocking system of divided and counter-weighted authority among the executive, legislative, and judicial branches of government. ". . . Roosevelt was savagely condemned for attempting to break down the delicate checks and balances. . . ." (p. 799)

13. **pinko** Disparaging term for someone who is not a "red," or Communist, but is presumed to be sympathetic to communism. "Critics deplored the employment of 'crackpot' college professors, leftist 'pinkos.'. . ." (p. 802)

14. **deficit spending** The spending of public funds beyond the amount of income. "Despite some $20 billion poured out in six years of deficit spending. . . ." (p. 803)

15. **left** (or **left-wing**) In politics, groups or parties that traditionally advocate progress, social change, greater economic and social equality, and the welfare of the common worker. (The **right** or **right-wing** is traditionally groups or parties that advocate adherence to tradition, established authorities, and an acceptance of some degree of economic and social hierarchy.) "He may even have headed off a more radical swing to the left. . . ." (p. 804)

PART II: Checking Your Progress

A. True-False

Where the statement is true, mark **T**. Where it is false, mark **F**, and correct it in the space immediately below.

____ 1. Roosevelt's call for a "New Deal" in the 1932 campaign included attacks on the Hoover deficits and a promise to balance the federal budget.

____ 2. The economy was beginning a turn upward in the months immediately before Roosevelt's inauguration.

____ 3. Congress rushed to pass many of the early New Deal programs that granted large emergency powers to the president.

____ 4. Roosevelt's monetary reforms were designed to maintain the gold standard and protect the value of the dollar.

____ 5. The Civilian Conservation Corps (CCC) and the Public Works Administration (PWA) were designed to reform American business practices.

____ 6. Two early New Deal programs, the National Recovery Administration (NRA) and the Agricultural Adjustment Administration (AAA), were both declared unconstitutional by the Supreme Court.

_____ 7. The primary agricultural problem of the Great Depression was declining farm production caused by the natural disasters of the period.

_____ 8. The Securities and Exchange Commission and the Public Utilities Holding Company Act both imposed new federal regulations to reform corrupt or self-serving business practices that injured the public.

_____ 9. The Tennessee Valley Authority (TVA) was designed primarily to aid in conserving water and soil resources in eroded hill areas.

_____ 10. The Committee for Industrial Organization (CIO) used sympathetic New Deal laws to unionize many unskilled workers previously ignored by the American Federation of Labor (AF of L).

_____ 11. Roosevelt's political coalition rested heavily on lower-income groups, including African-Americans, Jews, Catholics, and southerners.

_____ 12. After Roosevelt's Court-packing plan failed, the conservative Supreme Court continued to strike down New Deal legislation just as it had before.

_____ 13. After 1938 the New Deal lost momentum and ran into increasing opposition from an enlarged Republican bloc in Congress.

_____ 14. The New Deal more than doubled the U.S. national debt through "deficit spending."

_____ 15. By 1939 the New Deal had largely solved the major depression problem of unemployment.

B. Multiple Choice

Select the best answer and write the proper letter in the space provided.

_____ 1. Franklin Roosevelt's presidential campaign in 1932

    a. called for large-scale federal spending to reduce unemployment and restore prosperity.
    b. focused primarily on issues of international trade.
    c. promised to aid the ordinary person by balancing the federal budget and ending deficits.
    d. emphasized that there was no way out of the depression in the near future.

_____ 2. Eleanor Roosevelt became and influential figure in the 1930s especially by advocating the cause of

    a. the impoverished and dispossessed.
    b. feminists and proponents of sexual liberation.
    c. farmers and ranchers.
    d. immigrant ethnic groups and Roman Catholics.

_____ 3. The Roosevelt landslide of 1932 included the shift into the Democratic camp of traditionally Republican

    a. New Englanders.
    b. African-Americans.
    c. labor unions.
    d. southerners.

4. Roosevelt's first bold action during the Hundred Days was

    a. taking the nation off the gold standard.
    b. declaring a national bank holiday.
    c. legalizing labor strikes and job actions.
    d. doubling relief for the unemployed.

5. The *primary* purpose of the Civilian Conservation Corps (CCC) was

    a. to restore unproductive farmland to productive use.
    b. to protect wildlife and the environment.
    c. to provide better-trained workers for industry.
    d. to provide jobs and experience for unemployed young people.

6. Strong political challenges to Roosevelt came from extremist critics like

    a. Father Coughlin and Huey Long.
    b. Frances Perkins and Harry Hopkins.
    c. Henry Ford and Mary McLeod Bethune.
    d. John Steinbeck and John L. Lewis.

7. Roosevelt's National Recovery Administration (NRA) ended when

    a. Dr. Francis Townsend attacked it as unfair to the elderly.
    b. Congress refused to provide further funding for it.
    c. it came to be considered too expensive for the results achieved.
    d. the Supreme Court declared it unconstitutional.

8. Roosevelt's Agricultural Adjustment Administration met sharp criticism because

    a. it failed to raise farm prices.
    b. it actually contributed to soil erosion on the Great Plains.
    c. it raised prices by paying farmers to slaughter animals and not grow crops.
    d. it relied too much on private bank loans to aid farmers.

9. In addition to the natural forces of drought and wind, the Dust Bowl of the 1930s was also caused by

    a. Roosevelt's AAA farm policies.
    b. excessive use of dry farming and mechanization techniques on marginal land.
    c. the attempted shift from wheat and cotton growing to fruit and vegetable farming.
    d. the drying up of underground aquifers used to irrigate the Great Plains.

10. The so-called "Indian New Deal" included an emphasis on

    a. local tribal self-government and recovery of Indian identity and culture.
    b. the distribution of tribal lands to individual Indian landowners.
    c. the migration of Indians from rural reservations to the cities.
    d. programs to encourage businesses like gambling casinos to locate on Indian lands.

11. The major New Deal program that attempted to provide flood control, electric power, and economic development occurred in the valley of the

    a. Columbia River.
    b. Colorado River.
    c. Hudson River.
    d. Tennessee River.

____ 12. The Social Security Act of 1935 provided for

    a. electricity and conservation for rural areas.

    b. pensions for older people, the blind, and other categories of citizens.

    c. assistance for low-income public housing and social services.

    d. unemployment and disability insurance for workers.

____ 13. The new labor organization that flourished under depression conditions and New Deal sponsorship was

    a. the Knights of Labor.

    b. the American Federation of Labor.

    c. the National Labor Relations Board.

    d. the Committee for Industrial Organization.

____ 14. Among the groups that formed part of the powerful "Roosevelt coalition" in the election of 1936 were

    a. African-Americans, southerners, and Catholics.

    b. Republicans, New Englanders, and "Old Immigrants."

    c. midwesterners, small-town residents, and Presbyterians.

    d. businessmen, prohibitionists, and Coughlinites.

____ 15. Roosevelt's attempt to "pack" the Supreme Court proved extremely costly because

    a. the Court members he appointed still failed to support the New Deal.

    b. Congress began proceedings to impeach him.

    c. its failure ended much of the political momentum of the New Deal.

    d. many of his New Deal supporters turned to back Huey Long.

C. Identification

Supply the correct identification for each numbered description.

_____ 1. Term used by FDR in 1932 acceptance speech that came to describe his whole reform program

_____ 2. FDR's reform-minded intellectual advisers, who conceived much of the New Deal legislation

_____ 3. Popular term for the special session of Congress in early 1933 that passed vast quantities of Roosevelt-initiated legislation

_____ 4. The early New Deal agency that worked to solve the problems of unemployment and conservation by employing youth in reforestation and other socially beneficial tasks

_____ 5. Large federal employment program, established in 1935 under Harry Hopkins, that provided jobs in areas from road building to art

_____ 6. Widely displayed symbol of the National Recovery Administration (NRA), which attempted to reorganize and reform U.S. industry

_____ 7. New Deal farm agency that attempted to raise prices by paying farmers to reduce their production of crops and animals

_____ 8. The drought-stricken plains areas from which hundreds of thousands of "Okies" were driven during the Great Depression

_____ 9. New Deal agency that aroused strong conservative criticism by producing low-cost electrical power in competition with private utilities

_____ 10. New Deal program that financed old-age pensions, unemployment insurance, and other forms of income assistance

_____ 11. The new union group that organized large numbers of unskilled workers with the help of the Wagner Act and the National Labor Relations Board

_____ 12. New Deal agency established to provide a public watchdog against deception and fraud in stock trading

_____ 13. Organization of wealthy Republicans and conservative Democrats whose attacks on the New Deal caused Roosevelt to denounce them as "economic royalists" in the campaign of 1936

_____ 14. Roosevelt's scheme for gaining Supreme Court approval of New Deal legislation

_____ 15. Law of 1939 that prevented federal officials from engaging in campaign activities or using federal relief funds for political purposes

D. Matching People, Places, and Events

Match the person, place, or event in the left column with the proper description in the right column by inserting the correct letter on the blank line.

____ 1. Franklin D. Roosevelt

____ 2. Eleanor Roosevelt

____ 3. Banking holiday

____ 4. Harry Hopkins

____ 5. Father Coughlin

____ 6. Huey ("Kingfish") Long

____ 7. *Schechter* case

____ 8. Harold Ickes

____ 9. John Steinbeck

____ 10. John L. Lewis

____ 11. General Motors sit-down strike

____ 12. Alfred M. Landon

____ 13. Election of 1936

____ 14. John Maynard Keynes

____ 15. Justice Roberts

A. Republican who carried only two states in a futile campaign against "The Champ" in 1936

B. The "microphone messiah" of Michigan whose mass radio appeals turned anti–New Deal and anti-Semitic

C. Writer whose best-selling novel portrayed the suffering of dust bowl "Okies" in the Thirties

D. Supreme Court justice whose "switch in time" to support New Deal legislation helped undercut FDR's Court-packing scheme

E. Presidential wife who became an effective lobbyist for the poor during the New Deal

F. Louisiana senator and popular mass agitator who promised to make "every man a king" at the expense of the wealthy

G. Former New York governor who roused the nation to action against the depression with his appeal to the "forgotten man"

H. Dramatic CIO labor action in 1936 that forced the auto industry to recognize unions

I. Lopsided but bitter campaign that saw disadvantaged economic groups lined up in a kind of "class warfare" against those better off

J. Former New York social worker who became an influential FDR adviser and head of several New Deal agencies

K. Former bull moose progressive who spent billions of dollars on public building projects while carefully guarding against waste

L. Roosevelt-declared closing of all U.S. financial institutions on March 6–10, 1933, in order to stop panic and prepare reforms

M. British economist whose theories helped justify New Deal deficit spending

N. Supreme Court ruling of 1935 that struck down a major New Deal industry-and-labor agency

O. Domineering boss of the mine workers' union who launched the CIO

E. Putting Things in Order

Put the following events in correct order by numbering them from 1 to 5.

____ FDR devalues the dollar to about sixty cents in gold in an attempt to raise domestic prices.

____ Congress passes numerous far-reaching laws under the pressure of a national crisis and strong presidential leadership.

____ Republican attempts to attack the New Deal fall flat, and FDR wins reelection in a landslide.

____ FDR's frustration at the conservative Supreme Court's overturning of New Deal legislation leads him to make a drastic proposal.

____ Passage of new federal prolabor legislation opens the way for a new union group and successful mass labor organizing.

F. Matching Cause and Effect

Match the historical cause in the left column with the proper effect in the right column by writing the correct letter on the blank line.

Cause	**Effect**
____ 1. The "lame-duck" period from November 1932 to March 1933	**A.** Succeeded in raising farm prices but met strong opposition from many conservatives
____ 2. Roosevelt's leadership during the Hundred Days	**B.** Encouraged the CIO to organize large numbers of unskilled workers
____ 3. The Civilian Conservation Corps, the Works Progress Administration, and the Civil Works Administration	**C.** May have pushed the Court toward more liberal rulings but badly hurt FDR politically
	D. Caused a sharp "Roosevelt Depression" that brought unemployment back up to catastrophic levels
____ 4. New Deal farm programs like the AAA	**E.** Caused a political paralysis that nearly halted the U.S. economy
____ 5. The Tennessee Valley Authority	**F.** Provided federal economic planning, conservation, cheap electricity, and jobs to a poverty-stricken region
____ 6. The Wagner (National Labor Relations) Act	**G.** Provided federal jobs for unemployed workers in conservation, construction, the arts, and other areas
	H. Caused Roosevelt to propose a plan to "pack" the Supreme Court
____ 7. FDR's political appeals to workers, African-Americans, southerners, and "New Immigrants"	**I.** Pushed a remarkable number of laws through Congress and restored the nation's confidence
	J. Forged a powerful political coalition that made the Democrats the majority party

___ 8. The Supreme Court's conservative rulings against New
Deal legislation

___ 9. Roosevelt's attempt to "pack"
the Supreme Court

___ 10. The rapid cutback in federal
"pump-priming" spending in
1937

G. Developing Historical Skills

Reading Charts

Charts can classify complex information for ready reference. In this chapter they are an effective way to present the many New Deal laws, agencies, and programs. The chart dealing with the Hundred Days is on p. 781, and that dealing with the later New Deal on p. 784.

Answer the following questions.

1. Which Hundred Days agency whose primary purpose was recovery also contributed to relief and reform?

2. List three Hundred Days actions that were aimed *primarily* at recovery.

3. List three later New Deal measures aimed primarily at reform.

4. Which later New Deal law aimed primarily at relief also contributed to recovery and reform?

5. Which was the *last* of the later New Deal laws aimed primarily at providing relief?

6. Compare the two charts. What can you conclude about the Hundred Days compared to the later New Deal in relation to their relative emphasis on the three goals of relief, recovery, and reform? In which of the areas do you see the most continuity of purpose?

H. Map Mastery

Map Discrimination

Using the maps and charts in Chapter 34, answer the following questions.

1. *TVA Area*: In which four states was most of the Tennessee Valley Authority located?

2. *TVA Area*: How many major TVA dams were located in (a) Tennessee and (b) Alabama?

3. *The Rise and Decline of Organized Labor*: Before the organizing drives of the 1930s, which year saw the highest membership for organized labor?

4. *The Rise and Decline of Organized Labor*: About how many million members did the CIO *gain* between 1935 and 1945: 2 million, 4 million, 6 million, or 8 million?

Map Challenge

Using the graph of *The Rise and Decline of Organized Labor* on p. 797, write a brief essay explaining the changing fortunes of (a) organized labor in general and (b) the different types of unions—craft, industrial, and independent—from 1900 to 1998.

PART III: Applying What You Have Learned

1. What qualities did FDR bring to the presidency, and how did he display them during the New Deal years? What particular role did Eleanor Roosevelt play in FDR's political success?
2. How did the early New Deal legislation attempt to achieve the three goals of relief, recovery, and reform?
3. How did Roosevelt's programs develop such a strong appeal for the "forgotten man," and why did the New Deal arouse such opposition from conservatives, including those on the Supreme Court?
4. Discuss the political components of the "Roosevelt coalition" formed in the 1930s. What did the New Deal offer to the diverse elements of this coalition?
5. Was the New Deal essentially a conservative attempt to save American capitalism from collapse, a radical change in traditional American anti-government beliefs, or a moderate liberal response to a unique crisis?
6. How was the New Deal a culmination of the era of progressive reform, and how did it differ from the pre–World War I progressive era? (See Chapters 29 and 30.)

35

Franklin D. Roosevelt and the Shadow of War, 1933–1941

PART I: Reviewing the Chapter

A. Checklist of Learning Objectives

After mastering this chapter, you should be able to

1. describe the isolationist motives and effects of FDR's early foreign policies.
2. explain how American isolationism dominated U.S. policy in the mid-1930s.
3. explain how America gradually began to respond to the threat from totalitarian aggression while still trying to stay neutral.
4. describe Roosevelt's increasingly bold moves toward aiding Britain in the fight against Hitler and the sharp disagreements these efforts caused at home.
5. discuss the events and diplomatic issues in the Japanese-American conflict that led up to Pearl Harbor.

B. Glossary

To build your social science vocabulary, familiarize yourself with the following terms.

1. **Exchange rate** The monetary ratio according to which one currency is convertible into another, e.g., American dollars vis-à-vis German deutschmarks, which determines their value relative to one another. "Exchange-rate stabilization was essential to revival of world trade . . ." (p. 806)
2. **militarist** Someone who glorifies military values or institutions and extends them into the political and social spheres. "Yet in Tokyo, Japanese militarists were calculating that they had little to fear. . . ." (p. 807)
3. **totalitarianism** A political system of absolute control, in which all social, moral, and religious values and institutions are put in direct service of the state. "Post-1918 chaos in Europe, followed by the Great Depression, fostered the ominous spread of totalitarianism." (p. 809)
4. **quarantine** In politics, isolating a nation by refusing to have economic or diplomatic dealings with it. ". . . they feared that a moral quarantine would lead to a shooting quarantine." (p. 812)
5. **division** The major unit of military organization, usually about 3,000 to 10,000 strong, into which most modern armies are organized. " . . . he sent his mechanized divisions crashing into Poland at dawn on September 1, 1939." (p. 813)
6. **unilateral** In politics, concerning a policy or action undertaken by only one nation. "This ancient dictum [was] hitherto unilateral. . . ." (p. 815)
7. **multilateral** In politics, referring to a policy or action undertaken by more than one nation. "Now multilateral, [the Monroe Doctrine bludgeon] was to be wielded by twenty-one pairs of American hands. . . ." (p. 815)
8. **steppes** The great plains of southeastern Europe and Asia. "The two fiends could now slit each other's throats on the icy steppes of Russia." (p. 822)

9. **convoy (v.)** To escort militarily, for purposes of protection. (The escorting ships or troops is called a convoy.) "Roosevelt made the fateful decision to convoy in July 1941." (p. 823)

10. **warlord** A leader or ruler who maintains power by continually waging war, often against other similar rulers or local military leaders. ". . . Roosevelt had resolutely held off an embargo, lest he goad the Tokyo warlords. . . ." (p. 824)

11. **hara-kiri** Traditional Japanese ritual suicide. "Japan's *hara-kiri* gamble in Hawaii paid off only in the short run." (p. 825)

PART II: Checking Your Progress

A. True-False

Where the statement is true, mark **T**. Where it is false, mark **F**, and correct it in the space immediately below.

____ 1. Roosevelt's policy toward the 1933 London Economic Conference showed his concern for establishing a stable international economic order.

____ 2. Roosevelt adhered to his Good Neighbor principle of nonintervention in Latin America even when Mexico seized American oil companies in 1938.

____ 3. American isolationism was caused partly by deep disillusionment with U.S. participation in World War I.

____ 4. The Neutrality Acts of the mid-1930s prevented Americans from lending money or selling weapons to warring nations and from sailing on belligerent ships.

____ 5. Despite the neutrality laws, the United States provided some assistance to the Spanish Loyalist government in its Civil War with the Fascistic General Franco.

____ 6. The United States reacted strongly when Japan sank the American gunboat *Panay* in Chinese waters.

____ 7. The United States attempted to dissuade the Western democracies from pursuing their policy of appeasing Hitler's aggressive demands.

____ 8. The "cash-and-carry" Neutrality Act of 1939 allowed America to aid the Allies without making loans or transporting weapons on U.S. ships.

____ 9. The fall of France to Hitler in 1940 strengthened U.S. determination to stay neutral.

____ 10. Isolationists argued that economic and military aid to Britain would inevitably lead to U.S. involvement in the European war.

____ 11. Republican presidential nominee Willkie joined the isolationist attack on Roosevelt's pro-Britain policy in the 1940 campaign.

____ 12. The 1941 Lend-Lease Act marked the effective abandonment of U.S. neutrality and the beginning of naval clashes with Germany.

____ 13. The Atlantic Charter was an agreement on future war aims signed by Great Britain, the United States, and the Soviet Union.

___ 14. U.S. warships were already being damaged and sunk in clashes with the German navy before Pearl Harbor.

___ 15. The focal point of conflict between the United States and Japan in the pre–Pearl Harbor negotiations was Japan's refusal to withdraw from the Dutch East Indies.

B. Multiple Choice

Select the best answer and write the proper letter in the space provided.

___ 1. Roosevelt torpedoed the London Economic Conference of 1933 because

   a. he wanted to concentrate primarily on the recovery of the American domestic economy.
   b. he saw the hand of Hitler and Mussolini behind the conference's proposals.
   c. he was firmly committed to the gold standard.
   d. he wanted economic cooperation only between the United States and Britain, not the rest of Europe.

___ 2. Seeking to withdraw from overseas commitments and colonial expense, the United States in 1934 promised future independence to

   a. Puerto Rico.
   b. the Virgin Islands.
   c. the Philippines.
   d. Cuba.

___ 3. Roosevelt's Good Neighbor policy toward Latin America included

   a. a substantial program of American economic aid for Latin American countries.
   b. a renunciation of American intervention in Mexico or elsewhere in the region.
   c. an American military presence to block German influence in Argentina and Brazil.
   d. an American pledge to transfer the Panama Canal to Panama by the year 2000.

___ 4. The immediate response of most Americans to the rise of the Fascist dictators Mussolini and Hitler was

   a. a call for a new military alliance to contain aggression.
   b. a focus on political cooperation with Britain and the Soviet Union.
   c. support for the Spanish government against Fascist rebels.
   d. a deeper commitment to remain isolated from European problems.

___ 5. The Neutrality Acts of 1935, 1936, and 1937 provided that

   a. the United States would remain neutral in any war between Britain and Germany.
   b. Americans could not sail on belligerent ships, sell munitions, or make loans to nations at war.
   c. no belligerent could conduct propaganda campaigns, sell goods, or make loans within the United States.
   d. the United States would take the lead in neutral efforts to end the wars in China and Ethiopia.

6. The effect of the strict American arms embargo during the civil war between the Loyalist Spanish government and Franco's Fascist rebels was

a. to encourage a negotiated political settlement between the warring parties.
b. to strengthen the Spanish government's ability to resist Franco.
c. to push Britain and the Soviet Union to intervene in the Spanish Civil War.
d. to cripple the Loyalist government while the Italians and Germans armed Franco.

7. The policy of appeasing the Fascist dictators reached its low point in 1938 when Britain and France sold out Czechoslovakia to Hitler in the conference at

a. Geneva.
b. Versailles.
c. Munich.
d. Prague.

8. The "cash-and-carry" Neutrality Act of 1939 was cleverly designed to

a. guarantee that American policy would not benefit either side in World War II.
b. enable American merchants to provide loans and ships to the Allies.
c. prepare America for involvement in the war.
d. help Britain and France by letting them buy supplies and munitions in the United States.

9. The "destroyers-for-bases" deal of 1940 provided that

a. the United States would give Britain fifty American destroyers in exchange for eight British bases in North America.
b. the United States would give Britain new bases in North America in exchange for fifty British destroyers.
c. if America entered the war it would receive eight bases in Britain in exchange for American destroyers.
d. the British would transfer captured French destroyers to the United States in exchange for the use of American bases in East Asia.

10. The twin events that precipitated the reversal of American policy from neutrality to active, though nonbelligerent, support of the Allied cause were

a. the Munich Conference and the invasion of Poland.
b. the fall of France and the Battle of Britain.
c. the fall of Poland and the invasion of Norway.
d. the invasion of the Soviet Union and the German submarine attacks on American shipping.

11. In the campaign of 1940, the Republican nominee Willkie essentially agreed with Roosevelt on the issue of

a. the New Deal.
b. the third term.
c. Roosevelt's use of power in office.
d. foreign policy.

_____ 12. The Lend-Lease Act clearly marked

    a. the end of isolationist opposition to Roosevelt's foreign policy.
    b. an end to the pretense of American neutrality between Britain and Germany.
    c. a secret Roosevelt plan to involve the United States in war with Japan.
    d. the beginning of opposition in Congress to Roosevelt's foreign policy.

_____ 13. The provisions of the Atlantic Charter signed by Roosevelt and Churchill in 1941 included

    a. self-determination for oppressed peoples and a new international peacekeeping organization.
    b. a permanent alliance between Britain, the United States, and the Soviet Union.
    c. a pledge to rid the world of dictators and to establish democratic governments in Germany and Italy.
    d. an agreement to oppose Soviet communism, but only after Hitler was defeated.

_____ 14. By the fall of 1940, American warships were being attacked by German destroyers near the coast of

    a. Spain.
    b. Ireland.
    c. Iceland.
    d. Canada.

_____ 15. The key issue in the failed negotiations with Japan just before Pearl Harbor was

    a. the refusal of the Japanese to withdraw their navy from Hawaiian waters.
    b. Americans' insistence on their right to expand naval power in Asia.
    c. the Japanese refusal to withdraw from China.
    d. the Japanese refusal to guarantee the security of the Philippines.

C. Identification

Supply the correct identification for each numbered description.

_____ 1. International economic conference on stabilizing currency that was sabotaged by FDR

_____ 2. Nation to which the U.S. promised independence in the Tydings-McDuffie Act of 1934

_____ 3. FDR's repudiation of Theodore Roosevelt's corollary to the Monroe Doctrine, stating his intention to work cooperatively with Latin American nations

_____ 4. A series of laws enacted by Congress in the mid-1930s that attempted to prevent any American involvement in future overseas wars

_____ 5. Conflict between the rebel Fascist forces of General Francisco Franco and the Loyalist government that severely tested U.S. neutrality legislation

_____ 6. Roosevelt's 1937 speech that proposed strong U.S. measures against overseas aggressors

_____ 7. European diplomatic conference in 1938 where Britain and France conceded to Hitler's demands for Czechoslovakia

_____ 8. Term for the British-French policy of attempting to prevent war by granting German demands

_____ 9. Leading U.S. group advocating American support for Britain in the fight against Hitler

_____ 10. Leading isolationist group advocating that America focus on continental defense and non-involvement with the European war

_____ 11. Controversial 1941 law that made America the "arsenal of democracy" by providing supposedly temporary military material assistance to Britain

_____ 12. Communist nation invaded by Hitler in June 1941 that was also aided by American lend-lease

_____ 13. U.S.–British agreement of August 1941 to promote democracy and establish a new international organization for peace

_____ 14. U.S. destroyer sunk by German submarines off the coast of Iceland in October 1941, with the loss of over a hundred men

_____ 15. Major American Pacific naval base devastated in a surprise attack in December 1941

D. Matching People, Places, and Events

Match the person, place, or event in the left column with the proper description in the right column by inserting the correct letter on the blank line.

___ 1. Cordell Hull

___ 2. Adolf Hitler

___ 3. Benito Mussolini

___ 4. Gerald Nye

___ 5. Francisco Franco

___ 6. Ethiopia

___ 7. Czechoslovakia

___ 8. Poland

___ 9. France

___ 10. Charles A. Lindbergh

___ 11. Wendell Willkie

___ 12. Winston Churchill

___ 13. Joseph Stalin

___ 14. Iceland

___ 15. Hawaii

A. Courageous prime minister who led Britain's lonely resistance to Hitler

B. Leader of the "America First" organization and chief spokesman for U.S. isolationism

C. African nation invaded by an Italian dictator in 1935

D. Dynamic dark horse Republican presidential nominee who attacked FDR only on domestic policy

E. Fanatical Fascist leader of Germany whose aggressions forced the United States to abandon its neutrality

F. Instigator of 1934 Senate hearings that castigated World War I munitions manufacturers as "merchants of death"

G. Nation whose sudden fall to Hitler in 1940 pushed the United States closer to direct aid to Britain

H. Site of a naval base where Japan launched a devastating surprise attack on the United States

I. North Atlantic nation near whose waters U.S. destroyers came under Nazi submarine attack

J. Small East European democracy betrayed into Hitler's hands at Munich

K. The lesser partner of the Rome-Berlin Axis who invaded Ethiopia and joined the war against France and Britain

L. FDR's secretary of state, who promoted reciprocal trade agreements, especially with Latin America

M. Russian dictator who first helped Hitler destroy Poland before becoming a victim of Nazi aggression in 1941

N. East European nation whose September 1939 invasion by Hitler set off World War II in Europe

O. Fascist rebel against the Spanish Loyalist government

E. Putting Things in Order

Put the following events in correct order by numbering them from 1 to 5.

____ FDR puts domestic recovery ahead of international economics, torpedoing a major monetary conference.

____ Western democracies try to appease Hitler by sacrificing Czechoslovakia, but his appetite for conquest remains undiminished.

____ Already engaged against Hitler in the Atlantic, the United States is plunged into World War II by a surprise attack in the Pacific.

____ The fall of France pushes FDR into providing increasingly open aid to Britain.

____ Japan invades China and attacks an American vessel, but the United States sticks to its neutrality principles.

F. Matching Cause and Effect

Match the historical cause in the left column with the proper effect in the right column by writing the correct letter on the blank line.

Cause	Effect
____ 1. FDR's refusal to support international economic cooperation in the 1930s	**A.** Thrust the United States into an undeclared naval war with Nazi German in the North Atlantic
____ 2. Roosevelt's Good Neighbor policy	**B.** Prompted FDR to make his "Quarantine Speech," proposing strong action against aggressors
____ 3. Bad memories of World War I and revelations about arms merchants	**C.** Brought new respect for the United States and for democracy in Latin America
____ 4. The U.S. Neutrality Acts of the 1930s	**D.** Shocked the United States into enacting conscription and making the "destroyers-for-bases" deal
____ 5. Japanese aggression against China in 1937	**E.** Forced Japan to either accept U.S. demands regarding China or go to war
____ 6. Hitler's invasion of Poland	**F.** Caused the United States to institute a "cash-and-carry" policy for providing aid to Britain
____ 7. The fall of France in 1940	**G.** Deepened the worldwide Depression and aided the rise of Fascist dictators
____ 8. Willkie's support for FDR's pro-British foreign policy	**H.** Actually aided Fascist dictators in carrying out their aggressions in Ethiopia, Spain, and China.
____ 9. The U.S. embargo on oil and other supplies to Japan	**I.** Promoted U.S. isolationism and the passage of several Neutrality Acts in the mid-1930s
____ 10. Roosevelt's decision to convoy lend-lease shipments	**J.** Kept the 1940 presidential campaign from becoming a bitter national debate

G. Developing Historical Skills

Reading Text for Sequence and Context

In learning to read for and remember the historical sequence of events, it is often helpful to look for the context in which they occurred.

In the first list below are several major events discussed in the chapter. The second list contains the immediate contexts in which those events occurred. First, link the event to the appropriate context by putting a number from the bottom list to the right of the proper event. Then put the event-with-context in the proper sequence by writing numbers 1 to 7 in the spaces to the left.

Order	Event	Context
_____	Destroyer-for-bases deal	_____
_____	Atlantic Charter	_____
_____	Good Neighbor policy	_____
_____	U.S. Neutrality Acts of 1935–1936	_____
_____	Pearl Harbor	_____
_____	Lend-lease	_____
_____	Munich Conference	_____

Context

1. Failure of U.S.–Japanese negotiations
2. Decline of U.S. investment in Latin America
3. Nye Hearings and Italy's invasion of Ethiopia
4. Britain's near-defeat from German bombing
5. The fall of France
6. Hitler's threats to go to war
7. Hitler's invasion of Russia

H. Map Mastery

Map Discrimination

Using the maps and charts in Chapter 35, answer the following questions.

1. *Presidential Election of 1940*: In the 1940 election, how many electoral votes did Willkie win west of the Mississippi River?

2. *Presidential Election of 1940*: How many electoral votes did Willkie win east of the Mississippi?

3. *Main Flow of Lend-Lease Aid*: Which *continent* received the most U.S. lend-lease aid?

4. *Main Flow of Lend-Lease Aid*: Which nation received lend-lease aid by way of both the Atlantic and Pacific oceans?

PART III: Applying What You Have Learned

1. How and why did the United States attempt to isolate itself from foreign troubles in the early and mid-1930s?
2. Discuss the effects of the U.S. neutrality laws of the 1930s on both American foreign policy and the international situation in Europe and East Asia.
3. How did the Fascist dictators' continually expanding aggression gradually erode the U.S. commitment to neutrality and isolationism?
4. How did Roosevelt manage to move the United States toward providing effective aid to Britain while slowly undercutting isolationist opposition?
5. Was American entry into World War II inevitable? Is it possible the U.S. might have been able to fight *either* Germany *or* Japan, while avoiding armed conflict with the other?
6. How did the process of American entry into World War II compare with the way the country got into World War I? (See Chapter 31.) How were the Neutrality Acts aimed at the conditions of 1914–1917, and why did they prove ineffective in the conditions of the 1930s?

36

America in World War II,
1941–1945

PART I: Reviewing the Chapter

A. Checklist of Learning Objectives

After mastering this chapter, you should be able to

1. tell how America reacted to Pearl Harbor and prepared to wage war against both Germany and Japan.
2. describe the domestic mobilization for war.
3. describe the war's effects on American society, including regional migration, race relations, and women's roles.
4. explain the early Japanese successes in Asia and the Pacific and the American strategy for countering them.
5. describe the early Allied efforts against the Axis powers in North Africa and Italy.
6. discuss FDR's 1944 fourth-term election victory.
7. explain the final military efforts that brought Allied victory in Europe and Asia and the significance of the atomic bomb.

B. Glossary

To build your social science vocabulary, familiarize yourself with the following terms.

1. **concentration camp** A place of confinement for prisoners or others a government considers dangerous or undesirable. "The Washington top command . . . forcibly herded them together in concentration camps. . . ." (p. 829)
2. **bracero** A Mexican farm laborer temporarily brought into the United States. "The *bracero* program outlived the war by some twenty years. . . ." (p. 833)
3. **U-boat** A German submarine (from the German *Unterseeboot*). "Not until the spring of 1943 did the Allies . . . have the upper hand against the U-boat." (p. 841)
4. **depose(d); deposition** Forcibly remove from office or position. "Mussolini was deposed, and Italy surrendered unconditionally soon thereafter." (p. 843)
5. **beachhead** The first position on a beach secured by an invading force and used to land further troops and supplies. "The Allied beachhead, at first clung to with fingertips, was gradually enlarged, consolidated, and reinforced." (p. 846)
6. **underground** A secret or illegal movement organized in a country to resist or overthrow the government. "With the assistance of the French 'underground,' Paris was liberated. . . ." (p. 846)
7. **acclamation** A general and unanimous action of approval or nomination by a large public body, without a vote. "He was nominated at Chicago on the first ballot by acclamation." (p. 847)

8. **bastion** A fortified stronghold, often including earthworks or stoneworks, that guards against enemy attack. ". . . the 101st Airborne Division had stood firm at the vital bastion of Bastogne." (p. 848)

9. **genocide** The systematic extermination or killing of an entire people. "The Washington government had long been informed about Hitler's campaign of genocide against the Jews. . . ." (p. 849)

10. **bazooka** A metal-tubed weapon from which armor-piercing rockets are electronically fired. "The enemy was almost literally smothered by bayonets, bullets, bazookas, and bombs." (p. 854)

PART II: Checking Your Progress

A. True-False

Where the statement is true, mark **T**. Where it is false, mark **F**, and correct it in the space immediately below.

_____ 1. America's major strategic decision in World War II was to fight Japan first and then attack Hitler's Germany.

_____ 2. A substantial minority of Americans, particularly those of Germans and Italian descent, questioned the wisdom of fighting World War II.

_____ 3. Government-run rationing and wage-price controls enabled the United States to meet the economic challenges of the war.

_____ 4. New sources of labor such as women and Mexican *braceros* helped overcome the human-resources shortage during World War II.

_____ 5. World War II stimulated massive black migration to the North and West and encouraged black demands for greater equality.

_____ 6. A majority of women who worked in wartime factories stayed in the labor force after the war ended.

_____ 7. American citizens at home had to endure serious economic deprivations during World War II.

_____ 8. The Japanese navy established its domination of the Pacific sea-lanes in the 1942 battles of Coral Sea and Midway.

_____ 9. The American strategy in the Pacific was to encircle Japan by flank movements from Burma and Alaska.

_____ 10. In the first years of the war in Europe, Britain and the United States bore the heaviest burden of Allied ground fighting against Hitler.

_____ 11. Britain was reluctant to attack Germany directly across the English Channel because of its memory of World War I's heavy losses.

_____ 12. At the Teheran Conference in 1943, Stalin, Churchill, and Roosevelt planned the D-Day invasion and the final strategy for winning the war.

_____ 13. Liberal Democrats rallied to dump Vice President Henry Wallace from FDR's ticket in 1944 and replace him with Senator Harry S Truman.

_____ 14. Roosevelt died just a few weeks before the dropping of the atomic bomb and the surrender of Japan.

_____ 15. The United States modified its demand for "unconditional surrender" by allowing Japan to keep its emperor, Hirohito.

B. Multiple Choice

Select the best answer and write the proper letter in the space provided.

_____ 1. The fundamental American strategic decision of World War II was

   a. to attack Germany and Japan simultaneously with equal force.
   b. to concentrate naval forces in the Pacific and ground forces in Europe.
   c. to attack Germany first while using just enough strength to hold off Japan.
   d. to attack Germany and Japan from the "back door" routes of North Africa and China.

_____ 2. The major exception to the relatively good American civil liberties record during World War II was the treatment of

   a. American Fascist groups.
   b. Japanese-Americans.
   c. Mexican-Americans.
   d. German-Americans.

_____ 3. Wartime inflation and food shortages were kept partly in check by

   a. price controls and rationing.
   b. government operation of factories and railroads.
   c. special bonuses to farmers and workers to increase production.
   d. importation of additional fuel and food from Latin America.

_____ 4. The wartime shortage of labor was partly made up by bringing into the work force such groups as

   a. teenage and elderly laborers.
   b. Japanese and Chinese immigrants.
   c. Mexican _braceros_ and women.
   d. sharecroppers and inner-city residents.

_____ 5. Compared with British and Soviet women during World War II, more American women

   a. did not work for wages in the wartime economy.
   b. worked in heavy-industry war plants.
   c. served in the armed forces.
   d. worked in agriculture.

_____ 6. The Fair Employment Practices Commission was designed to

   a. prevent discrimination against blacks in wartime industries.
   b. guarantee all regions of the country an opportunity to compete for defense contracts.
   c. prevent discrimination in employment against women.
   d. guarantee that those who had been unemployed longest would be the first hired.

7. The wartime migration of rural African-Americans to northern urban factories was further accelerated after the war by the invention of

   a. the cotton gin.
   b. the gasoline-powered mechanical combine.
   c. synthetic fibers such as nylon that largely replaced cotton cloth.
   d. the mechanical cotton picker.

8. Besides African-Americans, another traditionally rural group who used service in the armed forces as a springboard to postwar urban life were

   a. Scandinavian-Americans.
   b. New England farmers.
   c. Indians.
   d. Japanese-Americans.

9. The Japanese advance in the Pacific was finally halted at the battles of

   a. Guadalcanal and Tarawa.
   b. Bataan and Corregidor.
   c. Guam and Wake Island.
   d. Coral Sea and Midway.

10. The essential American strategy in the Pacific called for

   a. securing bases in China from which to bomb the Japanese home islands.
   b. carrying the war into Southeast Asia from Australia and New Guinea.
   c. advancing on as broad a front as possible all across the Pacific.
   d. "island hopping" by capturing only the most strategic Japanese bases and bypassing the rest.

11. The U.S.–British demand for "unconditional surrender" was

   a. a sign of the Western Allies' confidence in its ultimate victory.
   b. designed to weaken Japan's and Germany's will to resist.
   c. a weak verbal substitute for the promised "Second Front."
   d. developed in close cooperation with the Soviet Union.

12. The American conquest of Guam and other islands in the Marianas in 1944 was especially important because

   a. it halted the Japanese advance in the Pacific.
   b. it made possible round-the-clock bombing of Japan from land bases.
   c. it paved the way for the American reconquest of the Philippines.
   d. it indicated that the Japanese would surrender without an invasion of the home island.

13. The most difficult European fighting for American forces through most of 1943 occurred in

   a. France.
   b. Italy.
   c. North Africa.
   d. Belgium.

_____ 14. Hitler's last-ditch effort to stop the British and American advance in the west occurred at

    a. the Battle of Normandy.

    b. the Battle of Château-Thierry.

    c. the Battle of Rome.

    d. the Battle of the Bulge.

_____ 15. The *second* American atomic bomb was dropped on the Japanese city of

    a. Nagasaki.

    b. Hiroshima.

    c. Kyoto.

    d. Okinawa.

C. Identification

Supply the correct identification for each numbered description.

_____1. A U.S. minority that was forced into concentration camps during World War II

_____2. A federal agency that coordinated U.S. industry and successfully mobilized the economy to produce vast quantities of military supplies

_____3. Women's units of the army and navy during World War II

_____4. Mexican-American workers brought into the United States to provide an agricultural labor supply

_____5. Symbolic personification of female laborers who took factory jobs in order to sustain U.S. production during World War II

_____6. The federal agency established to guarantee opportunities for African-American employment in World War II industries

_____7. U.S.-owned Pacific archipelago seized by Japan in the early months of World War II

_____8. Crucial naval battle of June 1942, in which U.S. Admiral Chester Nimitz blocked the Japanese attempt to conquer a strategic island near Hawaii

_____9. Controversial U.S.-British demand on Germany and Japan that substituted for a "second front"

_____10. Site of 1943 Roosevelt-Churchill conference in North Africa, at which the Big Two planned the invasion of Italy and further steps in the Pacific war

_____11. Iranian capital where Roosevelt, Churchill, and Stalin met to plan D-Day in co-ordination with Russian strategy against Hitler in the East

_____12. The beginning of the Allied invasion of France in June 1944

_____13. The December 1944 German offensive that marked Hitler's last chance to stop the Allied advance

_____14. The last two heavily defended Japanese islands conquered by the United States in 1945

_____

_____15. The devastating new weapon used by the United States against Japan in August 1945

D. Matching People, Places, and Events

Match the person, place, or event in the left column with the proper description in the right column by inserting the correct letter on the blank line.

____ 1. Henry J. Kaiser

____ 2. John L. Lewis

____ 3. A. Philip Randolph

____ 4. Detroit

____ 5. Jiang Jieshi (Chiang Kai-shek)

____ 6. Douglas MacArthur

____ 7. Chester W. Nimitz

____ 8. Dwight D. Eisenhower

____ 9. Winston Churchill

____ 10. Joseph Stalin

____ 11. Thomas Dewey

____ 12. Henry A. Wallace

____ 13. Harry S Truman

____ 14. Albert Einstein

____ 15. Hirohito

A. Commander of the Allied military assault against Hitler in North Africa and France

B. Japanese emperor who was allowed to stay on his throne, despite unconditional surrender policy

C. FDR's liberal vice president during most of World War II, dumped from the ticket in 1944

D. The Allied leader who constantly pressured the United States and Britain to open a "second front" against Hitler

E. Site of a serious racial disturbance during World War II

F. Leading American industrialist and shipbuilder during World War II

G. Commander of the U.S. Army in the Pacific during World War II, who fulfilled his promise to return to the Philippines

H. Inconspicuous former senator from Missouri who was suddenly catapulted to national and world leadership on April 12, 1945

I. Tough head of the United Mine Workers, whose work stoppages precipitated antistrike laws

J. Commander of the U.S. naval forces in the Pacific and brilliant strategist of the "island-hopping" campaign

K. Allied leader who met with FDR to plan strategy at Casablanca and Teheran

L. German-born physicist who helped persuade Roosevelt to develop the atomic bomb

M. Republican presidential nominee in 1944 who failed in his effort to deny FDR a fourth term

N. Head of the Brotherhood of Sleeping Car Porters whose threatened march on Washington opened job opportunities for blacks during World War II

O. U.S. ally who resisted Japanese advances in China during World War II

E. Putting Things in Order

Put the following events in correct order by numbering them from 1 to 4.

____ The United States and Britain invade Italy and topple Mussolini from power.

____ Japan surrenders after two atomic bombs are dropped.

____ The United States enters World War II and begins to "fight Hitler first."

____ The United States stops the Japanese advance in the Pacific and attacks Germany in North Africa.

F. Matching Cause and Effect

Match the historical cause in the left column with the proper effect in the right column by writing the correct letter on the blank line.

<table>
<tr><td align="center">Cause</td><td align="center">Effect</td></tr>
<tr>
<td>

___ 1. The surprise Japanese attack at Pearl Harbor

___ 2. Fear that Japanese-Americans would aid Japan in invading the United States

___ 3. Efficient organization by the War Production Board

___ 4. The mechanical cotton picker and wartime labor demand

___ 5. Women's role in wartime production

___ 6. American resistance in the Philippines and the Battle of the Coral Sea

___ 7. The American strategy of "leapfrogging" toward Japan

___ 8. The British fear of sustaining heavy casualties in ground fighting

___ 9. Conservative Democrats' hostility to liberal Vice President Henry Wallace

___ 10. Japan's refusal to surrender after the Potsdam Conference in July 1945

</td>
<td>

A. Kept the Western Allies from establishing a "second front" in France until June 1944

B. Slowed the powerful Japanese advance in the Pacific in 1942

C. Enabled the United States to furnish itself and its allies with abundant military supplies

D. Enabled the United States to set up key bomber bases while bypassing heavily fortified Japanese-held islands

E. Drew millions of African-Americans from the rural South to the urban North

F. Resulted in Senator Harry S Truman's becoming FDR's fourth-term running mate in 1944

G. Created a temporary but not a permanent transformation in gender roles for most women

H. Caused innocent American citizens to be rounded up and put in concentration camps

I. Created a strong sense of American national unity during World War II

J. Led the United States to drop the atomic bomb on Hiroshima in August 1945

</td>
</tr>
</table>

G. Developing Historical Skills

Reading Maps for Routes and Strategy

In order to understand the events and strategies of war, careful reading of military maps is essential. Attention to the routes and dates of the Allied armies, presented in the map of *World War II in Europe and North Africa, 1939–1945* on p. 844, will help you grasp the essentials of Allied strategy and the importance of the postponement of the "second front" in the west, as described in the text. Answer the following questions.

1. Where were (a) the Russians and (b) the Western Allies Britain and America each fighting in January and February of 1943?

2. Approximately where were the central Russian armies when the British and Americans invaded Sicily?

3. Approximately where were the central Russian armies when the British and Americans invaded Normandy in June 1944?

4. It took approximately ten months for the British and Americans to get from the Normandy beaches to the Elbe River in central Germany. How long did it take the Russians to get from Warsaw to Berlin?

5. Besides north-central Germany, where else did the British, American, and Russian invasion routes converge? From what two countries were the British and Americans coming? From what country was the southern Russian army coming?

H. Map Mastery

Map Discrimination

Using the maps and charts in Chapter 36, answer the following questions.

1. *Internal Migration in the United States During World War II*: During World War II, what was the approximate *net* migration of civilian population from the East to the West? (Net migration is the number of westward migrants minus the number of those who moved east.)

2. *Internal Migration in the United States During World War II*: Of the nine fastest-growing cities during the 1940s, how many were located in the West and South? (Consider Washington, D.C., as a southern city.)

3. *Internal Migration in the United States During World War II*: Which were the two fastest-growing cities in the North?

4. *United States Thrusts in the Pacific, 1942–1945*: Which *two* of the following territories were not wholly or partially controlled by Japan at the height of Japanese conquest: India, Philippines, Australia, Netherlands Indies, Thailand, and New Guinea?

5. *World War II in Europe and North Africa, 1939–1945*: From which North African territory did the Allies launch their invasion of Italy?

6. *World War II in Europe and North Africa, 1939–1945*: As the Russian armies crossed into Germany from the east, which three Axis-occupied East European countries did they move through?

7. *World War II in Europe and North Africa, 1939–1945*: As the Western Allied armies crossed into Germany from the west, which three Axis-occupied West European countries did they liberate and move through? (Do not count Luxembourg.)

8. *World War II in Europe and North Africa, 1939–1945*: Along which river in Germany did the Western Allied armies meet the Russians?

Map Challenge

Using the maps of both the Pacific (p. 840) and European (p. 844) theaters in World War II, write an essay explaining the principal movements of Allied armies and navies in relation to the principal Allied strategies of the war determined in the ABC–1 agreement and the various wartime exchanges and meetings among American, British, and Soviet leaders.

PART III: Applying What You Have Learned

1. What effects did World War II have on the American economy? What role did American industry and agriculture play in the war?

2. Discuss the effects of World War II on women and on racial and ethnic minorities. Is it accurate to see the war as a key turning point in the movement toward equality for some or all of these groups?

3. Ever since World War II, historians and other scholars have commonly spoken of "postwar American society." How was American society different after the war than before? Were these changes all direct or indirect results of the war, or would many have occurred without it?

4. How did the United States and its allies develop and carry out their strategy for defeating Italy, Germany, and Japan?

5. What were the costs of World War II, and what were its effects on America's role in the world?

6. Compare America's role in World War I—domestically, militarily, and diplomatically—with its role in World War II. (See Chapter 31.) What accounts for the differences in America's participation in the two wars?

37

The Cold War Begins, 1945–1952

PART I: Reviewing the Chapter

A. Checklist of Learning Objectives

After mastering this chapter, you should be able to

1. describe the economic transformation of the immediate post–World War II era.
2. describe the postwar migrations to the "Sunbelt" and the suburbs.
3. explain changes in the American population structure brought about by the "baby boom."
4. explain the growth of tensions between the United States and the Soviet Union after Roosevelt's death and Germany's defeat.
5. describe the early Cold War conflicts over Germany and Eastern Europe.
6. discuss American efforts to "contain" the Soviets through the Truman Doctrine, the Marshall Plan, and NATO.
7. describe the expansion of the Cold War to Asia and the Korean War.
8. analyze the postwar domestic climate in America and explain the growing fear of internal communist subversion.

B. Glossary

To build your social science vocabulary, familiarize yourself with the following terms.

1. **gross national product** The total value of a nation's annual output of goods and services. "Real gross national product (GNP) slumped sickeningly in 1946 and 1947. . . ." (p. 858)
2. **agribusiness** Farming and related activities considered as commercial enterprises, especially large corporate agricultural ventures. ". . . consolidation produced giant agribusinesses able to employ costly machinery." (p. 862)
3. **population curve** The varying size and age structure of a given nation or other group, measured over time. "This boom-or-bust cycle of births begot a bulging wave along the American population curve." (p. 866)
4. **precinct** The smallest subdivision of a city, as it is organized for purposes of police administration, politics, voting, and so on. "He then tried his hand at precinct-level Missouri politics. . . ." (p. 866)
5. **protégé** Someone under the patronage, protection, or tutelage of another person or group. "Though a protégé of a notorious political machine in Kansas City, he had managed to keep his own hands clean." (p. 866)
6. **superpower** One of the two overwhelmingly dominant international powers after World War II—the United States and the Soviet Union. "More specific understandings among the wartime allies—especially the two emerging superpowers—awaited the arrival of peace." (p. 870)
7. **exchange rates** The ratios at which the currencies of two or more countries are traded, which express their values relative to one another. ". . . the International Monetary Fund (IMF) [was established] to encourage world trade by regulating currency exchange rates." (p. 871)

8. **underdeveloped** Economically and industrially deficient. "They also founded the International Bank for Reconstruction and Development . . . to promote economic growth in war-ravaged and underdeveloped areas." (p. 871)

9. **military occupation** The holding and control of a territory and its citizenry by the conquering forces of another nation. ". . . Germany had been divided at war's end into four military occupation zones. . . ." (p. 873)

10. **containment** In international affairs, the blocking of another nation's expansion through the application of military and political pressure short of war. "Truman's piecemeal responses . . . took on intellectual coherence in 1947, with the formulation of the 'containment doctrine.' " (p. 874)

11. **communist-fronter** One who belongs to an ostensibly independent political, economic, or social organization that is secretly controlled by the Communist party. ". . . he was nominated . . . by . . . a bizarre collection of disgruntled former New Dealers . . . and communist-fronters." (p. 881)

12. **Politburo** The small ruling executive body that controlled the Central Committee of the Soviet Communist party, and hence dictated the political policies of the Soviet, Chinese, and other Communist parties (from "Political Bureau"). "This so-called Pied Piper of the Politburo took an apparently pro-Soviet line. . . ." (p. 881)

13. **perimeter** The outer boundary of a defined territory. ". . . Korea was outside the essential United States defense perimeter in the Pacific." (p. 883)

PART II: Checking Your Progress

A. True-False

Where the statement is true, mark **T**. Where it is false, mark **F**, and correct it in the space immediately below.

_____ 1. The American consumer economy began to grow dramatically as soon as the war ended, during the years 1945 to 1950.

_____ 2. The postwar economic boom was fueled by military spending and cheap energy.

_____ 3. Labor unions continued to grow rapidly in the industrial factories throughout the 1940s and 1950s.

_____ 4. The economic and population growth of the Sunbelt occurred because the South relied less than the North did on federal government spending for its economic well-being.

_____ 5. After World War II, American big cities became heavily populated with minorities, while most whites lived in the suburbs.

_____ 6. Government policies sometimes encouraged residential segregation in the cities and new suburbs.

_____ 7. Harry S Truman brought extensive experience and confidence to the presidency he assumed in April 1945.

_____ 8. The growing Cold War broke down the strong bonds of trust and common ideals that America and Russia had shared as World War II allies.

___ 9. The Western Allies pushed to establish a separate nation of West Germany, while the Russians wanted to restore a unified German state.

___ 10. The Truman Doctrine was initiated in response to threatened Soviet gains in Iran and Afghanistan.

___ 11. The Marshall Plan was developed primarily as a response to the possible Soviet military invasion of Western Europe.

___ 12. The fundamental purpose of NATO was to end the historical feuds among the European nations of Britain, France, Italy, and Germany.

___ 13. The postwar hunt for communist subversion was supposedly aimed at rooting out American communists from positions in government and teaching.

___ 14. Truman defeated Dewey in 1948 partly because of the deep splits within the Republican party that year.

___ 15. Truman fired General MacArthur because MacArthur wanted to expand the Korean War into China.

B. Multiple Choice

Select the best answer and write the proper letter in the space provided.

___ 1. Besides giving educational benefits to returning veterans, the Servicemen's Readjustment Act of 1944 (the GI Bill of Rights) was partly intended to

   a. prevent returning soldiers from flooding the job market.
   b. provide the colleges with a new source of income.
   c. keep the GIs' military skills in high readiness for the Cold War.
   d. help to slow down the inflationary economy that developed at the end of World War II.

___ 2. Among the greatest beneficiaries of the post–World War II economic "boom" were

   a. the industrial inner cities.
   b. farm laborers.
   c. labor unions.
   d. women.

___ 3. Among the causes of the long postwar economic expansion were

   a. foreign investment and international trade.
   b. military spending and cheap energy.
   c. labor's wage restraint and the growing number of small businesses.
   d. government economic planning and investment.

4. The two regions that gained most in population and new industry in the postwar economic expansion were

    a. the Northwest and New England.
    b. the Northeast and South.
    c. the Midwest and West.
    d. the South and West.

5. The federal government played a large role in the growth of the Sunbelt through

    a. federal subsidies to southern and western agriculture.
    b. its policies supporting civil rights and equal opportunity for minorities.
    c. housing loans to veterans.
    d. its financial support of the aerospace and defense industries.

6. Among the federal policies that contributed to the postwar migration from the cities to the suburbs were

    a. housing-mortgage tax deductions and federally built highways.
    b. public housing and Social Security.
    c. military and public-works spending.
    d. direct subsidies to suburban homebuilders.

7. The postwar "baby-boom" population expansion contributed to

    a. the sharp rise in elementary school enrollments in the 1970s.
    b. the strains on the Social Security system in the 1950s.
    c. the popular "youth culture" of the 1960s.
    d. the expanding job opportunities of the 1980s.

8. Among President Harry Truman's most valuable qualities as a leader were

    a. his considerable experience in international affairs.
    b. his personal courage, authenticity, and sense of responsibility for big decisions.
    c. his intolerance of pettiness or corruption among his subordinates.
    d. his patience and willingness to compromise with honest critics.

9. The primary reason that Franklin Roosevelt made concessions to Stalin at the Yalta Conference was that

    a. he sympathized with the Soviet need to dominate Eastern Europe.
    b. he wanted the Soviet Union to enter the war against Japan.
    c. he wanted the Soviets to agree to American domination of Central America and the Caribbean.
    d. he was afraid of a postwar confrontation with the Soviet Union over China.

10. Before World War II, both the United States and the Soviet Union

    a. had competed with Germany for the role of leading power in Europe.
    b. had concentrated on practical achievements rather than ideological issues.
    c. had attempted to build powerful armies and navies in order to gain global power.
    d. had been largely inward-looking and isolated from international affairs.

11. A crucial early development of the Cold War occurred when

    a. Germany was divided into an East Germany under Soviet control and a pro-American West Germany.
    b. American and Soviet forces engaged in armed clashes in Austria.
    c. the Soviets crushed anticommunist rebellions in Poland and Hungary.
    d. the French and Italian Communist parties attempted revolutions against their governments.

12. The NATO alliance represented an historic transformation in American foreign policy because

    a. it departed from the principles of the Monroe Doctrine.
    b. it put the United States into the position of guaranteeing the permanent subordination of Germany.
    c. it committed the United States to a permanent peacetime alliance with other nations.
    d. it meant establishing military bases outside the territory of the continental United States.

13. The Truman Doctrine originally developed because of the communist threat to

    a. Turkey and Greece.
    b. France and West Germany.
    c. Iran and Afghanistan.
    d. Poland and Hungary.

14. The crusade of Senator Joseph McCarthy was first directed especially at

    a. the Soviet Union
    b. potential communist takeovers of Western Europe.
    c. Republicans who refused to support Dwight Eisenhower.
    d. alleged communists inside the United States government.

15. The Korean War broke out in 1950 when

    a. Chinese communists invaded South Korea.
    b. the Soviet Union threatened to blockade Japan and South Korea.
    c. South Korea invaded North Korea.
    d. North Korea invaded South Korea.

C. Identification

Supply the correct identification for each numbered description.

1. Popular name for the Servicemen's Readjustment Act, which provided assistance to former soldiers

2. Shorthand name for the southern and western regions of the U.S. that experienced the highest rates of growth after World War II

3. New York suburb where postwar builders pioneered the techniques of mass home construction

4. Term for the dramatic rise in U.S. births that began immediately after World War II

5. Big Three wartime conference that later became the focus of charges that Roosevelt had "sold out" Eastern Europe to the Soviet communists

_____ 6. The extended post–World War II confrontation between the United States and the Soviet Union that stopped just short of a shooting war

_____ 7. Meeting of Western Allies during World War II that established the economic structures to promote recovery and enhance FDR's vision of an "open world"

_____ 8. New international organization that experienced some early successes in diplomatic and cultural areas but failed in areas like atomic arms control

_____ 9. Term for the barrier that Stalin erected to block off Soviet-dominated nations of Eastern Europe from the West

_____ 10. American-sponsored effort that provided funds for the economic relief and recovery of Western Europe

_____ 11. The new anti-Soviet organization of Western nations that ended the long-time American tradition of not joining permanent military alliances

_____ 12. Jiang Jieshi's (Chiang Kai-shek's) pro-American forces, which lost the Chinese civil war to Mao Zedong's (Mao Tse-tung's) communists in 1949

_____ 13. Key U.S. government memorandum that militarized American foreign policy and indicated national faith in the economy's capacity to sustain large military expenditures

_____ 14. U.S. House of Representatives committee that took the lead in investigating alleged procommunist agents such as Alger Hiss

_____ 15. The dividing line between North and South Korea, across which the fighting between communists and United Nations forces ebbed and flowed during the Korean War

D. Matching People, Places, and Events

Match the person, place, or event in the left column with the proper description in the right column by inserting the correct letter on the blank line.

_____ 1. Benjamin Spock

_____ 2. Hermann Goering

_____ 3. Joseph Stalin

_____ 4. Berlin

_____ 5. Iran

_____ 6. George F. Kennan

_____ 7. Greece

_____ 8. George C. Marshall

_____ 9. Japan

_____ 10. Nuremberg

A. Top Nazi official who committed suicide after being convicted in war-crimes trials

B. Physician who provided advice on child rearing to baby-boomers' parents after World War II.

C. Young California congressman whose investigation of Alger Hiss spurred fears of communist influence in America

D. Oil-rich Middle Eastern nation that became an early focal point of Soviet-American conflict

E. Originator of a massive program for the economic relief and recovery of devastated Europe

F. American military commander in Korea fired by Presiden Harry Truman

G. Former vice president of the United States whose 1948 campaign as a pro-Soviet liberal split the Democratic party

H. Site of a series of controversial war-crimes trials that led to the execution of twelve Nazi leaders

I. Wisconsin senator whose charges of communist infiltration of the U.S. government deepened the anti-red atmosphere of the early 1950s

____ 11. Richard Nixon

____ 12. Joseph McCarthy

____ 13. Henry A. Wallace

____ 14. Strom Thurmond

____ 15. Douglas MacArthur

J. Nation that was effectively converted from dictatorship to democracy by the strong leadership of General Douglas MacArthur

K. The tough leader whose violation of agreements in Eastern Europe and Germany helped launch the Cold War

L. Southern European nation whose threatened fall to communism in 1947 precipitated the Truman Doctrine

M. Territory deep inside the Soviet zone of Germany that was itself divided into four zones of occupation

N. Southern segregationist who led "Dixiecrat" presidential campaign against Truman in 1948

O. Brilliant U.S. specialist on the Soviet Union and originator of the theory that U.S. policy should be to "contain" the Soviet Union

E. Putting Things in Order

Put the following events in correct order by numbering them from 1 to 5.

____ The threatened communist takeover of Greece prompts a presidential request for aid and a worldwide effort to stop communism.

____ The collapse of Jiang Jieshi's (Chiang Kai-shek's) corrupt government means victory for Mao Zedong's (Mao Tse-tung's) communists and a setback for U.S. policy in Asia.

____ A new president takes charge of American foreign policy amid growing tension between America and its ally the Soviet Union.

____ A "give-'em-hell" campaign by an underdog candidate overcomes a three-way split in his own party and defeats his overconfident opponent.

____ Communists go on the offensive in a divided Asian nation, drawing the United States into a brutal and indecisive war.

F. Matching Cause and Effect

Match the historical cause in the left column with the proper effect in the right column by writing the correct letter on the blank line.

Cause	**Effect**
____ 1. Cheap energy, military spending, and rising productivity	**A.** Caused an era of unprecedented growth in American prosperity from 1950 to 1970
____ 2. The mechanization and consolidation of agriculture	**B.** Drew millions of white and black Americans to the Sunbelt after World War II
____ 3. Job opportunities, warm climates, and improved race relations	**C.** Led to the proclamation of the Truman Doctrine and hundreds of millions of dollars in aid for anticommunist governments
____ 4. "White flight" to the suburbs	**D.** Led to organization of the permanent NATO alliance
____ 5. The post–World War II "baby boom"	**E.** Caused the rise of big commercial agribusiness and spelled the near-disappearance of the traditional family farm
____ 6. The American airlift to West Berlin	**F.** Aroused Republican charges that Democrats Truman and Acheson had "lost China"

___	7. The British withdrawal from communist-threatened Greece	**G.** Broke a Soviet ground blockade and established American determination to resist further Soviet advance
___	8. The threat of Soviet invasion or U.S. isolationist withdrawal from Europe	**H.** Left America's cities heavily populated by racial minorities
___	9. General MacArthur's reform-oriented rule of occupied Japan	**I.** Led to the firm establishment of Japanese democracy and the beginnings of a great Japanese economic advance
___	10. Mao Zedong's (Mao Tse-tung's) defeat of Jiang Jieshi (Chiang Kai-shek)	**J.** Caused much school-building in the 1950s, a "youth culture" in the 1960s, and a growing concern about "aging" in the 1980s

G. Developing Historical Skills

Reading a Bar Graph

Read the bar graph of *National Defense Budget* on p. 861 and answer the following questions.

1. In what census year after World War II did the defense budget first decline as a percentage of the federal budget and a percentage of GNP?

2. In what census year after 1960 was the defense budget the same fraction of GNP as it was in 1950?

3. Which decade after World War II saw the largest increase in actual dollar outlays for defense?

4. By approximately what percentage of the federal budget did the defense budget increase from 1950 to 1960? By roughly what percentage did it decrease from 1970 to 1980? By what percentage did it increase from 1980 to 1990? By about what percentage did it decrease from 1990 to 1999?

H. Map Mastery

Map Discrimination

Using the maps and charts in Chapter 37, answer the following questions.

1. *Postwar Partition of Germany*: Which of the Big Four had the smallest occupation zone in postwar Germany?

2. *Postwar Partition of Germany*: Which of the three *Western* occupation zones was closest to Berlin?

3. *Postwar Partition of Germany*: Which two other nations did the American occupation zone border on?

4. *The Shifting Front in Korea*: When General MacArthur attacked at Inchon, did he land above or below the thirty-eighth parallel?

5. *The Shifting Front in Korea*: Besides China, what other nation bordering North Korea presented a potential threat to American forces?

6. *The Shifting Front in Korea*: After the armistice—signed on July 27, 1953—which of the two Koreas had made very slight territorial gains in the Korean War?

Map Challenge

Using the map of *Population Increase, 1950–2000* on p. 863, write an essay explaining the differences in the regional impact of post–World War II migration and population growth from 1950 to 1998. What states and regions exhibited exceptions to the general patterns of growth?

PART III: Applying What You Have Learned

1. How and why did the American economy soar from 1950 to 1970?
2. How have economic and population changes shaped American society since World War II?
3. What were the immediate conflicts and deeper causes that led the United States and the Soviet Union to go from being allies to bitter Cold War rivals?
4. Explain the steps that led to the long-term involvement of the United States in major overseas military commitments, including NATO and the Korean War. How did expanding military power and the Cold War affect American society and ideas?
5. Discuss President Harry Truman's role as a leader in both international and domestic affairs from 1945–1952. Does Truman deserve to be considered a "great" president? Why or why not?
6. Why did World War II—unlike World War I—lead to a permanent end to American isolationism? (See Chapter 31.) How did the long American tradition of isolation from permanent foreign entanglements create tensions in U.S. policy during the early Cold War?

38

The Eisenhower Era,
1952–1960

PART I: Reviewing the Chapter

A. Checklist of Learning Objectives

After mastering this chapter, you should be able to

1. explain how Eisenhower's leadership coincided with the American mood of the 1950s.
2. describe Ike's initially hesitant reactions to McCarthyism and the early civil rights movement.
3. describe the approach that Eisenhower and Dulles took to the Cold War and nuclear policy.
4. list the basic elements of Eisenhower's foreign policy in Vietnam, Europe, and the Middle East.
5. describe the vigorous challenges Eisenhower faced from the Soviet Union and indicate how he responded to them.
6. describe the new American economy of the 1950s.
7. explain the changes in American "mass culture" in the 1950s, including the rise of television and the computer.

B. Glossary

To build your social science vocabulary, familiarize yourself with the following terms.

1. **plebiscite** In politics, a single-question universal election or referendum, in which a ruler or government seeks approval of a policy or a mandate to continue in office. "In future years, television made possible a kind of 'plebiscitarian' politics. . . ." (p. 888)
2. **McCarthyism** The practice of making sweeping, unfounded charges against innocent people with consequent loss of reputation, job, and so on. "But 'McCarthyism' has passed into the English language as a label for the dangerous forces of unfairness. . . ." (p. 891)
3. **brass** High-ranking military officers. "The military brass at first protested. . . ." (p. 894)
4. **taboo** A social prohibition or rule that results from strict tradition or convention. ". . . Warren shocked the president and other traditionalists with his active judicial intervention in previously taboo social issues." (p. 895)
5. **self-incrimination** Sworn testimony in a trial or other legal proceeding that forces a person to admit to criminally indictable acts; the Fifth Amendment to the U.S. Constitution forbids compelling such testimony. "The millionaire Teamster chief . . . invoked the Fifth Amendment against self-incrimination 209 times. . . ." (p. 902)
6. **embezzlement** The fraudulent appropriation or theft of funds entrusted to one's care. "He was later sentenced to prison for embezzlement." (p. 903)
7. **secondary boycott** A boycott of goods, aimed not at the employer or company directly involved in a dispute but at those who do business with that company. ". . . antilaborites also forced into the bill prohibitions against 'secondary boycotts'. . . ." (p. 903)
8. **thermonuclear** Concerning the heat released in nuclear fission; specifically, the use of that heat in hydrogen bombs. "Thermonuclear suicide seemed nearer in July 1958. . . ." (p. 904)
9. **confiscation** The seizure of property by a public authority, often as a penalty. "Castro retaliated with further wholesale confiscations of Yankee property. . . ." (p. 905)

10. **Pentecostal** A family of Protestant Christian churches that emphasize a "second baptism" of the holy spirit, speaking in tongues, faith healing, and intense emotionalism in worship. "'Televangelists' like the Baptist Billy Graham, the Pentecostal Holiness preacher Oral Roberts. . . ." (p. 911)

PART II: Checking Your Progress

A. True-False

Where the statement is true, mark **T**. Where it is false, mᵃrk **F**, and correct it in the space immediately below.

____ 1. Eisenhower presented himself to the country as a strongly partisan Republican president.

____ 2. Eisenhower initially hesitated to oppose Senator Joseph McCarthy because of McCarthy's political popularity and power.

____ 3. McCarthy lost his power when he attacked alleged communist influence in the U.S. Army.

____ 4. The Supreme Court ruled in *Brown* v. *Board of Education* that blacks should be provided additional educational benefits in order to equalize public education.

____ 5. Eisenhower used his influence as president to support blacks' push for civil rights in the schools and elsewhere.

____ 6. Eisenhower endorsed a major growth of military spending on conventional and nuclear forces to counteract the Soviet Union in the Cold War.

____ 7. Eisenhower tried but failed to repeal most of the New Deal economic and social legislation.

____ 8. In the Hungarian crisis, the United States retreᵃted from Secretary of State Dulles's talk of "rolling back" communism and liberating the "captive peoples" of Eastern Europe.

____ 9. Eisenhower sent the first contingent of American troops to Vietnam in 1954 in order to prevent the communist Vietnamese from defeating the French.

____ 10. The Suez crisis was caused by Egyptian President Nasser's nationalization of the Suez Canal.

____ 11. The Soviet *Sputnik* satellite raised American fears that the Soviet Union had forged ahead of the United States in rocketry, science, and education.

____ 12. In the 1950s Latin Americans sometimes demonstrated hostility toward the United States for supporting anticommunist dictators and ignoring Latin American interests.

____ 13. Senator Kennedy was able to successfully neutralize the issue of his Roman Catholicism during the 1960 campaign.

____ 14. Feminist Betty Friedan's manifesto *The Feminine Mystique* was aimed primarily at reviving labor militancy among working-class women in factories and shops.

____ 15. Social critics like David Riesman and Daniel Bell attacked the conformity and consumer-ism that they believed was undermining the older American character and work ethic.

B.   Multiple Choice

Select the best answer and write the proper letter in the space provided.

____ 1. In the 1952 campaign, the Eisenhower-Nixon ticket made the first really effective use of

    a.   the Cold War as a campaign issue.
    b.   television.
    c.   political advertising.
    d.   political appeals targeted at special-interest groups.

____ 2. As president, Eisenhower enjoyed great popularity by presenting a leadership style of

    a.   reassurance, sincerity, and optimism.
    b.   aggressiveness, boldness, and energy.
    c.   political shrewdness, economic knowledge, and hands-on management.
    d.   vision, imagination, and moral leadership.

____ 3. The Korean War ended with

    a.   an agreement to unify and neutralize Korea.
    b.   a peace treaty that provided for withdrawal of American and Chinese forces from Korea.
    c.   an American and South Korean military victory.
    d.   a stalemated armistice and continued division of North and South Korea.

____ 4. Senator Joseph McCarthy's anticommunist crusade finally collapsed when

    a.   the Cold War wound down.
    b.   Eisenhower publicly attacked him as a threat to the Republican party.
    c.   McCarthy failed to force the alleged communists out of the federal government.
    d.   McCarthy attacked the U.S. Army for alleged communist influence.

____ 5. The precipitating event that made Dr. Martin Luther King, Jr. the most prominent civil rights leader was

    a.   the lynching of Emmett Till.
    b.   the Little Rock school crisis.
    c.   the Montgomery bus boycott.
    d.   the passage of the 1957 Civil Rights Act.

____ 6. The primary impetus for civil rights within the federal government came from

    a.   the Supreme Court.
    b.   Congress.
    c.   President Eisenhower.
    d.   the armed forces.

7. Martin Luther King, Jr.'s civil rights organization, the SCLC, rested on the institutional foundation of

   a. black business.
   b. the black churches.
   c. black colleges.
   d. northern philanthropic foundations.

8. Eisenhower's basic approach to domestic economic policy was

   a. to seek to overturn the Democratic New Deal.
   b. to propose major new federal social programs.
   c. to turn most New Deal programs over to the states.
   d. to trim back some New Deal programs but keep most in place.

9. Despite his fiscal conservatism, Eisenhower actually outdid the New Deal with his massive federal spending on

   a. a continental interstate highway system.
   b. a system of medical care for the elderly.
   c. intercontinental military bombers and civilian aircraft.
   d. agricultural subsidies for American farmers.

10. The United States first became involved in Vietnam by

    a. providing economic aid to the democratic Vietnamese government of Ngo Dinh Diem.
    b. providing economic aid to the French colonialists fighting Ho Chi Minh.
    c. providing aid to Ho Chi Minh in his fight against the French colonialists.
    d. sending American bombers to defend the French at Dien Bien Phu.

11. Senator John F. Kennedy's main issue in the campaign of 1960 was that

    a. as a Catholic he would better be able to deal with Catholic Latin America.
    b. the United States should seek nuclear disarmament agreement with the Soviets.
    c. the United States had fallen behind the Soviet Union in prestige and power.
    d. the Eisenhower administration had failed to work hard enough for desegregation.

12. When the 1950s began, a majority of American women were

    a. working in blue-collar factory or service jobs.
    b. raising children and not employed outside the home.
    c. pursuing training and education to prepare them for the new positions in service and high technology.
    d. agitating for federal child care and other assistance to enable them to assume a larger place in the work force.

13. The primary force shaping the new consumerism and popular culture of the 1950s was

    a. the computer.
    b. magazines like *Playboy*
    c. television.
    d. evangelical Protestantism.

___ 14. One major breakthrough in American literature in the early post–World War II years was

    a. the realistic depiction of war and industrial poverty.

    b. angry social criticism of the "American dream."

    c. satirical and comic novels by Jewish writers.

    d. an optimistic vision of nature and love in the work of American poets and playwrights.

___ 15. A key economic transformation of the 1950s was

    a. the displacement of large corporations by smaller entrepeneurial businesses.

    b. the growth of "white collar" jobs into a majority that increasingly replaced "blue collar" factory labor.

    c. the turn from World War II military and defense industries to civilian production.

    d. the replacement of "mass consumer production" by "target marketing" aimed at particular segments of the population.

C. Identification

Supply the correct identification for each numbered description.

_____ 1. Term for making ruthless and unfair charges against opponents, such as those leveled by a red-hunting Wisconsin senator in the 1950s

_____ 2. Supreme Court ruling that overturned the old *Plessy* v. *Ferguson* principle that black public facilities could be "separate but equal"

_____ 3. The doctrine upon which Eisenhower and Dulles based American nuclear policy in the 1950s

_____ 4. An Asian alliance, set up by Secretary Dulles on the model of NATO, to help support the anticommunist regime in South Vietnam

_____ 5. The British-and-French-owned waterway whose nationalization by Egyptian President Nasser triggered a major Middle East crisis

_____ 6. A soviet scientific achievement that set off a wave of American concern about Soviet superiority in science and education

_____ 7. Major international corporation that symbolized the early computer and "information age"

_____ 8. High-flying American spy plane, whose downing in 1960 destroyed a summit and heightened Cold War tensions

_____ 9. Latin American nation where a 1959 communist revolution ousted a U.S.-backed dictator

_____ 10. Betty Friedan's 1963 book that launched a revolution against the suburban "cult of domesticity" that reigned in the 1950s

D. Matching People, Places, and Events

Match the person, place, or event in the left column with the proper description in the right column by inserting the correct letter on the blank line.

___ 1. Dwight D. Eisenhower

___ 2. Joseph R. McCarthy

___ 3. Earl Warren

___ 4. Martin Luther King, Jr.

___ 5. Ho Chi Minh

___ 6. Ngo Dinh Diem

___ 7. Betty Friedan

___ 8. Adlai E. Stevenson

___ 9. Billy Graham

___ 10. James R. Hoffa

___ 11. John Foster Dulles

___ 12. Nikita Khrushchev

___ 13. Fidel Castro

___ 14. Richard Nixon

___ 15. John F. Kennedy

A. Eloquent Democratic presidential candidate who was twice swamped by a popular Republican war hero

B. Anticommunist leader who set up a pro-American government to block Ho Chi Minh's expected takeover of all Vietnam

C. Latin American revolutionary who became economically and militarily dependent on the Soviet Union

D. Eisenhower's tough-talking secretary of state who wanted to "roll back" communism

E. Red-hunter turned world-traveling diplomat who narrowly missed becoming president in 1960

F. Black minister whose 1955 Montgomery bus boycott made him the leader of the civil rights movement

G. The soldier who kept the nation at peace for most of his two terms and ended up warning America about the "military-industrial complex"

H. Popular religious evangelical who effectively used the new medium of television

I. Youthful politician who combined television appeal with traditional big-city Democratic politics to squeak out a victory in 1960

J. Blustery Soviet leader who frequently challenged Eisenhower with both threats and diplomacy

K. Reckless and power-hungry demagogue who intimidated even President Eisenhower before his bubble burst

L. A Vietnamese nationalist and communist whose defeat of the French led to calls for American military intervention in Vietnam

M. Writer whose 1963 book signaled the beginnings of more extensive feminist protest

N. Tough Teamster-union boss whose corrupt actions helped lead to passage of the Landrum-Griffin Act

O. Controversial jurist who led the Supreme Court into previously off-limits social and racial issues

E. Putting Things in Order

Put the following events in correct order by numbering them from 1 to 5.

___ Major crises in Eastern Europe and the Middle East create severe challenges for Eisenhower's foreign policy.

___ An American plane is downed over the Soviet Union, disrupting a summit and rechilling the Cold War.

___ Eisenhower refuses to use American troops to prevent a communist victory over a colonial power in Asia.

____ Eisenhower orders federal troops to enforce a Supreme Court ruling over strong resistance from state officials.

____ Eisenhower's meeting with Soviet leader Khrushchev marks the first real sign of a thaw in the Cold War.

F. Matching Cause and Effect

Match the historical cause in the left column with the proper effect in the right column by writing the correct letter on the blank line.

Cause	Effect
____ 1. Joseph McCarthy's attacks on the U.S. Army	A. Set off "massive resistance" to integration in most parts of the Deep South
____ 2. *Brown* v. *Board of Education*	B. Led to continuing nuclear tests and the extension of the arms race
____ 3. Governor Orval Faubus's use of the National Guard to prevent integration	C. Caused the United States to begin backing an anticommunist regime in South Vietnam
____ 4. The 1956 Hungarian revolt	D. Created widespread resentment of the United States in parts of the Western Hemisphere
____ 5. The Communist Vietnamese victory over the French in 1954	E. Forced Secretary of State Dulles to abandon his plans to "roll back" communism
____ 6. Nasser's nationalization of the Suez Canal	F. Exposed the senator's irresponsibility and brought about his downfall
____ 7. The fears of both the United States and the Soviet Union that the other nation was gaining a lead in rocketry and weapons	G. Forced President Eisenhower to send federal troops to Little Rock
____ 8. The downing of the U-2 spy plane	H. Undermined the Paris summit and weakened Eisenhower's goodwill diplomacy
____ 9. American intervention in Latin America and support for anticommunist dictators in that region	I. Enabled the Democrats to win a narrow electoral victory in 1960
____ 10. Kennedy's television glamour and traditional political skills	J. Led to the 1956 British-French-Israeli invasion of Egypt

G. Developing Historical Skills

Comparing and Interpreting Election Maps

Read carefully the maps for the elections of 1956 (p. 902) and 1960 (p. 907). Answer the following questions.

1. Which was the only nonsouthern state to vote for Democrats Stevenson in 1956 and Kennedy in 1960?

2. Which three southern states (states of the old Confederacy) voted for Republicans Eisenhower in 1956 and Nixon in 1960?

3. Which two southern states switched from Republican in 1956 to Democratic in 1960?

4. How many more electoral votes did Kennedy get in the West (not counting Texas) in 1960 than Stevenson got in the same region in 1956?

5. How many electoral votes did Kennedy win from states that Stevenson also carried in 1956? (Note the divided electoral vote in one state.)

PART III: Applying What You Have Learned

1. In what ways was the Eisenhower era a time of caution and conservatism, and in what ways was it a time of dynamic economic, social, and cultural change?
2. How did Eisenhower balance assertiveness and restraint in his foreign policies in Vietnam, Europe, and the Middle East?
3. What were the dynamics of the Cold War with the Soviet Union in the 1950s, and how did Eisenhower and Khrushchev combine confrontation and conversation in their relationship?
4. How did America's far-flung international responsibilities shape the U.S. economy and society in the Eisenhower era? Was the American way of life fundamentally altered by the nation's new superpower status, or did it remain largely sheltered from world affairs?
5. How did television and other innovations of the "consumer age" affect American politics, society, and culture in the 1950s?
6. Despite widespread power and affluence, the 1950s were often described as an "age of anxiety." What were the major sources of anxiety and conflict that stirred beneath the surface of the time? Could they have been addressed more effectively by Eisenhower and other national leaders? Why or why not?

39

The Stormy Sixties,
1960–1968

PART I: Reviewing the Chapter

A. Checklist of Learning Objectives

After mastering this chapter, you should be able to

1. describe the high expectations Kennedy's New Frontier aroused and the political obstacles it encountered.
2. analyze the theory and practice of Kennedy's doctrine of "flexible response" in Asia and Latin America.
3. describe Johnson's succession to the presidency in 1963, his electoral landslide over Goldwater in 1964, and his Great Society successes of 1965.
4. discuss the course of the black movement of the 1960s, from civil rights to Black Power.
5. indicate how Johnson led the United States deeper into the Vietnam quagmire.
6. explain how the Vietnam war brought turmoil to American society and eventually drove Johnson and the divided Democrats from power in 1968.
7. describe the cultural rebellions of the 1960s, and indicate their short-term and long-term consequences.

B. Glossary

To build your social science vocabulary, familiarize yourself with the following terms.

1. **free world** The noncommunist democracies of the Western world, as opposed to the communist states. "But to the free world the 'Wall of Shame' looked like a gigantic enclosure around a concentration camp." (p. 919)
2. **nuclear proliferation** The spreading of nuclear weapons to nations that have not previously had them. "Despite the perils of nuclear proliferation or Soviet domination, de Gaulle demanded an independent Europe. . . ." (p. 919)
3. **exile** A person who has been banished or driven from her or his country by the authorities. "He had inherited . . . a CIA-backed scheme to topple Fidel Castro from power by invading Cuba with anticommunist exiles." (p. 921)
4. **peaceful coexistence** The principle or policy that communists and noncommunists—specifically, the United States and the Soviet Union—ought to live together without trying to dominate or destroy each other. "Kennedy thus tried to lay the foundations for a realistic policy of peaceful coexistence with the Soviet Union." (p. 923)
5. **détente** In international affairs, a period of relaxed agreement in areas of mutual interest. "Here were the modest origins of the policy that later came to be known as 'détente.'" (p. 923)
6. **sit-in** A demonstration in which people occupy a facility for a sustained period to achieve political or economic goals. "Following the wave of sit-ins that surged across the South. . . ." (p. 923)

7. **establishment** The ruling inner circle of a nation and its principal institutions. "Goldwater's forces had . . . rid[den] roughshod over the moderate Republican 'eastern establishment.'" (p. 929)

8. **literacy test** A literacy examination that a person must pass before being allowed to vote. "Ballot-denying devices like the poll tax, literacy tests, and barefaced discrimination still barred black people from the political process." (p. 931)

9. **ghetto** The district of a city where members of a religious or racial minority are forced to live, either by legal restriction or by informal social pressure. (Originally, ghettoes were enclosed Jewish districts in Europe.) ". . . a bloody riot exploded in Watts, a black ghetto in Los Angeles." (p. 932)

10. **black separatism** The doctrine that blacks in the United States ought to separate themselves from whites, either in separate institutions or in a separate political territory. ". . . Malcolm X trumpeted black separatism. . . ." (p. 932)

11. **hawk** During the Vietnam War, someone who favored vigorous prosecution or escalation of the conflict. "If the United States were to cut and run from Vietnam, claimed prowar 'hawks,' other nations would doubt America's word. . . ." (p. 935)

12. **dove** During the Vietnam War, someone who opposed the war and favored de-escalation or withdrawal by the United States. "New flocks of antiwar 'doves' were hatching daily." (p. 935)

13. **militant** In politics, someone who pursues political goals in a belligerent way, often using paramilitary means. "Other militants . . . shouted obscenities. . . ." (p. 938)

14. **dissident** Someone who dissents, especially from an established or normative institution or position. ". . . Spiro T. Agnew [was] noted for his tough stands against dissidents and black militants." (p. 939)

15. **coattails** In politics, the ability of a popular candidate at the top of a ticket to transfer some of his or her support to lesser candidates on the same ticket. "Nixon was . . . the first president-elect since 1848 not to bring in on his coattails at least one house of Congress. . . ." (pp. 939–940)

PART II: Checking Your Progress

A. True-False

Where the statement is true, mark **T**. Where it is false, mark **F**, and correct it in the space immediately below.

____ 1. Kennedy's attempt to control rising steel prices met strong opposition from big business.

____ 2. The Kennedy doctrine of "flexible response" was applied primarily to conflicts with Soviet communism in Europe.

____ 3. The U.S.-supported coup against the corrupt Diem regime brought South Vietnam greater democracy and political stability.

____ 4. Kennedy financed and trained the Cuban rebels involved in the Bay of Pigs invasion but refused to intervene directly with American troops or planes.

____ 5. The Cuban missile crisis ended in a humiliating defeat for Khrushchev and the Soviet Union.

____ 6. Kennedy encouraged the civil rights movement to become more outspoken in its opposition to segregation and discrimination.

_____ 7. Johnson's landslide victory came in every part of the country except the traditionally Republican Midwest.

_____ 8. The Gulf of Tonkin Resolution authorized the president to respond to naval attacks but kept the power to make war in Vietnam firmly in the hands of Congress.

_____ 9. Johnson's Great Society programs attempted to balance the federal budget and return power to the states.

_____ 10. The nonviolent civil rights movement, led by Martin Luther King, Jr., achieved great victories in integration and voting rights for blacks in 1964 and 1965.

_____ 11. The urban riots of the late 1960s demonstrated that the South had not been improved by the civil rights movement.

_____ 12. The campaigns of Senators McCarthy and Kennedy forced Johnson to withdraw as a presidential candidate and promoted de-escalation of the Vietnam War.

_____ 13. The deep Democratic divisions over Vietnam helped elect Nixon as president in 1968.

_____ 14. One major American institution largely unaffected by the cultural upheaval of the 1960s was the Roman Catholic Church.

_____ 15. The "sexual revolution" of the 1960s included the introduction of the birth control pill and the increasing visibility of gays and lesbians.

B. Multiple Choice

Select the best answer and write the proper letter in the space provided.

_____ 1. President Kennedy's proposals for increased educational aid and medical assistance
   a. succeeded because of his skill in legislative bargaining.
   b. were traded away in exchange for passage of the bill establishing the Peace Corps.
   c. were stalled by strong opposition in Congress.
   d. were strongly opposed by business interests.

_____ 2. The industry that engaged in a bitter conflict with President Kennedy over price increases was
   a. the aircraft industry.
   b. the meat industry.
   c. the steel industry.
   d. the oil industry.

_____ 3. The fundamental military doctrine of the Kennedy administration involved
   a. "flexible response" to "brushfire wars" in the Third World.
   b. a massive nuclear retaliation against communist advances.
   c. a heavy buildup of conventional armed forces in Western Europe.
   d. reliance on rapid-response jet and helicopter air power.

4. The first major foreign-policy disaster of the Kennedy administration came when

    a. Middle East governments sharply raised the price of imported oil.
    b. American-backed Cuban rebels were defeated at the Bay of Pigs.
    c. Khrushchev threatened American interests in the Cuban missile crisis.
    d. American forces suffered severe battlefield losses in Vietnam.

5. The Cuban missile crisis ended when

    a. the American-backed Cuban invaders were defeated at the Bay of Pigs.
    b. the United States agreed to allow Soviet missiles in Cuba as long as they were not armed with nuclear weapons.
    c. the Soviets agreed to pull all missiles out of Cuba and the United States agreed not to invade Cuba.
    d. The United States and the Soviet Union agreed that Cuba should become neutral in the Cold War.

6. The Kennedy administration was pushed into a stronger stand on civil rights by

    a. the civil rights movement led by the Freedom Riders and Martin Luther King, Jr.
    b. the political advantages of backing civil rights.
    c. the pressure from foreign governments and the United Nations.
    d. the threat of violence in northern cities.

7. Lyndon Johnson won an overwhelming landslide victory in the 1964 election partly because

    a. he repudiated many of the policies of the unpopular Kennedy administration.
    b. he promised to take a tough stand in opposing communist aggression in Vietnam.
    c. Republican candidate Senator Barry Goldwater was seen by many Americans as a "trigger-happy" extremist.
    d. Johnson had achieved considerable personal popularity with the electorate.

8. President Johnson was more successful in pushing economic and civil rights measures through Congress than President Kennedy because

    a. he was better at explaining the purposes of the laws in his speeches.
    b. the Democrats gained overwhelming control of Congress in the landslide of 1964.
    c. Republicans were more willing to cooperate with Johnson than with Kennedy.
    d. Johnson was better able to swing southern Democrats behind his proposals.

9. The Civil Rights Act of 1965 was designed to guarantee

    a. desegregation in interstate transportation.
    b. job opportunities for African-Americans.
    c. desegregation of high schools and colleges.
    d. voting rights for African-Americans.

10. Most of the racial riots of the 1960s occurred in

    a. northern inner-city areas.
    b. southern inner-city areas.
    c. white neighborhoods where black families attempted to move in.
    d. college campuses.

11. Escalation of the aerial bombardment in Vietnam

    a. bolstered the stability of the South Vietnamese government.
    b. forced the Viet Cong and North Vietnamese to turn to conventional warfare.
    c. strengthened the Viet Cong and North Vietnamese will to resist.
    d. enabled the United States to limit the use of ground forces in Vietnam.

12. Opposition to the Vietnam War in Congress was centered in

    a. the House Foreign Affairs Committee.
    b. the Senate Armed Services Committee.
    c. the Republican leadership of the House and Senate.
    d. the Senate Foreign Relations Committee.

13. The antiwar presidential candidates whose political showing forced Johnson to withdraw from the race were

    a. Nelson Rockefeller and Ronald Reagan.
    b. Eugene McCarthy and Robert Kennedy.
    c. J. William Fulbright and George McGovern.
    d. George Wallace and Curtis LeMay.

14. One dominant theme of the 1960s "youth culture" that had deep roots in American history was

    a. conflict between the generations.
    b. distrust and hostility toward authority.
    c. the widespread use of mind-altering drugs.
    d. a positive view of sexual experimentation.

15. The cultural upheavals of the 1960s could largely be attributed to the "three P's" of

    a. pot, promiscuity, and publicity.
    b. presidential failure, political rebellion, and personal authenticity.
    c. poverty, protest, and the "pill."
    d. population bulge, protest against racism, and prosperity.

C. Identification

Supply the correct identification for each numbered description.

_____ 1. Kennedy administration program that sent youthful American volunteers to work in underdeveloped countries

_____ 2. High barrier between East and West erected during the 1961 Berlin crisis

_____ 3. Elite antiguerrilla military units expanded by Kennedy as part of his doctrine of "flexible response"

_____ 4. An attempt to provide American aid for democratic reform in Latin America that met with much disappointment and frustration

_____ 5. Site where anti-Castro guerrilla forces failed in their U.S.-sponsored invasion

_____ 6. Tense confrontation between Kennedy and Khrushchev that nearly led to nuclear war in October 1962

_____ 7. New civil rights technique developed in the 1960s to desegregate lunch counters and other public facilities in the South

_____ 8. LBJ's broad program of welfare legislation and social reform that swept through Congress in 1965

_____ 9. The 1964 congressional action that became a "blank check" for the Vietnam War

_____ 10. Law, spurred by Martin Luther King, Jr.'s march from Selma to Montgomery, that guaranteed rights originally given blacks under the Fifteenth Amendment

_____ 11. Racial slogan that signaled a growing challenge to King's non-violent civil rights movement by militant younger blacks

_____ 12. The Vietnamese New Year celebration, during which the communists launched a heavy offensive against the United States in 1968

_____ 13. Student activist protest at the University of California that criticized corporate interests and impersonal university education

_____ 14. Student organization that moved from nonviolent protest to underground terrorism within a few years

_____ 15. Site of an off-duty police raid in 1969 that spurred gay and lesbian activism

D. Matching People, Places, and Events

Match the person, place, or event in the left column with the proper description in the right column by inserting the correct letter on the blank line.

___ 1. John F. Kennedy

___ 2. Robert S. McNamara

___ 3. Nikita Khrushchev

___ 4. Martin Luther King, Jr.

___ 5. Lyndon B. Johnson

___ 6. Barry M. Goldwater

___ 7. James Meredith

___ 8. Malcolm X

___ 9. Mario Savio

___ 10. Eugene J. McCarthy

___ 11. Robert F. Kennedy

___ 12. Richard M. Nixon

___ 13. George C. Wallace

___ 14. Hubert Humphrey

___ 15. Alfred Kinsey

A. First black student admitted to the University of Mississippi, shot during a civil rights march in 1966

B. Cabinet officer who promoted "flexible response" but came to doubt the wisdom of the Vietnam War he had presided over

C. New York senator whose antiwar campaign for the presidency was ended by an assassin's bullet in June 1968

D. Former vice president who staged a remarkable political comeback to win presidential election in 1968

E. Charismatic Black Muslim leader who promoted separatism in the early 1960s

F. Minnesota senator whose antiwar "Children's Crusade" helped force Johnson to alter his Vietnam policies

G. Early student activist and leader of the Free Speech Movement at the University of California

H. Nonviolent black leader whose advocacy of peaceful change came under attack from militants after 1965

I. Vice president whose loyalty to LBJ's Vietnam policies sent him down to defeat in the 1968 presidential election

J. Charismatic president whose brief administration experienced domestic stalemate and foreign confrontations with communism

K. Third-party candidate whose conservative, hawkish 1968 campaign won 9 million votes and carried five states

L. Aggressive Soviet leader whose failed gamble of putting missiles in Cuba cost him his job

M. Controversial Indiana University "sexologist" who documented Americans' changing sexual behavior

N. Conservative Republican whose crushing defeat opened the way for the liberal Great Society programs

O. Brilliant legislative operator whose domestic achievements in social welfare and civil rights fell under the shadow of his Vietnam disaster

E. Putting Things in Order

Put the following events in correct order by numbering them from 1 to 5.

____ A southern Texas populist replaces a Harvard-educated Irish-American in the White House.

____ An American-sponsored anticommunist invasion of Cuba fails.

____ Kennedy successfully risks nuclear confrontation to thwart Khrushchev's placement of Russian missiles in Cuba.

____ A candidate running on a "peace" platform obtains a congressional "blank check" for subsequent expanded military actions against the Communist Vietnamese.

____ Communist military assaults, political divisions between hawks and doves, and assassinations of national leaders form the backdrop for a turbulent election year.

F. Matching Cause and Effect

Match the historical cause in the left column with the proper effect in the right column by writing the correct letter on the blank line.

Cause	Effect
____ 1. Kennedy's unhappiness with the corrupt Diem regime	**A.** Pushed Johnson into withdrawing as a presidential candidate in 1968
____ 2. Khrushchev's placement of missiles in Cuba	**B.** Brought ever-rising American casualties and a strengthened will to resist on the part of the Communist Vietnamese
____ 3. Johnson's landslide victory over Goldwater in 1964	**C.** Led to a U.S.-encouraged coup and greater political instability in South Vietnam
____ 4. The Gulf of Tonkin Resolution	**D.** Helped push through historic civil rights legislation in 1964 and 1965
____ 5. Martin Luther King, Jr.'s civil rights marches	**E.** Brought along huge Democratic congressional majorities that passed a fistful of Great Society laws
____ 6. Angry discontent in northern black ghettos	**F.** Helped Nixon win a minority victory over his divided opposition
____ 7. American escalation of the Vietnam War	**G.** Became the questionable legal basis for all of Johnson's further escalation of the Vietnam War
____ 8. The Communist Vietnamese Tet Offensive in 1968	**H.** Led to a humiliating defeat when Kennedy forced the Soviet Union to back down
____ 9. Senator Eugene McCarthy's strong antiwar campaign	**I.** Sparked urban riots and the growth of the militant "Black Power" movement
____ 10. The deep Democratic party divisions over Vietnam	**J.** Led to an American military request for 200,000 more troops as well as growing public discontent with the Vietnam War

G. Developing Historical Skills

Interpreting Line Graphs

Read the line graph of *Poverty in the United States* on p. 931 carefully and answer the following questions.

1. In what year did the number of people below the poverty line return to approximately the same level it had been at in 1964?

2. In what two years did the percentage of the American population below the poverty line reach its lowest point since 1960?

3. Between what years did the absolute numbers of people below the poverty line *rise* slightly at the same time those in poverty *declined* slightly as a percentage of the total population? What would explain this difference?

4. The number of people in poverty in 1966 was about the same as the number in poverty in which subsequent year?

H. Map Mastery

Map Discrimination

Using the maps and charts in Chapter 39, answer the following questions.

1. *Vietnam and Southeast Asia*: Besides North Vietnam, which two other Southeast Asian countries bordered on South Vietnam?

2. *Presidential Election of 1964*: How many electoral votes did Barry Goldwater win outside the Deep South in 1964?

3. *Presidential Election of 1968*: What four northeastern states did Nixon carry in 1968?

4. *Presidential Election of 1968*: Which five states outside the Northeast did Humphrey carry in 1968? (One of them is not in the continental United States.)

Name_____ Section_____ _____ Date_____

Map Challenge

Using the electoral maps of the five elections of 1952, 1956, 1960, 1964, and 1968 (pp. 889, 902, 906, 928 and 940 (in Chapters 38 and 39), write a brief essay describing the changing fortunes of the Republican and Democratic parties in different regions of the country from 1952 to 1968. Include a discussion of which states and regions remained relatively loyal to a single party, which shifted loyalties, and which were most contested. What are the most plausible explanations for these patterns?

PART III: Applying What You Have Learned

1. What successes and failures did Kennedy's New Frontier experience at home and abroad?
2. How did the civil rights movement progress from difficult beginnings to great successes in 1964–1965 and then encounter increasing opposition trom both black militants and "white backlash" after 1965?
3. What were Johnson's major domestic achievements, and why did they come to be overshadowed?
4. Why did the Vietnam War, and the domestic opposition to it, come to dominate American politics in the 1960s?
5. How was the cultural upheaval of the 1960s related to the political and social changes of the decade? Is the "youth rebellion" best seen as a response to immediate events, or as a consequence of such longer-term forces as the population bulge and economic prosperity? What were the long-term results of the "counter-culture" in all its varieties?
6. What led the United States to become so deeply involved in the Vietnam War? (See Chapters 37 and 38 for background on the Cold War, anticolonialism, and earlier events in Vietnam.)

40

The Stalemated Seventies, 1968–1980

PART I: Reviewing the Chapter

A. Checklist of Learning Objectives

After mastering this chapter, you should be able to

1. describe Nixon's policies toward the war in Vietnam and Cambodia.
2. analyze Nixon's domestic policies and his appeal to the "silent majority."
3. describe the American withdrawal from Vietnam, the final communist victory there, and the "new isolationism" represented by the War Powers Act.
4. discuss the Watergate scandals and Nixon's resignation.
5. explain the related economic, energy, and Middle East crises of the 1970s and indicate how Nixon, Ford, and Carter attempted to deal with them.
6. analyze the successes and failures of the détente with Moscow and the opening to Beijing (Peking) pursued by the American administrations of the 1970s.
7. describe the rise of the new feminist movement, and the gains and setbacks for women and minorities in the 1970s.
8. discuss the Iranian crisis and its political consequences for Carter.

B. Glossary

To build your social science vocabulary, familiarize yourself with the following terms.

1. **moratorium** A period in which economic or social activity is suspended, often to achieve certain defined goals. "Antiwar protestors staged a massive national Vietnam moratorium in October 1969. . . ." (p. 948)
2. **Marxism** The doctrines of Karl Marx, advocated or followed by many modern Socialists and communists. "The two great communist powers . . . were clashing bitterly over their rival interpretations of Marxism." (p. 950)
3. **anti-ballistic missile** A defensive missile designed to shoot down or otherwise protect against an offensive missile attack. "The first major achievement was an anti-ballistic missile (ABM) treaty. . . ." (p. 951)
4. **devaluation** In economics, steps taken to reduce the purchasing power of a given unit of currency in relation to foreign currencies. " . . . he next stunned the world by taking the United States off the gold standard and devaluing the dollar." (p. 954)
5. **obstruction of justice** The crime of interfering with police, courts, or other officials to thwart the performance of their legal duties. "Many were involved in a criminal obstruction of justice through tangled cover-ups. . . ." (p. 955)
6. **audit** To examine accounts or records in order to determine their accuracy and legitimacy—a process performed by officials appointed for that purpose. "Even the Internal Revenue Service was called upon by Nixon's aides to audit or otherwise harass political opponents. . . ." (p. 955)

7. **echelon** An ordered subdivision of military troops or of a military or political headquarters. "John Dean III . . . testified glibly . . . as to the involvement of the top echelons in the White House. . . ." (p. 956)

8. **executive privilege** In American government, the claim that certain information known to the president or the executive branch of government should be unavailable to Congress or the courts because of the principle of separation of powers. "He took refuge behind various principles, including separation of powers and executive privilege. . . ." (p. 956)

9. **appropriation** The direct approval, by Congress or other legislative bodies, for the executive to spend money for a specified purpose. (**Authorization** is the prior budgeting of an overall sum for an agency or activity, but does not include permission to spend.) "Finally, with appropriations running short, Nixon agreed to a compromise. . . ." (p. 957)

10. **recession** A moderate and short-term economic downturn, less severe than a depression. (Economists define a recession as two consecutive quarters, i.e., six months, of declining gross domestic product.) "Lines of automobiles at service stations lengthened as tempers shortened and a business recession deepened." (p. 958)

11. **sheik** A traditional Arab clan chieftain or ruler. "The Middle Eastern sheiks [had] approximately quadrupled their price for crude oil. . . ." (p. 958)

12. **illegitimacy** The condition of being contrary to or outside of the law or formal rules. "The sour odor of illegitimacy hung about this president without precedent." (p. 960)

13. **born-again** The Evangelical Christian belief in a spiritual renewal or rebirth, involving a personal experience of conversion and a commitment to moral transformation. ". . . this born-again Baptist touched many people with his down-home sincerity." (p. 967)

14. **balance of payments** The net ratio, expressed as a positive or negative sum, of a nation's exports in relations to its imports. (It may be calculated in relation to one particular foreign nation, or to all foreign states collectively.) "The soaring bill for imported oil plunged America's balance of payments deeply into the red. . . ." (p. 971)

15. **ayatollah** A supreme religious leader in the Shi'ite branch of Islam. "Ayatollah Ruhollah Khomeini, the white-bearded Muslim holy man who inspired the revolutionaries. . . ." (p. 974)

PART II: Checking Your Progress

A. True-False

Where the statement is true, mark **T**. Where it is false, mark **F**, and correct it in the space immediately below.

____ 1. Nixon's "Vietnamization" policy sought to bring an immediate negotiated end to the Vietnam War.

____ 2. Nixon's 1970 invasion of Cambodia provoked strong domestic protests and political clashes between "hawks" and "doves."

____ 3. Nixon and Kissinger's diplomacy attempted to play the Soviet Union and China off against each other for America's benefit.

____ 4. Nixon attempted to reverse what he saw as the Warren Supreme Court's excessive turn toward "judicial activism."

____ 5. Nixon consistently opposed the expansion of social security and pro-environmental legislation.

___ 6. The basic issue in the 1972 Nixon-McGovern campaign was inflation and the management of the economy.

___ 7. The 1973 Paris agreement on Vietnam provided for a cease-fire and American withdrawal but did not really end the civil war among the Vietnamese.

___ 8. The strongest charge against Nixon during Watergate was that he had used government agencies to burglarize and harass opponents and cover up the Watergate crimes.

___ 9. The disclosure of the secret bombing of Cambodia led Congress to acknowledge the president's sole authority to take military action in defense of America's national security.

___ 10. The 1973 Arab-Israeli War and OPEC oil embargo added to the inflation that began in the wake of the Vietnam War.

___ 11. Conservative Republicans strenuously opposed Nixon's resignation and urged him to fight to stay in office even after the Watergate tapes were released.

___ 12. President Ford attempted to stop the final communist victory in Vietnam by attacking the captured ship *Mayaguez*.

___ 13. The women's movement achieved success in the 1970s by allying itself with the rising antiwar and black power movements of the decade.

___ 14. The Camp David accords brought an end to the Middle East conflict and the oil crisis and thus substantially eased inflation in the United States.

___ 15. The Iranian revolution against the shah brought the United States into a confrontation with militant Muslim leaders of the country.

B. Multiple Choice

Select the best answer and write the proper letter in the space provided.

___ 1. A primary cause of the economic decline that began in the 1970s was

    a. an international trade war.
    b. a rise in the price of agricultural goods.
    c. the breakup of efficient American companies.
    d. a decline in worker productivity.

___ 2. The severe inflation of the 1970s was largely caused by

    a. Lyndon Johnson's effort to maintain the Vietnam War and the Great Society programs without raising taxes.
    b. Nixon's decision to devalue the dollar and take the U.S. off the gold standard.
    c. the higher prices for scarce natural resources like iron, coal, and lumber.
    d. the strong demands of unionized workers for substantial wage increases.

3. President Nixon's "Vietnamization" policy provided that

    a. the United States would accept a unified but neutral Vietnam.

    b. the United States would escalate the war in Vietnam but withdraw from Cambodia and Laos.

    c. the United States would gradually withdraw ground troops while supporting the South Vietnamese war effort.

    d. the United States would seek a negotiated settlement of the war.

4. The antiwar movement expanded dramatically in 1970 when

    a. the massacre of civilians at My Lai by some U.S. soldiers was revealed.

    b. Nixon ordered further bombing of North Vietnam.

    c. the communist Vietnamese staged their Tet Offensive against American forces.

    d. Nixon ordered an invasion of Cambodia.

5. Nixon attempted to pressure the Soviet Union into making diplomatic deals with the United States by

    a. playing the "China card" by opening U.S. diplomacy and trade with the Soviets' rival communist power.

    b. using American economic aid as an incentive for the Soviets.

    c. threatening to attack Soviet allies such as Cuba and Vietnam.

    d. drastically increasing spending on nuclear weapons and missiles.

6. The Supreme Court came under sharp political attack especially because of its rulings on

    a. antitrust laws and labor rights.

    b. voting rights and election laws.

    c. criminal defendants' rights and prayer in public schools.

    d. environmental laws and immigrants' rights.

7. The most controversial element of Nixon's "Philadelphia Plan" was

    a. its guarantees of women's equal right to employment in the construction trades.

    b. the extension of "affirmative action" to promote the employment of groups of minorities and women.

    c. its insistence that employers and labor provide financial compensation to individuals who had suffered discrimination.

    d. its attempt to get around Supreme Court decisions prohibiting racial and sexual discrimination by business and labor.

8. Some of President Nixon's greatest legislative successes came in the area of

    a. upholding civil rights.

    b. stopping the growth of inflation.

    c. protecting the environment.

    d. maintaining foreign-policy cooperation with Congress.

9. Among the corrupt Nixon administration practices exposed by the Senate Watergate Committee was

a. payments to foreign agents.
b. bribes to congressmen and senators.
c. the illegal use of the Federal Bureau of Investigation and the Central Intelligence Agency.
d. the illegal use of the Environmental Protection Agency and the Treasury Department.

10. The War Powers Act was passed by Congress in response to

a. the Watergate scandal.
b. President Nixon's secret bombing of Cambodia.
c. the end of the war in Vietnam.
d. the Arab oil embargo.

11. The Arab oil embargo of 1973–1974 affected the American economy primarily by

a. causing the successful introduction of alternative energy sources.
b. leading the United States to open Alaskan and offshore oilfield to exploration.
c. increasing American investment in the Middle East.
d. ending the era of cheap energy and fueling severe inflation.

12. Gerald Ford came to be president because

a. he had been elected as Nixon's vice president in 1972.
b. he was speaker of the House of Representatives and was next in line after Nixon resigned.
c. he was elected in a special national election called after Nixon resigned.
d. he had been appointed vice president by Nixon before Nixon resigned.

13. Despite numerous successes for the women in the 1970s, the feminist movement suffered a severe setback when

a. the Supreme Court began to oppose the extension of women's rights.
b. the Equal Rights Amendment failed to achieve ratification by the states.
c. Congress refused to extend women's right to an equal education to the area of athletics.
d. the declining economy created a growing gap between men's and women's earning power.

14. President Carter's greatest success in foreign policy was

a. handling the Arab oil embargo and the energy crisis.
b. negotiating successful new agreements with the Soviet Union.
c. negotiating the Camp David peace treaty between Israel and Egypt.
d. maintaining peace and stability in Central America.

15. President Carter's greatest problem in foreign policy was

a. the Panama Canal issue.
b. the Soviet invasion of Afghanistan.
c. the continuing Arab-Israeli confrontation.
d. the Iranian seizure of American hostages.

C. Identification

Supply the correct identification for each numbered description.

_____ 1. Nixon's policy of withdrawing American troops from Vietnam while providing aid for the South Vietnamese to fight the war

_____ 2. The Ohio university where four students were killed during protests against the 1970 invasion of Cambodia

_____ 3. Top-secret documents, published by *The New York Times* in 1971, that showed the blunders and deceptions that led the United States into the Vietnam War

_____ 4. The first major achievement of the Nixon-Kissinger détente with the Soviet Union, which led to restrictions on defensive missile systems

_____ 5. Nixon's plan to win reelection by curbing the Supreme Court's judicial activism and soft-pedaling civil rights

_____ 6. Term for the new group affirmative action policy promoted by the Nixon administration

_____ 7. A Washington office complex that became a symbol of the widespread corruption of the Nixon administration

_____ 8. The law, passed in reaction to the secret Cambodia bombing, that restricted presidential use of troops overseas without congressional authorization

_____ 9. Arab-sponsored restriction on energy exports after the 1973 Arab-Israeli war

_____ 10. Nixon-Ford-Kissinger policy of seeking relaxed tensions with the Soviet Union through trade and arms limitation

_____ 11. International agreement of 1975, signed by President Ford, that settled postwar European boundaries and attempted to guarantee human rights in Eastern Europe

_____ 12. Proposed constitutional amendment promoting women's rights that fell short of ratification

_____ 13. Supreme Court decision that declared women's right to choose abortion.

_____ 14. *Two* historic sites seized by American Indian activists in 1970–1972 to draw public attention to Indian grievances

_____

_____ 15. Provision of the 1972 Education Amendments that prohibited gender discrimination and opened sports and other arenas to women

D. Matching People, Places, and Events

Match the person, place, or event in the left column with the proper description in the right column by inserting the correct letter on the blank line.

____ 1. Richard Nixon   **A.** The Muslim religious leader who dominated the 1979 Iranian revolution

____ 2. Spiro Agnew   **B.** The first appointed vice president and first appointed president of the United States

____ 3. Rachel Carson   **C.** Supreme Court justice whose "judicial activism" came under increasing attack by conservatives

____ 4. Daniel Ellsberg

____ 5. Henry Kissinger

____ 6. Earl Warren

____ 7. George McGovern

____ 8. Sam Ervin

____ 9. Gerald Ford

____ 10. John Dean

____ 11. James Earl Carter

____ 12. Anwar Sadat

____ 13. Allen Bakke

____ 14. Shah of Iran

____ 15. Ayatollah Ruhollah Khomeini

D. Nixon's tough-talking conservative vice president, who was forced to resign in 1973 for taking bribes and kick-backs

E. Talented diplomatic negotiator and leading architect of détente with the Soviet Union during the Nixon and Ford administrations

F. Egyptian leader who signed the Camp David accords with Israel

G. California medical school applicant whose case led a divided Supreme Court to uphold limited forms of affirmative action for minorities

H. Environmental writer whose book *Silent Spring* helped encourage laws like the Clean Water Act and the Endangered Species Act

I. South Dakota senator whose antiwar campaign was swamped by Nixon

J. Former Georgia governor whose presidency was plagued by economic difficulties and a crisis in Iran

K. Former Pentagon official who "leaked" the Pentagon Papers

L. Winner of an overwhelming electoral victory who was forced from office by the threat of impeachment

M. White House lawyer whose dramatic charges against Nixon were validated by the Watergate tapes

N. North Carolina senator who conducted the Watergate hearings

O. Repressive pro-Western ruler whose 1979 overthrow precipitated a crisis for the United States

E. Putting Things in Order

Put the following events in correct order by numbering them from 1 to 6.

____ The overthrow of a dictatorial shah leads to an economic and political crisis for President Carter and the United States.

____ An impeachment-threatened president resigns, and his appointed vice president takes over the White House.

____ A U.S. president travels to Beijing (Peking) and Moscow, opening a new era of improved diplomatic relations with the communist powers.

____ The American invasion of a communist stronghold near Vietnam creates domestic turmoil in the United States.

____ The signing of an agreement with North Vietnam leads to the final withdrawal of American troops from Vietnam.

____ A plainspoken former governor becomes president by campaigning against Washington corruption and for honesty in government.

F. Matching Cause and Effect

Match the historical cause in the left column with the proper effect in the right column by writing the correct letter on the blank line.

Cause	Effect
___ 1. Nixon's "Vietnamization" policy	**A.** Spawned a powerful "backlash" that halted federal day care efforts and the Equal Rights Amendment
___ 2. The U.S. invasion and bombing of Cambodia	**B.** Caused Senate defeat of the SALT II treaty and the end of détente with Moscow
___ 3. Nixon's trips to Beijing (Peking) and Moscow	**C.** Brought about gradual U.S. troop withdrawal but extended the Vietnam War for four more years
___ 4. The Warren Court's "judicial activism"	**D.** Prompted conservative protests and Nixon's appointment of less activist justices
___ 5. Pressure on Moscow and renewed bombing of North Vietnam	**E.** Led to the taking of American hostages and new economic and energy troubles for the United States
___ 6. The growing successes of the women's movement in areas of employment and education	**F.** Brought about a cease-fire and the withdrawal of American troops from Vietnam in 1973
___ 7. Nixon's tape-recorded words ordering the Watergate cover-up	**G.** Caused protests on U.S. campuses and congressional attempts to restrain presidential war powers
___ 8. The communist Vietnamese offensive in 1975	**H.** Brought an era of relaxed international tensions and new trade agreements
___ 9. The Soviet invasion of Afghanistan	**I.** Caused the collapse of South Vietnam and the flight of many refugees to the United States
___ 10. The 1979 revolution in Iran	**J.** Proved the president's guilt and forced him to resign or be impeached

G. Developing Historical Skills

Understanding Political Cartoons

The more controversial a major political figure, the more likely he or she is to be the subject of political cartoons. Richard Nixon was such a controversial figure, and the cartoons in this chapter show several views of him. Answer the following questions.

1. What is the view of Nixon's diplomacy in the cartoon *Balancing Act* on p. 951? What is the significance of his unusual "balance bar?"

2. In the cartoon of *Nixon, the Law and Order Man* on p. 960, what aspect of Nixon's earlier career is satirized? What details suggest the cartoonist's view of Nixon's Watergate strategy?

3. In the cartoon *How Long Will Nixon Haunt the GOP* on p. 960, what is the cartoonist suggesting about Ford's pardon of Nixon? What alleged quality of Nixon's is common to both this cartoon and the previous one on *Nixon, the Law and Order Man*?

4. In the cartoon *Who Lost Vietnam* on p. 962, Nixon is satirized, but less harshly than in the other cartoons. What changes the perspective on him here?

PART III: Applying What You Have Learned

1. What policies did Nixon pursue with Vietnam, the Soviet Union, and China, and what were the consequences of those policies?

2. In what ways did Nixon's domestic policies appeal to Americans' racial and economic fears, and in what ways did he positively address problems like inflation, discrimination, and pollution?

3. How did Nixon fall from the political heights of 1972 to his forced resignation in 1974? What were the political consequences of Watergate?

4. How did the administrations of the 1970s attempt to cope with the interrelated problems of energy, economics, and the Middle East?

5. Why can the 1970s be characterized as a "decade of stalemate?" What caused the apparent inability of the federal government to cope with the new problems of the time?

6. In what ways were the foreign policy and economic issues of the 1970s similar to those of the whole post-World War II era, and in what ways were they different? (See Chapters 37, 38, and 39.)

41

The Resurgence
of Conservatism, 1981–1992

PART I: Reviewing the Chapter

A. Checklist of Learning Objectives

After mastering this chapter, you should be able to

1. describe the rise of Reagan and the "new right" in the 1980s, including the controversies over racial and social issues.
2. explain the "Reagan revolution" in economic policy and indicate its immediate and long-term consequences.
3. describe the revival of the Cold War in Reagan's first term.
4. discuss the American entanglement in Central American and Middle Eastern troubles, including the Iran-contra affair.
5. describe the end of the Cold War, and the results for American society abroad and at home.
6. explain America's growing involvement in Middle East conflict, including the Persian Gulf War and its aftermath.
7. explain the Clinton victory in 1992, and Clinton's attempt to navigate between traditional Democratic values and resurgent right in the Republican party.
8. recount the successes and failures of the Clinton administration, and the causes and consequences of his impeachment.

B. Glossary

To build your social science vocabulary, familiarize yourself with the following terms.

1. **neoconservatives (neoconservatism)** Political activists and thinkers, mostly former liberals, who turned to a defense of traditional social and moral values and a strongly anticommunist foreign policy in the 1970s and 1980s. "Though Reagan was no intellectual, he drew on the ideas of a small but influential group of thinkers known as 'neoconservatives.'" (p. 977)
2. **supply side** In economics, the theory that investment incentives such as lowered federal spending and tax cuts will stimulate economic growth and increased employment. "But at first 'supply-side' economics seemed to be a beautiful theory mugged by a gang of brutal facts. . . ." (p. 981)
3. **red ink** Referring to a deficit in a financial account, with expenditures or debts larger than income or assets. "Ironically, this conservative president thereby plunged the government into a red-ink bath of deficit spending. . . ." (p. 981)
4. **oligarchs** A small, elite class of authoritarian rulers. ". . . the aging oligarchs in the Kremlin. . . ." (p. 982)
5. **indictment** In law, a formal statement of charges of legal violations presented by a prosecutor. "Criminal indictments were later brought against several individuals tarred by the Iran-contra scandal. . . ." (p. 986)

6. **welfare state** The political system, typical of modern industrial societies, in which government assumes responsibility for the economic well-being of its citizens by providing social benefits. "They achieved, in short, Reagan's highest political objective: the containment of the welfare state." (p. 987)

7. **leveraged buy-out** The purchase of one company by another using money borrowed on the expectation of selling a portion of assets after the acquisition. "A wave of mergers, acquisitions, and leveraged buy-outs washed over Wall Street. . . ." (p. 990)

8. **logistical (logistics)** Relating to the organization and movement of substantial qualities of people and material in connection with some defined objective. "In a logistical operation of astonishing complexity, the United States spearheaded a massive international military deployment on the sandy Arabian peninsula." (p. 995)

9. **sect** A separatist religious group that claims for itself exclusive knowledge of truth and a superior method of salvation over against all other religious organizations. "That showdown ended in the destruction of the sect's compound and the deaths of many Branch Davidians. . . ." (p. 1001)

10. **paramilitary** Unauthorized or voluntary groups that employ military organization, methods, and equipment outside the official military system of command and organization. "The last two episodes brought to light a lurid and secretive underground of paramilitary private 'militias'. . . ." (p. 1001)

11. **immunity** In law, a guarantee against prosecution for crime granted to a potential defendant in exchange for some benefit to the state. " . . . the tobacco firms would win immunity from further litigation, including at the federal level." (p. 1004)

12. **vouchers** Officially granted certificates for benefits of a particular kind, redeemable by a designated agency or service provider. "Bush championed private-sector initiatives, such as school vouchers. . . ." (p. 1010)

PART II: Checking Your Progress

A. True-False

Where the statement is true, mark **T**. Where it is false, mark **F**, and correct it in the space immediately below.

_____ 1. Conservative Christian groups provided an important component of Reagan's "new right" coalition.

_____ 2. The Supreme Court's *Bakke* decision upheld the principle of racial quotas in college and medical school admissions.

_____ 3. Once in office, Reagan backed away from most of his ideologically conservative election promises and concentrated on practical management of the economy and relations with the Russians.

_____ 4. The fact that Reagan's "supply-side" economic proposals bogged down in Congress demonstrated the continuing stalemate between Congress and the executive branch.

_____ 5. "Reaganomics" was successful in lowering interest rates and balancing the budget but had difficulty bringing down inflation and creating economic growth.

_____ 6. Reagan's revival of the Cold War in the early 1980s caused rising military budgets and growing doubts about American policy in Western Europe.

_____ 7. Reagan pursued a tough policy of military intervention and aid in opposition to leftist governments in Central America and the Caribbean.

_____ 8. Soviet leader Mikhail Gorbachev's policies of *glasnost* and *perestroika* helped reduce Soviet-American conflict in Reagan's second term.

_____ 9. The Iran-contra affair involved the secret exchange of weapons for American hostages and the illegal transfer of funds to Nicaraguan rebels.

_____ 10. One of the greatest American concerns during the Persian Gulf War was that Iraq would use its stockpile of chemical and biological weapons.

_____ 11. Bill Clinton's presentation of himself as a "new" Democrat was designed to emphasize his commitment to reversing past Democratic party positions on civil rights.

_____ 12. Clinton's ambitious reform goals suffered a severe setback when his health-care proposal failed.

_____ 13. After victory in the 1994 congressional elections, the militant conservatism of Speaker Newt Gingrich stumbled when it shut down the federal government for a time.

_____ 14. Clinton put conservative Republicans on the defensive by fighting hard for traditional Democratic policies like defense of social welfare and support for affirmative action.

_____ 15. George W. Bush defeated Albert Gore in the Electoral College but not in the popular vote.

B. Multiple Choice

Select the best answer and write the proper letter in the space provided.

_____ 1. In the 1980 national elections,

   a. Edward Kennedy challenged incumbent President Carter for the nomination of the Democratic party.
   b. although Ronald Reagan won the presidency, both houses of Congress still had Democratic party majorities.
   c. third-party candidate John Anderson won three states and seventeen Electoral College votes.
   d. Ronald Reagan won the presidency by the closest margin since the Kennedy-Nixon election of 1960.

_____ 2. The "new-right" movement that helped elect Ronald Reagan was spearheaded by

   a. fiscal conservatives.
   b. evangelical Christians.
   c. gold-standard advocates.
   d. midwesterners

3. Many "new-right" activists were most concerned about

   a. cultural and racial issues.
   b. economic questions.
   c. foreign policy.
   d. Medicare and Medicaid programs.

4. Of all the social issues, the most politically explosive for the "new right" was

   a. affirmative action.
   b. the teaching of evolution in public schools.
   c. balancing the federal budget.
   d. sex and violence on television.

5. That preference in the admission policies of institutions of higher education could not be based on ethnic or racial identity alone was the Supreme Court's decision in

   a. *Roe* v. *Wade*.
   b. the *Bakke* case.
   c. *Brown* v. *Board of Education*.
   d. the *Miranda* decision.

6. Ronald Reagan was similar to Franklin D. Roosevelt in that both presidents

   a. disliked big business.
   b. championed the common person against vast impersonal menaces.
   c. were raised in wealthy families.
   d. favored social engineering by the government.

7. Ronald Reagan differed from Franklin D. Roosevelt in that Roosevelt

   a. saw big government as the foe of the common person, and Reagan said the foe was big business.
   b. appealed to the working class and Reagan appealed only to the rich.
   c. advocated a populist political philosophy and Reagan did not.
   d. branded big business as the enemy of the common person, while Reagan branded big government as the foe.

8. Conservative Democrats who helped Ronald Reagan pass his budget and tax-cutting legislation were called

   a. boll weevils.
   b. Sagebrush rebels.
   c. scalawags.
   d. neoconservatives.

9. The Iran-contra scandal reflected a sharp conflict between Congress and President Reagan over

   a. U.S. aid for rebels against the leftist government of Nicaragua.
   b. the American policy of refusing to trade arms for U.S. hostages in the Middle East.
   c. the attitude of American Christian and Jewish leaders toward Iran's Islamic Revolution.
   d. the U.S. economic boycott of Fidel Castro's Cuba.

_____ 10. Two hotly debated cultural issues that embroiled the Supreme Court during the Reagan-Bush administrations were

    a. hairstyles and rock music.

    b. affirmative action and abortion.

    c. child-rearing practices and television.

    d. language teaching and dress in the workplace.

_____ 11. The major American and Allied success in the Persian Gulf War was

    a. the overthrow of Saddam Hussein.

    b. the liberation of Kuwait from Iraqi rule.

    c. the freeing of the Kurds from Iraqi oppression.

    d. the achievement of an enduring peace in the Middle East.

_____ 12. Two areas where the first Clinton administration experienced the most success in domestic affairs was

    a. health care reform and gay rights.

    b. political campaign reform and term limits.

    c. gun control and deficit reduction.

    d. immigration reform and improved race relations.

_____ 13. Clinton worked to promote free trade through his advocacy of

    a. NAFTA, GATT, and the World Trade Organization (WTO)

    b. NATO, the UN, and the PLO.

    c. greater emphasis on human rights as the key factor in U.S.-China relations.

    d. closer ties between the United States and the former Soviet Union and Yugoslavia.

_____ 14. The two charges for which President Clinton was impeached and tried were

    a. violation of the War Powers Act in the bombing of Serbia and excessive use of force in the Branch Davidian assault.

    b. abuse of the power of presidential pardon and the Whitewater scandal.

    c. obstruction of justice and perjury before a grand jury.

    d. adultery and violation of moral norms of the presidency.

_____ 15. The fundamental issue in the presidential election of 2000 was

    a. foreign policy toward China, Russia, and Latin America.

    b. trade policy toward Europe and nations of the Third World.

    c. whether to use projected budget surpluses for tax cuts or for debt reduction and Medicare.

    d. whether to build a unilateral American missile defense system.

C. Identification

Supply the correct identification for each numbered description.

_____ 1. Outspoken conservative movement of the 1980s that emphasized such "social issues" as opposition to abortion, the Equal Rights Amendment, pornography, homosexuality, and affirmative action

_____ 2. Evangelical Christian organization that aroused its members to fervent support of Reagan and the Republican party in the 1980s

3. The economic theory of "Reaganomics" that emphasized cutting taxes and government spending in order to stimulate investment, productivity, and economic growth by private enterprise

_____ 4. The protest movement, supported by Reagan Interior Secretary Watt, that attempted to reduce federal environmental controls on industrial activities in the West

_____ 5. Conservative southern Democrats who supported Reagan's economic policies in Congress

_____ 6. Polish labor union crushed by the communist-imposed martial-law regime in 1983

_____ 7. The leftist revolutionary rulers of Nicaragua, strongly opposed by the Reagan administration

_____ 8. Popular name for Reagan's proposed space-based nuclear defense system, officially called the Strategic Defense Initiative

_____ 9. Physical symbol of the Cold War and divided Europe that came down in 1989

_____ 10. Nation whose invasion by Iraq in 1990 led to the Persian Gulf War

_____ 11. Conservative campaign platform that led to a sweeping Republican victory in the 1994 mid-term elections

_____ 12. International trade organization that prompted strong protests from anti-global trade forces in Seattle, Washington in 1999

_____ 13. Clinton Arkansas investment deal that spurred a federal special prosecutor and led to widespread investigations of his administration

_____ 14. Colorado high school where a deadly shooting in 1999 stirred a national movement against guns and gun violence

_____ 15. Third party led by environmentalist Ralph Nader that took votes from Democratic presidential nominee Albert Gore in 2000 election

D. Matching People, Places, and Events

Match the person, place, or event in the left column with the proper description in the right column by inserting the correct letter on the blank line.

____ 1. Jimmy Carter

____ 2. Edward Kennedy

____ 3. Ronald Reagan

____ 4. Oliver North

____ 5. Sandra Day O'Connor

____ 6. Mikhail Gorbachev

____ 7. George Bush, Sr.

A. Texas billionaire who won many votes as independent candidate in 1992 and 1996

B. Son of a former president who narrowly defeated Albert Gore in the disputed 2000 presidential election

C. Soviet leader whose summit meetings with Reagan achieved an arms-control breakthrough in 1987

D. Supreme Court Justice who was narrowly confirmed despite charges of sexual harassment

E. Iraqi dictator defeated by the United States and its allies in the Persian Gulf War

F. Brilliant legal scholar appointed by Reagan as the first woman justice on the Supreme Court

G. Well-meaning but luckless president whose reelection attempt was swamped by the 1980 Reagan landslide

____	8. Albert Gore	H.	Clinton's vice president who won popular vote but lost electoral vote in 2000 presidential election
____	9. Saddam Hussein	I.	The first baby-boomer president, and the second U.S. president to be impeached and acquitted
____	10. George Walker Bush	J.	Prominent child care advocate and health care reformer in Clinton administration; won U.S. Senate seat in 2000
____	11. Clarence Thomas	K.	Liberal Democratic senator whose opposition to Carter helped divide the Democrats in 1980
____	12. William Clinton	L.	Long-time Republican political figure who defeated Dukakis for the presidency in 1988
____	13. H. Ross Perot	M.	Promoter of the "Contract with America" and the first Republican Speaker in 40 years
____	14. Hillary Rodham Clinton	N.	Marine colonel involved in the Iran-contra affair
____	15. Newt Gingrich	O.	Political darling of Republican conservatives who won landslide election victories in 1980 and 1984

E. Putting Things in Order

Put the following events in correct order by numbering them from 1 to 6.

____ Reagan easily wins reelection by overwhelming divided Democrats.

____ The United States and its allies defeat Iraq in the Persian Gulf War.

____ Republicans win Congress and confront President Clinton on taxes and spending.

____ Reagan's "supply-side" economic programs pass through Congress, cutting taxes and federal spending.

____ George Walker Bush defeats Albert Gore in a razor-close election.

____ President Clinton is impeached on charges of perjury and obstruction of justice and acquitted in a U.S. Senate trial.

F. Matching Cause and Effect

Match the historical cause in the left column with the proper effect in the right column by writing the correct letter on the blank line.

	Cause		Effect
____	1. The growth of the "new-right" movement focused on social issues	A.	Led to a breakoff of arms-control talks, U.S. economic sanctions against Poland, and growing anxiety in Western Europe
____	2. Reagan's crusade against big government and social spending	B.	Brought about an overwhelming Republican victory in the 1984 presidential election
____	3. By 1983, Reagan's "supply-side" economic policies	C.	Resulted in the failure of the American marines' peacekeeping mission in 1983
____	4. The revival of the Cold War in the early eighties	D.	Helped curb affirmative action and limit the right to abortion.
____	5. Continued political turmoil and war in Lebanon	E.	Led to sharp cuts in both taxes and federal social programs in 1981
		F.	Strained relations with America's European allies

_____ 6. Reagan's hostility to leftist governments in Central America and the Caribbean

_____ 7. Reagan's personal popularity and Democratic divisions

_____ 8. Reagan's "Star Wars" plan for defensive missile systems in space

_____ 9. The huge federal budget deficits of the 1980s

_____ 10. Reagan's and Bush's appointments of conservative justices to the Supreme Court

_____ 11. The Reagan administration's frustration with hostages and bans on aid to Nicaraguan rebels

_____ 12. Violent episodes like the Oklahoma City bombing and the Columbine school shootings

_____ 13. The Congressional Republicans' ideological rhetoric and government shutdown of 1995

_____ 14. The Monica Lewinsky affair

_____ 15. The U.S. Supreme Court's intervention in the 2000 election

G. Curbed inflation and spurred economic growth but also caused sky-high deficits and interest rates

H. Prompted Congress to pass the Gramm-Rudman-Hollings Act calling for automatic spending cuts and a balanced budget by 1991

I. Helped fuel Ronald Reagan's successful presidential campaign in 1980

J. Caused the U.S. invasion of Grenada and the CIA-engineered mining of Nicaraguan harbors

K. Encouraged the public and the Clinton administration to press for tougher gun control

L. Enabled Clinton to regain political momentum and defeat Bob Dole in 1996

M. Was a windfall for prosecutor Kenneth Starr and laid the basis for Clinton's impeachment

N. Halted Florida's vote counting and permitted Bush to declare victory over Gore

O. Led to the Iran-contra affair

G. Developing Historical Skills

Using Chronologies

Properly read, chronologies provide handy tools for understanding not only the sequence of events but also their historical relations.

Examine the Chronology for this chapter (p. 1012), and answer the following questions.

1. In which year did a number of events indicate deep Soviet-American tension and a revived Cold War?

2. How many years did it take after the first Reagan-Gorbachev summit to reach agreement on the INF treaty?

3. List three events *prior* to the Persian Gulf War in 1991 that reflect growing American involvement in the Middle East.

3. List three events between the imposition of sanctions against Poland (1981) and the dissolution of the Soviet Union (1991) that show the *progress* in easing Cold War tensions.

5. How many years elapsed between the Persian Gulf War and the U.S.-British air strikes against Iraq under the Clinton administration?

PART III: Applying What You Have Learned

1. What caused the rise of Reagan and the "new right" in the eighties, and how did their conservative movement affect American politics?
2. What were the goals of Reagan's "supply-side" economic policies, and what were their short-term and long-term effects?
3. What led to the revival of the Cold War in the early 1980s and to its decline and disappearance by 1991?
4. Describe the major changes affecting American foreign policy from 1982 to 1992 in Central America, the Middle East, and Eastern Europe. Which of these changes occurred as a result of American policy and which occurred primarily as a result of developments within those regions?
5. What were the successes and failures of the Bush administration? Was Bill Clinton's election a positive mandate for change, or was it primarily a repudiation of the Bush record?
6. How did the antigovernment mood of the 1990s affect both Bill Clinton and his Republican opponents? In what ways did Clinton attempt to uphold traditional Democratic themes, and in what ways did he serve to consolidate the conservative Bush-Reagan era?
7. What new foreign policy challenges did the United States face after the end of the Cold War? What were the principal themes of U.S. relations with the world in the Clinton administration?
8. Some historians have compared the "Reagan revolution" with the New Deal because of the way it seemed to transform radically American economics and politics. Is this a valid comparison? Is it correct to see the "Reagan legacy" as a reversal or overturning of the New Deal and the Great Society of Lyndon Johnson?

42

The American People
Face a New Century

PART I: Reviewing the Chapter

A. Checklist of Learning Objectives

After mastering this chapter, you should be able to

1. describe the changing shape of the American economy and work force, and the new challenges facing the United States in an international economy during the "information age."
2. explain the changing roles of women since World War II and the impact of those changes on American society.
3. analyze the difficulties affecting the American family, and explain the new power of the elderly.
4. describe the impact of the newest wave of immigration from Asia and Latin America and the growing voice of minorities in American society.
5. describe the difficulties and challenges facing American cities, including poverty and drug abuse.
6. describe the changing condition of African-Americans in American politics and society.
7. discuss the major developments in American culture and the arts since World War II.

B. Glossary

To build your social science vocabulary, familiarize yourself with the following terms.

1. **biosphere** The earth's entire network of living plants and organisms, conceived as an interconnected whole. ". . . the fragile ecological balance of the wondrous biosphere in which humankind was delicately suspended." (p. 1016)
2. **nuclear family** A parent or parents and their immediate offspring. "The nuclear family, once prized as the foundation of society. . . ." (p. 1020)
3. **undocumented** Lacking official certification of status as a legal immigrant or resident alien. ". . . attempted to choke off illegal entry by penalizing employers of undocumented aliens. . . ." (p. 1023)
4. **amnesty** An official governmental act in which some general category of offenders is declared immune from punishment. ". . . by granting amnesty to many of those already here." (p. 1023)
5. **civil trial** A trial before a judge or jury instigated by a private lawsuit in which one party seeks relief, compensation, or damages from another. A **criminal trial** is instigated by an indictment for criminal law violations brought by a state prosecutor on behalf of the government ("the people"); it may result in fines, imprisonment, or execution. "In a later civil trial, another jury found Simpson liable for the 'wrongful deaths' of his former wife and another victim." (p. 1025)

PART II: Checking Your Progress

A. True-False

Where the statement is true, mark **T**. Where it is false, mark **F**, and correct it in the space immediately below.

_____ 1. The communications and genetics revolutions in postwar America created new social and moral dilemmas as well as widespread economic growth.

_____ 2. The United States remained the world's richest nation with the highest per capita income in the 1990s.

_____ 3. Continuing discrimination as well as different career patterns still caused women to receive lower wages than men in the late 1990s.

_____ 4. By the 1990s almost all women without children at home were employed, but a majority of mothers remained outside the workplace.

_____ 5. One of the greatest problems caused by the weakening of the family was the growing poverty of America's elderly.

_____ 6. One factor that made Hispanic immigration to the U.S. unique was the close proximity of Mexican-Americans to their former homeland across the border.

_____ 7. The fastest growing American minority in the 1980s and 1990s was African-Americans.

_____ 8. By the late 1990s, a majority of Americans lived in suburbs rather than central cities or rural areas.

_____ 9. The large-scale Los Angeles riots of 1992 occurred in reaction to the jury's verdict in the O. J. Simpson murder case.

_____ 10. African-Americans attained considerable success in both local and national political leadership positions in the 1980s and 1990s.

_____ 11. The rise of a substantial black middle class after the 1980s created a growing division between the well-off and poor within the African-American community.

_____ 12. The rise of television and rock music caused a sharp decline in the number of Americans who were consumers of the "high culture" of museums and symphony orchestras.

_____ 13. The 1980s and 1990s witnessed the decline of regional themes in American writing and culture.

_____ 14. American playwrights and theatre audiences generally turned away from sensitive subjects like the AIDS epidemic.

_____ 15. Environmental concerns and disillusionment with wealth caused some late twentieth-century Americans to advocate a "no-growth" economy for the country.

B. Multiple Choice

Select the best answer and write the proper letter in the space provided.

____ 1. The "flagship business" of the heavy industrial economy of the *early* twentieth century was

    a. the International Business Machines Company.
    b. the Microsoft Corporation.
    c. the U.S. Steel Corporation.
    d. the General Mills Corporation.

____ 2. The primary engine driving the U.S. economy of the 1990s was

    a. scientific knowledge.
    b. corporate mergers and acquisitions.
    c. labor union activism.
    d. international investment in American companies.

____ 3. The earliest great successes of the "genetic revolution" occurred in

    a. improving the human gene pool.
    b. increasing crop yields and curing genetic diseases.
    c. providing new sources for human organ transplants.
    d. artificial insemination and human cloning.

____ 4. Compared to other countries' median incomes, Americans in the 1990s were

    a. still the wealthiest people in the world.
    b. in the middle third of the world's income levels.
    c. seeing a steady decline in their average incomes.
    d. no longer at the top but still among the world's most affluent people.

____ 5. The most striking development in the American economic structure in the 1980s and 1990s was

    a. the growing inequality between rich and poor.
    b. the slow general decline in the American standard of living.
    c. the growing reliance on investments and real estate rather than jobs for income.
    d. the increasing concentration of wealth in certain regions and affluent suburbs.

____ 6. Which of the following was *not* among the causes of the income gap in the United States?

    a. intensifying global economic competition
    b. the shrinkage in manufacturing jobs for unskilled and semi-skilled labor
    c. the decline of labor unions.
    d. the weakening family structure

____ 7. The most dramatic change in the patterns of women's employment from the 1950s to the 1990s was

    a. the end of "occupational segregation" in certain female job categories.
    b. that the majority of mothers with young children went to work outside the home.
    c. that women were unable to break through into traditional single-sex colleges and universities.
    d. that married women worked at a higher rate than single women.

8. Perhaps the most significant sign of the weakening of the traditional American family was

    a. that television no longer portrayed family situations.
    b. that a majority of children no longer lived with their birth parents.
    c. that families were increasingly slow to form at all.
    d. that the elderly were no longer likely to live with their adult children.

9. The increasingly longer lives of America's senior citizens were often eased by

    a. the ability of the potent elderly lobby to obtain government benefits for seniors.
    b. the willingness of younger generations to provide income support for aged parents.
    c. the large-scale migration of senior citizens to the West Coast.
    d. the more positive portrayals of the elderly in movies and television.

10. The deepest problem caused by federal programs like Social Security and Medicare in the twenty-first century was likely to be

    a. that benefits could not keep up with rising inflation.
    b. that the Social Security and Medicare trust funds would exercise too great a control over the economy.
    c. that the higher taxes necessary to support benefits would create a generational war with younger workers.
    d. that the health care system could no longer meet the rising demand for services to the elderly.

11. The "new immigrants" of the 1980s and 1990s came to the United States primarily because

    a. they wanted jobs and economic opportunities unavailable in their homelands.
    b. they were fleeing religious and political repression.
    c. they admired American cultural and intellectual achievements.
    d. they wanted to strengthen the minority voting bloc to the United States.

12. The largest group of the "new immigrants" came from

    a. East Asia.
    b. Mexico and other Latin American countries.
    c. Africa and the Middle East.
    d. South Asia.

13. The period between 1920 and the mid-1990s will likely be seen as a unique but passing age in American demographic history because

    a. a majority of people lived in the Northeast rather than the South and West.
    b. a majority of people were of European rather than African-Americans or Hispanic ancestry.
    c. a majority of people were the children or grandchildren of immigrants.
    d. a majority of people lived in central cities rather than in rural areas or suburbs.

14. An increasingly important development among African-Americans since the 1960s has been

    a. the growing equality of incomes within the community.
    b. the inability of African-Americans to break through into politics or the arts.
    c. the growing gap between successful affluent African-Americans and those in poverty.
    d. the concentration of nearly all African-Americans in the central cities.

___ 15. The most striking development in American literature in the past two decades has been

    a. the importance of the fantastic literature of absurdism and "black comedy."

    b. the rise of writers from once-marginal regions and ethnic groups.

    c. the focus on themes of nostalgia and lost innocence.

    d. the rise of social realism and attention to working-class stories.

C. Identification

Supply the correct identification for each numbered description.

_____ 1. The computer corporation that symbolized the U.S. economy in the 1990s much as U.S. Steel did in 1900

_____ 2. Health care program for the elderly, enacted in 1965, that created large economic demands on the American economy by the 1990s

_____ 3. Law of 1986 that granted amnesty to past illegal immigrants and penalized employers of future illegal workers

_____ 4. The largest of the "new immigrant" groups

_____ 5. Organization headed by Cesar Chavez that worked to improve conditions for migrant workers

_____ 6. City where major racial disturbance erupted in 1992

_____ 7. American region that saw a particularly rich literary revival in the 1980s and 1990s

_____ 8. Zora Neale Hurston's 1937 novel that received widespread new attention because of interest in feminist and African-American literature

_____ 9. Avant-garde painting movement pioneered by Jackson Pollock and others in the 1940s and 1950s

_____ 10. Oil tanker whose 1989 spill off the coast of Alaska sparked deep concern over oil drilling and transportation on the world's oceans

D. Matching People, Places, and Events

Match the person, place, or event in the left column with the proper description in the right column by inserting the correct letter on the blank line.

___ 1. O. J. Simpson

___ 2. L. Douglas Wilder

___ 3. Carol Mosely-Braun

___ 4. Larry McMurtry

___ 5. Norman MacLean

___ 6. August Wilson

___ 7. Toni Morrison

A. Leading Indian writer, author of *House Made of Dawn*

B. Pioneer artistic creator of "abstract expressionism" in the 1940s and 1950s

C. The first African-American state governor

D. Irish-American writer whose memoir *Angela's Ashes* revived interest in the older European immigrant groups

E. African-American writer of the 1930s whose works were rediscovered and gained popularity in the 1980s and 1990s

F. Playwright who deployed gritty American slang in socially critical dramas like *Glengarry Glen Ross*

G. Former football star whose murder trial became a focus of racial tension

H. Author of *Beloved* and winner of the Nobel Prize for Literature

_____ 8. N. Scott Momaday

_____ 9. David Mamet

_____ 10. Zora Neale Hurston

_____ 11. Jackson Pollock

_____ 12. Frank McCourt

I. Western writer who portrayed small towns in *Last Picture Show* and the cattle-drive era in *Lonesome Dove*

J. First African-American woman elected to the U.S. Senate

K. African-American playwright who portrayed the psychological costs of the northern migration

L. Former English professor who wrote memorable tales of his Montana boyhood

E. Putting Things in Order

Put the following events in correct order by numbering them from 1 to 5.

_____ F. Douglas Wilder is elected the first African-American governor.

_____ Congress passes the Immigration Reform and Control Act to try to thwart illegal immigration.

_____ Jackson Pollock and others pioneer "abstract expressionism" and the leading form of modern American painting.

_____ Los Angeles experiences a major riot as the result of a racial incident involving police brutality.

_____ California voters approve Proposition 209 in an attempt to overturn affirmative-action policies.

F. Matching Cause and Effect

Match the historical cause in the left column with the proper effect in the right column by writing the correct letter on the blank line.

Cause	Effect
_____ 1. Decline of manufacturing jobs and higher pay for educated workers	A. Made the American southwest increasingly a "bi-cultural" zone
_____ 2. The computer revolution and the new trend toward "genetic engineering"	B. Changed both child-rearing patterns and men's social roles
_____ 3. Expanding economic opportunities for women	C. Brought major literary prominence to minority and Western writers
_____ 4. Rise of the median age of the population since the 1970s	D. Contributed to sharply increased income inequality in the U.S.
_____ 5. Growing numbers and political power for Hispanic Americans	E. Made the elderly a powerful political force
_____ 6. The growth of the African-American middle class and their migration to the suburbs	F. Further isolated the poverty-stricken lower class in the inner cities
_____ 7. Poverty and economic upheavals in Latin America and Asia	G. Made New York City the art capital of the world
	H. Created the highest rates of immigration to the United States since the early 1900s
	I. Led California voters to pass measures restricting the use of racial categories
	J. Expanded the economy but threatened many traditional jobs while creating new ethical dilemmas for society

    ___   8. The resentment against many
                   affirmative action measures

    ___   9. The rise of previously "marginal"
                   ethnic groups and regions

    ___   10. The success of modernist
                   American art movements since
                   the 1940s

PART III: Applying What You Have Learned

1. What were the consequences of the dramatically changed American economy in the 1990s? What caused the rapidly increasing gap between rich and poor in this period?

2. How did women's new economic opportunities affect American society? What barriers to women's complete economic equality proved most difficult to overcome?

3. How did the "new immigration" and the rise of ethnic minorities transform American society in the 1990s? Were the effects of the new immigration similar to that of earlier waves of immigration, or fundamentally different?

4. How were the changes in American society reflected in literature and the arts in the 1980s and 1990s?

5. What social and moral challenges seem most urgent as America enters a new millennium? How are these challenges rooted in American history, and how does understanding that history contribute to engaging these problems?